Boy,
Am I Ever Lucky!

The Life and Times of Robert J. Zoller

A book by

Bob Zoller

You may contact the author at the following address:

Robert J. Zoller
Lakehouse West
3435 Fox Run Rd., #123
Sarasota, FL 34231-7342
941-923-7525

First published by Dog Ear Publishing
4010 W. 86th Street, Ste H
Indianapolis, IN 46268
www.dogearpublishing.net

ISBN: 978-159858-570-4

This book is printed on acid-free paper.

Printed in the United States of America

Dedicated to my daughter, Kristin Johnson,
who worked a lot harder on this project
than I did.

PREFACE

I'm 91 years old now and it's time to write about my life if I'm ever going to. When I was growing up in a small midwestern town, I read a lot and I was fascinated by "the world out there". I wanted to see it—all of it, or as much as possible—and I decided that fame and fortune weren't as important as experiencing far-away places, and hopefully, a lifetime of adventure.

In my third year of college the wanderlust became especially strong. Edwin C. Kepler, one of the best friends I ever had, transferred to the University of Iowa. So I pledged him to my fraternity and moved him in as my roommate. Like me, he was curious about the world out there and wanted to experience it first-hand. We read a lot of travel poetry and were especially influenced by Richard Halliburton, who dropped out of Princeton and wrote "The Royal Road to Romance" about his adventures bumming around the world.

So we decided to drop out of college and follow our dreams—to China, India, Australia and many other places—maybe even Katmandu!

Things had changed since Halliburton's day. China and Japan were at war, so Americans could no longer go there. Halliburton worked his way across the Pacific on a tramp steamer, but the maritime unions put a stop to that. Neither of us had any money, but we were both good writers and the Des Moines Register might agree that two young Iowa boys, seeing the world on a shoestring, would be a continuing story worth publishing. We expected they would pay us for the articles we would send back. If we ran out of money we could surely find jobs to keep us in food and shelter.

We were serious about going. We even got our passports and planned how to take everything we needed, but still travel light.

Kepler's family supported our plans but mine surely did not. They thought I was suddenly brain-damaged, but I was determined to go without their approval. It was my mother who changed our plans. She simply asked me to finish college first—

something she said nobody in our immediate family had ever done. I couldn't say no.

So at the end of the school year, Kepler dropped out and hitchhiked to New Orleans—to start "letting life happen to him." Got a job as a reporter on the Times-Picayune. I would return to SUI for my senior year and later, we'd get together and give it another try.

It never happened. But maybe it's just as well.

Looking back at my life, I now believe that many of us don't plan our lives and then make the plans happen. Life just happens to us. At this stage of my game, I am supremely happy with the way things turned out. I think about my many years on this earth and I'm a bit surprised how good they have been – and I keep telling myself, "Boy, Am I Ever Lucky!"

NO, REALLY, I WASN'T ALWAYS AN OLD MAN – I WAS YOUNG … ONCE UPON A TIME.

THE ARCHER. I was no Robin Hood, but I was one of the best marksmen in Waverly – mainly because there wasn't much competition. (I made the bow and all the arrows for my Archery merit badge at Boy Scout Camp.)

PART 1. OFF TO A GOOD START

LIFE IN WAVERLY. I arrived on April 21, 1916. I'm not sure this was planned, as my siblings, Edward and Helen, were 11 and 9 at the time. Later, I was told they almost named me "Donald" and I'm glad they didn't.

I don't remember much of anything until my first day in kindergarten, and one recess when a weird kid was running around yelling (to no one in particular), "Liar, liar, pants on fire, nose as long as a telephone wire!"

I do remember growing up when boys wore knee pants and black stockings – until about ten years old when they graduated to long pants. In winter, getting dressed, the trick was to get the stockings over your long underwear as neatly as possible. It wasn't easy.

Life wasn't easy in those days. In winter, our only heat was a Royal Oak stove. When it was ten below zero outdoors, our bedrooms stayed about six below. After Dad got a good fire going in the morning, I would bolt from my bed and dash to the heat to get dressed.

Waverly, Iowa – where I grew up – had an Opera House. They never had any operas there, but I appeared on its stage one time – briefly – in a kindergarten skit. I was skinny then, so I played the part of Jack Spratt: some fat girl, of course, played my wife. I think we just sat there at a table, holding knives and forks, while somebody recited the poem.

When the program was over, I went to the cloakroom to bundle up for the walk back home. I couldn't find my stocking cap and neither could the teacher. When everyone had gone, there was one dirty, ragged old cap left. I put up a fight, but my teacher made me wear it, because there was almost a blizzard outdoors. On the way home, I threw the ugly sucker over the bridge railing and down into the icy waters of the Cedar River. I probably froze my ears before I got home, but I don't remember.

I do remember there was hell to pay the next day when the teacher showed up with my stocking cap and wanted the ratty one back for the kid who took mine.

I told her I lost it. She probably went to her grave trying to figure out that one.

In an early school picture—first grade, I believe—I looked pretty neat: my mother always kept me fairly well dressed and better scrubbed than most of my classmates. Many years later, I ran into Jeanette Hemingway, a classmate of mine from kindergarten through college. She told me, "I'll remember you as the kid who always had his shoes shined."

BIG HORSES, LITTLE HARRY, AND THE DIME

Years before I began keeping a diary, one thing happened that I still remember exactly as it happened – just like yesterday, but it was 80 years ago.

A bunch of us, eight or nine kids, all about ten years old – headed out to play in the woods. It was a nice summer day. Sometimes we'd take off our shirts, strip to the waist and pretend we were Indian braves. I remember that I had just spent a week on my uncle's farm and was bragging about riding horses, probably creating the impression that I was a much better cowboy than I actually was.

On the way home, we short-cutted through a large pasture where six horses were grazing. They were big horses. Really big! Draft horses, not quite the size of Clydesdales, but not a lot smaller, either.

John Mooney suggested that if I was so good, I should prove it by riding one of these. I said, "O.K., but you'll have to help me catch one." It never occurred to me I'd need a stepladder to get up that high – or that none of these horses were apt to agree with Mooney's suggestion.

We walked toward the horses. They didn't seem too friendly. They eyed us, and walked away. They kept walking away. Someone came up with the idea that we should surround them. Approach from all sides and hem them in. (Bad idea!)

We were all the same age, but Harry Rathe – not one of our usual gang, but kind of a tag-along that day – was the smallest kid there. He was a funny-looking kid with flaming red hair. Wearing a funny little hat with a very small brim. As we approached from all directions, one of the big horses, facing away from Harry, suddenly ducked his head and kicked both back legs way up in the air, a good six feet, like a bronco at a rodeo!

He kicked the hat right off Harry's head! And Harry immediately dived to retrieve it!

We all stood stunned – scared to death! Then we looked at Harry and could see the horse's flying hoof had grazed his forehead and removed a piece of skin the size and shape of a dime!

It was just starting to ooze blood, and we all knew that a half-inch closer and Harry's face would have been removed, or maybe his entire head!

Little Harry would have died instantly. Gospel truth.

DANGEROUS DAYS

Looking back on my early years, I often wonder how boy-children and teenagers stayed alive long enough to become adults. I remember (vaguely) being about five years old when Mike Rhode, my father's delivery man, found me on the Third Avenue bridge, sitting outside the railing, holding a rope and dangling my coaster wagon down to the shallow water and rocks some 25 feet below. If the wagon hit the water, the current would have pulled me right down after it! And why I was there alone, at five years old, makes me wonder.

A couple of years later, I remember going with older boys to a deep-water swimming hole in the lower Cedar River. It was called "The Log" – because a water-logged tree trunk had laid on the bottom for years. I couldn't swim a stroke. The older boys could, but not very well. I remember wading in water up to my ears until I could get out to, and up on, the log. It was slimy-slippery and I knew if I slipped off, or was pushed off on the far side, I'd be in fast-flowing water over my head and I'd drown.

I didn't want to seem "chicken" so I hung around longer than I should have, and finally had just enough good sense to get off the log and wade back to shore.

Worse yet, in my early teens, on a warm Spring day, hundreds of people were on our Main Street bridge, watching a spectacular show: the break-up of thick river ice and the Spring flood washing it down the river.

Five of us kids were a mile or so down the river, in Brooks' Woods, watching the raging floodwaters filled with slush, with huge "icebergs" bigger than cars and everything in between. And the floodwaters, a good ten feet over normal, were racing downstream at maybe 30 or 40 miles-an-hour. A raging torrent!

Boys that age get stupid at times and we talked about diving in. I was the best swimmer and, therefore, got elected. I declined, but the discussion continued, and eventually I got naked, tried to pick a spot between the biggest "icebergs", and dived in! It was a terrible shock! I swam about four fast strokes into the floodwaters, then turned and swam out – *about 150 yards downstream!*

The others ran down to me, carrying my clothes. I was in pain. A few seconds in ice water and my skin was burning, not cold. That's all I remember, but I remember that exceedingly well. (Looking back, I realize that it was an incredibly stupid, dangerous thing to do!)

In high school, Joe Roe was the wildest kid in our gang. The two of us were riding in a Model T Ford roadster as he drove into town onto E. Bremer Avenue, breaking all speed limits (substantially) – right down the middle of the grassy medians that divided the highway – *while sitting up on the back of the driver's seat and steering with his feet!*

Another time, he got his sister's new Terraplane (then said to be the fastest stock car made) and he proved it could do 100 m.p.h. on Highway 218 south to Janesville – curves included – with ten of us jammed into the car, leaving Joe hardly any elbowroom for his driving.

There were many other examples, too numerous to mention.

GROWING UP. FUN AND GAMES.

I went to Lincoln grade school, one block from where we lived in an apartment above Dad's meat market. I was a good student but none of us cared at all about scholastic achievement. Sports were everything—football, basketball and track. We played baseball, but considered it a minor sport.

I think it was remarkable that as grade school kids we played football games and held track meets, East vs. West—with no adults involved in any way. (We didn't have any basketball courts until Junior High). For our track meets, we dug a sizeable pit on our school grounds (without asking or telling anyone) and filled it with sawdust so we could use it as a landing site for high jump, broad jump, and pole vault. With scrap lumber from a nearby lumber yard we built the "standards" to hold the crossbars, which were bamboo from Kaiser's furniture store—as were, in a heavier version, our pole vaulting poles (taped with electrical tape to enhance gripping and prevent splitting.) More scrap lumber was used to build high and low hurdles. There was no coaching—we taught ourselves everything, and built everything we needed.

IN FOOTBALL, we watched high school games and practices and taught ourselves the rules, strategy, trick plays (both run and pass) and the mechanics of blocking and tackling. In those days nobody made football uniforms for kids so we improvised those, too. We folded towels under our sweaters to act (not very well) as shoulder pads. I tried cardboard as hip and thigh pads but that didn't work. No helmets. A lot of us got hurt. Some broke arms and wrists and Roger Herman broke his nose three times.

I was fairly good but I played mostly with kids older and bigger. As a matter of fact, I never got very big and this was one of the things in my life that really bothered me. I ended up about 5'9" and mostly 132-148 lbs. in high school. Still I was good enough to play three years of high school football and basketball.

No "platoons" in football those days, everyone went both ways. I was good on defense—a sure tackler and I don't remember anyone ever completing a pass on me. My senior year, against a bigger school, Charles City, we got beat 19-0 and I made seven consecutive tackles playing safety!

On offense I played two years as a wingback and my senior year I was the quarterback. I received some area recognition but was always overshadowed by Johnny Weires, who was fast and big for those days. Johnny was no brain surgeon in the "smarts" area and was held back early on, so he was a year or two older than his classmates and this was a major advantage. Johnny was a very good athlete and considered one of the best ball carriers of those times.

As a sophomore I played on one of Waverly's best-ever teams. We were undefeated and un-scored on until the last game of the season, which we won easily but were scored on, due to an unfortunate series of events, in the worst downpour I ever played in.

In my very first game, against Cedar Falls, our quarterback gave me the ball on my very first play. Lefty Flood opened a big hole and I went for 10 yards. On the bottom of a big pile I saw a fist coming down on my face, and somebody really hung a beauty on me—right on my nose! (No face guards in those days.) The referee saw it and penalized them 15 yards. *If I had quit football right then and there, I'd probably still hold the state record for averaging 25 yards per carry!*

In a game against powerhouse West Waterloo, I ran a kickoff back 90 yards for a touchdown. In the same game a year before, I ended up in the hospital. They had an all-state guard who outweighed me by 60 lbs. He put a block on me that must have been a beautiful thing to watch. Dislocated my elbow and they couldn't get it back in place, on the field or in the locker room. Hence, the hospital and anesthesia.

One good thing came out of it. The next day, the Waterloo Courier reported the event, headlined: "ZOLLER, STAR WAVERLY HALFBACK, IS INJURED." (A nice compliment – not really accurate, but appreciated.)

I had a bunch of bad luck that Junior year. The dislocation happened in early September. I was able to play again in early October, but a gang of us went stupid on Halloween. We raided a couple of vegetable gardens near Wartburg College, gathered a few dozen 5-lb. squashes and "bowled" them down the hallways of the college dormitories. But the college guys didn't take the bait and come out to confront us. We left, but three of us came back later and ran into some 30 or more irate college athletes ready to kill us. I ran and dodged the flying squashes, doing pretty well until, full speed, I ran into a steel cable I couldn't see in the dark. I ended up nearly unconscious with a broken collarbone. That ended my football season and adversely affected my whole basketball season as well.

I remember a Nashua running back named Charlie Dan – listed at 175 pounds, but I think he may have been 190. And he was a sprinter. But mostly he was tough. I heard he drank, got into fights at Saturday night dances, and I suspect he may have been older than high school rules allowed. I weighed exactly 132 in my sophomore year and Charlie had me by a good 50 pounds. Before the Nashua game I worried all week about tackling Charlie Dan. (I figured not only "hurt", but maybe "crippled or killed".) But that was the game in the incredible rainstorm. Ankle-deep mud. The weather saved me: in the muck, he went down easily! (I told you I was lucky!)

My final game in my senior year, also against Nashua, was played in a raging blizzard. We nearly froze and nobody came to watch. Football players didn't wear gloves in those days so there were a lot of fumbles. We won easily, but the wind was a problem. I was the punter and everytime I kicked into the wind, we lost yardage!

BASKETBALL. The game was a lot different in those days. No professional players, no NBA. A few big companies began to head in that direction: they hired the best college players for regular jobs, but they also played basketball. (You kind of got the idea they didn't do much but play basketball.) A league was formed, mostly in the Midwest, and Rath Packing Co. of Waterloo fielded a team.

My brother took me to a number of the games in Waterloo. I'd watch great players and copy their style. Our high school coach, K.V. Stevenson, was ultra-conservative—lay-ups and two-handed set shots (from short range) were about all his system allowed. Once in awhile I'd sneak in a one-hander and he didn't much like that. Some people thought I was a show-off but I surely was one of our better shooters. When I was a senior, Independence had an excellent team. They beat us but I had a good night and kept the game close. Afterward, Coach said, "I don't care what the drugstore cowboys say, you shoot any way you want!"

Almost 60 years after our playing days were over, and just before he died, Marshall Carpenter wrote me a letter and said, "Back in the 1930's, you were the first guy in Waverly ever to shoot with one hand!" I was happy that he remembered.

Basketball was much different in those days. A lot slower. Teams with a good lead could stall. There was no shot clock, no half-court line you had to cross by a certain time. And after every score the game stopped and went back for another center-jump. (What were they thinking?) So there wasn't a lot of scoring. Sometimes I might score 14 points and we would win 24 to 12!

As a senior I was the top scorer and I was told my total was the second highest in our history (to that date). My good friend and great athlete, Bill Leary, had just a couple more points, two years before. But he played a game or two more than I did.

I seemed to get better after high school. At Iowa they wouldn't even give me a look-see—I wasn't big enough for Big Ten ball. But we had a great Delta Chi team that won the All-Fraternity Championship, then the All-University title. Our football players—Marion Harris, a reserve tackle and John Hild, fullback and linebacker, played guards. Bob Lannon, all-Big Ten end, was center, and Neil Overton and I were the forwards. (Lannon and Overton both played for Winner, S.D. state champions in high school.) Our varsity Hawkeyes weren't having a very good year and at several Big Ten games we heard people yelling, "We want Delta Chi!"

DIRTY TRICK. The sports editor of the Daily Iowan really embarrassed me. I was on the sports desk, covering (among other things) inter-fraternity basketball. I wrote up the story of us winning the championship game, being very careful not to claim any credit for myself. Most readers don't know that reporters who write the story do not write the headlines, and only the editors decide who gets by-lines. But our editor saw an opportunity he couldn't resist. So he headlined my story: "ZOLLER STARS AS DELTA CHI WINS TITLE" – and added the by-line: "BY BOB ZOLLER"! It took a lot of explaining by me and I'm sure I was never able to undo the damage!

After I left high school Waverly got a new coach, Walton S. Koch. He thought his team was getting a bit over-confident so he asked a couple of us former players, now home from college over the Christmas holidays, if we would play them on New Years Eve.

We liked the idea. The game was promoted by our local newspaper, scheduled at 7 p.m. so it wouldn't interfere with later festivities, and the public was invited to attend. The gym was jammed with local fans. It was handled like a real game, uniformed referees and all the trimmings. It was a great success and it continued for several years. I played in all of them and was often the high point man. The Alumni won them all. One year our starting five was the leading scorers from five consecutive years in high school—Marshall Carpenter, Wayne Sparks, me, Bob Nygren, Pep Grawe. Sparks, by the way, became Captain of the team at Carleton College and a Little All-American.

JOHN MOONEY, FRIEND AND COMPETITOR

Football and basketball were the "biggies" in those days but if you played either of them, Coach made you go out for track. I was a pole-vaulter—not very good. Fairly fast, but not the best. As a senior I was lead-off man on our half-mile relay team and the best javelin thrower in school.

At this point I have to tell you about John Mooney, a kid I grew up with from Kindergarten through four years of college. We were friends but John wanted so much to be an athlete that he became overly competitive and developed a mean streak. He was my age, about the same size, so he tried to beat me in everything, and he never could. He lived on the east side of town and his girlfriend, Marian Miller, lived on a farm just west of town. So John jogged the whole distance every evening, going and coming, and considered it Spartan training for distance running.

One day he challenged me to race him—a mile. I suggested why not a whole track meet, every event? He agreed. I conceded the mile and the half-mile events (mainly because I was too lazy to run them) and he conceded the pole vault and the javelin throw. We then competed in six or seven events and I won them all—so he feigned injury and gave up.

One year John was the other lifeguard at the local pool when Walt Koch, pool manager, suggested that we establish pool records for the various swimming events—to give the local athletes something to shoot for in the years to come. I was the fastest swimmer in town so Koch timed me at various distances for the freestyle and backstroke, and declared these pool records. I also set a record for distance, underwater.

For some reason I didn't do the breaststroke so Mooney practiced that several times a day for several weeks. Then he took a couple days off and hitchhiked to Iowa City to meet with Iowa's great swim coach, Dave Armbruster, to check his stroke and suggest improvements. On his return, John got Koch to time him and set a couple of breaststroke records.

About ten minutes later I got Koch, dived in and quickly broke both of John's new records! (I know, it was a mean thing to do. Maybe one of the worst things I've ever done. But I felt he deserved it.)

We both went to U. of Iowa. Neither family could afford it, so we both got jobs to help out. We went our separate ways, except that as sophomores, we both were sports reporters for The Daily Iowan. I was in Journalism only one year. John made it a career. After he graduated, he went back for another year to become the Sports Editor—and locally famous. (Or maybe infamous.)

He wrote critically of the Hawkeye football team, even suggesting drug abuse, stirring up a hornet's nest! One day the football team physically threw him out of their practice and warned him never to come back!

Not long after, he left school and it was considered a sure thing the University had asked him to do so. He had a job with The Chicago Tribune—briefly. That didn't work out. Then he landed a job with the Salt Lake Tribune and stayed there throughout his working life. And, surprise! He became the best-known sports writer and editor in the history of Utah! When he retired, it seems everyone rich and famous in Utah attended his party, including the governor! And most of the state's nationally known athletes.

Passing through Utah in 1940, I stopped to see him as he arrived at his office. He had gained so much weight (at least 100 lbs.) he looked entirely different. Even his voice had changed. We talked old times for an hour or two. Years later, in the late 1970's, I was on the Isle of Capri and ran into people from Salt Lake City.

"Do you know John Mooney?" I asked. "Everyone in Utah knows John Mooney," they said. I asked them to give him a phone call when they got home. "Tell them you met a guy in Italy who said, "Anything you can do, I can do better—and that includes writing!" They said OK and asked my name. "No name needed," I said. "He'll know who."

About 10 years ago, I decided to write him a long letter about my life and his, and praising his success. He answered—a long and very nice letter. I felt we were friends again.

That was shortly before I heard he had died.

SWIMMING: THE THING I DID BEST

When I was 12, I entered my first-ever race—in the Cedar River, starting at the dam (dry, at the time) and about 180 yards to a life raft opposite the bathing beach. About 35 swimmers, all ages. We were to race all at the same time, but there were two age groups. I finished 3rd overall, and by far the winner of the younger age group.

After that, several summers at Boy Scout Camp where they had a pool, daily swimming and weekly races. Here I discovered I could swim faster than most kids, even the older ones, from Waterloo, Cedar Falls and other towns in the area.

LIFEGUARD—probably smiling at a pretty girl.

SWIMMERS OUT OF THE WATER The kid is Nip Blake from California. At 15, he looked like a young Buster Crabbe, the movie Tarzan.

In 1934 a lot of guys applied for the job as Life Guard at the Waverly Beach. I got it, succeeding well-known Waverly athletes Charlie Lowder and Alec Miller. I'm convinced I was the fastest swimmer of that era, but Charlie Lowder was the best. (He was built like a Greek god and was a varsity swimmer at Iowa State University.)

Incidentally, this wonderful job I got by beating out so many other applicants paid $30 a month—for which I worked every day (7 days a week)— 9 to 12 in the mornings (clean-up) and 1 to 9 p.m., guarding. But I did get a break on some rainy days when I could close up early because nobody wanted to swim anyway.

During my year at the Cedar River beach, somebody heard that Iowa Falls had a swim team and a Dual Meet in Waverly was arranged. When they arrived in regulation tank suits, and even had a coach (!), I was ready to concede defeat. I can't remember much about it, but the pick-up team I put together did win the meet—mainly because I won everything I entered—even the diving, which was a major surprise.

The only swim coach we ever had in Waverly was me. Except for Charlie Lowder, I was the only Senior Red Cross Lifeguard. Our new pool opened in June 1935 and several hundred people, who couldn't (or wouldn't) swim (or bathe) in the muddy Cedar River, suddenly developed a new interest in swimming. I kept busy teaching children and adults basic and advanced swimming. Walt Koch, the pool manager, and Wayne Sparks, the other guard, stood by and watched. I did all the work. But I didn't mind—because I never gave it a thought.

I'll never forget the day when all the beginners took their swimming tests. They had to venture into deep water for the first time. Maybe 70 or 80 of them, one at a time, had to jump in feet first, come up, level off, swim to the middle of the pool, make a sharp turn and swim back. Most were nervous about their first time in water over their heads and had some difficulty going from vertical to horizontal—the whole idea, of course, of the jump in and the sharp turn. I had to go in to rescue at least 20 of them. All in one morning. Quite a workout.

We had a "big deal" dedication of our new swimming pool. Somehow I got put in charge, planned the whole thing, got Coach Armbruster to attend with several of his All-American swimmers and divers, and got my brother Ed (Jack) to serve as MC. He was a bit nervous, and I suspect had been imbibing more than somewhat to reinforce his courage. So I ended up having to MC the event as well as doing most everything else. But a large crowd attended and it was a complete success.

ICE WATER AND SOMETHING TO BRAG ABOUT

Dorothy Sparks (Wayne's older sister) and Dorothy Moeller (newspaper lady, wife of Les Moeller, editor) were big wheels in the local Red Cross. They decided Waverly should have a Senior Red Cross Life Saving Examiner. There were none in the area and I was the logical choice. But I had just turned 19, and 21 was the minimum age for this lofty position so I was not acceptable. But I was the only "Senior Lifeguard" which was required before one could try for promotion to Examiner. So the ladies persisted and finally got the Red Cross headquarters in St. Louis to grant me a dispensation.

At that time New Hampton had also built a beautiful new pool, much better and twice the size of Waverly's. They had four lifeguards, all qualified, who wanted to take the tests for Examiner. So St. Louis agreed to send a Special Examiner to New Hampton and I would have to go there so all five of us could be tested at the same time.

The tests lasted all day, for two days. The two Dorothys agreed to drive me there, wait all day, and drive me home. After everything was arranged, Mother Nature intervened and presented a major problem—unseasonably cold weather—actually *unbelievably* cold weather! Trying to perform effectively in the icy water was almost impossible. (We didn't actually turn blue, but we felt like it!) Someone suggested we wait a few days but that wasn't possible. So we struggled through the first day's schedule, in some pain, but no life-threatening problems.

On the morning of the second day all four New Hampton guards quit. I wish I could have, but the ladies had worked hard to get St. Louis to waive the age requirement, then driven me to New Hampton two days in a row, so I couldn't quit on them. I stayed and passed everything. Then the Special Examiner told me I had just become the youngest Red Cross Life Saving Examiner in the United States!

Ironic, I suppose, but the sport I was best at, I disliked the most. At the University of Iowa I did so well in the interfraternity and all-University swimming races that Coach Armbruster asked me to join the varsity—quite a compliment as Iowa was rated in the top three colleges, nationally, in this sport. (Michigan, Yale and Iowa.) But I knew the varsity swimmers had to get to the Field House in the wee hours of the morning, swim several miles, then return after classes and put in an hour or two more. I couldn't believe anything was worth all that.

In 1935, I became the youngest Red Cross Life Saving Examiner in America.

I like to believe I was the fastest swimmer in Northeast Iowa, but always greatly disadvantaged competing with swimmers who trained all year in indoor pools and who had the coaching I never had. Nobody taught me how to swim, and nobody taught me how to race. I never learned to make turns effectively. I suspect there were many fine points I didn't know but the main thing is, you can never be very good without total dedication, and years of practice. My opportunity to swim was restricted to three months in the summer and most of that time I had to guard the lives of the paying customers.

Besides, I wasn't endowed with ideal physical equipment. Not with my size 7 1/2 feet and small hands. Most good swimmers today are big— some 6'4" to 6'6" and with long arms, big hands and feet. Michael Phelps, who won 8 medals (6 gold!) at the last Olympic Games, has size 14 feet!

But swimming was good to me, in many ways. For one thing, girls seem to go for lifeguards. On slow days at the pool I was sometimes invited for "underwater smooching". If the girls were pretty it was a "fringe benefit". Maybe fifty years after I left Waverly, Eileen Donovan Bodeker told me, "I remember you as what my granddaughters now call a "hunk"!

And for many years after I left Waverly when I went back for a visit, invariably someone would come up to me and tell me, "You taught me how to swim!"

NEVER A DIVER. MAYBE I COULD HAVE BEEN.

With proper coaching and equipment, I might have become a pretty good diver. I was about the right size. But nobody in Waverly knew anything about diving, so I had to figure it out on my own. The river beach had only one (primitive) diving board and it was an odd height above the water. The new pool wasn't much better. It did have a conventional one-meter springboard. At the 3-meter level, just a solid platform.

Not bad! (I'd give it maybe a 10?)

To compete in college or AAU diving events, I would have to perfect 10 different dives, all from 3-meter springboards. We didn't have a 3-meter springboard and I never learned all the dives. I really beat myself up trying to learn a double-somersault off the 3-meter platform. I'd spin so fast I couldn't tell where I was in the air, so I'd either land on my face or snap open too soon and land flat on my back. The first was the worst: I peeled my eyelids back and hurt my eyes. If I tried to read anything, it became painful. Doc Robertson, our town's best eye specialist, told me I had scar tissue on my eyeballs! He prescribed reading glasses, which I used for awhile. Eventually, the pain went away.

However, I did coach Jim Clark and Bud Kirkland, taught them the 5 dives they needed for the Junior competition, and they went to the State AAU meet and finished first and second! Every year we had a big water show at the pool and the three of us would put on a triple-diving exhibition.

In 2004, when I was 88 years old, I went to Waverly for my last visit. At the High School Reunion, Dr. William Wehrmacher came to me, and shook hands and said, "I always remember you as the best diver I ever saw!" (Remarkable, I think, considering I wasn't really a diver at all.) But it was nice to hear.

ON MY HONOR, I WILL DO MY BEST...

BOY SCOUTS. I joined when I was 12. By 14, I was the youngest Eagle Scout in Waverly. I loved overnight hikes, getting close to nature, sleeping under the stars. And learning a lot about many things. It seems that all the good kids in Waverly were Boy Scouts. George Beebe and Bev Ladage were two years older, but we worked together on a lot of merit badges and made Eagle about the same time. Jack Wright, who was knowledgeable about almost everything, became our Scoutmaster and a life-long friend.

The Wapsipinicon Area Council had a camp—Ingawanis—on the Cedar River about six miles from Waverly. In summer, Scouts came from all over. It cost $5 a week and my family finally gave into my begging. I only got one week but I applied for a job and was hired as Dishwasher. No salary but you got the camping. Later I was promoted to Cook's Help. I stayed all summer. Next year I was a Tribe Leader. I spent my summers there for five years and loved it. The year I graduated from high school they wanted me as the Waterfront Director. But I got a paying job as the Waverly Life Guard.

Scouting and Ingawanis were valuable parts of my life. I cannot imagine anything better for a young man growing up. Being out in the woods all summer, meeting good kids from a dozen other communities, becoming a leader, being molded and guided by the Scout's Oath and the Scout Laws—it was about as Norman Rockwell All-American as you can get.

I think I've been "a good kid" all my life and Scouting was a major reason why.

INTELLECTUAL PURSUITS

I mentioned before that sports were everything and nobody (including me) paid much attention to doing well in reading, writing and arithmetic. We never heard about "nerds" in those days but we had a few. We called them "greasy grinds"—they were the Rodney Dangerfields of those times and they "got no respect". Henry Moulds is the one I remember best: he didn't play football and he got good grades—studied all the time. I was the opposite, except I got good grades too. *But until I enrolled at the University, I never even once encountered the concept of homework.*

For a couple of years in high school they gave State Tests—every class, every school in Iowa. As a sophomore I scored our school's highest in three subjects; Gail Jackson 2, Wayne Sparks, Vince Carstensen, Bill Draeger and Henry Moulds (!) one each. Four of us scored high enough to be invited to compete in the State Finals in Iowa City. Superintendent T. M. Clevenger drove us in his Buick—Sparks, me and two others (girls, but I can't remember who). Clevenger gave Sparks his car for the night before the tests. Wayne knew an Iowa City girl and she got a date for me. We found out later that most of our competitors were coached by their teachers and crammed all day and most of the night before the tests, but we didn't study at all. We stayed out until 2 a.m. And we didn't win anything either. But I enjoyed telling everyone over the next few years that I was "the second-year Latin champion of Northeast Iowa!"

In my senior year they gave a special statewide test in World History. Ruth Geiger and I tied for the top grades in our school. One year they gave all high school students in Iowa an I.Q. test. This created an uproar of protest – the ones who scored lowest would be scarred for life! So they never published the results and never gave I.Q. tests again. Years later, my cousin, Dorothy Strotman, served as Secretary to the Waverly Superintendent of Schools. Going through old files, she discovered the long-hidden I.Q. scores and wrote me that I was No. 1. She told me my score which I can't remember. (At age 87, I took another I.Q. test because I suspected my memory was slipping. I was right: I missed several of the memory questions. But my overall score was still good enough to apply for membership in Mensa.)

In college, in my first English class, we all had to write themes on subjects of our choosing. Two weeks later, I was one of twenty-five Freshmen (of more than 3,000) selected for Honors English.

In Law School, I maintained a low profile, but when the grades came out I beat Phil Allen and Howard Davidson (both Presidents of Delta Chi before me) and Wayne Sparks. Phil later became a political commentator on radio in the Midwest (like Rush Limbaugh, only Phil was liberal). Davidson graduated from Harvard Law. Sparks was smart, had graduated from Carleton College, was a doctor's son, and unlike me, loaded with confidence.

I finished near the top of my class – not sure where, but I suspect in the top three (or better) as I was offered a scholarship and bid to the staff of the Iowa Law Review, a very special honor.

At this point I interrupt this totally immodest recitation of my achievements to tell you something you should know—if you don't already know it: the "authorities" and the majorities are not always right. Sometimes, if you become well-informed, you can catch them doing things that are incredibly stupid. In fact, I've been pretty much made a hobby of discovering dumb things by people who should know better.

One of these dumb decisions bothered me more than somewhat. I had decided if I had any talent it was probably that I could write well and should major in Journalism. My sophomore year I was a sports reporter for The Daily Iowan, considered one of the best student newspapers in America. All reporters were required to keep "string books". Whatever you got published, you'd clip and paste in your string book and turn it in every week. The faculty staff would check everyone's published work and the best stories would be labeled (in red pencil) as "Good". Then each week the list of "Goods" would appear on the school's bulletin board. Over the year, I headed the list more times than any student on The Daily Iowan.

Every week the number of column inches also was measured—apparently to provide some indication of each reporter's effort and activity. I never thought about that much—until the grades came out and I was given "C"! Then I found out that *grades were based on column inches, and nothing else!* Forget the "Goods"! I had concentrated on sports-related feature stories. Meanwhile, students who understood the system would spend hours every week typing box scores of football, basketball, (etc.) off the Associated Press, INS and UPI wire services and rack up maybe 200 column inches of *typing* to my 45 or 60 of *creative writing!*

Some system! They ignore their own evaluation of good writing and give the top grades to people who type a lot! I confronted the Dean (the fairly famous Frank Luther Mott) and let off a lot of steam—and got nowhere. All by itself this system cost me Phi Beta Kappa! That's something I earned and would like to have had. Such stupidity in an institution of higher learning!

NOT GOOD, JUST LUCKY!

Until now I've talked a lot about my little triumphs. But I need to say again: *intelligence is a gift. Nobody ever earns it, and the fortunate people who have it have no right to claim any credit.*

I'm not sure I lived up to my potential. In my early years I lacked confidence, viewing myself as a small town boy from a family of modest means with no educational credentials. I never worked very hard; I was satisfied with things as they happened to me. I never pushed hard to excel, either in high school or college. (I wish I had.)

I took a college course which required that we keep a (loose-leaf) diary and turn it in every Monday. Not the usual, about girlfriends or the basketball game, but our involvement in things cultural, philosophical, educational. Attending a lecture, reading a book—and what we thought as a result of what we heard or read. I liked the idea. So I kept diaries for many years, although not always on intellectual matters. And they really helped me greatly in writing this book. (Some of these are among my "stuff". If anyone finds them and reads them, please be informed: my world was entirely different than the one you live in. If I use an "X" or a star with a young lady's name, *it meant I kissed her* – and nothing more!)

"ROOTS". (WAY OUT ON A LIMB OF MY FAMILY TREE.)

Genealogy buffs hope to trace their families back to noble ancestors, or at least to important people. My ancestors were poor German farmers that came to this country hoping to escape poverty. With hard work they survived, but it wasn't easy, and nobody became rich or famous – until my generation when one of my cousins became a key member of the famous "Whiz Kids" at Ford Motor Co.

I never knew any of my grandparents – they all died before I was born.

DAD'S FAMILY, THE ZOLLERS. Both of his brothers lived all their lives in Waverly. Otto, a grocery store clerk was a miser. (I guess he had to be, to survive on a clerk's salary.) Jeremiah ("Dell") never saved a nickel in his life. He was a "Lost Weekend" type. Stayed sober sometimes for a couple of months, then "went off on a toot" and would disappear for a week or two. Worked for my father because nobody else would hire him. (I liked Dell a lot.)

Of Dad's three sisters, "Mate", lived in Waterloo, had a large family and I barely knew them. Nora ("Node") lived in Janesville, not far from Waverly. Wife of a rural mail carrier. Lived to be 100. Harriet ("Aunt Hat") had a withered hand, but was the most elegant of the group. Lived in Minneapolis with husband "Jurg" Jurgenson, a car salesman. It seemed they always owed us money, lived a lot better than we did, and never paid us back. (I liked Aunt Hat because I got to see a lot of lakes and she made great orange cream pie.)

My paternal grandfather was quite a guy. Dad never said anything about him, but some of the old-timers in Waverly told me he was a retired blacksmith and the strongest man in town. When traveling strong men would come to amaze the locals with feats of strength (in one of the pool halls), somebody would send a kid to go get old John Zoller to defend the honor of Waverly. The feature act was always a test of strength and legend has it that my grandfather – said to be a retired blacksmith – won more than his share.

I was also told old John was the "best swimmer in that part of the country" – a dubious distinction because most people couldn't swim in those days – or never did.

THE CLIPPING. When I was in Junior High, I was snooping through my father's old roll-top desk and found a lengthy (full-page) newspaper story about the old guy's service in the Civil War. It was yellow with age, probably 50-some years old. It said he was captured and sent to a prison camp in the South, on the west bank of the Mississippi River.

One night a considerable number of the prisoners attempted to escape. Most made it to the river, but the Rebel troops began shooting. Some prisoners were killed or wounded, most surrendered and only one managed to escape, swimming the Mississippi River. Guess who?

Of course, this sounds like something somebody made up. But Grandfather was known as a super-swimmer. He did get home safely and the newspaper must have checked the story which they labeled "remarkable".

I also found a picture of the old guy who had long hair, a full beard and looked very heavy – no neck at all! It reminded me of pictures of Henry Wadsworth Longfellow. (Or was it John Greenleaf Whittier?)

Years later, when I returned from my war – Dad died in 1941 – I asked my family if I could have the clipping and the picture, and they all said they never saw them or knew they existed.

THE RITTERS. I knew we had some "shirt-tail" relatives in Waverly called the Ritters. One was a somewhat disreputable character called "Scrib" who Dad never acknowledged. I lived in Waverly 24 years and never knew much about him, even where he lived. He did have a son, Erv ("Little Scrib") who became locally famous as our community's No. 1 bootlegger, and during prohibition, even Waverly's "important people" had to depend on him for anything alcoholic. Erv thrived and became a natty dresser.

MOTHER'S SIDE: THE REITHS. Mom's parents, also from Germany, lived on a farm 20 miles from Waverly, near Oran. Three boys: John and Frank, and George who died young. Four girls: Irene, Clare (my mother), Ann and Rose. John farmed all his life, followed politics and world news (via an old crystal set radio) and I remember him as seeming to produce more saliva than most people. Drooled a lot. His son Louie, inherited that, and grandson Leo also was somewhat on the juicy side.

Frank didn't take to hard work, like farming. Dabbled in real estate, in Des Moines. He and his wife produced only one child, but he was a good one – Francis, the "Whiz Kid".

Irene (Woods) was kind of the boss of the bunch. My mother and Ann just faded into the background. Rose was a real character: left home at 16, supported herself, never married but had a good time from sixteen to a ripe old age. One time, she told Laura, my wife, "I never married, but I never missed a thing."

SURVIVAL ITEM. John's son, Johnny, got lucky: he and his hired man were plowing when a storm came up, so they left their tractors and ran to shelter. Lightning struck – killed the hired man and the farm dog, and knocked Johnny unconscious. His shoes were blown off his feet and found more than fifty feet away! The keys and coins in his pocket were melted and fused into a solid mass. But Johnny came to, went home, was checked by a doctor (who made house calls in those days!) and suffered no permanent damage whatever.

I had a whole bunch of cousins, but I never spent much time with them except Ann's kids – they lived in Waverly. Ruth, Dorothy and "Junior" Strotman were all very bright, and Ruth was a beauty. She's still alive (at 95) and we stay in touch. As a youngster, I spent a couple of weeks every summer at Irene's farm, riding horses. Francis Woods (much older than I) enjoyed bullying me. But the girl, Evelyn, was my age and we got along fine.

I seldom saw the future Whiz Kid, but I remember him as a 12-year-old at a family reunion. I knew he was "special" because he liked pie, cake and candy but never ate any because he knew it wasn't good for him! (I'd never run into that before.)

I later learned – from Aunt Rose – who also lived in Des Moines – that he was always at the top of his class in high school and college (Drake) and had organized a dance band and earned good money, both in high school and college. On graduation, General Electric recruiters sent him to Schenectady for management training.

His career was remarkable. More on that a bit later on.

MY IMMEDIATE FAMILY

Dad quit school when he was in the 5th grade, later worked in a factory that made oak barrels. But he did OK, fed his family, and became the Town Marshall. (I still have his .32 caliber Smith & Wesson revolver.) He had a good mind, read newspapers a lot, but never spent much time expressing his opinions. Never talked much at all.

THE FATHER-SON TALK. I was already in high school when he thought it was time for a discussion about sex. So one day he asked me, "You know about that stuff?" I said, "Yes". And that was the end of our conversation.

He spent most of his life owning a meat market specializing in quality meats, and was best known for his "Home Grown Baloney". Everyone said it was the very best and when local people moved to California, they had it mailed to them from time to time. If Ed had been smarter, or I had been older, we might have built a business to give Oscar Meyer a run for his money.

Mother was a farm gal, a schoolteacher briefly, and seemed content to remain as unobtrusive as possible.

Brother Ed – everyone called him "Jack" – was a "fun person" who concentrated on having a good time – usually involving liquid refreshment. Everyone liked him. When big name bands came to Waterloo, he somehow got acquainted and they all would end up at his apartment partying for the rest of the night. Dorothy Lamour, a singer at the time, was one who joined the "after hours" group at his place.

People often told me they couldn't believe Ed and I were really brothers. I was the Eagle Scout; he got kicked off the football team for smoking. After one semester at Gates Business College, he worked in a clothing store, but spent most of his life as a cigarette salesman. He took up magic and became locally famous. After he retired, he spent most of his time in front of TV. No interest in local, state or national affairs, only sports and entertainment. I kidded him about being "the laziest white man I ever saw". And that if Olive, his wife, died before he did, he'd starve to death, because he never learned where the kitchen was, or how to open the refrigerator!

I always gave him a hard time, but he never got mad at me. Had a lot of bad habits, but I admit, my brother was more likeable than I ever was, and a lot better looking.

My sister Helen was a nurse, and a very good one. She was a bit on the hefty side in high school and I remember she beat up Eldon Laird when he beat up my brother. When Bill McHugh, older than I, punched me, she sought him out and beat up on him, too. At about 30, she left and worked a couple years in Newark, NJ. She came back slimmed down and smartly dressed. Eventually, she married Harry McDonnell, which I thought was a big mistake. The only good thing that happened was a daughter named Vicki – a real winner.

So – that's where I came from. Mate's son, Johnny Nettleton, moved to Chula Vista, CA, owned a food market, seemed successful, but committed suicide. His son, Steve, went into the business and ended up owning a chain of supermarkets all over California, and flew his own airplane to manage them.

Node's son, Donnie Shepard, was my age. I remember him as a tough kid. When he was 12, he fell into a ditch-digging machine. It mangled a leg and he was hospitalized for well over a year, and finally died. Local newspapers did frequent stories about his courage in a losing battle and this made him locally famous.

Otto and his wife Gertrude lived in abject poverty – there was a lot of that going around in those days. Otto died, Gertrude survived a few more years. When she passed on, it turned out that Otto had done some investing (General Motors, et al) and apparently hit the jackpot. Also apparently, they had no idea what money was for. So it all went to relatives, friends and charities – way over $100,000, probably twice that much! Maybe equivalent to a million or two today!

Another thing I surely wonder about. People weren't overly sociable in those days – parties, dinners, etc. Never in my lifetime do I recall Otto or Dell or any of their families ever setting foot in our house! Or any of us in theirs. I know there were no bad feelings involved. That's just the way they were. Strange.

Later I'll tell you about the girl I married and the children we produced, our granddaughters and so on. But all that happened after I grew up and left Waverly to "let life happen to me".

THE BOY-GIRL THING

I guess Adam and Eve didn't have a lot of choices. But most of the human race ever since has spent a great deal of time looking for the right person to "partner" with—usually someone of the opposite sex—and in many cases (hopefully at least) someone who "turns them on".

The entire process varies with the beliefs and customs of the tribe, or society, the times and many other factors. Sometimes neither party gets any say in the matter: their weddings are "arranged". Some pair off early in life, some get married because they have to, and some take a long time to find their "soul mates". Some never do. Many marriages last a lifetime and too many end in divorce.

My marriage lasted a lifetime—sixty-one years—very good years.

While my brother and my daughter were involved in divorces, almost all of my friends stayed married for their lifetimes. Ed Kepler was divorced twice and I was Best Man at his second wedding. I was also Best Man at my brother's second wedding. And Best Man a third time for a couple whose name I do not know!

That last one was kind of an oddball situation—after The War, about 57 years ago. Our Catholic priest, Father Mahoney, was the chaplain at Fort Ritchie, an Army post near where we lived. One day he told me a Catholic soldier had met a local girl and they decided to get married. The soldier had no Catholic friends and I guess the Best Man had to be Catholic. Would I do the soldier a favor? I agreed. When I arrived at the Chapel, I found the soldier was a black man, his bride was white. Father Mahoney hadn't mentioned that to me. He knew he didn't have to.

I believe the reason practically everyone I ever knew well had marriages that lasted is because of the whens and wheres of our lives. I keep telling you, our world was different.

I like girls. Always did. But early on, I never met any that interested me greatly—football, for example, was much more important. Our Boy-Girl activities were frequently group activities. Some paired off: "went steady". But mostly, one guy would get his father's car, pick up two more guys and three girls and "cruise"—which mainly involved driving back and forth (slowly to save gas) on "main street" (Bremer Avenue) for an hour or two. We'd talk and laugh and that was about it.

Sometimes six or a dozen of us would go on a "blanket party"—out in the woods, to a campground perhaps, build a fire, roast marshmallows, and talk. Sometimes (usually?) there would be some "smooching" or "necking". But always good, clean fun. Everybody in Waverly knew everybody in Waverly, and reputations were carefully guarded.

Of course, our community never outlawed human nature. All of us weren't altar boys. All girls weren't virgins. But everyone knew who was what. Kenny Dean, for example, mentally undressed every female of our species, and talked about it. So we called him "Dirty Dean" and didn't like him much. A few – very few – of the local girls were known to be "easy" and almost everyone knew who they were. But kissing was as far as the good kids went.

The first girl I ever kissed was Mary Louise Seeley. She grew up in Waverly, but on the West Side, so I didn't know her well. Her family moved to Des Moines, but she came back to visit one summer, told Mary Spalding (I believe) she wanted a date with me. I remembered her as being pretty, so I liked the idea. I was 16 and I could drive, so I got my Dad's car. We went "cruising", the two of us in the front seat and another couple in the back seat. Just past St. Mary's Cemetery I turned onto a country road and noticed my date was sitting very close to me, friendly-like, so I leaned over and kissed her. In the process I forgot to steer and pulled the car left and right down into a deep ditch! Why, that top-heavy old 1926 Buick didn't tip over, I'll never know. I just kept driving down the ditch, maybe 60 or 80 yards, and it got somewhat less deep so I drove it right back up on the road. We all breathed easier and I never made the same stupid mistake again.

THE FIRST NAKED LADY I EVER SAW.

About four years before my first kiss, I found out what a naked lady looks like! Quite an experience. I decided to write about it because this is an account of my growing up in a small Midwestern town in the first half of the 20th century and I want it to be authentic. I'm reporting all the things that make me look good, so it's necessary to tell you I did some things I'm not especially proud of.

Besides, we all know this Boy-Girl thing has been going on since the dawn of human history, so why pretend it hasn't entered into all our lives? (In addition, I now look back on a life of so many missed Boy-Girl opportunities that in retrospect I view this guy I'm writing about as a "Little Lord Fauntleroy.") Or a nerd without a pocket protector. And I'm not proud of it!

I was 12, at the old Cedar River beach. Some kid told me if I got up on the roof of the bathhouse, I could look down into the girls' dressing room. Without giving it adequate thought, I climbed up from the men's side, up the peaked roof of the central building and, lying prone, peered down—and hit the jackpot! The girls' side had partitions to provide privacy and you couldn't see anybody there. But in the center aisle, right out in the open and facing me, was a totally naked lady drying off before getting dressed! I was surprised and thrilled, dumbfounded and scared to death, all at the same time, all within 3 seconds! (Or possibly, five.)

I knew her immediately: it was Mary Ladage, Bev's sister! Her body was perfect, a work of art! This was a big surprise because I never noticed it when she was dressed. (She always had a fairly unattractive "Ella Cinders" hairdo and when you looked at her that's mostly what you saw.)

But panic was my principal reaction as I realized anyone a hundred yards away could see me on the roof and know what I was doing there. As I scrambled back down, I had visions of lifelong disgrace and years in Fort Madison—Iowa's State Penitentiary!

This may or may not have been the worst thing I've done. But I didn't get caught. (I keep telling you, I'm lucky!) Later, of course, I realized at least several dozen other young guys had made the same trip. But I bet they never saw Mary Ladage!

I LEARNED ABOUT LIFE AS A LIFEGUARD

Lifeguards have some advantages in this Boy-Girl thing and I was no exception. I had a good body and I got a nice tan and spent several summers mostly in bathing suits. At the pool, I would sometimes dive, and divers look pretty good in the middle of a swan dive or layout half gainer. So once in awhile, as mentioned before, I'd get an invite for "underwater smooching". I was no "dreamboat" like Bob Schulze but I was OK and I did quite well.

One time at the pool, Ann Nygren and Alene Klaudt asked me to judge which one had the best boobs. I figured they just did it to shock me, so I didn't take the bait: I just immediately declared them both losers!

Alene was a good athlete—golf and tennis. She started going steady with Lee Reinhardt and therefore no longer available for dating. But one time a group had made plans to attend a special dance in Waterloo and, last minute, Lee couldn't go. So somebody asked me to fill in as Alene's date. I did, and on the way home four of us rode in the back seat, which was kind of crowded (or cozy, as the case may be), and Alene kissed me. I was surprised and pleased and we smooched all the way back to Waverly. This was a rather strange situation because (1) Alene was unquestionably one of the best kissers I met in my entire life, and (2) we never dated again. She went back to being Lee's steady and they were married not too long after.

I repeat for emphasis: in those days kissing was the big deal. One of my lifeguard summers (and now I am bragging), I went smooching with three girls—separately—in one evening! And none of them knew about the others!

This, of course, took some doing. First you have to have a car. And then you need a bit of luck. The first was Mary Ellis, youngest and prettiest of the three Ellis girls. I was driving around, picked her up and she mentioned she had to be someplace and didn't have much time. I parked near the golf course and we smooched. It was nice, and according to my diaries that happened with me and Mary Ellis a number of times. But later she started going steady with a very fine looking young guy, Billy Brooks, from Shell Rock. And they got married.

The second was Mary Ellen Stoeber, a visitor from Chicago. She had relatives in Waverly and came for several weeks, every summer. Young and pretty. Hung around the pool a lot. So we arranged to get together that evening, parked and smooched. Her local relatives were keeping her on a fairly tight leash so she had to be home at a time when my evening was, at least somewhat, still young. (More on Mary Ellen Stoeber later.)

ABOUT LORAINE. FIRST LOVE?

The third young lady was Loraine Sherf, and she was the most important of the three. New Year's Eve, months before that, I was stagging it to the big dance at Electric Park in Waterloo. Several guys in my gang were also dateless; we were all home from college over the Christmas holidays.

That's when I saw this girl I thought was interesting (i.e., good looking) and I asked if anyone knew who she was. I was told, "Forget it, She goes steady with the guy she's dancing with. They go to ISTC." (Iowa State Teachers College, now the University of Northern Iowa.) Later, when the music stopped, I took a chance and asked her and the guy with her for a dance. I was surprised they said O.K. (My guess is, he had to go to the Men's room and figured I was no serious competition.)

As we danced—and afterwards from other people—I learned her boyfriend was Noel Bacon, head cheerleader and Big Man on Campus; they planned to marry after graduation; and she had just moved to Waverly! When I got another look at Noel, I could see he was taller than I and better looking. So prospects seemed slim, but when summer came and Loraine was in Waverly (and Noel wasn't), I gave her a call. As I remember, she made excuses at first, but on the night of my Trifecta, she said OK and we cruised and talked and when I took her home we kissed goodnight. It was no smooching party but it wasn't just a perfunctory peck on the cheek either!

She also told me Noel had graduated and had gone to California with a couple of college chums—something all Iowa lads (including me) had high on their list of Things to Do. Unfortunately, she reminded me they planned to get married when he got back.

But "when the cat's away, the mice will play" and our summer was a bit like that. Loraine became as close to being a "girlfriend" as I had ever had. It became an exceptionally nice summer! Times being what they were, we seldom did anything but ride around, talk, find a place to park and smooch. And we did a lot of that. I even wrote a poem, "To Loraine".

Then, in mid-summer, Loraine drove down to the pool and told me what I expected but didn't want to hear. "Noel's back." There goes a really good deal, I thought. This was goodbye? "He wants me to go with him and spend a week with his family." I knew this meant planning the wedding.

I didn't say goodbye. I figured that was up to her. But then she asked me, "What do you think I should do?" This was a bombshell! Like I'm involved in the decision? Apparently, she was pondering a choice! For once in my life I didn't know what to say. Noel had proposed marriage, and was planning on it. I considered marriage a matter that might come into my life some years into the future. I couldn't imagine why, but it seemed like she wanted to know where I stood on the subject. And I suddenly came to believe that if I told her what I thought she wanted to hear, she *might* break it off with Noel!

I tried to choose my words well. I can't remember what they were but they suggested it might be best to visit his family, if they were expecting her. She said OK. But three days later she was back at the pool. "We broke up," she told me.

I felt badly about this—sorry for Noel, and rather amazed at what had happened. We continued to see each other everyday until I returned to college. She got a schoolteacher job at a small town about 50 miles from Waverly. While I was thinking how nice it would be to be with her again over the holidays, I knew it wasn't fair to let her believe I was really a prospective marriage candidate.

My friend Pep Grawe had told me on several occasions that he much admired Loraine and it was too bad I had gotten there first. So I told him I was ready to break it off and suggested he move in and take my place. "I feel that Loraine is vulnerable." I said. "Your job is to make sure she doesn't get involved with some cowboy up there where she'll be teaching school." Pep figured that would be a great idea and said he would handle it.

But he didn't. I tried to ease out gracefully but she kept writing me letters and every time we both got back to Waverly we dated and it was just like always. She told me she had met a young truck driver named "Skeeter" and he was after her. He was harmless, she said, but fun-loving and something of a clown. I didn't think Skeeter was anything but bad news.

June 8, 1938—the day before I left Waverly to start my summer job in Newton—I was the Toastmaster at Waverly's Music-Alumni Dinner Dance and I took Loraine. That night she told me she loved me but I had never indicated any interest in a permanent relationship. And if I had no marriage plans, she'd probably marry Skeeter. I said I couldn't marry her or anyone—and not because of her. It was my "no job, no prospects and no idea of how I might make a living" problem.

Later she married Skeeter, and without ever meeting the guy, I knew it was an incredible mismatch. And it was.

NOEL BACON, FLYING TIGER

I felt badly about this whole affair, although I had never said or done anything to encourage this lovely lady to break up with Noel Bacon. Noel, meantime had become something of a celebrity, having been maybe the first Iowa boy to join Gen. Chennault's famous Flying Tigers. This was about as glamorous and adventurous as one can get, and the Iowa newspapers covered the story, big-time. I was impressed—and even more sorry that Loraine had passed up a good man like this to get involved with a guy like Skeeter.

And now, to complete this story: fast-forward to Phase 2 of my life—but just briefly. When the war ended, the USS Corregidor and I were in Pearl Harbor. A lot of my closest friends had already left my ship, and a new LCDR, an aviator, had come aboard. I liked the guy and he invited me to join him for the cocktail hour at the Officers Club. We ordered our drinks and then I spotted an old friend and left to say hello. When I returned to our table another officer was there and my new friend introduced him. "This is an old Flying Tiger buddy of mine," he said, "Meet Noel Bacon."

"I already have," I said. We shook hands. "I'm sorry," I told him. (It was all I could think of to say.) "It's OK," he said, "These things happen. No hard feelings."

All this happened years after the day at the pool when Loraine asked, "What do you think I should do?" So I was surprised Noel knew me when we met in Pearl Harbor. But he did, immediately. We talked. "She was a great gal," I said. "A real lady," Noel said. Then we raised our glasses. "To Loraine!" This happened several times in the next hour or two. "To Loraine!" Not surprising, I realized later I had too much to drink.

On one of my postwar visits to Waverly, John Meyer told me Loraine had remarried, and this one was a better deal for her. I forget the name and what he did for a living, but they lived nearby Shell Rock, pretty much a suburb of Waverly. John said he would see her in Waverly now and then, and she still looked great. I was happy to hear this.

As a retired naval officer, I belong to the Military Officers Association and they send me their monthly magazine. Every issue lists the names of officers who died. Maybe eight or ten years ago, Noel Bacon's name appeared, and I decided to let Loraine know. John Meyer supplied her married name and address and I wrote her a letter. I said I hoped she was well and happy, that Noel had died, and about our meeting in Pearl Harbor. I tried not to open any old wounds, but maybe I did. She never replied—and I don't blame her.

MONEY IS IMPORTANT WHEN YOU DON'T HAVE ANY

What a difference 60, 70 or 80 years make! Compared with today when poverty is defined as not having a separate television set for each person who lives there, most of us in Waverly were poor, but we didn't know it.

Through high school and college, boys and girls dated "on the cheap"—mostly we just drove around or parked and talked. Roy's Place had great 5¢ hamburgers but it was no secret that we always took the girls home before going to Roy's Place. And sometimes we didn't even have the nickel or dime to go there alone.

I went through college on a shoestring, as the saying goes. And at one time I didn't even figure a shoestring would be available. My high school coach K.V. Stephenson knew I was bright so when I was a junior, he suggested I try for an appointment to West Point. But he said I would need to take a course in Solid Geometry. T. M Clevenger, Supt. of Schools, arranged a class for me in my senior year. He taught it himself, and I was the only one in the class!

But I never took the shot at West Point because only a few appointments were available and the U.S. Congressman who arranged these appointments usually gave them in return for political contributions, or so I was told. My family had no political clout or connections.

But things looked brighter for me when Jim Watson, president of Delta Chi fraternity at the University of Iowa, got in touch with my brother in Waterloo and said, "I've been hearing some good things about your kid brother, and I want to talk to him about joining Delta Chi." Ed told him I wasn't planning on college, much less joining a fraternity. But Watson said he wanted to talk to me, and when he did, he said he could arrange a halftime board job to help with expenses. I did a bit of arithmetic and as a result I was able to tell my parents if they could come up with $500 a year, I could go to college.

Mother was the one that made sure I got the $500. Bob Schulze and I went together—Bob's folks drove us to Iowa City. We both pledged Delta Chi. I immediately bonded with Bob Lannon, Neil Overton and John Hild. I found out a lot of students were barely financially able. Being a "state school" it was the cheapest place we could go. Food was the biggest expense and there weren't nearly enough halftime board jobs to go around. They were rare and of great value.

The year before, Hild was a key football recruit. They gave him a janitor's job at the Field House but it wasn't enough to buy food. So he got an all-night job at a filling station and he spent every night of his freshman year pumping gas and sleeping in a chair.

Lannon and Hild knew all the athletes and told me about two recruits from Chicago who were sent to Iowa by a rich alumnus with his promise to send them monthly checks. But something got mixed up, the checks didn't arrive on time, so the two of them spent the first month sleeping under the Iowa River bridge and stealing vegetables out of local gardens to eat!

My boy-girl relationships were severely hampered by my lack of funds. I simply had little money to spend on dates. No Junior Proms or Military Balls or Senior Hops. The best place to meet girls was the daily Tea Dances at the Student Union but you had to buy refreshments. I could manage only our Delta Chi party and one or two of the major dances a year. I had dates but until I was a Senior, never a steady girlfriend at college. Only about three girls are worth mentioning. The governor of Iowa was a man named Hickenlooper. He was popular and used his strange name as a political plus, always telling jokes about it. He had twin daughters, both at SUI when I was there. One time I had a date with one of them—one date only—and I can't remember how it happened or anything about it, except it was considered something difficult to do and something to be proud of. I recall that after it happened, a lot of students knew me who had never heard of me before.

The second was Fran Pohlad, a big city gal from Chicago. She was a knockout, so pretty I would never have had the courage to approach her. For some reason unknown to me, she approached me! Twice a week I had this class I previously mentioned—the one that required keeping a diary. I would get there early because they always had classical music playing. With most of the seats unoccupied, Fran would come sit beside me. We would talk, and when the professor arrived and embarked on his 50-minute lecture, she would write me notes—on matters totally unrelated to the subject at hand.

She was unusually friendly and I enjoyed this so much we finally began dating. She was two years older than I, having worked as a model at Marshall Fields in Chicago before starting in college. In the spring, we'd go canoeing on the Iowa River and that was about as romantic as you could get. The House Mother at Delta Chi wasn't enthusiastic about this relationship— she thought Fran was too sophisticated for me and figured I'd get hurt. I had no illusions about how long I could hold off the competition, but my philosophy was to "enjoy it while you can!"

COLLEGE HUMOR'S "NATIONAL COED OF THE MONTH"

In those days there was a national magazine called College Humor—kind of a "girlie" magazine that in those gentle days was about as close to Playboy as you could get. Big national circulation. So while Fran was my girlfriend (or so I hoped) the May issue came out and it featured several pages of Fran as the national "Coed of the Month!" No nudity in those days, but a lot of "undergarment shots" showing the lady in various stages of undress! This was semi-embarrassing to us because on our dates for the next couple of weeks, wherever we went, the students would cheer and applaud! (It seems everyone at SUI read that issue of College Humor!)

Almost immediately after, the Des Moines Register—Iowa's major newspaper—ran a picture of Fran and the story about her. I don't remember this but I found it mentioned in an old diary which also said Fran didn't like what they wrote about her.

As I expected, the affair ended at the end of the school year. We all went home and Fran never came back to SUI. It was great while it lasted. Like Loraine, Fran told me she loved me and that I was "No. 1". Unlike Loraine (and a lot like me), Fran had much to accomplish before settling down with anyone.

R. J. ZOLLER, ESQUIRE? MAYBE, MAYBE NOT.

SEPTEMBER 1937. Still wondering how I should spend the rest of my life, I decided maybe I should become a lawyer. I enrolled in the SUI College of Law, along with fraternity brothers Phil Allen and Howard Davidson, and Waverly friend Wayne Sparks.

For several reasons this school year became one of the worst times of my entire life. I was elected President of Delta Chi and became a member of the Iowa Men's Interfraternity Council. Trying to run the fraternity and cope with a Law faculty who tried to produce good lawyers by snowing us under workloads that demanded 20 hours of intense, undivided attention everyday, was difficult enough. Then Delta Chi raised the monthly House Bill at the same time my folks asked me if I could survive on $400 for the year.

The two weeks I worked my board job were OK, but I couldn't pay my board bill for the rest of the month. To cut expenses for those two weeks I tried to eat out on ten or fifteen cents a day (you could get small hamburgers for a nickel, or thin milkshakes for a dime.) It wasn't easy, but I got some help when Phil and Sewell Allen got food packages from home and shared them with me. And old John Becker, our janitor, knew I had problems and some-time after midnight, when everyone was asleep except us law guys, he'd smuggle "left-overs" up to my study room.

The situation got even worse right after the holidays when the several Delta Chi professors who really ran our fraternity told Lannon, Overton and me they had to terminate our half-time board jobs. I knew this was fair: they helped us for three years and needed the jobs to pledge other members. But it was a major blow, made even worse as they expected me to eat there full time and pay the bill. And I just didn't have the money.

So, for much of that year, I spent a lot of time being hungry. I knew that my folks would find the money if I told them, but I chose not to. With old John Becker (and Ma Becker, our cook) and the Allen brothers and a few others who helped on occasion, I could survive. And I did.

Actually the lack of sleep bothered me more. We would study until 3 or 4 a.m. on a fairly regular basis. (Really studying was a totally new experience for me.) Sewell Allen had a part-time job with a local law firm. With all the distractions of fraternity living, we law guys would go downtown to Sewell's office in the evenings and study there. Midnight or 1 a.m. we'd start home but always stop at a restaurant that stayed open all night because all the budding artists, playwrights, poets and actors hung out there and gave the restaurant an extra source of income.

Phil Allen knew them all—he had been a Theater Guy. The four of us would see how much money we had among us. If we were lucky enough to have that much, 20 cents would get us each a cup of coffee. Often, we didn't have that much, so Phil would go table-to-table asking for contributions from his arty friends. Most of them had little money but gave what they could. We always got the coffee. Over the year, I met almost everyone in the College of Fine Arts. I don't remember him (he wasn't famous at the time) but I'm sure I met and talked with Tennessee Williams.

ENTER SALLY. About the only good thing that happened to me in this otherwise lousy year was Sally Larson. I met her at Delta Chi in November '37. She was an Onawa girl and Onawa was like Waverly where everybody knew everybody. So the Allen brothers, and the five or six other Delta Chi's they had pledged, all knew Sally. She was quite a gal—pretty, smart and practical. And just the girl for me because she knew my financial situation and told me early on, "You don't have to spend any money on me!"

We hit it off and we went steady all that year. Like a sailor with a girl in every port, I had two that whole year, Sally at college and Loraine when I got home!

Somewhere along the line Loraine heard about Sally, and then Sally heard about Loraine. Both were mad at me, but then the competition began. I'll tell you now, both were wonderful people, both decided I was their guy, and both hinted at marriage (because I didn't). Both would have been good wives, but for me the timing was all wrong.

Sally was awfully good to me. She invited me to a lot of dances and parties, picking up all or most of the costs. She came from a family of modest means but had pledged a sorority, took part in Theater, and earned extra money typing for several professors.

Except for Sally and Loraine, my last year of college was like Hell Week for the full nine months. Not enough to eat (sometimes), not nearly enough sleep, fighting with Delta Chi faculty—including O.K. Patton, my Contracts Professor, who ran Delta Chi. Worst of all, I found Law School a major mistake, for several reasons: (1) I hated Law, found it dull. Not at all like Perry Mason criminal law, but more like CPA work on property, torts, contracts, etc. (2) As a lawyer I envisioned a life in Waverly or somewhere like it and no chance for the travel and adventure I wanted. (3) Or, I could go to a big city and get a law clerk job, and get paid a grocery clerk's salary, briefing cases for the partners and guys who owned the firm. (4) Few clients hired young lawyers—they got the older ones who had experience and connections. (5) Most of my class had jobs already waiting for them, with fathers or brothers in the business. (6) Unlike today when both government and business hire thousands of lawyers each year, it wasn't like that in the 1930's and early '40's. There was the FBI: they hired a few and took their pick of the very best from Harvard, Columbia, Yale and Stanford – and that was about it.

Having decided against a law career, what then? What would I do for a living? This quandary was probably the worst thing of all. All my buddies had decided their futures and selected college courses accordingly. Hild was already a school teacher; Lannon was an all-Big Ten end and several pro teams had contacted him, but he was set to join the coaching staff at Syracuse; Overton and Bob Schulze had one more year in Dental College. And so on. I had top grades in Law school and a record of scholastic excellence, but nothing specific to sell. I didn't even know what kind of job to try for. This was frustrating beyond belief!

If I knew then what I know now I wouldn't have worried so much. NOW I know, as I said at the beginning—"Life is what happens to you when you're not looking."

PEOPLE I FOUND INTERESTING. MAYBE YOU WILL, TOO

At Delta Chi we all had study rooms, usually two to a room. But we didn't sleep there. Half of the third floor was our dormitory—filled with double-decker steel frame bunks. No heat. Windows on three sides and they were never closed. The wind whipped through, and in winter it was like sleeping outdoors. A test of manhood. Only the sissies left when the room temperature dropped below zero. (Actually—this is true—one time it was a record 30° below zero outdoors and 27° below in the dorm!)

Nobody had heating pads. But you should see us dress for bed, starting with long underwear or sweat suits and 3 or 4 pairs of socks, then almost everything in our wardrobe. I had the top bunk in the corner. Then an open window. And then Overton in a top bunk. In the morning, Neil could be under 8 inches of snow! And I couldn't see him at all!

Overton was the son of a doctor, in Winner, SD, on the edge of the Rosebud Indian Reservation. The only boy, with a couple of sisters. One of the funniest guys I ever met. Weird. On a double-date, four of us were talking in a restaurant. Suddenly we noticed Neil was quietly "diapering" two of his fingers with a paper napkin! He devised contests (which he usually won)—one event was to spread a newspaper on the living room rug, then get on your stomach, with your hands behind your back, and CRAWL UNDER THE NEWSPAPER! (This was a time trial.) One more: the broad jump—but you were jumping out into the Iowa River!

Overton looked nothing like an athlete, but he was good at everything. State high school champion in the pole vault. With Lannon, they won a state championship in football (and maybe basketball, too.) After graduation, he set up a dental practice in Cedar Falls, then in Ottumwa where he met and married Maxine, became a Navy dentist until he retired in Pensacola. They had a whole bunch of kids.

Lannon had a good and easy college life because of football. He was big and fast, an all-Big Ten end, and elected the Most Valuable Player at SUI his senior year. He was well known among the student body and elected or appointed to lots of committees. Fell hard for Marian Grantham and they married when seniors. Produced three great sons. After coaching at Syracuse, Bob became Ass't Sales Manager of Will & Baumer Candle Co. Retired to play golf in Southern Pines, NC.

John Hild was one of the two strongest men I ever knew. (Mike Rhode, who worked for my father for many years, was the other.) John played fullback and linebacker for the Hawkeyes and was once called "the roughest, toughest player ever to wear the Old Gold uniform."

I'll never forget: one year, final exam week, practically the entire Student Body was celebrating, and most of them were roaring drunk. By 1 a.m. my gang was trying to sleep in our dorm. Some Delta Chis and a bunch from the fraternity next door, a medical fraternity, were making a lot of noise on our front lawn. Apparently the visitors were spoiling for a fight—there was a lot of shouting and this was disturbing our attempts to get some sleep.

Marion Harris, a very large brother who played football, leaned out the window and told them to "Pipe down!" Some guy on our lawn yelled back, "Come down here and say that!" Harris yelled, "You come up here!" We all yelled, "Harris, get back in bed!" Then suddenly the second floor entrance to our dorm was flung open and some madman yelled, "Where's the guy who wants to fight!"

"I'm coming!" several of us yelled, and we jumped out of bed and headed down the stairs. I was second in line—thank goodness! Hild got there first, but coming out of the dark into bright lights he couldn't see, and the invader swung as hard as he could, and hit Hild right in the face! Hild grabbed him and threw him down on the landing. He got up and said, "Just come here and fight!"

Big mistake! Hild started swinging as he descended the four or five steps to the landing and he hit the guy so hard that blood splattered on the walls. Then we grabbed him, went down and tossed him out on the lawn, where he splashed, as the lawn was saturated with spring rains. The guy was totally unconscious. I never saw anyone get hit like that and I thought maybe Hild had killed him! His buddies were dumfounded—because this guy was Otis Wolfe, a very large man who two years before had been the All-University Heavyweight Boxing Champion! (Later, I learned Otis was a nice guy when sober but totally nasty and belligerent when drunk. I think Hild cured him. Years later he was one of the most respected doctors in Iowa.)

Glen Cunningham was a famous runner who held the world record for the mile run, I think in the 1930's, just before Roger Bannister, the Englishman, became the first human to run a 4-minute mile. Cunningham had come from Kansas to SUI to study for a Ph.D. in something and I saw him at the Field House. He called me over, introduced himself (I already knew who he was) and then asked me a favor. "You're about my size," he said. "I need a workout. Wrestle with me." So I did. I was honored. I was also tossed around a lot! He was years older than I and much stronger. It was no match. But I'm glad it happened.

Larry Griswold, gymnastics coach at SUI, became famous as one of America's greatest "clown divers". He was the star of The Diving Collegians, a main attraction at the World's Fair in Chicago. He was a pioneer in trampoline and developed the Nissen and Leonard balancing act that was of Cirque du

Soleil quality about 60 years ahead of the remarkable performances we see on television today.

The year I worked on the Daily Iowan, I handled publicity and produced the show program for the Iowa Circus which Griswold created, planned, directed and starred in. So we became friends, and Larry played the major role in one of the best weekends I had at Iowa—because it was great fun, and didn't cost me a nickel!

The Hawkeyes played a football game at Illinois, an important Big Ten game. Lannon got me a free ticket and Griswold drove me there and back at no charge. I ate and slept at the Illinois Chapter of Delta Chi. So my entire trip and weekend didn't cost me anything. (And we won the game.)

George Nissen became the Big Ten tumbling champion, but the University wouldn't pay to send him to the National Intercollegiate Championships in New York. So Nissen hitch-hiked, going and coming, and won the national championship! After graduation, he became rich and famous as a leading—or *the* leading—manufacturer of trampolines and the balance beams and all the other equipment you see when you watch gymnastics competition at the Olympic games. Knowing what to look for, I could always see the name NISSEN on the Olympic equipment.

IS THERE LIFE AFTER COLLEGE?

I graduated from S.U.I. in 1938. Being out of college seemed strange, and it was made considerably worse because when I should have been out marketing my skills, I wasn't aware of any that were marketable! So I went home, embarrassed to be unemployed and still relying on my family for food and lodging. My second day home, my mother woke me up and said, "Coach Armbruster is on the phone." (Armbruster was the famous swimming coach at SUI.) He asked if I had a job. I said no. He told me to get to Newton, Iowa and see Dr. Wood, Chairman of the Maytag Park Board about the head lifeguard job. He told me, "It's only 3 months, but this is the best lifeguard job in the State of Iowa." In 20 minutes, I was on the road hitchhiking.

Coach also said that every year he sent an All-American swimmer to this special job in Newton, but the last two had disappointed the Park Board. "Your job," he told me, "is to get me out of the doghouse, and I know you will."

Dr. Wood talked to me briefly, then had one of his office assistants take me in his car to "interview" with other members of the Park Board. I was already impressed because the assistant was a very pretty girl named Helen Berlau—whom I hoped to date if I got the job. I was hired and asked to start a week later.

When I arrived, I learned I had two fulltime assistant lifeguards, both just out of high school – Jack Marion and Jack Nichols – and a part-timer, "Peanut" Niebur. When I met them and they learned I was not another All-American, I could see I had a problem. Marion and Nichols were both champion swimmers, freestyle and backstroke respectively. I knew I needed to earn their respect and the way to do that was to beat them at their specialties. I knew it was risky, but my first day on the job before the pool opened, I challenged them, beat Marion and then beat Nichols. After that, Peanut decided not to race me. We became good friends and got along exceptionally well all summer.

GREATEST SUMMER EVER—AND ONE MISTAKE

It all had to do with girls—handling the pool job was a piece of cake. It didn't take me long to decide that Newton had more beautiful young ladies than I had ever seen in one place before. Before I even got to call Helen Berlau, I met Arla Ruth Taylor who worked with me at Maytag Pool. She had just graduated from ISTC (now U. of Northern Iowa) and was my first date, on my first night. And the first Newton gal I kissed. That night she and I became good friends. She didn't want to go steady but was willing to smooch when neither of us had a date—and sometimes we even smooched at the pool when nobody was looking!

On that first date she took me to Roswell's—a large drugstore where the owner had put in a dance floor and a jukebox so the young people would have a place to meet and hang out—and not go to Des Moines. (A couple of Newton kids had died in car crashes going to or from Des Moines.) Roswell's was wonderful. Crowded every evening. No charge except a Coke or some ice cream—which was great for me as I was still "living on a shoestring".

My job paid $80 a month—not much, but my "room rent" was free because I had a cot and a locker at the pool. As Head Guard, I had teaching privileges—every morning until the pool opened at 1 p.m. I charged 50 cents an hour for private lessons for beginners or advanced swimmers. This helped. Later in the summer I offered group rates: 10 cents an hour for groups over 10 people—and some 30 or so kids came regularly, not to learn anything, just to have more "pool time". Most were good swimmers so I taught them speed swimming and lifesaving – a profitable idea I wish I'd thought of sooner.

My only expense was food, but I had college training on how to survive on almost nothing. Jack Marion told me where to go for great pork cutlet sandwiches. They were great indeed and that's what I ate most of the summer. And milk shakes, of course.

Marty O'Conner was pool manager, probably 27 or 28 years old. Good guy. Had been a good college basketball player somewhere, I think Carleton. My first week in Newton they were still doing some work at the pool so I had no place to sleep. So Marty called his younger brother who was a star basketball player, just graduated from Drake. Bucky had a spare bed and let me stay there as long as I needed. He became a good friend.

Bucky, whose real name was Frank, later became one of the best basketball coaches in University of Iowa history—I believe the best! Unfortunately, he was killed in an auto accident at the height of his career.

Jack Marion, one of my lifeguards, was a good-looking dude—18 years old (as were most of the people I hung with that summer). He had a great body and either a great tan or was naturally dark-skinned. He appeared part Mexican or part Samoan—I never asked. I noticed a lot of girls liked Jack Marion.

Jack Nichols, the other lifeguard, was tall, slim, blond and low-key. I met his parents when they invited me to his birthday dinner. Jack was a good kid. I liked him. He was killed while in the Air Corps in World War II.

"Peanut" Niebur, a part-time lifeguard, was short, unhandsome, a clown and a tough kid. I never saw him with a date and I suspect he was too busy stealing hubcaps. That summer in Newton, Maytag workers went on strike, and violence erupted, so badly that the National Guard took over Newton! They also took over the big room I was using at the pool—and I had to move to a smaller area at the pool until they left town.

During the violence, Peanut's older brother was a leader of the strikers and was arrested and charged with kidnapping! (I don't remember how that turned out.)

There were others at the pool, but they are not part of my story.

But Mary Dickinson surely was.

MARY DICKINSON. THE GIRL WHO HAD EVERYTHING.

The first time I saw Mary (at Roswell's) I thought she was one of the most beautiful girls I'd ever seen. I introduced myself and asked her to dance. After that she invited me to sit with her and her girlfriends. We talked and danced all evening. Then I walked her home (she lived only about three blocks away). And we kissed goodnight—but she lacked experience and didn't do very well. So I showed her how, and the second one will live in my memory forever!

I couldn't believe my good luck. I was truly in love—immediately. We kissed several times, then said goodnight—but not until I asked her to meet me at Roswell's the following evening.

And so began one of the memorable events of my life—a wonderful relationship that I handled incredibly badly. Had I not turned totally stupid, my life may have been different from then on. But I'll tell you the good part first.

Mary had just turned 18 and just graduated from high school. She told me I was the second boy ever to kiss her—and I suspect the first one must have been 10 or 12 at the time. Most of the girls I met were going steady and I couldn't understand why the local lads weren't standing in line to get with Mary. Jack Marion explained it: Mary was a goddess—untouchable. Too perfect. Too religious. She sang at Catholic Mass every Sunday as the principal soloist. Her parents were very close friends with Father McCann the Pastor, who in turn was a real buddy of Fred Maytag, who owned Newton. Marion was quite impressed that Mary and I became "an item"—as were many of the Newton lads.

The more I learned about Mary the more I admired her. First and foremost, she made no secret of her feelings for me. (I think it was partly because I was the first real boyfriend in her life; partly because I was the Head Life Guard, sent to Newton by a nationally known swimming coach and therefore a person of some special interest to all the young people; a Red Cross Life Saving Examiner; a Catholic who met her after Mass every Sunday, a college graduate, and because I knew more about about most things than she did.)

Many years later I had a beautiful Alaskan Malamute named "Sioux". I remember a judge who gave her Best of Breed and then explained, "In judging, I start with perfection, then search for faults, and deduct for the number of faults and their importance. With this dog, I just can't find any faults!"

Mary was like that. I couldn't find any room for improvement. Even her family was perfect. Her father was the Sales Manager of Automatic Washing Machine Company (and a couple of years later, Sales Manager of Amana Industries). Her mother was a fine looking woman and a great mother—to two sons and four daughters! Mary was the oldest, then Cathy, Willard, Greg, Betty and one very young daughter whose name I can't remember.

Almost immediately, I was invited for Sunday dinners, right after church, along with Father McCann. Apparently I passed muster because I then was tendered a standing invitation—for every Sunday dinner for the rest of the summer! It became apparent I was viewed as a prospective son-in-law. And I was passing all the tests.

But all of a sudden, reality hit me—the horrible realization that this wonderful summer would end and I'd be back home with no job, no prospects, no idea of what to do for a living. And Mary would be off to college. How in the world could I make anything good out of this masterpiece of lousy timing?

That's when I did everything wrong. I should have sat down with Mary and her parents and explained how I felt and the situation I was in. Instead, I went totally stupid. The best thing I could think of was to ease out of the relationship, gradually. It wouldn't be easy: I don't say this to represent myself as God's gift to women, but it was crystal clear that I had become the most important thing in Mary's life. She was totally in love and would have married me that summer if I asked her.

Looking back, I cannot understand why I did what I did. I think I've been a pretty decent guy all my life but I'm ashamed of the way I treated Mary. While I continued to be with her all the rest of the summer, I began to date other girls, and as time went on it became less Mary and more the other girls. I still loved her, still ate Sunday dinners at the Dickinsons and she was my last goodbye when I left Newton.

To me, the Summer of 1938 was remarkable. To my knowledge (and chagrin) I've never been considered one of the best looking guys in Waverly or in college. But I surely was in some demand among the young ladies of Newton. And this was their "A" team!

BETH FELLOWS, FOR EXAMPLE. A BLONDE BEAUTY

Eighteen, just out of high school. Her father was a successful dentist, and like the Dickinsons, the Fellows were upscale, Country Club people. Beth spent June at a summer camp so I didn't meet her until July 5, at Roswell's. She was going steady with Paul Young, but it wasn't long before she was coming to the pool everyday and smiling a lot—at me. Mary left town for a few days, so I got a date with Beth and we hit it off and I began to wonder why I was so lucky. A few days later I dated Beth again. Paul found out and vented his rage on Beth (and fortunately, not on me!) Mary also found out. Told me she "really liked me a lot and was jealous of Beth."

A couple of days later Beth said she was in love with me.
She left for another summer camp in Minnesota and soon after arriving she sent me a Special Delivery letter. She wrote again, about every four days. Don't ask me how, but Paul Young and Mary both heard about this. Ann Rash told me Paul Young had even complained to Beth's parents and was bad-mouthing me to all the other guys in his group.

AND THERE WERE SEVERAL OTHERS

Ann Rash, incidentally, was making her own moves. Another "rich kid"—her father was General Manager of the J.C. Penney store. She signed up for private swimming lessons although she was an expert swimmer. I had to teach her things like the Japanese crawl (which they used to dominate at the 1936 Olympic Games). Ann was aggressive, inviting me here and there but with Mary and Beth she didn't stand a chance. I do remember one rainy day she brought picnic food and we had lunch in one of the cabins in Maytag Park.

One day during the swim lesson she asked if I remembered the Gantner ads. (They involved underwater smooching.) I figured why not. So we did. Again, her boyfriend found out and now Butch Hastings joined Paul Young and I began to worry I might get waylaid some night on my way back to the pool.

I also had a couple of dates with Helen Berlau and it was apparent she liked me and would have enjoyed further association. Smooching, of course. (Forget baseball, smooching was America's pastime – at least at that time, in that place!)

One night at Roswell's I met and danced with Cathy Bradley. She was a student at SUI, quite well known as one of the more popular girls on campus. Like Fran Pohlad, Cathy (I thought) was out of my league, dating only the big wheels, so surely she wouldn't have given me the time of day. But now she was friendly, so one night when Mary and Beth were unavailable, I asked her for a date. She already had one, but suggested the next night, and I viewed this as encouraging. We dated several times that summer. On the first date I found out why they called her "Stonewall Bradley", but on the others, the wall came tumbling down. (Or so to speak.) By August she was passing me a list of the evenings when she would be available! Cathy was very pretty and a great smoocher, and naturally, I was flattered.

At this point I should tell anyone reading this that I'm well aware my Boy-Girl relationships have dominated much or most of my recent reporting. Please understand that I had just turned 22, an age when most healthy people are shopping around, hoping to find the ones they want to be with for the rest of their lives. For reasons explained, I wasn't looking for anything permanent, but never before had I encountered so many pretty girls, nice girls and such nice relationships. Rest assured that my Boy-Girl stuff will soon be replaced by more important events.

I had my final college date with Sally Larson on June 6 that summer, said goodbye and left Iowa City. I told her I wasn't coming back. But she wouldn't give up. She wrote me several letters and visited me in Newton three times. On her last visit, apparently believing that lack of money was my problem, she said she now had a "pretty good job" with the University, and with my scholarship and her income we could get by. I had to explain that she had misjudged my situation, my plans were drastically changed, and besides that I was in love with Mary Dickinson. (That did it.)

Besides the girls, the dating, and getting several of the Newton boys a bit upset about the girls and the dating, several other things did happen that summer. I heard the U.S. Army Air Corps was recruiting college graduates and I applied. I knew I could pass their tests and I could be a good flyer. But I loused up this one with honesty: on a long questionnaire I said I had hay fever and they turned me down. So much for honesty being the best policy. (Had they let me join in the summer of 1938 I would probably have ended up full Colonel or Brigadier General: they promoted their officers much faster than any other branch of our military services.)

I saved nine people from drowning that summer. No big deal.

JULIE HAMILL

I planned, produced and MC'd a very fine Water Show with swimming races, clown diving, water safety demonstrations, etc. Beth's older sister turned out to be the fastest girl swimmer in Newton. Peanut and Marion were great in the clown diving. But the star of the show was Julie Hamill.

I was sitting in the guard tower one day when I started to dive in because I saw a head bobbing about a foot underwater in the deep end. But I held up for another look. Then I saw a little girl doing something I'd never seen before. She would take a breath and descend to the bottom of the pool, then push up until she could grab another breath, and go down again. Every time she came up, she would be leaning a bit forward so she would gain five or six feet. She was getting in deeper all the time, so I blew my whistle and when she looked at me, I motioned her back into the shallow end. Then I went to talk to her. She couldn't swim a stroke. She had no fear whatever. She was 8 years old. The water was well over her head, even at the ropes. I got her name and phoned her parents, suggesting they send her to me for lessons. And they did.

Three weeks later the feature act of the Water Show was 8-year-old Julie Hamill! I told the audience her story, then had her swim 100 yards, demonstrating five different strokes, all beautifully done. Then I told her to go up on the high board, and I threw three quarters in three different places in the 12-ft. deep diving zone and said, "Julie, go get them." She dived in and in what seemed like a full minute underwater, she came up with all three!

There was a huge crowd. The Park Board, the Dickinsons and other Newton VIP's were all there. They all burst into cheers and the applause lasted for several minutes. They were impressed. And so was I.

John Mooney stopped in to say hello. I don't remember where he was going or why. Waverly kid Max Eggleston (who I guess was about 16 years old) came to visit and stayed with me for three days. I fixed a place for him to sleep at the pool and took him to Roswells. An old boyfriend of Arla Ruth's came to see her, and he turned out to be Dick Penly from Waterloo, a close friend of mine—from Boy Scout camp!

GRISWOLD THE GREAT

One morning a guy yelled at me from just outside the pool. It was Larry Griswold. Said he was passing through and just stopped to say hello. En route to Marshalltown to star in their big Water Show the following night. Said come and join the fun. Gave me five comp tickets. Marion volunteered to stay and work, so Peanut and Nichols and Nichols' girlfriend and I drove to Marshalltown. When we took our seats in the audience, Griswold sat with us—part of his act. Dressed in street clothes, suit and tie and he even had a hat. Near the end of the show the divers were competing, diving beautifully. Griswold, playing drunk, began to criticize the divers. "Lousy dive," he'd say. "I'd give it a 3!" Many people could hear him.

Then he started to get me into the act. "My kid brother can do that one better," he yelled. The Security people started up and he pulled me down the aisle. "Show 'em," he said. People thought it was for real—Griswold had done this a hundred times and was good at it. When Security got near, I went back and sat down and Griswold bolted into the audience and down to the 3-meter board. With Security in pursuit, he scrambled up the tower. One of the guards grabbed his pant legs and pulled down his pants and revealed oversize boxer shorts—white, with big red hearts! And the audience caught on.

His act was remarkable. You had to see it to believe it. And of course he winds up with a spectacular dive no one has ever seen. I think it was a full twisting 3 1/2, but I really don't remember. He does all this in street clothes.

My three months in Newton were among the most memorable of my life. "The best of times and the worst of times." Two other people deserve mention – Andrew Cummings whom I liked a lot and spent many evenings with, on double-dates. His parents owned a small drugstore and they were

Scottish, with brogues so thick I had difficulty understanding them. He also had a younger brother, John, and a sister, Dorothy, at Grinnell College.

Then there was Marianna Dunn. She was Mary's best friend and a member of Mary's singing trio. Like so many Newton girls she was beautiful, and very witty, fun to be with. One time when Mary was out of town I asked Marianna to go out with me. She said she would love to, but would never do anything to offend Mary. As a result, she was the only gal in Newton I wanted to kiss and never did (that summer).

LEGAL EAGLE. Arla Ruth Taylor came to work one day, obviously upset. She told me she had contracted to buy an expensive set of encyclopedias, which she thought would be useful as she started her teaching career. It was one of those deals where you buy one a month until two years or so later you own the whole set. After one or two, she decided she had made a bad decision and tried to cancel. The publisher's legal department informed her that she had violated the contract and now owed the $280 (or whatever) for the entire set. Payment was due in 30 days.

I told her, "Have no fear; Super Freshman Law Student is here!" I sent home for my Contracts set of briefs, and when they arrived I wrote a letter (representing myself as "legal counsel" for Arla Ruth) citing the case of So-and-So versus So-and-So—and Arla Ruth never paid anything and never heard from them again! *(Question: Aside from Perry Mason and me, did you ever hear of any other lawyer who never lost a case?)*

I hated for this summer to end. I had made so many great friends and the young ladies had treated me so well I began to think I was quite a guy—although I never fully understood my good fortune in this regard. I knew the Park Board would give me an excellent report when they contacted Coach Armbruster. But I knew it was all over now and I was returning to unemployment, uncertainty and confusion.

I was so sorry about Mary Dickinson that I hoped to help her get started with the right people when she enrolled at SUI. She was so beautiful I felt every guy on campus would go for her and a lot them could mess up her life, and my job was to do all possible to make sure that didn't happen. So I wanted her first contact at SUI to be a nice guy, and that would be Neil Overton.

One thing puzzled me greatly. Mary's mother liked me a lot and I'm sure, as I said before, the Dickinsons seemed to view me as their prospective son-in-law. Then Beth came into the picture. Actually she never really took Mary's place but became an extremely pleasant way for me to ease out of Mary's life. When this began to happen I surely didn't feel I should be joining the Dickinson family (and Father McCann) every Sunday for dinner. The first Sunday I didn't show up, Mrs. D. got in touch and really scolded me. Neither of us got into details, but I then continued to show up every Sunday. And I did, indeed, feel welcome.

Actually, for more than the next two years—in fact until I left Iowa for good—the Dickinson's became my "home away from home", every time I got to Newton. Even if I popped in unannounced, I was always urged to stay for dinner. And several times I even stayed overnight.

AFTER NEWTON, THE REST OF THE YEAR 1938

This was not a particularly enjoyable time of my life—after my wonderful summer in Newton ended. I was still hurting badly about not knowing what to do for a living. Because I wanted to get out of Waverly—although I've always believed it to be one of the best small cities anywhere—I finally decided to aim for a career in the Foreign Service. The tests were difficult because they wanted only the brightest and best, but I knew with some preparation, I could pass any test. But developing the ability to converse in a foreign language would take some doing. (I rather deferred that problem, to concentrate on geography, world history, geopolitics and any and all subjects I figured I would need to know. (Maybe I'd move to Montreal or New Orleans, live with a French family and learn the language.)

I could devote full time to my studies at home. I subscribed to TIME and KEN, a new magazine that covered the subjects I needed to know. I could use the high school library, Wartburg's library and, of course, the Waverly Public Library.

For a few months I studied a lot. But I got down to SUI and Delta Chi several times to ensure Mary Dickinson and Neil Overton hit it off—and they did. Giving up Mary was difficult for me but I knew it had to be done. (After more than 65 years I still have some feelings for the gal.) Beth Fellows and I were still "going steady" but Beth enrolled at Grinnell College and we couldn't get together often because I had no car. And this is no way to pursue a romance.

I got to SUI several times that autumn. I could usually find a ride, especially on football weekends. Early on, I would sometimes date Mary and sometimes she would go with Overton and get me a date. I even spent a little time with Sally. I would always stay—and usually eat—at Delta Chi, and this helped conserve my limited finances.

Homecoming Weekend at SUI was great for me. Arla Ruth Taylor, Marianna Dunn and many from Newton were there. Arla Ruth was my Friday date. Saturday, Mary was my date. That night at the fraternity house there was a lot of smooching going on and, since Marianna decided I no longer was Mary's boyfriend, she kissed me a lot, was as good as I knew she would be, and I also knew that finally I had smooched with every really beautiful girl in Newton, bar none!

When I hitchhiked home from my lifeguard job in early September, I had $287, not bad, since my total salary for the summer was $240—I had lived on my income from the swimming lessons. Most of it was gone by late October because I stopped being frugal, trips to Iowa City, cokes and movies, and I needed some new clothes. Ed Kepler returned from New Orleans and he and Merle both enrolled at ISTC in Cedar Falls. Eddie Harden had graduated from Wartburg and, like me, he was unemployed. One day he called and told me he had a job for the two of us—peddling bills! *Two college graduates doing a job normally done by school kids!* But we earned $2.50 each! (Next month we did it again.)

I had many things to distract me from my studies. Trips to Iowa City. Beth at Grinnell needed my attention. (She wrote she heard about Marianna and me and was jealous!) Father Maguire contacted me, asked for me to rejuvenate the Young Catholics Club. I did, recruited a group, was elected President and then had to chair meetings, plan social events, etc. (I was very successful.) Bud Hayes, Chamber of Commerce Secretary, ran for U.S. Congress and became the Democratic Party's nominee. He asked me to accompany him to other towns in the area where he talked to various groups. Then he told me he had to resign his Chamber of Commerce thing and I should take over the job!

"You can handle it," he said. "Doesn't pay much but you'll have a nice office. I know your friends are interfering with your studying. You can lock the door, take the phone off the hook and have complete privacy." He made it sound like something to consider. I was broke and needed some walking-around money. Bud earned $125 a month and had to live totally on that. (He wasn't married.) I was still eating (sometimes) and sleeping at home. The Board of Directors picked me over several other applicants but they knew I lived at home (the cheapskates!) and offered me only $85 a month, on a "trial basis," but said they'd do better if I worked out OK.

I was only 22 and some thought they needed an older man. Bud Hayes was about 50. When I got the job I was the youngest C. of C. executive in Iowa. And the youngest Who's Who in Iowa. I got a raise to $100 a month— with a bonus of $150 at year-end if I did well on the job. My folks, incidentally, never asked me to pay anything for room and board.

The salary was enough for me to have fun and (in late March) buy a new Dodge automobile. With wheels, a lot of my life got simpler and much better.

These are the highlights from September 1938 to December 1940, when I said goodbye and embarked on a whole new life: Buying the Dodge was a major achievement. Unless you dwell in midtown Manhattan, you can't really live without wheels—in 1939 or now. Getting the C. of C. job was important. Some parts of it were fun. They piled on the work—a lot of evening meetings of the Board, committees, etc. They made me the County Commissioner of Scouting, which included Boy Scouts, Girl Scouts and Cub Scouts. I headed up the Infantile Paralysis Fund Drive—and later, practically every fund drive, and there were many of them.

I knew how to use newspaper publicity and I wrote all the stuff myself. Les Moeller was an excellent editor who ran the local paper until Pep Grawe, who inherited it, was old enough to take over. (Les became President of the Iowa Daily Press Association and later Dean of the School of Journalism at S.U.I.) Les liked me and appreciated my talents so he published everything I wrote and sometimes even asked me to cover high school basketball games or other local events, which I did for free.

We were a farm-based community, so Dairy Day was a major annual event. To promote it, I created a fictional character named "Agatha Hogwash" and claimed she was a three-time national champion cow milker, just moved to a farm in Bremer County. One of the big events was The Milkmaid Contest and half the idiots who read my pre-event publicity (which went on for several weeks) actually thought Agatha was a real person. There was a gawky high school kid, John Krause, who I photographed in a wig, sunbonnet and ladies clothes. We passed *her* off as Agatha Hogwash and we ran "her" pictures with my stories, and it was probably one of the best promotions of those times.

The Chamber was mainly a Retail Merchants' Association. I took a larger view: it should be the principal organization of community leaders dedicated to making Waverly grow and become the best possible place to live. So I wrote some letters and articles that persuaded most of the doctors, lawyers, dentists, CPA's, and educators (high school and Wartburg College) and other community leaders to join us. The result was the largest growth in the Chamber's history and one of the largest memberships in Iowa.

Wartburg College was a Lutheran institution and a number of students came from Canada. As a young guy I got acquainted with several of the students and hung out with them. They liked Waverly but complained, "No Hockey!" I eventually fixed that, working with the new manager of our A+P store, just arrived from Minnesota where he had played a lot of hockey.

We convinced a few of the larger local firms to put up the money and sponsor teams, and we organized the first and only Waverly Hockey League in our community's history. We built a regulation rink in a cove in the Cedar

River, and bought regulation goals and protective pads for the goalies. We apportioned the Canadians among the teams, and locals (including me) filled the rest of the positions. I played defense, wasn't a great skater but became one of the better "body-checkers." I played rough (harking back to my old football days) and limped a lot until the season was well over. When an all-star team was selected to play Iowa Falls, I was on it. When I left town, so did ice hockey.

I was in many activities, and in the local papers practically all the time, and previously well-known for my years as the lifeguard, so I'm sure I became one of the best-known Waverly residents of those times. I was spending a lot of time with Fred Studier, Treasurer of Lutheran Mutual Life Insurance Co. (and the C. of C.), liked and admired the man greatly—as did everyone in Waverly. War was raging in Europe and Hitler, for good reasons, was becoming the most hated man in the world. In America, the nation was divided: should we go get him, or mind our own business?

What bothered me is that all the old guys who wouldn't have to go and risk never coming back, spent a lot of time telling guys like me to go and fight. I remembered that a lot of young Americans lost their lives in World War I, and it seemed that nothing much changed as a result. Fred Studier agreed wholeheartedly. So I wrote a couple of articles—one for the Waverly papers, which got everyone in town in an uproar (pro and con)—and one for the Des Moines Register. The one published in the Register was picked up and reprinted in Vox Populi—or was it "We the People?"—the "National Yearbook of Public Opinion".

I'll never forget catching hell from old Guy Vanderveer (the banker who ran Waverly). He really lit into me. He didn't call me a coward, but came pretty close. I wasn't used to scathing denunciation and it bothered me more than somewhat. So a year or so later, I returned to Waverly as a brand new naval officer, donned my uniform and walked into the State Bank and confronted the old guy and probably said, "I want you to know I'm on my way to face the enemy, and this country isn't even at war yet! I'm the first in Waverly to do this. Any questions or comments?" (It was a happy moment in my life.)

My brother Ed—everyone else called him Jack—married Olive Gilbert in February 1940. I was the best man. The bridesmaid, Mildred McGowan, and I drove the newlyweds from Waterloo to Fort Dodge for their honeymoon. Back in Waterloo, I got in a bunch of smooching—she was several years older than I, but very pretty.

MY FIRST LOOK AT DEATH, CLOSE UP

I used to hire Bob Harris when some C. of C. job required extra help. One day, just before noon, I sent him to the newspaper office to deliver a news release. On return, he told me someone had just phoned in about an accident—the train had run over some hobo on the Great Western tracks about a mile east of Waverly. So we jumped into my car and went to take a look. The track is elevated where the accident was said to have happened. I climbed up the embankment and saw a body, maybe 100 yards away. We were the only ones there. I ran ahead of Bob to the body. The train had cut the man in two, right through his belt line. He was on his back staring upward. *I was shocked! It was a friend of mine, Larry Hertlein!*

Larry was an accountant, well known in Waverly. He had been gassed in France in the first World War and bothered by it greatly for many years. Spent several years in a Veterans Hospital. Later he married—his wife was one of my favorite teachers—and almost everyone in Waverly considered them the best-looking couple in town. They lived just a block or so from the C. of C. office and Larry used to walk to work, stopping in my office for a few minutes of small talk almost every day. It was suicide, of course, but why? Later I found out the mental problems from the gassing, considered cured, had returned and was being aggressively treated. Apparently he gave up hope.

I was greatly disturbed by this event. And you know what? As Bob and I had left my office and got into my car to go see what happened, Mrs. Hertlein drove past on her way home for lunch, and waved at me!

MORE ABOUT BETH

As mentioned before, when you're 22 years old, you are greatly interested in girls or something is seriously wrong. Mary was gone—but never forgotten—and Beth had told me she was in love with me before I left Newton. She was at Grinnell College; I was in Waverly with no money (or very little) and no automobile at that time. So we didn't see each other often. On the bright side, Beth wrote often. But I knew a real knockout like Beth Fellows was avidly pursued—perhaps by the entire male student body at Grinnell. And I was dating in Waverly, at ISTC, and on all my trips to Iowa City.

I did get to Grinnell a couple of times that Fall. And then on New Year's Eve Beth took me to her Country Club Dance in Newton where I saw almost everyone including the Dickinsons, Beth's parents and sister, and this was a memorable evening. Beth looked spectacular and I decided I really did love her! I even "pinned" her—the fraternity pin thing that college guys substituted for engagement rings.

On New Year's Day, a Sunday, I went to Mass, talked with Cathy Bradley, went to see Arla Ruth Taylor, then (again) for a big noontime Sunday dinner at the Dickinsons (with Mary and Father McCann), took Mary to Roswells, met Marianna and her new boyfriend, Henry Kling (a rich farmer, nephew of Henry Wallace, Vice President of the U.S. under FDR). Then to Beth's home for evening dinner with her family and Mr. and Mrs. Neal Hammer. (He was Secretary of the Newton C. of C.) This was a pleasant affair but again I felt like a prospective son-in-law under scrutiny—like interviewing for the job.

I must admit, Beth was wonderful that weekend. But I never forgot my $85 a month "trial job", my ambition to see the world, and above all, my decision to find my role in life before getting married.

Beth invited me to special functions (like formal dances, etc.) at her college a few times and continued to write often. But I think we both gradually came to understand that without the commitment of marriage this couldn't last without more time and attention than either of us could give. On July 2, 1939 we smooched as usual and then we agreed to go our separate ways.

Beth transferred to SUI in September. A year before, when Beth and I were an item, Bill Green had asked me about her—in a way I thought a bit unusual, almost like "Are you going to make this permanent or can I move in, later on?" (Not in those words.) But that Fall at SUI he did move in. Marianna Dunn married Henry Kling in December and Beth and Bill came to the wedding together—engaged. They later married, a very good marriage for both: Beth was a beauty and Bill Green was probably the best athlete Newton ever turned out, a local hero, and a great football player at SUI. (He was the hero of consecutive wins over Notre Dame and Minnesota, both national powers.) He made Maytag a career and had good jobs. They remained Midwesterners all their lives and were able to maintain close touch with all their high school and college friends in Iowa. Their lives were much different than mine, but for them, I'm sure it was just about perfect.

Marianna's marriage wasn't so good. A year later I attended the Iowa Junior Chamber of Commerce Convention in Mason City and encountered Henry Kling in a hotel room, with a woman, and roaring drunk. When he recognized me, he winked and said, "Don't tell Marianna!" Awhile later, they divorced. (From the time I met him, I knew he was a jerk. Not good enough for Marianna.)

ANOTHER BREAKUP. Overton and I were both invited to Marianna's big wedding and the Dickinsons asked us to stay with them. I felt like an oddball with no date. Someone fixed me up, but I don't even remember who my date was—some sorority gal from Iowa State. I didn't know about it until weeks later, but Neil and Mary parted ways that night. I was surprised, but I suspect Mary was more ready to get married than Neil was, that he was just starting his dentistry practice and not quite ready for additional responsibilities.

After Overton, Mary started going with a local fellow named Emmitt Martin. I didn't really know him, but I did know he was surely lucky to get a wonderful young lady like Mary Dickinson.

In October of that year—1940—they got married. He opened an undertaking business in New Hampton and they spent their lives in Iowa. My Midshipman School roommate, Jerry Carney, a native of New Hampton, retired there. In our annual exchange of Christmas cards his wife told me Mary sang in the church choir, still very beautiful. Just a couple of years ago Emmitt died of cancer. And later Mary had a serious fall and was quite badly injured. After so many years I still felt terribly sorry for her.

Overton went into the Navy as a dentist, made it his career and retired as a Captain. His first Navy assignment was in Ottumwa, Iowa where he met and married a pretty girl (Maxine) and raised a large family, retiring in Pensacola, Florida. We kept in touch. Several years ago Neil had a stroke and was never the same. Then he died of a heart problem. Maxine still lives in the same house and five of her six kids all live in Pensacola. (How lucky can you get?)

If I had not had what my family considered "some pretty wild ideas," I could have been a "happy camper" in Iowa, maybe even in my hometown. Most people seemed to think I was a successful young man, but I couldn't figure out where I might be, ten years down the road. My job was kind of fun. I played hockey in the winter, basketball practice with the high school team, took up golf and played a lot, swam and dived in the summertime, and even took up drinking alcoholic beverages—but always with considerable restraint

MY LAST TWO YEARS IN WAVERLY

My closest friends were Overton, Ed and Merle Kepler (all in Cedar Falls)— Jack Wright, Larry Hegg, Paul Scharf, Pete Cordt, Bob Harris and about 150 other Waverly guys I had known for many years—some a bit older and most a few years younger. No steady girlfriends.

I was always on the go – golfing, to Cedar Falls, to the movies. (I can't believe how many double features I saw from 1934 to the end of 1940 – every film Hollywood ever made, I believe!) Jerry Behonek, a Delta Chi brother at

SUI, transferred to ISTC so he and Overton and the Keplers and I seemed always to have something going on. I must have had a few dozen dates (mostly blind) with ISTC girls but only three were memorable because they were considered among the best the college had to offer – but after a couple of dates with each, there was no interest by any of us.

A man named John Ennis had a popcorn machine on wheels which he took to high school football games. It had a public address system and somehow I ended up being the play-by-play announcer during the action, and inserted a few "commercials" between plays and during timeouts. The commercials were for John's refreshments, and to get as many young people as possible to come to the Legion Hall dance after the game. You see, I rented the hall and the jukebox and hoped to make a profit. Depending on the attendance, I might net as much as $17 (the most ever) but usually $2.50 to $7.50 – but every little bit helped. (Things were much different in those days. Obviously.)

Lutheran Mutual Life Insurance Co. was an important business in Waverly. They had a new President, just arrived from Minneapolis. He had two sons: the older one, Jimmy Hegg, was a well-known singer and MC at Curly's Bar, a nightspot in Minneapolis. The younger son, Larry, moved to Waverly with the family. Larry was my age. We became friends. He was an artist, had studied at Eastern schools and with Diego Rivera, the famous Mexican. He rented an "apartment" over a store downtown and used it as a studio to paint and sculpt. Larry was a fun guy, had a pixy-like sense of humor. Jimmy Hegg was engaged to be married and his girlfriend had a younger sister, Ruth Roseland, who (I guess having nothing better to do) came to Waverly with the Heggs.

Ruth was quite a gal. Daughter of a Lutheran minister, but she surely didn't look like one. She had long red hair, a shapely body, and was attractive in a rather spectacular way. I remember seeing her walking down Waverly's "Main Street" in high heels, short shorts, a tight tee-shirt, with her long red hair, and the Hegg's black Scotty dog on a leash. I can tell you she really attracted attention!

So – Ruth became my girlfriend. This was never a serious relationship although a lot of smooching was involved. And it was nice. I could go to Hegg's and see Larry and Ruth at the same time. She was good company. I didn't need any more blind dates. She was a very good dancer. And I made a lot of the local boys jealous.

Pete Cordt, manager of the canning factory – probably our city's largest industry – was a bachelor who looked liked a rugged outdoorsman and I found him to be a man of many talents. On summer evenings, dozens of Waverly ladies of all ages would stroll past his home to admire his beautiful flower gardens. If he was outside, he'd welcome them for a closer look and explain the many varieties that made his home a showplace. He had a great "club basement" with fireplace, a good sound system, full kitchen and an organ on which he could play anything you asked for. He was a gourmet cook and the best host in town. Lucky for me, I became (along with Jack Wright, Larry and Ruth) one of his most frequent guests. For me, Tom Collins – Pete and Jack's suggestion for a beginner – became a regular libation, and Pete always had great food at every get-together.

Jack and Barbara, his wife, had a cabin in the woods, three or four miles out of town, and I spent a lot of pleasant evenings there in my final years in Waverly. If it rained, we went inside and built a fire in the fireplace. If decent weather, we had a big campfire outside. Either place, Tom Collins. Jack cooked great hamburgers. Sometimes, steaks.

A lot of the really fun stuff of those days was hanging around with Overton and the Keplers in Cedar Falls with headquarters at the A.D.A. fraternity house. Overton thought up weird contests, as previously mentioned, and Ed Kepler was foolish enough to try competing with Overton (who seldom lost contests of any kind). My role mainly was observer, although I sometimes intervened to prevent serious injuries when I saw them coming – usually when they'd been drinking.

One time, the two were gone when I arrived in Cedar Falls so Merle and I did something and then I went to sleep in Ed's bed. Ed and Neil returned, argued, then Ed ran out and locked me and Neil in the room. Neil, woozy, thought he could get Ed to unlock the door by starting a fire in the wastebasket. When the flames scorched the ceiling, I made him put it out. Ed had gone to Neil's hotel, got into his room and slept there.

Despite the many friends, and never running out of things to do, these were not great days for me. I could see no future worth thinking about, and no idea how to plan for it. I decided I had to get out of Waverly. Jack Wright, Larry Hegg and Kepler, of course, thought I should go. Jack told me he always wanted to do something similar, procrastinated, then one day he was married, had a son, and the opportunity had passed. He said, "Go! If you get stranded anywhere in the world and run out of money, I'll send what you need to get home."

He also said we would need a password so if I ever asked for money, he would know it was really me. I figured I'd leave the country from San Francisco so that would be the password, "San Francisco". This came in handy later on.

Ed Kepler graduated from ISTC and he got a part time job on the Des Moines Register and a reporter job with the Associated Press, also in Des Moines. Things change. Time marches on.

BIG CHANGE FOR ME. On July 1, 1940 I submitted my resignation to the Board of the Waverly Chamber of Commerce. This was pretty big news in town – a topic of major discussion. Nobody except my best friends could understand why. Nor could my family, although by now they did understand I was adult, competent, and somewhat bull-headed.

The Board voted me a bonus of $75 and asked me to help find a replacement. There were 192 applications for my job! I was told that the Iowa Falls Chamber of Commerce heard about it and said they wanted me to come take over there. I didn't even go to take a look.) I recommended Roy Swanson from Cherokee for the Waverly job, and they hired him.

CALIFORNIA HERE WE COME!

I spent my days in Waverly going over all my clothes and keepsakes, planning a long absence. Sold a lot of clothes to friends, most notably my tuxedo to Virgil Lagomarcino. I mention this because about 40 years later we met at a Waverly reunion and he was about nine sizes larger than I was! And I also reread all the letters from old girlfriends I had received through the years. This was good for my ego.

After many goodbyes, I left Waverly on August 8, 1940. First stop, Des Moines. Ed Kepler always said when I was ready to go, he would, too. Couldn't find him. Tried for 2 or 3 hours. Decided to go on to Jack Wright's cabin in Estes Park, CO., phone Kepler and have him join me there. At the last stoplight heading west out of Des Moines, before open country, the light changed to amber. For the first time I can ever remember, I slowed to a stop. (I always drove through amber lights, and still do.) *This unusual decision to stop, I am sure, changed my whole life forever after!*

While I waited for the green, Ed Kepler walked across the street right in front of my car. I said, "Pack. Let's go." He hesitated. "Bad timing," he said. "I just got this job with Associated Press. I'd like to keep it long enough to include it on my resume." Then he said, "Just this morning I saw the announcement of a new program to recruit naval officers. They send you on a month's cruise in the Caribbean. By the time you get back, I'll be ready to go."

"I don't want to join the navy," I said. "They sign you up for four years and then you're stuck." Kepler said, "No, if you don't want to go on, you don't have to." I couldn't believe that. We went to Navy Recruiting to check it out. Kepler was right and he said, "You want to travel, here's a free cruise. Boy, are you lucky!"

Right then and there I took the physical, passed, and being a college graduate and single, I was fully qualified. So, I signed on the dotted line. I thought the cruise would start immediately but they said college graduates all over the country were signing up. It might be a couple of months. They'd let me know.

OFF TO COLORADO. Jack, Barbara and baby Bill were at the cabin in Estes Park. They had been there awhile and Jack had to get back. They left a few days after I arrived. But Barb and her baby came back; Jack had taken a train home. The reason: just as they were ready to leave (from Barbara's parents home in Ault) they learned there were fourteen cases of infantile paralysis in Waverly! So Barb and the baby would stay a few weeks in Ault.

I had the cabin alone. I liked the solitude. Before the Wrights left, we had driven up over the timberline – more than 12,000 feet elevation – and it began to snow. In August. The next day Jack and I rode in the big Estes Park Rodeo parade. Some guy in the crowd called my name. It was Matt Heartney from Des Moines, a law school classmate of mine two years before. He said he was at the Stanley Hotel and I should call him. I did and was invited to spend the evening there. The Stanley was lavish. The Heartneys were well-heeled. I was invited back the next night for dinner, and it was not only great but a lot fancier than I was used to. After playing games all evening, I took part in The Great Stanley Hotel Icebox Raid. I never saw anything like that in my life. They were right to call it "Great".

Matt was going to post-graduate studies at Yale in the fall. After that, of course, he had a job waiting in his father's law firm. I was unemployed. But I decided I wouldn't trade lives with him anyway!

My old girlfriend, Beth Fellows, was spending a few weeks at the Cheley Colorado Camps, so I drove up, surprised her, and spent the evening. She invited me back, but when I popped in, unannounced, a few days later I couldn't find her. (Big camp). I didn't try really hard – there would be no smooching as she was getting ready to marry Bill Green.

The day before I left, I climbed a small mountain, all alone, way up to the final auto-size boulder that topped it off. This wasn't the sheer cliff, hang-on-by-your-fingertips kind of mountain like you see in the movies, but it was a strenuous climb and when I sat on its peak, I felt a sense of achievement. A problem came up when I sat there too long watching the sun sinking below the great mountains to the west, so I didn't leave a lot of daylight for the trip back down. I arrived in the dark, but I made it safely. When I thought about it, I decided it was pretty stupid to do that all alone, and without telling anyone where I was going.

ON THE ROAD AGAIN

The next day I drove south – Boulder, Denver, Colorado Springs, Pueblo and Trinidad (where I crawled into the back seat and slept from midnight to 6 a.m.). On my whole trip, going out and coming back, I never spent a dime for hotel or motel. Slept in the back seat. Except in Mexico.

To Las Vegas (NM), Santa Fe, Albuquerque, then decided to go to Mexico. Slept in Socorro, NM. Next day, Las Cruces and El Paso. Crossed into Old Mexico at Ciudad Juarez. Didn't feel totally comfortable in Juarez but I bought some Mexican money and checked into Hotel Rio Bravo (a real flea-bag). Wandered around town, had a Tom Collins in a bar where some Indian and his wife were celebrating. Troubadours sang and played Mexican music and the Spanish classics – very enjoyable. Had a good chicken dinner for $1.30 (Mex) – *26 cents American!*

The next day, I wrote letters, sent out my laundry, joined three young New York guys, bought a small hand-woven wool rug for $1.30 (U.S.) and a western-style belt for 75 cents. After siesta (I'm catching on), a filet mignon dinner at the best restaurant I could find. It was very good and cost a whopping 29 cents (U.S.). At the hotel that night I encountered my first (and only) bedbugs!

Back in the USA, to Las Cruces, then across the desert and into the mountains. Drove until well after midnight and just as I was crossing the Great Divide in the midst of the Apache Forest, I stopped and slept. Awfully cold, but I saw the sunrise from the mountaintops, and it was beautiful driving through the forest at dawn. Spent the day at the Petrified Forest and the Grand Canyon. Slept in a little Arizona town, where prices were high – gas, a good dime a gallon higher than anywhere else, and a light breakfast cost 46 cents! Next day at Boulder Dam, then Lake Meade Beach to swim. On to Las Vegas (primitive compared to the glitter and glamour there today.) It was 114° when I crossed the desert – mile after mile at 70 mph. No air conditioning. Sometimes I drove with bare feet hanging out the window. (Don't ask me how.)

GLORIOUS, GLAMOROUS GOLDEN CALIFORNIA

Arrived at Nip Blake's house in Glendale. They invited me to stay with them; I did, for three days, then went to USC campus and moved into a fraternity house where Waverly friend, Kenny Koch, was staying for summer school, in dentistry.

From August 24 until leaving California on Sept. 19, I had a great time with Nip and Kenny Koch and old Waverly girlfriend, Mary Spalding. Mary and I grew up together – Waverly schools and SUI, dated a bit. She met Don Herrick at SUI; they married, moved to Hollywood where he established a dental practice. I swam in the Pacific and dived off the 10-meter platform at the Olympic pool. (The diver who followed me was Dr. Sammy Lee, reigning Olympic champion. He did better.)

Nip took me to a "Fiesta" where I saw the most beautiful horses ever. Leo Carillo was the Grand Master – a movie star and (later) TV star, "The Cisco Kid". Nip's girlfriend had a sister and they got me a date with her, a couple of times. The girls were nieces of the famous evangelist, Aimee Semple McPherson. (That name may mean nothing to you. But just before that, she was one of America's biggest news stories: a famous religious leader and radio personality disappears for weeks and nobody knows where she is! It turned out she was "shacking up" with a lover, and you can imagine what newspapers all over the U.S. (and I believe most countries of the world) did with that!

Next to Disney, of course, one of the leading producers of animation films (cartoons) in those days was an outfit called "Harmon-Ising". Koch was a personal friend of partner, Hugh Harman, and he took me to meet the guy. We were invited to his apartment and stayed for drinks and dinner.

PRACTICAL JOKES. I got to know the other students living at Kenny's fraternity house, and went out with them quite often. The one I remember best was a "cowboy" from Arizona – his folks owned a sizeable ranch. We got to playing practical jokes on each other. I think I started it by short-sheeting his bed. I can't remember all the pranks – there were too many. I do remember, just before I left California, I put black shoe-polish on the underside of every door handle and dresser-pull in his room. So I figured I won. But guess what – that was September 1940. More than five years later – after I returned home from the war – I got out my civilian clothes, donned my best suit (a double-breasted navy pinstripe that I bought for my brother's wedding). Then I put my hand in a pocket and found every pocket in the suit was filled with white talcum powder! What a mess! Possibly this is one of the longest-running practical jokes in history! (Or maybe not.)

I continued to see a lot of movies but in the LA area they were all double-features, plus vaudeville – for as little as 20 cents! I remember one other thing: at a major shopping area near the USC campus, I saw people looking into the window of a bank building. I joined them, and saw my first television. A sign explained that this moving picture we were seeing was coming "through the air" from downtown Los Angeles, six miles away! I watched for awhile. You could barely see whatever they were showing. Mostly it was snow. I was totally unimpressed. (Now as a retired old man, TV is one of the best friends and constant companions in my life.)

HOMEWARD BOUND. (NON-STOP, ALMOST.)

The Navy called and I was ordered to report to the USS Illinois, a training ship, in New York City, on September 30. Mary Spalding Herrick had not been to Iowa for a couple of years so we planned that she would go back with me. Kenny had a girl cousin from Readlyn (just a few miles from Waverly) who was living in LA and she wanted to ride along. We decided to enlist a fourth passenger, so I put an ad in the paper, and a young guy from Lincoln, Nebraska, joined the party. (Many or most people driving long distances those days advertised for passengers to help share expenses.) We were a compatible group.

It was 3 p.m. when we left LA. Arrived in Las Vegas, ate, looked around and all agreed to skip sleeping and drive right on through. We could change drivers and the others could doze off. I didn't get any sleep until 5 a.m. and we arrived in Salt Lake City before seven. We ate breakfast, saw the Mormon Tabernacle and killed time until John Mooney arrived at the Telegram. Mary, John and I were all in the WHS Class of '34, and the SUI Class of '38. We had a lot to say, but miles to go, so we left a couple of hours later. Drove all day to Cheyenne, ate there, kept going, drove all night through Nebraska and left Vic out in Lincoln at 7 a.m.

My diary said we stopped in Cedar Falls so I could go to Confession. I guess I was more religious in those days than I remember. Arrived in Waverly at 3 p.m., just 46 hours after leaving LA. Spent some time with parents, got together with Jack Wright, Larry and Ruth that evening. Had about five days at home, doing the usual. Met with Don Cass (SUI) and his Waterloo friends, Jack Althouse and Fred Joyce who also are going to the USS Illinois, and we agreed to meet at the Park Central Hotel in New York on September 28. We all had different travel arrangements. Wayne Sparks drove Ruth and me to Waterloo on 9/26. We spent an evening at the Tavern before I boarded a train after midnight for the trip to New York.

On Sunday 9/29, Joyce and I went to the World's Fair – after I attended Mass at St. Patrick's. Saw Billy Rose's Aquacade and almost everything else.

HOWDY, SAILOR!

Next day, I reported for duty with 500 other college graduates from all over the U.S. We were taken out to the USS Arkansas (battleship) anchored in the Hudson River. They gave us "sailor suits" and we slept that night in hammocks! Then we sailed out to the open sea – leaving NY was a magnificent sight – and encountered strong winds and heavy seas. Lots of seasick sailors, but not me.

We headed south and every day it was sunny and much warmer and the sea changed from drab gray to beautiful blue. The Arkansas was one of our oldest battleships, built in 1912. 1500 men on board. College guys were all given numbers – I was 106. Our sister ship, the USS New York, joined us en route to Guantanamo Bay, a naval base on the east end of Cuba. We had a couple of days there and then to Colon, Panama, on the Atlantic side of the canal. After a day in Colon, we rode a primitive railroad 50 miles through the jungle and along the canal to Panama City on the Pacific side. My Waterloo gang spent most of liberty in bars, but I wandered around to see and enjoy all the things that were new and different.

On October 10, I received an invitation to the marriage of Mary Dickinson and Emmett Martin scheduled for Oct. 19. 30 days on the Ark was mostly lectures, study, standing watches, becoming seamen. I loved it. I saw a sailor hit by a car in Colon – they drive on the left side of the street and pedestrians from the U.S. look the wrong way. Our main battery is 12-inch (diameter of the shell) guns. Each gun weighs 62 1/2 tons, the shells about 900 lbs. each. We fired the big guns (target practice) with the candidates all lined up, watching, on deck. Wow! The concussion blew the hat off a sailor beside me and the handkerchief out of the hands of a guy blowing his nose. I was told one of us suffered a detached retina.

I was also told that Oct. 21 was a historic day. For the first time ever, a U.S. battleship fired on another U.S. battleship! We and the crew were confined below the main deck and the Ark was full of top brass from Washington. In Hampton Roads, VA, the Ark and the Wyoming anchored 1000 yards apart. To test the effectiveness of the armor plate on older battleships, we fired at the #5 barbette of the Wyoming four times with our 12-inch guns. We never learned the results and were warned not to talk about it ashore.

THE BEST LAID PLANS…

I had no intention of becoming a naval officer. I was just getting a free vacation and killing time until Kepler would join me on our Great Adventure. Then Congress passed a draft law and, obviously, everything changed.

Suddenly, I felt I had to pass the tests and be recommended for Midshipman School. First the physicals. I was number 106 so I heard a lot of guys were failing. When I took all the tests I went before the Senior Medical Officer who looked at my chart and said, "What's the matter with you, young man?" My heart sank. What had they found? Cancer or what? "I don't know of anything wrong, sir," I answered. "Neither do we." He smiled and told me, "You're 106, and so far, the only one we can't find anything wrong with!"

Near the end of the cruise, Lieutenant Commander Sid Bunting – the guy who determined our fate – interviewed everyone who passed the physical. I heard he believed strongly that you had to be extremely competent in mathematics to be a naval officer. I had no college math and figured that would send me back to civilian life where I'd be drafted by the Army and spend the next years slogging through the mud of Europe.

When I faced him, the first thing he said was, "No math!" But I was prepared. I told him, "I had solid geometry in high school. I'm a close friend of the head of the Math Department at Wartburg College in my hometown. If you'll recommend me for a Midshipman School months from now, I'll spend those months doing nothing but studying math." He said he liked my attitude and would recommend me for the classes starting December 16 at Northwestern University. (Once again, I got lucky.)

(Shortly after I was commissioned and assigned to the USS Rapidan, Sid Bunting came aboard as my new Commanding Officer!)

79 candidates failed the physical. (All of us had to pass at least two previous Navy physicals to get this far.) And 19 more were listed as "both physically unfit and inept." I knew seven of these guys. I met a lot of great young men from all over the U.S. on this cruise. The best of the bunch was a Notre Dame grad, George Petritz. We became very good friends. More on Petritz later.

AFTER THE ARK. October 25. Back in New York, I checked into a Manhattan hotel, I bought a paper and saw that Syracuse was playing Columbia in NYC the next day. Found out where they were staying, phoned Lannon, who invited me to a big Syracuse Club party at the Biltmore at 7 p.m. Cocktails and lavish food. Met a lot of coaches and sports writers and ended up with a bunch at some nightclub with great entertainers – until 3 a.m.

Next day I saw a big parade for Presidential candidate, Wendel Willkie, down Broadway. Lannon had given me a ticket to the game and I saw I was a bit late, and was actually running to the subway. As I rounded a corner I crashed into a man rushing the other way. We hit hard, both of us almost went down. But he smiled – a rather silly grin, and I recognized him – Joe E. Brown, the comedian, the guy with the big mouth! I had seen in the paper, he was starring on Broadway in "Harvey".

At the football game I sat with two other Lannon friends from SUI – Wendy Delzell and his wife. I knew them, a very handsome couple, big wheels at SUI. I even remembered Wendy as an excellent basketball player at one of the Cedar Rapids high schools. Lannon and I spent the evening at the New Yorker, after which I put him on a midnight train to Syracuse, then went to a stage show on 42nd Street. Sunday, after Mass, I subwayed to the Polo Grounds to watch the Chicago Bears beat the NY Giants. It was the first professional game I ever saw. Some guy booted a 52-yard field goal, considered very good at that time.

IN WAVERLY FROM OCTOBER 29 UNTIL DECEMBER 15. Life was about the same as earlier this year. I dated a lot – mostly Ruth (but this was cooling). One trip to Iowa City and Delta Chi, lots of Cedar Falls and Waterloo. Pep Grawe and Wayne Sparks were back in Waverly and I spent time with them as well. I played a lot of basketball, working out with the WHS team. The only change was trying to study spherical trigonometry (but the distractions were major and many).

John Chellevold, head of Wartburg College's math department, said he would help. But I didn't need him. I breezed through a book Jack Wright gave me, and by the time I arrived at Midshipman School, I could navigate by spherical trigonometry – solving the Celestial Triangle. Of course, I found out nobody did that anymore, so I promptly put it out of my mind forever.

December 15 was the day I said my goodbyes and left Waverly "forever". Until then, Waverly was my home, but not anymore. Ruth, Larry and I spent the evening at Pete Cordt's – sort of a "going away party". Then Jack took me through a very heavy snowstorm to Oelwein to catch a midnight train to Chicago. Waverly was pretty much snowed in, so I drove my car down "Main Street" until I got near Dad's market, then I pulled over toward the curb and plowed into a snowdrift and left it there.

I think this may be the way you can tell a small town: you can leave your car in a snowdrift on the main street in the center of the business district – and leave town (except for occasional visits over the years) for the rest of your life!

And so ends Part 1 of my life. I would rate it, "So Far, So Good". Or maybe a bit better than that.

PART 2. MY WAR. THE BIG ONE.

Midshipman School • Meeting Laura • Newport • Dad Dies • Captain Tuck • Portland and Payson • Action in the North Atlantic • Almost Overboard • Iceland • Our "Perfect Storm" • 12/7/41 • Worst Christmas! • Greenland • The Wedding • Casablanca • "Muledriver's Revenge" • Rapidan Torpedoed • "Kaiser Coffins" • USS Corregidor • "Assistant Captain?" • War in the Pacific • Liscome Bay Disaster • Takin' Makin, Kwajelein, Tarawa • New Guinea • Saipan: Kamikazes! • Guam • Typhoon! • Anti-Submarine Warfare • War Ends. We Win!

Part 2 of my life was getting ready for war, and being in it – full scale, lock, stock and barrel, go for broke. There was a lot of this going on, all over the world. It was one of the most crucial and dramatic periods in world history.

For me, many anxious moments – and lots of very good luck – without which I wouldn't be around to write about it now. It was a most interesting time to be a young man. Life changed drastically for millions in America, and in almost all parts of the world.

Mine began by boarding the train in Oelwein, Iowa, at about midnight, December 15, 1940. I said "thank you" to good friend, Jack Wright, who braved the blizzard to get me to the station on time. As I walked down the aisle looking for a seat, a young man looked at me and said, "I think I know you. Bob Zoller?" He was Jerry Carney from New Hampton.

I laughed. "You're the guy who broke Merle Kepler's nose!" I'd heard the story. He and Merle had tangled in football and again in basketball. Carney was a hotheaded Irishman, about three years younger than me, a good high school athlete.

He had really hung one on Merle in one of their games. Carney and I then discovered we were both heading for Midshipman School and agreed to be roommates.

It was a rough train ride. The seats were uncomfortable; neither of us
slept much. In Chicago, Joyce met us at Grand Central Station. We took a
streetcar to the "downtown campus of Northwestern University" and were
assigned a room in a residential hotel the Navy had taken over, Tower Hall. It
was just off N. Michigan Avenue, near the Old Water Tower, a few blocks north
of the Chicago River. From our room on the 5th floor we could look down on
Rush Street and its bars, nightclubs, and ethnic restaurants.

Six of us were roommates: Mulcare, Baum, Barry, Joyce, Carney and
me. Baum was Jewish, all the rest of us were Catholics – except Joyce wasn't
as "orthodox" as the rest of us. Nearly a thousand young college graduates
became Midshipmen and 740 of us graduated and became naval officers. We
all studied hard. Long hours. On Christmas Day, I went to Mass and spent all
the rest of the holiday studying.   Being a good student, I had no problems –
except one. Halfway through, they gave us another physical – and I did not
pass the eye test! After all I had done, if I had to go back to Waverly I would
feel like a total failure!

Lucky for me, a huge number of others also couldn't meet the Navy's
standard. And I'm sure somebody in Washington decided they had too much
time and money invested in us, and they needed new officers badly, now.
Besides, all of us had passed several previous eye tests, so it must be too much
studying under bad lighting, and therefore probably a temporary condition.
(Or so they hoped.)

A guy named Halloway, in the next room, came up with a copy of the
eye chart and we all memorized it before the next test. When I was given the
exam I read a memorized line of letters OK, BUT IT WAS THE WRONG
LINE! I know the eye doctor caught it, but he just laughed and went on. So I
passed – as did everyone else.

Scholastically, I did extremely well. They tested us frequently and
posted the grades. I beat everyone in my room on every exam and was always
near the top for the whole school.

We wore our Midshipman uniforms on all liberties and Chicago
seemed a bit surprised: we were constantly asked, "What are you?" On Christmas Eve, Joyce and I were down in the Loop and we passed a bar just as a
drunk was thrown out. The guy doing the bouncing looked at us and asked
about our uniforms. When we told him, he got all sentimental and told us how
proud he was that we were getting ready to fight for our country. Then he
insisted we come inside for free drinks. He was the owner – Barney Ross, former Lightweight boxing champion of the world.

On New Years Eve, Joyce and I cruised the Loop. Ran into Wendy
Delzell and his wife (whom I'd seen recently at the Syracuse game in New

York) and hung out with them. Wendy popped for a couple rounds of drinks. Then we split and discovered we could go into any hotel, go up on the elevator, get off on any floor, pick any room putting out a lot of noise, knock on the door and be enthusiastically invited to join the party! The uniforms paid all our New Years Eve celebration costs!

SMALL WORLD NOTE. At one of the hotel room wingdings, whom should I run into but Gertrude Lynch, my high school music teacher! She was a single lady, really whooping it up on New Years Eve in the Big City! She was "feeling no pain" and kept telling me how much she always liked me. I already knew that: when I was a senior she picked me to play the lead in the annual Waverly High School Operetta. This was somewhat remarkable because I was probably the worst singer in school – I couldn't carry a tune in a basket. I had refused the offer: if I tried to sing the several solos, she would have been fired. She had insisted, so we compromised by having the chorus sing all my "solos" with me, and they were instructed to sing loud to make sure nobody could hear me! This had to be a first and certainly an only – in Waverly and probably in the history of U.S. high school operettas!

THE YEAR 1940 was an extremely important year – for the world, and for me personally. Adolf Hitler and his German military machine conquered all of Europe, including France, and then started in on England. Led by Winston Churchill, the British resisted with great courage, but it seemed only a matter of time before they, too, would surrender or be destroyed. In America, these events were (justifiably) viewed with alarm. Hitler was a madman with a mission: to exterminate the Jewish people and rule the world. Franklin Delano Roosevelt, our President, tried to help the English people but his options were limited. Our military, all branches, had been neglected: we were not a major military power at the time. We were trying to rebuild, as rapidly as possible. I was part of the program – a very small part, but it was happening in all branches of our service. I knew for sure it was only a matter of time before our nation would go to war.

1941: A YEAR EVEN MORE IMPORTANT, TO ME AND THE WORLD.

After New Years Eve, I was flat broke – not a dime to my name. But January 6 was payday: the magnificent sum of $25!

February 2. ENTER LAURA, "the light of my life and the solace of my declining years!" (Or something like that.) This was surely one of the most important events of my life. It was a miracle *that* it happened, and *how* it happened. Two people in a city of three million who got to just the right place, at precisely the right time!

It was a Saturday and I had the duty, so I was one of twenty or so Midshipmen restricted for the full day and assigned various duties. It only happened to each of us about twice in the 90 days our training lasted. When I reported, I was told my duty was Classroom Messenger. "But there are no classes on Saturday," I told them. "Well," the officer said, "you're on duty anyway. Have a seat over there and we'll let you know if anything comes up."

Actually, I sat there all day, waiting. A couple of times I was asked what I was doing. I told them, and they said, "Oh, yeah. Well, just wait." About seven o'clock some officer said I could go to my room and study, but since I was "on duty," I couldn't leave the building.

I went to my room. It seemed the entire building, except for the duty office, was deserted. I began to ponder the idea of sneaking out – nobody would ever know. Then I did. This was risky and totally unlike me. I went to a tavern across the street because a lot of Middies hung out there and maybe someone I knew would be there. Baum was there.

We discussed how to spend the evening. Maybe go to the Loop and run into our gang? "By the way," I told Baum, "just before I left the duty office, a phone call came in, from that YWCA up the street. They're having an Open House and have a lot of girls and not enough men. They invited all the Midshipmen." We agreed to check it out. When we got there, it was intermission. The band was taking a break. We looked around – it didn't seem too promising – so we started to leave. Then a Hostess (who probably outweighed me by 30 pounds) grabbed my arm and said, "You can't leave. Here's a girl I want you to meet!" She started steering me to a wallflower that I certainly did not want to meet.

I had to do something quickly. I saw four girls in a circle, near the bandstand. They looked better. I broke the death grip the Hostess had on my arm and said, "I just saw a girl from my hometown! I've got to say hello or her father will be mad at me." She wasn't sure, so she kept an eye on me, and I headed toward the four, and just then the band began to play. I could see the faces of three of them, at least somewhat, but the one facing away from me had an especially attractive posterior. So I touched her shoulder, she turned, and I asked her to dance with me.

Jackpot! She was beautiful and a wonderful dancer. I was impressed. We danced two or three numbers and then I suggested we might leave and go to some other place, like one of the ethnic restaurants on Rush Street – or wherever. She said, "I can't leave, I'm on a date!"

She pointed him out. He was standing in a corner, holding the two plates of (I'm sure) melting ice cream he'd gone to pick up during intermission! I made sure to get her phone number. And thus began a romance that lasted 61 years!

I told you it was a miracle that we met. A whole bunch of things had to happen to get us to the right place at the right time. *If any one of these had not taken place*, our chances of finding each other would have been zero to none!

- The stoplight in Des Moines had to change at just the right time.
- I had to stop on Amber – completely foreign to my nature.
- Kepler had to be on the far west side of the city.
- Kepler had to walk right in front of my car.
- Kepler had to have seen the news about the new Navy V-7 program on the Associated Press wire, that very morning.
- Kepler had to talk me into joining the V-7 program, to kill time. Or at least check it out.
- I had to investigate, pass the physical, and sign up.
- The Navy had to call me for that particular cruise.
- On the Arkansas, I had to learn about Lt. Cmdr. Bunting's obsession with mathematics, and be ready to suggest a solution.
- Bunting had to buy my suggestion.
- Bunting had to assign me to the Dec. 16 school in Chicago.
- Of all possible duties on all possible days, I had to get Classroom Messenger, on this particular Saturday.
- An officer finally said I could go to my room.
- I decided to go AWOL, the first, and only time in my life.
- I had to have overheard the YWCA Open House invitational phone call.
- Baum had to agree to check it out.
- We had to arrive there right at intermission.
- The Hostess had to insist I not leave.
- Laura's date had to leave her to go for the ice cream.
- I had to approach the four girls instead of the wallflower.
- I had to pick Laura (over the three others) to dance.
- She had to say OK, and then give me her phone number.
- And, by the way, it was the first time Laura had ever attended a YWCA Open House!

For the rest of my time in Chicago, it was courtship at every opportunity. We had Saturdays and Sundays off and liberty every weekday from 5 p.m. to 10 or 11 p.m. I spent every possible moment with Laura. She lived with her mother and older sister, Josephine, and they accepted me 100%. I was invited for dinner, often. In due time I was leaving my civilian clothes there so I didn't have to wear my uniform on all our dates. Because I didn't have to be back on Sundays, I'd sleep there after our Saturday dates. Then (they were Polish and Catholic), we'd go to Mass on Sunday.

We didn't have a lot of time. In the middle of March I'd be commissioned and sent to sea. I'd have ten days leave to go home to pack and say my goodbyes, so I convinced Laura to come to Waverly to meet my family and friends.

Before we leave Chicago, a few more things you should know. Not very important, but one day Carney and I went to the YWCA, played one-on-one basketball. He was good, but I beat him.

I took Laura to the Graduation Ball and she was the most beautiful lady there. That night I gave her my fraternity pin, (the college guys' version of engagement) although we had never talked marriage.

THE BAD NEWS. When I failed the eye exam, I was told not to use my eyes, and this lasted a couple of weeks. My grades took a dive – I had been way up at the top. I still did well. But I was disappointed. Win some and lose some.

ABOUT LAURA'S FAMILY, THE NIEWINSKIS.

Laura's mother was a remarkable woman. Grew up in a large family on a farm in Poland. Only 16 years old, she had fallen in love with America, based on what she had heard. She went to her father and asked for her share of the inheritance so she could leave and go to the United States. He agreed and she left and never saw any of her family again. Traveling "last class" she arrived in New York, knowing nobody there – 16 years old, and unable to speak English! She found out that Chicago had the most Polish people, so she went there, got a job in the garment industry, and eventually married a young Polish man, also an immigrant. They had two daughters, and when Laura was about five, her father was involved in an accident at work and died. Her mother worked hard and was good at her job. She supported herself and gave her daughters a good life. Josephine became a successful businesswoman and, as I believe I mentioned, Laura became my wife.

Actually, Laura wasn't her real name. She was Aurelia Niewinski, but her family always called her Laura, so I did, too. Being Polish, she was just a bit different than the girls I knew in Iowa and I found this interesting. We went to a lot of ethnic restaurants and nightclubs – German, Hungarian, Polish, etc. And her family lived near a Jewish neighborhood so I got to sample a lot of wonderful Jewish food. Because of Laura, however, I developed one very bad habit: staying up late. According to my diary, our dates usually ended at 4:30

or 5:30 a.m. when I didn't have to get back to Tower Hall earlier. (Years later, Bob Hope made the song famous, "Two sleepy people, by dawn's early light – and too much in love to say good night." That was us.)

When Laura came to Waverly during my 10-day leave, I introduced her to family and friends and everyone seemed to like her a lot. Except, my sister had reservations (as I expected she would) because Laura was a beauty operator and Helen had always expected I would marry a Senator's daughter, or some such. Laura had a Chicago friend, an older woman, now living in Cedar Falls. Laura phoned her to tell her she was in Waverly, visiting her new boyfriend. She said I had been one of the lifeguards at the Waverly Swimming Pool. "Oh," her friend said, "is he the one with the pretty legs?" (It really happened!)

My father had been sick for some time and the local doctors decided he should go to a specialist at University Hospital in Iowa City. So one day after Laura returned to Chicago, Helen and I drove Dad to Iowa City to see a fairly-famous Dr. Steindler. Then we received the bad news – cancer, and terminal. My last few days were hectic. We closed the meat market, put everything up for sale, including the building. Jack Wright agreed to put a retail flower shop where the market had been and I'm sure this was more a favor to my family than a business decision. Everything was changing.

I was broke again. Didn't have enough money to report to my ship in Mobile, Alabama. I went to see Ed Englebrecht at the Waverly Savings Bank to borrow $150. I told him my Dad would co-sign the note. He laughed and said my signature was good enough (even though I was leaving Waverly "forever"). Another benefit of small town living in those times.

THE USS RAPIDAN, MY HOME FOR THE NEXT TWO YEARS

Again Jack Wright took me to Waterloo to catch the "Rocket" to St. Louis. By air to New Orleans, where I visited the French Quarter on a big party night – "Spring Festival". Boarded the USS Rapidan (oil tanker) in the shipyards in Mobile, Alabama, where it was being upgraded and repaired. (I couldn't figure why they assigned a fighting man like me to a sea-going filling station, when a battleship or aircraft carrier would be so much more appropriate!)

Ensign John Mundy became my new best friend almost immediately. (64 1/2 years later, as I write this, he still is.) Philadelphian, graduate of the Pennsylvania School Ship (Merchant Marine) and Naval Reserve officer.

Soon to be married to Evelyn Toy, "the girl next door". John was a good officer who always seemed to be in charge when bad things happened. He had a
wonderful sense of humor, and he really kept me laughing when, as you will
see, there wasn't a hell of a lot to laugh about.

Sam Houston was "the Bull Ensign" and a great officer. He and
Wilbur Ulle, an engineering officer, were also from the Pennsylvania School
Ship. LCDR Sid Bunting (from the Arkansas) came aboard as our new C.O.
and LCDR Skahill was the Exec. Paul Pomeroy Stewart, from my class at
Abbott Hall (actually Tower Hall) and I were the only "90-Day Wonders".
Except for us, the Captain, the Exec and the Supply Officer (all Annapolis),
the Medical Officer and our Chief Engineer, all other officers were from the
Merchant Marines.

Paul Revere McGlohon was our Chief Engineer, a remarkable man.
Talk about "a canny Scot"! This guy, on the one hand, was a real life version
of the fictionally famous Colin Glencannon, chief engineer of the H.M.S.
Inchcliffe Castle – and, on the other hand, one of the wisest men I ever knew.
Mac was a "Mustang" – up from the ranks – a Chief Warrant Officer, and
therefore the lowest ranked officer in our Wardroom. But he had the respect
of all the officers on board. Ensign Ulle outranked him, but served as his
assistant.

Lucky for me, McGlohon liked me and became my mentor. He
watched me to observe how I handled things, then later and privately, would
tell me nicely what I should have done. He decided early that he didn't like
Paul Pomeroy Stewart and most of the rest of us didn't either. Stewart was
pompous – a pain in the neck, and parts lower down. He was good looking,
had been in radio and done some theater so he affected a "stage voice" (in the
manner of Ted, the newscaster on the old Mary Tyler Moore show. It didn't
work well for him.)

Stewart had married immediately after getting his commission and
brought his wife to Mobile. On Easter, they invited three of us Ensigns to dinner. After drinks, the lady brought out a beautiful roast turkey, and when Paul
began to carve, there was a Poof! And a terrible odor filled the room! She
didn't know you were supposed to remove all that stuff inside. As I remember,
we went directly to dessert. She was a nice lady and I really felt sorry for her.

Except for Sam Houston (engaged) and Mundy, who married shortly,
Ulle and I were the only two unmarried officers on the ship. Wilbur looked a
lot like John Garfield of the movies, except for his hair. Apparently, he was
aware of this because he always acted like Garfield. But he was good at getting dates wherever we went.

The Gunnery Officer was Lt. Hanson. He was about fifty and he
looked like a man who spent too many years outdoors in the hot sun – which

apparently he was. He claimed he once served as Captain of some rich guy's yacht, when President Roosevelt came aboard for a fishing vacation. But the fish wouldn't bite and FDR was most unhappy. Hanson told him, "You want fish? I'll get you fish." Then he filled up a burlap bag with shrimp and took a baseball bat and clobbered the bag until all the juices were seeping out, and put it over the side. In a few minutes FDR was reeling in the big ones, having a great time. According to Hanson's story, the President told him, "I owe you one. Let me know if I can ever help." (Some of the officers believed this, but some didn't.)

Lt. Merrit D. Mullen is a guy you will learn to know (and maybe hate) as my Rapidan story continues. In the Merchant Marines he was known as "Muledriver Mullen". It had something to do with a maritime strike, but I never knew what. He was the ship's First Lieutenant – in charge of many things like taking on and off-loading our liquid cargo, maintenance of most everything except the Engineering, Gunnery and Navigation things. He was bald, bull-necked and reminded me of Eric Von Stroheim, an old movie actor who usually played bad guys. Only a bit fatter.

Lt. Joe Gillis was our Navigator. Big, sad-faced, reminded me of Slim Summerville, another movie actor. Taught me a little about taking star sights, but he always used the good sextant with the telescope attached and I got the old clunker without a scope and so I had difficulty getting a good sight.

Our Doctor and our Supply Officer were replaced soon after I arrived, so I won't tell you about them..

MOBILE AND OTHER PORTS OF CALL

Mobile, Alabama, was kind of fun, giving me my first look at the Old South – Bellingrath Gardens, the Azalea Trail, etc. Laura was writing every day. This helped, but also reminded me of what I was missing. I liked the balmy weather and the smell of summer, which I noticed on the last leg of my trip from Iowa. I kept in touch with Waverly and heard a lot of my buddies had been drafted. Nazi Germany controlled all of Europe, except England and Russia. Sam had me doing a lot of decoding work. I paid off the Waverly Savings Bank loan and my old Delta Chi debts. I even got offered a Civil Service job – Chief Clerk at a U.S. Army Air base in Florida, at $192 a month – more than my Ensign's salary of $125 a month, plus a little extra for a "food allowance". (The Navy feeds enlisted men; Officers pay all their food costs but the Navy provides a Steward, cooks and mess attendants. All these were Puerto Rican, Filipino or black.)

When we left Mobile we sailed up the Mississippi River to Baton Rouge where I visited Delta Chi on the LSU campus and had a good evening. Then to Charleston, SC, where Mundy went ashore alone and came back that night as a married man! Evelyn had met him there, they married, but had little time for a honeymoon as we sailed immediately to Norfolk. Evelyn arrived soon after, so several of us helped our newlyweds celebrate. When it got pretty late, three of us – I think Ulle, Stewart and I – discovered we missed the last bus back to the base and didn't have enough money for a taxi. So John and Evelyn said not to worry, "Stay with us." *Believe it or not, we joined them in their hotel room on what could be considered as their wedding night!* There were twin beds and a very large closet and somehow we three "supernumeraries" slept there. (I use the word "slept" loosely.) But we did not peek.

Being a naval officer wasn't easy work. I rose at 3:30 a.m. everyday at sea and stood the 4 – 8 watch with Lt. Gillis as Junior Officer of the Watch, and to learn navigation. Still doing a lot of decoding and trying to learn as much seamanship as possible. Arrived Newport, RI on 7 May. Narragansett Bay was full of ships. We anchored a full six miles from the Newport pier.

ADVENTURES IN NEWPORT

And here I encountered my first really sticky situation. A storm blew in and by late in the evening the Bay was choppy and dangerous for small boats. We were also surrounded by fog so dense you couldn't see anything five feet in front of you. About 10:30 p.m. the Exec sent for me. We had a liberty party in Newport, some sixty or so enlisted, and we had to pick them up at midnight. I was to be the officer-in-charge. (The Navy always puts an officer in charge of sticky situations – so you can blame him if bad things happen, not the higher ups, if they didn't send an officer.)

The presumption was that I would be able to go six-plus miles in heavy seas in pea-soup fog more competently than the petty officer coxswain, enlisted bow hook, and engineer who would have handled it in fair weather. The fact was I knew nothing about small boats. This was a 50-foot motor launch but I didn't know anything about them either.

I went up to the bridge, checked the charts and the gyro compass and saw we should start out on a bearing of 190 degrees and we'd have to make two course changes en route. They gave me a magnetic compass which was totally useless because it never pointed to North, just to the closest big ship. Visibility was practically zero. We couldn't see a ship until we were about to crash into them – and the harbor was full of ships. I finally decided our best bet was to call up to the people on the ships, when we encountered them, and ask them to point the way we should go to the Newport pier. So we kind of felt our way and somehow arrived O.K.

Of course, the liberty party was more than somewhat drunk. We got back all right, found the Rapidan (but I have no idea how) and then the trick was to get the men aboard by their climbing up the sea ladder. The boat was riding up and down on huge waves and each man would try to grab the ladder when the boat was way up near the deck of the ship – quite a trick since a couple seconds later it would drop down about fifteen or twenty feet. We were lucky until a ship's cook – one of our oldest and drunkest – lost his grip near the top of the ladder and fell twelve or fifteen feet back onto the edge of the boat and then into the sea.

One of the men and I fished him out and back into the boat. He was terribly injured; I'd guess a broken back. They lowered a stretcher, we got him aboard and the doctor ordered another boat to take him ashore to the Naval Hospital. Lucky for me, they gave that trip to another officer. I never heard whether the man lived or died.

When the weather cleared, I fell in love with Newport. It was beautiful, quaint and colonial. I'd heard about the estates of the "old money" people and "top of the heap" socialites and enjoyed my solo walking tours through those neighborhoods. It was May and Newport was in bloom. The USS Albemarle pulled in and Russell Peabody (of Tower Hall and THE Boston Peabody's) sent me a message to meet him ashore and we had a good reunion. Both our ships were scheduled to be there a couple weeks and Peabody suggested we both take a few days leave and go to visit his family. He guaranteed a great time – golf, riding horses, parties, whatever, anytime and all the time. In case you aren't up on your American history, the Peabody's were one of the great families in Boston history – super-rich, philanthropists (millions donated, mainly to education, etc., back to the late 1700's). So the small town lad from Iowa, great-grandson of impoverished German farmers, was quite flattered at Peabody's invitation.

Unfortunately, the Navy kept it from happening. All of a sudden, the Albemarle received orders to sail. Russ met me briefly in town, and handed me a paper with addresses, phone numbers and other information I would need – to go to the Peabody's in Boston without him! I was overwhelmed! He said he'd call ahead and let them know I was coming; said his sister would take over and make sure I enjoyed the visit – whatever I wanted to see and do.

Later on I'm going to write about "Rich Kids I Have Known". But I wanted to tell you about Peabody now. What a nice thing for him to do! I declined his offer, just didn't think it was right to go without him. Knowing what I know now, I'd have gone – just one more thing in my life to tell about.

JOLLY OLD BOSTON, HOME OF THE BEAN AND THE COD

I did go to Boston, but not to Peabody's. I had never been to Boston and I thought maybe this was my only chance. (Of course, I was in and out of Boston many times, later on.) I went to Cambridge, the Harvard Campus, to see if I could find my old Delta Chi roommate, Howard Davidson, who was now attending Harvard Law. And I did. We had a great reunion. After a couple hours catching up, Howie had to study for another exam but said I should come back in the evening and plan to stay overnight. So I left and went sightseeing until 9 or 10 p.m., then back to Howie's room where we talked until 3:30. He and his Jewish roommate were very hospitable. I left in the morning, went to Mass and spooked around Boston all of Sunday, and back aboard the ship at 1 a.m. Monday.

DAD DIES. BACK TO WAVERLY.

Next trip, up the Mississippi River to Baton Rouge. There was a letter from home, that Dad was seriously ill, and I should come home if possible. I went to see the Captain who said, sorry, he had just received an "ALLNAV", (a message to all ships) from Washington, saying no officer could be given leave if his ship was scheduled for an overseas destination. And he showed me our orders to proceed from Baton Rouge to Bermuda. So I sent a telegram explaining why I couldn't be there. When we stopped in New Orleans to load a cargo of oil in drums I received another telegram that Dad had died.

Sunday, June 8, we left New Orleans at 6 a.m. A couple of hours later – more than halfway downriver to the sea – the Captain's Yeoman came to tell me the C.O. wanted to see me right away. And I was told our orders had been changed and I could go on leave. But I'd have to get ready fast and I would be put ashore, God knows where, and be on my own from that time on. I grabbed a suitcase, some clothes and what money I had and the Captain slowed the big ship as much as possible (a very dangerous maneuver in a river) and a boat crew dumped me out on the eastern shore.

I had been warned it might be swampland, maybe even an island. All the Captain could tell me was the road was east of the river. Watching for snakes and alligators, I headed east and made it to the road OK. It was hot and it was Sunday. No buses on Sundays, I'd have to hitchhike. No traffic in either direction. I sat on my suitcase for an hour. Finally a bread-delivery man saw me and stopped. He was headed south but said I better get in, he'd take me to a grocery store, maybe somebody there would be going north. He did and nobody was, so an hour later he picked me up and we headed toward New Orleans, more than fifty miles away.

The driver was white and a black couple, man and woman, were up front with him. I rode in the back of the panel truck – no seat, no A/C and not much air. It was a sweatbox. A two-hour ordeal. Surely, a totally improper situation for a lean, mean, fighting machine and card-carrying member of The Greatest Generation! But I got to New Orleans, flew to St. Louis and took a bus the rest of the way. Home by 1 a.m. on June 10, and Dad's funeral was that day. My mother held up well. I saw a lot of relatives at the funeral. The Waverly papers did a major story about my trip home.

Then it was hello and goodbye all over again. Wayne Sparks was drafted, Jack Wright out of town. Larry Hegg arrived from art school in Minneapolis. I saw the Heggs, Pete Cordt, Fred Studier. Helped Mother get organized and then left for Chicago.

BOSTON, NORFOLK, AND AN EVENING WITH CAPTAIN TUCK

Had three glorious days with Laura. A telegram arrived with orders to join my ship in Boston, ASAP. When I got there the town was full of British sailors: the HMS Rodney, battle cruiser that helped sink the Bismarck, was in Boston for repairs. I also discovered that a lot of our Pacific fleet was now on our east coast because of the war.

On June 22 I stood the first of my top watches at sea, en route to Norfolk. That's about three months after receiving my commission. I was told that in peacetime, the Annapolis boys (with four years of schooling) usually trained a full year as Junior Officers before given the full responsibilities of top watches at sea. So, I guess I was really a "90-day wonder." (Kind of proud of myself.)

In Norfolk we docked alongside the carrier Yorktown, so I called on Fred Joyce and ate with him on board. He gave me a tour of his huge ship and then we saw a movie and ended our evening at the Officers Club. On June 26, we moved to the Navy Yard for repairs on our gasoline tanks – a 6-day job. Wilbur got us dates – his was with the daughter of The Captain of the Yard, a four-striper in charge of the huge repair facility and the thousands of Navy and civilians who worked there. As usual, Ulle picked college girls, too young for me. We went to some big, fancy Ball, danced a few and then went back to the Captain's home to sample Betsy's record collection. Even the music was "too young" for me. I left the others and began to wander around the house.

I came across a room – a large Study, I'd say – and there was a fire burning in the fireplace. It looked cozy and I moved closer, just then noticing a man in an easy chair, reading a book. "Good evening," he said. "Care to join me?" Then he shook my hand and introduced himself. "Captain Tuck. Royal

Navy." It turned out he was the C.O. of the HMS Illustrious – the aircraft carrier that played the major role in sinking the Bismarck, the German super battleship generally considered the greatest warship ever built – in one of the most important naval battles ever!

He was an impressive man. I apologized for disturbing his reading. "I can read anytime," he told me. "I'd much rather talk with you." He asked all about me and really seemed interested. Our lives and backgrounds were so different it made for an interesting meeting. We hit it off. He rang for a member of the staff and we ordered our beverages – Scotch, as I remember (which I don't much care for, but it seemed appropriate. And he had sandwiches made for us, later on. He was, of course, a houseguest of Captain Baker. The Illustrious needed after-battle repairs and would be fixed up by the Norfolk Navy Yard. Captain Baker and his wife were at the fancy Ball at the "O" Club, and Wilbur and the girls stayed in the Club Basement listening to Betsy's records. So we remained undisturbed, just the two of us, until after 2 a.m. For me, this was a memorable evening.

Two days later, Captain Tuck was promoted by the Queen and, in an appropriate ceremony on the Illustrious, he was replaced as C.O. by Lord Louis Montbatten!

Our next trips were to Charleston, Key West and Houston. I got the opportunity to explore and get acquainted with all three, and this was the part of Navy life I enjoyed the most. It was fun going up the Houston Ship Channel from Galveston. Then, en route to Guantanamo via the Straits of Yucatan. The days were hot, the nights, beautiful. I got a cot and most nights I slept near one of the 3-inch AA guns, under the stars. And most nights I got rained on, heading for cover when the first drop hit.

Next stop, St. Thomas, the Virgin Islands. Saw my first "bum boaters", the native kids who come alongside as you enter the harbor: you toss coins in the water and they dive down to get them. Walked around Charlotte Amalie, the capital city, bought a "Zombie" for 10 cents – (enough rum for five people), swam, and in the evening went way up on the mountain to a beautiful resort, "Estates Constant", formerly referred to as "the white man's club". Fantastic views, good service, a quiet evening of books, music, darts, drinks.

Back to Galveston and Houston where a lot of mail caught up with us. From Andy Cumming who joined the Naval Reserve Air Corps (he said Overton was in Newfoundland) – from Ed Kepler who is in the V-7 program and will be at Abbott Hall with Al Folkers in September – (he said Merle enlisted in the Army and is in Alaska) – from Bill Leary who, along with Lefty Flood, is at Camp Claiborne near New Orleans, and they both hate it – from Laura, of course – from the family who said they sold "my home" in Waverly, and reported the Jay twins had a double wedding, Eleanor and Bill Mooney, Lenore and Vince Carstensen. I knew Vince was now a doctor and he and Lenore were at an air base near Houston. I planned to visit, but there wasn't time so I sent a letter. I also wrote Les Moeller.

After Houston, Norfolk. Laura came from Chicago with Stewart's wife, to spend her vacation with me. Thirteen glorious days (when I wasn't working aboard ship) – sun and swimming, dancing (Glen Gray at the Surf Club), Virginia Beach, a champagne party on Laura's 22nd birthday, dinners aboard ship and at the "O" Club, etc. The wives all thought Laura was great, and everyone tried to marry us off.

PORTLAND AND A RICH KID NAMED PAYSON

August 31: Portland, Maine. Anchored in Casco Bay, and wow! is it cold! My memories of Portland are extremely pleasant, due mainly to a college student named Elliot Payson, a bunch of his buddies and the gang of girl-friends they hung out with. Soon after the Rapidan arrived, a beautiful (expensive) speedboat came alongside. Three fine looking young men asked permission to come aboard, and then said they just wanted to welcome the U.S. Navy and issue an invitation to any unmarried officers to join them at a Country Club dance that night. Wilbur and I were the only unattached. We accepted, and they came back and picked us up, about 1700 (5 P.M.). First stop was a formal cocktail party at Skip Allen's house (complete with butlers!) – then to Peggy Coleman's house for dinner. (Peggy was 18 and a student at Smith College.) The dance was a Charity Ball – "V for Victory" – but Elliot picked up the ticket cost for Wilbur and me. He also said there hadn't been time to line up dates for us but all the guys in his group arranged to have their dates dance one dance with each of us!

These were all rich kids – really rich – attended prep schools, the best colleges – Smith, Vassar, Mary Baldwin, Princeton, Dartmouth, Harvard, Yale – all had fancy sport cars, power boats and family yachts – were extremely well-dressed, well-educated – and they treated us like visiting royalty! At intermission, Elliot took us to his home on "Falmouth Foreside", an impressive estate on Casco Bay. As we approached, I saw a large white-fenced field with a dozen horses. "Like to ride?" he asked. "We've got the horses and you're welcome any time. If I'm tied up, my sisters would be pleased to ride with you." Then he told us their sailboats and (several) speedboats were also available "anytime".

The Payson home was huge. I don't remember much about it except he took us into a large room that looked like a library, then pushed a button and the whole wall rolled away to reveal the largest privately owned bar I had ever seen! I didn't really want a drink but somehow it seemed appropriate that I should have one.

I was mightily impressed with Elliot Payson. What a kind, generous young man – so hospitable to a couple of Navy ensigns he had never seen before. He told me they hadn't had much Navy in Portland – I guess because it was relatively close to Newport's large Narragansett Bay and to Boston. He seemed interested in, and well versed on, world affairs and said he knew that Wilbur and I would soon be at war and deserved to be honored for that. I noticed also that all of his college buddies we met at the party that night obviously considered him their leader and agreed to whatever he decided to do.

Before we left Portland I learned the Paysons were probably the wealthiest of families and top of the heap, socially. Years later, I found out that a Mrs. Payson – Elliot's mother or sister, possibly – was the owner of the N.Y. Mets baseball team.

Wilbur and I had hit the jackpot, but unfortunately Elliot and all the others were leaving for college shortly. There was a very rich old lady living in a very large (hunting lodge-style) home on her own private island – "Clapboard Island" – in Casco Bay. Every year, just before all the affluent college kids returned to their studies, she would have a big send-off party – cocktails and a lavish buffet dinner – strolling musicians, dancing and about everything else you can think of – for (I'd guess) well over a hundred of the beautiful young people. Maybe 200. It was really big. Maybe twenty or thirty uniformed waiters just for passing hors d'oeuvres and bringing the drink orders. I had never seen anything quite like this, and it occurred to me how different were these young people from my fraternity brothers at SUI, most of whom were pinching pennies, and working (if they were lucky enough to get a job), just to make it through four years of college.

Wilbur and I were invited to this impressive affair and I'm not sure if Elliot arranged it, or whether the lady, Mrs. Brown, had invited all young officers on the few Navy ships we had in Casco Bay. My diary says I left the island with Peggy Coleman in her 30 ft. Chrysler Cruiser at 30 knots (!) and we went to her house on the Bay. There were others with us, but I don't remember who.

Other Portland items: Sam took 10 days leave and went to New York to marry "Shortstop". I took over for him as Communication Officer and 2nd Division Officer. There was a picture of Captain Tuck in LIFE magazine. I dated Patricia Webster and she invited me to visit her at Stoneleigh College in Rye, NH – "soon".

Then something I now consider strange happened. My log says, "Welcome news came, and we prepared to get underway for Argentia, Newfoundland to join a convoy bound for Iceland. At last, a real adventure!" What was I thinking? Going to war even before our war began, and getting shot at, maybe torpedoed and killed, is "welcome news"?? NOW I know that was weird, but I was young and stupid then, and that reaction was totally consistent with my thirst for adventure at that time.

Looking back, and having taken advantage of many years to get a lot smarter, I now know that war is not really an "adventure". In fact, it is surely the dumbest thing ever invented by the human race as an accepted method of solving problems.

Before we left Portland, Lt. Hanson seemed more upset about convoy duty in the N. Atlantic than any of our officers. I think he was older than our C.O., Exec or others on board and I later observed that, commissioned or enlisted, the older the man, the more fearful of dying. We had heard about oil tankers (like us) being torpedoed by German U-boats and, it seems, always with "no survivors". So Hanson went ashore our last day in Portland and we think he tried to call FDR.

ARGENTIA AND THE NORTH ATLANTIC

We arrived in Placentia Bay, Newfoundland on 27 September. This is where FDR and Winston Churchill met just a couple weeks before. The world press considered it a news event of major importance, calling it The Atlantic Conference and saying only that it took place "somewhere in the North Atlantic" and that we gave the British fifty old 4-stack destroyers in return for the right to use the Royal Navy's bases, worldwide. But one didn't have to have an I.Q. over 6 to know they probably discussed the U.S.A. declaring war on Germany, and when.

This harbor, also called Argentia Base, was very large and an awful lot of our Navy's ships were there, getting ready to take on the Germans, I'm sure. Peabody's Albemarle and Joyce's Yorktown were there. But the big news was that someone decided that our place in the convoy to Iceland would be taken by our sister ship, the Salinas – because we were having some problems with our engines and the Salinas was a knot and a half faster and more able to keep up with the speed of the convoy. I was disappointed because we missed the opportunity to be the first American warship (if you can call a tanker a warship) to be included in an all-British convoy. Keep in mind, the British were at war, and we were not.

But we were scheduled for the next one, leaving soon. Meanwhile, we gave the Salinas all our life jackets before she sailed; a couple new officers came aboard, (our whaleboat having picked them up) and I was on deck to watch our boat approach and for some reason it started to sink some 60 or 70 yards away and the new officers and the boat crew had to swim the rest of the way! Hal Sutherland and Leo "Fighter" Foley were our new officers. More on them later.

The weather there in the Fall of the year was cold and windy. We encountered heavy gales, so bad we lost another boat, this time a 30-ft motor launch, and I had the deck duty where I had to be on the bridge hours on end, taking bearings to ensure we weren't dragging anchor and maybe ending up on the rocks. One day, in better weather, a couple of us took a 12-mile hike through the mountains. Joyce invited me to dinner a couple of times but I couldn't get a boat to take me there. The Navy had issued us some cold weather clothing (and I bought some long johns –Hanson called them "long-handled drawers" – in Portland) so I began to wear a wool shirt and winter clothing.

And, what do you know, *Hanson's orders to shore duty in Galveston, TX, arrived!* Hanson just smiled and told us, "The important thing is *who* you know". We all decided his story about FDR was undoubtedly true.

Sam became Gunnery Officer and I became the new Communications Officer, with Ens. Sutherland as my assistant. I got a stateroom all by myself. And like most of our officers, I began to grow a beard. All of a sudden the Navy began to send almost all its communications in code. Fortunately, they issued us an electronic coding machine. (We named it "The Jeep".) All messages are directed to certain addressees, which could be a single ship, a specific class of ships or an entire fleet, or ALL NAVS which mean the entire U.S. Navy worldwide. The rules are that you decode only messages directed to you or to a group that includes you. But our C.O. wanted me to decode *all* messages so he would "know what was going on." This became an impossible situation, so bad that I complained and so the captain appointed a Coding Board – several officers who didn't stand watches – the doctor, supply officers, etc.

With all the watch standing and communications work, I believe I've never worked longer or harder in my life. My longest "vacation" at this time was an afternoon of touch football ashore – 25 officers and enlisted men. My team won 14 – 2 and I threw a touchdown pass to Boatswains Mate First Class Lytle (who two years later became a commissioned officer) and got our other score myself on a 70-yard run after intercepting a pass in the last minute! (Not bad for "an old sea dog".)

Got a lot of mail before we left, a couple from Ed Kepler who told me when he graduates from Abbott Hall he will request assignment to the Rapidan so we can fight this war together. News that Larry Hegg has been drafted

– is anyone left in Waverly? Another letter from Patricia Webster, the Portland rich girl, which made me feel good (but in fact, at this time of my writing, I cannot remember her at all). And, as always, several from Laura, which made me feel even better.

PRIMITIVE "O" CLUB, AND WAS THAT A MALAMUTE?

One other Newfoundland memory. Where the Navy goes, an Officers Club immediately follows. As soon as we heard about it, we went there. A boat took us ashore. We climbed out on the rocks and scaled a small cliff, and there it was: a Quonset hut – a small one, only for the bottled refreshments and the guy who poured them. You didn't go in, you got your drink and sat out-doors on one of the felled logs and drank it there. Your choice was easy: you were told, "Today we got rye." That was it.

But it was a sunny day and warmer than usual. Pleasant. I didn't care for rye, but it was something to do. I looked around and saw a big dog chained to a tree. "Beautiful animal," I said. "Anyone know what breed it is?" Some-one said it was an Alaskan Malamute. "I'd go pet him," I said, "but he looks like he'd take my arm off!" I was assured he was friendly so I went over, got acquainted, and talked to him. We immediately became friends, and I told myself that some day I would have an Alaskan Malamute dog.

Before we left Newfoundland, they gave me a Colt .45 automatic pis-tol (and ammo) and was told to wear it when I was Officer of the Deck and if we ever had to abandon ship. I learned all U.S. merchant ships were being armed with 5-inch guns and Armed Guard (Navy) crews. Then we got word that a U.S. destroyer, the Kearney, had been torpedoed while on convoy duty in Icelandic waters.

On 21 October, three destroyers tied up alongside to be refueled. All three had been with the Kearney when it was hit, and the officers we talked to all told the same story: the Kearney didn't sink but they saw three tankers hit, blow sky high and come down in pieces with no survivors! This wasn't exactly good news for us, in view of the fact we were about to leave on the same 1500-mile trip in the same kind of ship carrying the same cargo. I knew we would have 325,000 gallons of high octane aviation gasoline in our forward tanks and I would spend practically all of my time, day and night, eating, sleeping and standing watches right on top of them!

MY WAR IN THE NORTH ATLANTIC

We "shoved off" on 29 October. Joined a convoy of 42 ships, over half of which were tankers. One Icelandic ship and the Rapidan, and all the rest were British. We sailed with orders not to fly our American flag. I guess Washington wanted us to be an "equal opportunity sinkee" for the Nazi U-boats. Our escort was five U.S. destroyers. I don't remember if they flew American flags or not. I guess it wouldn't make any differences: any German U-boat officer could easily recognize them as U.S. Navy ships.

Late evening of our second day, we received a secret message: the Salinas – returning from the trip originally scheduled for us – had been torpedoed! Hit twice, but still afloat and making for the nearest land.

During my 20-24 (8 p.m. to midnight) watch on our forward 5-inch battery, two of my lookouts saw a torpedo wake crossing our bow by 20 yards and missing all ships! I was inclined to doubt their report but afterwards Lt. Mullen who was OOD on the bridge said he also saw it.

On the third day, a secret message informed us that the U.S. destroyer Reuben James had been torpedoed and went down. No word on survivors or any details. Just five days previously we had fueled the Reuben James in Argentia. Additional bad news arrived when the Commodore of our convoy signaled all ships to increase speed to 9.75 Knots, and "If you can't keep up, you are on your own." (With our recent engine troubles we were not at all sure our old bucket could keep up – and we all knew that stragglers were sitting ducks for the U-boats who trailed the convoys specifically to blow them up.

With all the bad news – if anyone enjoyed impending doom, this was a good place to be – four ensigns (including me) were assigned "Watch and watch" duty on our two 5-inch guns, starting as we left Argentia and continuing night and day until we reached Iceland. That's theoretically four hours on and four hours off – around the clock. Actually, it's five hours on and three off because you have to get ready (put on several layers of clothing in view of the North Atlantic weather, and fortify with hot coffee to prevent freezing. Then four full hours at the gun, usually in icy spray, and after that another half hour to get out of wet clothing and for a lot of hot coffee, to defrost.

And the three hours off were not all for sleeping. Maybe three in the middle of the night, but all others for one's regular job – communications (decoding) in my case.

Mundy and I alternated on the forward gun, Stewart and Sutherland on the one on the fantail. Our gun crews had it easier, one in three (on 4 hours, off 8). And the exec let them take shelter (they were just a few feet away, but out of the weather and could lie down and even take naps) while the officers had to be out in the open, on our feet, the full time on watch. It was an ordeal that lasted night and day for more than ten days.

SKAHILL SPOOKS

Lt. Cdr. Skahill, our exec, was a major pain in the posterior. He was scared to death and at times seemed totally weird. One night – sometime between midnight and 0400 – he appeared at my gun station and yelled "MAN THE GUN!" My crew ran out of the shelter and took their positions. "TRAIN ON TARGET BEARING 3-2-0," he ordered. We did. "LOAD!" came the order. Strange, I thought: we never loaded a shell and the silk bags filled with high-explosive gunpowder unless we then fired the piece. But we loaded. "COMMENCE FIRING!" he yelled. My crew looked at me. "COMMENCE FIRING!" he screamed. "CHECK FIRE!" I yelled. He was livid. "I SAID, COMMENCE FIRING! SHOOT THAT SUB BEARING 320!" He was waving his arm, pointing at a dark blob a mile or so ahead of us. "Sir," I told him, That's one of our escort destroyers!"

On Navy ships like ours, the Commanding Officer lives and eats by himself. The Executive Officer heads the Wardroom Mess and he and all officers except for those on watch eat together. At breakfast the following morning, Skahill didn't say anything until he finished eating. Then he announced, "I want you all to be especially careful. I hope you junior officers, particularly, won't mistake one of our escorts for an enemy submarine and open fire." (Yes, I thought, like *I* would make that mistake and *you* would be there to keep it from happening!)

Skahill also reported to the Captain on the bridge when he forgot to put his pants on over his long underwear! I think Mundy and I had actually pushed the exec over his limit. We turned to humor to relieve our own anxieties by talking constantly, at every meal, about being sunk. This was before the Reuben James went down. We agreed that if the Rapidan was the first U.S. Navy ship to be torpedoed and sunk, surely Hollywood would turn our story into a movie. We discussed a scene in the engine room with Wilbur in water up to his neck. With calm, John Garfield-style bravery, he simply reaches into his shirt pocket and withdraws a thoroughly water-soaked cigarette, puts it into his mouth and tries to light it as the water slowly rises to cover him completely.

We talked about which big movie stars would play each of us. Mundy suggested Gary Cooper for him. (That was before Clint Eastwood, who would have been an even better Mundy.) I wanted Errol Flynn. We talked about getting up a pool on our demise and argued whether winning should be determined by picking the date and time the torpedoes hit us – or where they hit – or time from the explosion to the ship being totally underwater.

All this drove Skahill crazy. At first he pretended he didn't hear us. But we turned our discussion to the number of survivors, then agreed that wouldn't work because there would be no survivors. "Not with us sitting on top of 325,000 gallons of high octane avgas!" That did it! He looked a bit "gray around the gills" and immediately demanded that we "knock it off!"

Early in our trip, as we rounded Cape Race (where the U-boats gathered for their best hunting) one of our escorts picked up a floating lifeboat containing three dead sailors and one who survived. They transferred the survivor, a hardy Norwegian, to the Rapidan (because we had a doctor and medical facilities). But I was too busy to pay a lot of attention and I don't really know the rest of the story. I do know he survived and we probably put him ashore for further treatment in Iceland.

The voyage was pretty hairy at times. We received reports of German submarines almost daily. And almost daily our escorts would go high-tailing through the convoy, dropping depth charges, blowing hell out of the ocean, the fish, and, hopefully, an occasional U-boat. I heard they claimed to have gotten three of them.

The enemy was not the entire problem. On this trip I learned several things. First, winter weather in the N. Atlantic is hazardous even in peacetime. Off Greenland, we encountered heavy seas so bad we couldn't stand our gun watches on the 5-inch guns without getting washed overboard. (So did we get a chance to sleep instead? No, we just switched to the 3-inch guns, located one deck higher up.) We lost equipment, washed overboard, and my diary says we nearly lost a 3rd class Gunners Mate named Minard as well. (A year or so later, Minard made Chief and he was my right-hand man because a year or so later I was then the ship's Gunnery Officer.

CONVOYS, COMMODORES AND CONFUSION

It wasn't too bad on this trip because the convoy was mainly British. But just being in a convoy is pretty sticky most of the time because you have a bunch of merchant ships of varying sizes, types and handling characteristics, trying to keep station in heavy seas and fog and running without any lights at night. Collision was a hazard equal to the threat of torpedoes. It was much worse in later convoys because (a) more ships – sometimes 120 – were involved. (b) They were mostly old rust buckets taken out of "moth balls", inactive for twenty years and resurrected only because of the war – and their ancient engines weren't all that dependable, either. (c) The best of the merchant ship officers had Naval Reserve commissions and (like Sam and Mundy) were called up by the Navy. That left a lot of inexperienced (sometimes incompetent) officers on many of the merchant ships. And, (d) each convoy was under the command of a "Commodore", and these were mainly retired Admirals, many of whom should have stayed retired. To put it bluntly, they simply did not know how to handle a 120-ship convoy – there were none of these in peacetime.

They did dumb things – things that risked hundreds (maybe thousands) of lives. Example: course changes. In the big convoys you have 120 ships spread out over miles of ocean – 12 abreast, in lines 10 ships deep. The Convoy must maintain radio silence. So, the Commodore uses flag signals during daylight, directing a course change of, say 60 degrees to the left, at 1:30 a.m. Some ships can't even see the Flag Ship, but the signal gets there by all the ships repeating it. If all goes well (and the weather is good), at 1:30 a.m. you can see (dark blobs) the ships closest to you. At that time all twelve of the ships leading their columns turn left 60 degrees. All the ships behind them wait until they reach the spot where the ship ahead has turned (as near as they can guesstimate it) and then they turn. Now all ships inside the turn (on the left side of the convoy) are ahead of those on the right. So, these have to slow down and ships on the right must speed up. It will take many hours to get the formation back in order.

That's if all goes well. What if the weather is bad – overcast, no moon or stars. You can't see anything except maybe a ship or two just ahead, rather indistinct blobs. Or maybe in rain or heavy fog, you can't see anything! And what if (for some reason totally unknown to rational man) the idiot Commodore –ten or fifteen minutes before the 1:30 a.m. turn – uses a whistle signal) to change 30 degrees to the left now? First of all, many or most ships won't hear a whistle signal, especially in heavy weather. So maybe some ships turn left and some don't. But even those who hear the signal are totally confused. Does he mean 30 degrees now, and 60 more at 1:30? Or 30 degrees now *instead of* the scheduled 60 at 1:30?

You don't believe this could happen? I've seen it happen! Several times in the Atlantic and (similar situations) at least twice in the Pacific!

ICELAND. BLEAK, GRAY AND SOMEWHAT UNIQUE

Well, we got to Iceland A-OKAY. Iceland was gray, drab, treeless, but I still found it interesting. Not as cold as its name and latitude suggests – the Gulf Stream warms it a bit. Some geography books have said the climate is much like that of Philadelphia. But I've lived in Philadelphia so I believe that's probably what the Iceland Chamber of Commerce would like to have you believe. But for sure it's not as cold as Newfoundland or Nova Scotia, and much warmer than Greenland, which is really cold.

And come to think of it, it's not totally treeless. There is one – at an outlying Officers Club. It's an artificial palm tree – in no way as good as the real McCoy, but sometimes you just take what you can get. And at this latitude, at this time of the year, daylight arrives about 8:45 a.m. and it's dark by 4 p.m.

The land is gray, the buildings are gray, and so are most of the people who live there. The place would look a lot better if the buildings were all pastel colors, like in Casablanca. Most of the native men seemed pretty dull, like almost everything else – except the girls looked much brighter, in every regard. The economy is based on codfish (which should tell you something). I don't remember seeing a lot of sunshine – and I was there on several occasions – but, all in all, I found Iceland interesting. It is unique. No other place on earth is like it. And to summarize, I'd say it has one thing in common with New York City: it's a nice place to visit, but I wouldn't want to live there.

Iceland was once volcanic and some of it still is. In a sense, they mine heat there. All the private and public buildings and most of the homes are heated with hot water from geysers and underground hot springs in some sort of public system.

Somebody had written me that Overton was assigned to a Marine unit now based in Iceland. So I wasted no time getting in touch. I found the camp, met his buddies and we had the first of our several reunions. In Reykjavik (Capital city, 40,000 pop.) I ran into a Waverly kid, Dan Gardner, who was a petty officer on some Navy ship. I also ran into Ens. O'Meara of Abbott Hall who told me Ens. Wade of our class died on the Reuben James. We found the Borg Hotel to be the best place to hang out. The food was good – except I discovered their "beef steak" was sometimes Icelandic pony – and about 9 p.m. they had an orchestra and dancing, and the "Stulkas" (local girls) were pretty, spoke English and were all good dancers. The only problem: the town was teaming with servicemen – Army, Navy, Marines and Coast Guard, from U.S., Britain, Canada, Norway and even a few from France. So the Borg was crowded, but we met some young British soldiers who were nice guys and fun to be with, and I enjoyed comparing their lives with ours.

ME AND MY BUDDY, DOUG

We spent a lot of time refueling cruisers, battleships and destroyers, some in Reykjavik harbor and more in a larger fiord nearby called Hvalfjordur. We didn't have a chaplain on the Rapidan and I missed going to Mass, so on a mid-November Sunday I learned the battleship Mississippi had Catholic services so I got a boat to take me there. When I arrived, the ship was quiet, being

Sunday, and as I went aboard I was welcomed by the Officer of the Deck, a man I recognized as Douglas Fairbanks, Jr.

He was, of course, the son of Douglas Fairbanks, Sr., and both of them were famous movie stars – real A-1, top-notch, cream-of-the-crop Hollywood royalty. After Mass, my boat was supposed to return and pick me up, but was late – about an hour and 15 minutes late. I didn't mind because I got to spend the time with a famous movie star. Just the two of us! And the guy turned out to be extremely friendly and interesting. We talked about the war, about movies, about the Navy. He told me the Mississippi had lost two officers overboard, in heavy seas, on the way to Iceland. When my boat finally arrived, we shook hands, said goodbye and wished each other good luck.

A week or two later I learned he had been detached from duty on the Mississippi and assigned as U.S. Liaison Officer with the elite British Commandos, now under the command of Lord Louis Montbatten! (How glamorous can you get?)

HURRICANE, AND UNESCORTED, A SITTING DUCK

November 25, we sailed south out of Iceland in a small convoy scheduled to meet up with a large convoy coming from Europe a day or two later. But the big convoy was late, and we had to kill time until they reached the rendezvous. I spent Thanksgiving Day back on the watch-and-watch schedule. We never even saw the lead ships of the convoy until Friday, the 28th, and before we could join up, a hurricane hit us. By Dec. 2, the storm was the worst I'd ever seen, and it scattered the whole convoy as every ship headed into the wind and tried to survive on its own.

We were taking huge waves over our main deck so standing the gun watches became impossible. On December 4 – after steaming at reduced speed all night (just enough to maintain steering control) and totally alone, unescorted – our engines broke down, we lost all steering, and we drifted broadside to the trough of the sea. I began to pray a lot, and I'm sure every officer and man on board was wondering if this wasn't the last hours of the Rapidan, and all of us. Tankers are pretty stable, but we were in imminent danger of capsizing. All we could do is hang on to something to keep from going overboard or being tossed into something a lot harder than we were.

I knew that McGlohon and Ulle were down in the engine room trying to get us going again. I was on the bridge with the Officer of the Deck, the Navigator and the Captain. I was the Junior Officer of the Watch but with everyone there senior to me, I had little to do. (I did help them worry!) Bunting was a good officer but suddenly he looked quite old, I thought. We hung on for eight or ten hours if memory serves me right, and then Mac got the engines going again and we were able to head into the sea and stop worrying about capsizing. The next day, the weather improved some, but we were alone and a sitting duck for any U-boat that might find us.

I've had a fairly large number of scary situations in my life – mostly in the war, of course – and this was surely one of them. This brief narrative, I know, is not a good description of the event. I am not doing it justice. All I can say is that now, some 63 years later, I get upset just thinking about it. I remember that nobody talked much when it was happening, and even Mundy (who always seemed to see the funny side of imminent disaster) had nothing whatever to say. I hope you saw the movie called "The Perfect Storm" (starring George Clooney, circa 2003). If you did, you will have a better idea of this 2 or 3-day ordeal that I seem unable to describe effectively.

After the hurricane, as I mentioned, the problem was being alone, unescorted. Our engines were still a problem. My personal log says we were cruising at 6 knots. (6-knot convoys were called "suicide fleets".) "Sitting duck" is another term that comes to mind. We surely hoped one or more of the escorts would find us but we traveled alone. We were following a zig-zag pattern, so our overall progress was pretty slow. It was 22 days before we arrived in Norfolk. (But the good news was: we survived and arrived alive!)

AIR RAID ON PEARL HARBOR!

Captain Bunting spent ungodly hours on the bridge, and I don't remember seeing Skahill at all. The Captain seemed older and more frail every day. Then one day between my gun watches, I was breaking down encoded messages and one of them said, AIR RAID ON PEARL HARBOR. THIS IS NOT A DRILL. EXECUTE PLAN ABLE. It was December 7, 1941. I took the news to Bunting. "What's plan Able?" he asked. "I don't think we have a Plan Able," I said. "It's probably for our combat ships." (A wild guess, but he seemed to buy it.)
A bit later, more messages:

SUNDAY 7 DECEMBER 1941 JAPAN ATTACKS U.S. BASES IN PACIFIC AT 0730, DECLARING WAR, DAMAGING OKLAHOMA AND WEST VIRGINIA IN PEARL HARBOR, BOMBING OAHU, PEARL HARBOR, HONOLULU, PHILIPPINES, GUAM, MIDWAY AND WAKE. U.S. NAVY EXECUTES WAR PLAN 46 AGAINST JAPAN. MONDAY U.S. CONGRESS DECLARES WAR AGAINST JAPAN AS OF SUNDAY DECEMBER 7.

WEDNESDAY 10 DECEMBER GERMANY AND ITALY DECLARE WAR ON U.S.A.

THURSDAY 11 DECEMBER U.S.A. DECLARES WAR ON GERMANY AND ITALY.

So now it's official. When we reached the safety of Norfolk Naval Base I settled down and wondered about our incredible good fortune. How we managed to stay afloat in our Perfect Storm. And 22 days unescorted? Where were the German submarines? I found out, somewhat later, that the Nazi General Doenitz, had recalled every U-boat in the Atlantic so the CO's could attend a major meeting in Germany (or occupied France) – to introduce a new attack strategy, "The Wolfpack". There simply were no enemy submarines in the Atlanta during our long, slow voyage from Iceland! Talk about luck!

AMERICA AT WAR

With our entry into the war, America changed – a lot. Mobilizing and blacking out. Rationing began. Pearl Harbor losses were a lot worse than we were told, and the public was never told how bad they were, until much later. I learned the Oklahoma was destroyed, 2000 of our service men died and 2000 more were seriously injured. Japs sank the HMS Prince of Wales and HMS Repulse off Malaga, bombed Manila and Cavite, and landed troops in the Philippines. Our bombers sank the battleship Haruna, a cruiser and a destroyer. But so far (and for some time after) the Japs were winning the war.

The Yorktown was in Norfolk so I went aboard to have dinner with Fred Joyce. The Albemarle arrived so Russ Peabody joined us. But I had to leave as the Rapidan was ordered to proceed to Baltimore. In peacetime, Navy officers do not wear uniforms ashore. But now we were told to send all our civilian clothing off the ship. Sutherland, Leo "Fighter" Foley and I went ashore in uniform on 17 December. We went into one of the largest restaurant/nightclubs in town and the band immediately began to play "Anchors' Aweigh," and a good 150 people all stood up and cheered!

It was a welcome (and surprising) reception. Then somebody bought us a round of drinks. Foley stood up, raised his glass and shouted, "Thank you! The next round is on us!" Sutherland and I grabbed him, sat him down and told him, "Shut up, you idiot!" Come to think of it, that was typical Fighter Foley.

I applied for leave. Didn't think I would get it because I had a long list of communications-related alterations and repairs which had to be done. But they went better than expected and Sam Huston said he'd get all the unfinished jobs done for me. So I was given seven days, after I convinced a skeptical Skahill that most jobs were completed and Sam was following the few remaining. I emphasized that if any questions arose, see Sam for the answers. I phoned the Niewinskis and they offered to have my Christmas there with them and they would invite my family to come to Chicago and we'd have a great holiday, all together.

What could be better? I left the ship a couple minutes after midnight so I could make my leave last every minute of the seven days. Sat up all night on the train. I noticed all the metal insignia on my uniform cap was looking pretty bad due to salt in the spray at sea, so, in Chicago, I went first to Marshal Fields to buy replacement insignia. So – who's working behind the counter? Mary Ellen Stoeber, my sometimes smooching partner, in my lifeguard days in Waverly!

Got in touch with Midshipman Kepler, of course, and he joined us at Niewinskis' and spent all of Sunday with us. Laura and I spent an evening at the Aragon ballroom, where we had gone on our first date. Then came the bad news: a telegram ordering me to report to the Rapidan by 1300 (1 p.m.) on Christmas Day! I phoned my family in Iowa but they had made their plans and decided to come anyway, arriving in the morning – Mother, Helen, Ed and Olive. I just had time to get them settled in and we all had to leave to get me to the station. My Aunt Rose met us at the station, too. She had heard about the reunion and decided to join in. A quick goodbye and I was en route to Baltimore for my worst Christmas ever – at least up to that time.

One good thing had happened: everyone (including Kepler) decided they really liked Laura and her family, and urged me to "get going and do something about it." Even my family!

IN WHICH I CONTEMPLATE MURDERING SKAHILL

Back in Baltimore, I reported aboard immediately and asked, "When do we get underway?" Then the news: *we weren't*. We had no orders to leave! I could have murdered Skahill! I went to his cabin. "You called me back, all the way from Chicago, on Christmas Day!" He cleared his throat, "Yes," he said, "I was wondering about a couple jobs on your list." I had to weigh my words carefully. "Commander," I said, "*I told you*, Sam was following up and all you had to do was ask him!"

I was irate but not stupid. I said nothing more. There's an old saying about the military: "You can't pee uphill." (Something like that.)

On a brighter note, all of us had known for some time that Stewart's wife was pregnant. I'd guess within ten minutes of the time Paul Pomeroy knew it, everyone knew it. He kept telling everyone who would listen, and he seemed to believe it was something unusual, as if nobody had ever done it before. And worse yet, he insisted the child was a boy. He talked about his son. Always his *son*. Someone asked how he could be sure it was a boy. I was there when Stewart actually said, "What else could it be?" I volunteered, "Maybe a girl?" He snorted and walked away.

Then I heard the Blessed Event took place while I was spending my Christmas vacation sitting on trains. Mundy had the deck when Stewart came back on board. "Everything O.K.?" he asked. Stewart handed him a cigar. "What was it?" Mundy asked. Stewart mumbled something and Mundy asked again, "Boy or girl?" Stewart told him, "A girl." Mundy's response was pure Mundy. "*I presume you drowned it*," he said.

CHANGE OF COMMAND

Captain Bunting was a rather strange person. He came from a good family, a wealthy family, and he looked it. I heard his family was super-military, that they had produced several Admirals and Generals and he seemed well on his way. Early 40's, prematurely gray, handsome and well-dressed. You should see his wife! A good ten years younger and a knockout! But he surely wasn't one of the boys. Aloof. All business. He never socialized with any of us, ever. I never heard him say anything personal or humorous to anyone in all the time he was aboard.

He was an excellent officer, but it turned out that the danger we faced in our trip to Iceland and back got to him, more than to any of his officers – except Skahill, of course. By the time we got back he was a sick man, and almost immediately he was detached and we had a new C.O. I don't remember him even saying goodbye – to any of us. I did hear he was promoted to Commander, but then I never heard of him again. Skahill remained our Exec and did not get a promotion.

Howard D. McIntosh was our new C.O. and as different as he could be. He was short, and reminded me of a movie actor named Charlie Ruggles. He quickly became one of us, in several ways. In port, he hung out with us, which Bunting never did. Instead of handling everything himself, he let us take a lot of responsibility. He didn't spend much time looking over our shoulders. He trusted us, and we all liked having him aboard.

Some other new officers came aboard. Tony Apuzzo was our new doctor – a Catholic (obviously) and this meant I had someone to go to Sunday Masses with me. Lt. (j.g.) Jerry Cherry who spoke Virginian with an accent) was our Supply Officer. And when I walked in to the Wardroom someone asked me, "Guess who's coming aboard?" I said I had no idea. "Joe Lykes!" I said, "Who's Joe Lykes?" Then I learned from the several of my shipmates who had come from the Merchant Marine that Lykes was the heir apparent of the Lykes "Dynasty". His family owned the largest steamship company under U.S. registry – dozens of ships, maybe a hundred, mostly freighters – and "about half of Cuba" (cattle, citrus) – a lot of Florida (more cattle, citrus, and a whole lot of other stuff. Very impressive.

CHRISTMAS DAY 1941. I was an unhappy camper aboard the Rapidan in Baltimore. In the evening, I went ashore by myself, wandered around, doing a lot of thinking. In view of the war and the realities of my life in those unpredictable times, I decided I was indeed in love and should get married, if Laura agreed.

December 26: Joe Lykes told me he had a married sister in Baltimore and planned to visit her and her husband, and invited me to join them. I don't remember who, but two of our other officers also went along. We had cocktails and wonderful hors d'oeuvres at his sister's apartment, and were there for two or three hours. Then Joe took us to the best restaurant in Baltimore – Miller Brothers. He told us to order "anything and a lot" as this party was on him. The small town boy from Iowa was mightily impressed. The Maitre D' and the waiters recognized Joe and rolled out the red carpet. Joe was recommending various selections and instructing the waiters on just how he wanted the food prepared. Then he said he'd order the wine, a very special Moiselle he had discovered in Hamburg (Germany, of course) in 1937. It was, indeed, a grand feast and a memorable evening, and I figured, with this rich kid on board we have really hit the jackpot!

The next day we sailed from Baltimore to Norfolk. We completed some sea trials, then tied up and I had the deck all day starting at noon on the 30th. Got some good letters that made me feel better – from Laura, from Bob Lannon and family, and even from Mrs. Dickinson, Mary's mother – who obviously, after 3 1/2 years, had not forgotten me.

NEW YEARS EVE. Hal, Wilbur and I took a cab from the Naval Operating Base to Norfolk and ran into Tony Apuzzo. The four of us ate at a Chinese restaurant, then saw a movie and after that, went over to the Portsmouth Navy Yard to celebrate the arrival of 1942 at the Officers Club. Ran into Priscilla and Betsy – the girls Wilbur and I were with the night I met Captain Tuck.

They invited us to their table. John and Evelyn Mundy joined us. At midnight I was dancing with some pretty young thing whose name I don't even remember – and thinking of Laura and wishing it were her.

I was quite sad and lonely, as I usually am on New Years Eve.

AND SO ENDS AN EVENTFUL 1941. WHAT'S NEXT?

1942. A new officer – Ensign Lawrence "Laurie" Crawford – reported for duty. Joe Lykes and I ate dinner at some place called "The Albany". A petty officer from the Rapidan was there and he sent a bottle of champagne to our table. He was Coxswain Slater who told us he "won $100 on one toss of the dice last night" and wanted to share his good fortune. Gambling was strictly forbidden aboard Navy ships but in wartime very few ships followed those rules.

January 2. Hal Sutherland, Doc Apuzzo, Wilbur Ulle and I went to a Yacht Club because Crawford invited us and guaranteed a good party. We met a lot of nice (and nice looking) girls, and then Captain McIntosh, Mundy and Cherry and their wives joined us and it was, indeed, a good party. Captain McIntosh had just been promoted to Commander. Matter of fact, everyone got pretty drunk, except me and Doc. At midnight they played The Star Spangled Banner and Wilbur got in trouble when some super-patriotic officer saw him slouching and holding a cigarette. Captain Mac intervened and got it cooled down. Wilbur felt bad. Alice Cherry consoled him. Wilbur felt grateful and began to snuggle up. Jerry Cherry passed out. Mundy and I got a big kick out of watching it all happen. I decided our new Captain, who obviously couldn't hold his liquor, was going to be something of a problem, but in all, a really good Joe and a lot more fun than Captain Bunting.

We departed Norfolk for Halifax, Nova Scotia on January 5 and arrived there on January 9. I liked going to Halifax – another opportunity to visit where I'd never been. But I knew that after that it would be Iceland again. We had five good days in Halifax. Because of the war, it was crowded with military from all over. Someone – Capt. McIntosh (?) – had arranged a party involving cocktails at the Lord Nelson Hotel, then meeting our dates (seven very nice, upper crust Nova Scotia girls), then to a dinner dance at the Nova Scotian main ballroom. Very nice, very British-Canadian. (Boy, do they stand at attention when they play "God Save the Queen" – or King, I can't remember.)

The next day, Crawford, Lykes, Mundy and I had tea at the Lord Nelson. Then we picked up our dates for dinner – mine was the daughter of a

Royal Canadian Air Force Colonel. Her name was Gwynne Lawrence, sister of Mundy's date. Afterwards all of us went to the home of the Lawrence sisters for the rest of the evening.

Halifax was interesting, cold and under a deep blanket of snow. Before we left we were issued sheepskin-lined overcoats for arctic watch-standing and I bought a pair of sheepskin-lined Wellington boots, because I saw so many British and Norwegian officers wearing them. They seemed just right for the N. Atlantic.

And the best thing that happened: Laurie Crawford was assigned to relieve me as Communications Officer! (Joy!)

January 13-24. En route to Reykjavik in a small convoy (36 ships, British, Swede, Norwegian and Free French). We spent a lot of time at General Quarters (battle stations) because our escorts were chasing submarines and dropping depth charges much of the time. On the first day we heard (radio) that a ship, the Cyclops, was torpedoed some distance behind us, and another one right ahead in the path we are taking and where we will be at dawn tomorrow. (90 died and 80 were rescued by the escorts in that one.) On January 15, news of two more sinkings – one well behind us and the other just ahead, off Cape Race. On the 16th, more General Quarters, more escorts dropping depth charges, and news of a sinking ship dead ahead of us. This time we passed some debris and a swamped lifeboat with nobody in it. And later, a huge oil slick.

MORE ICELANDIC ADVENTURES

But we made it O.K. and resumed our Icelandic routines. Phoned Overton and he drove to town in a Jeep and took Hal Sutherland and me back to the Marines Officers Club for the evening. Drinking, bull sessions, and a lot of group singing, and that's about all there is, but better than nothing.

The main excitement took place late one night when a group of us were catching the midnight boat back to the ship after an evening at the Borg Hotel. The boat was the Captain's Gig, that had two partially covered compartments, for officers in the back and enlisted men, forward. We were all on board when Merritt D. (Muledriver) Mullen arrived with a drinking buddy to whom he had offered a ride back to his ship. There wasn't enough room in the officer's compartment so Mullen looked around and ordered McGlohon (our Ch. Warrant Officer Chief Engineer) to "Get up front with the enlisted men!" And he did it in his characteristic tactless manner. We were all somewhat shocked. (Partly because we all liked McGlohon, and nobody liked Mullen.)

McGlohon said nothing but obviously he was steamed. When we arrived at the ship, I tried to lighten things up a bit with Mac, and I said – jokingly – "You aren't letting him get away with that, are you?" He looked at me and said, "Stay out of this, Robert." (I followed him to his stateroom but he shut his door in my face. A moment later, he came out carrying one of those 2-foot long flashlights and headed for Mullen's room, entered and closed the door. "Stand up, you *#@*%#x!!" Then crash, lickety-whop, bam! And he stormed out and went back into his own room.

I immediately found Mundy and told him what happened. We were elated – but deeply concerned. The lowest ranking officer on board just beat up the highest ranking, except for our C.O. and the Exec. – in wartime! Serious business. A General Court Martial offense. We surely didn't want McGlohon to spend the rest of life in Naval prison for doing what we all would have liked to do.

The word spread and every officer was a bit early to the breakfast table, as we all wanted to see what Mullen looked like. When he arrived, we weren't disappointed. His face was a mess! Two black eyes, a Band-Aid over his nose, cuts on his chin and both cheeks, even on his forehead, and a great deal of swelling. He said nothing. McGlohon skipped breakfast. We wondered if he was confined to his stateroom (– they don't put officers in the brig).

The outcome? Nothing happened! It wasn't difficult to figure out. Good-guy Captain McIntosh had decided that if McGlohon and Mullen had tangled, it was probably Mullen's fault. There were no charges filed and no further discussion. Case closed!

We spent most of our time refueling ships of all kinds, from Corvettes up to battleships. Doc, Leo Foley and I went to Mass every Sunday at an Icelandic Catholic Church that had a special Mass for servicemen. A British Army chaplain (Father Gaffney) was the priest and we became friends and had coffee and cookies with him after Mass, every time we attended. Four new ensigns, all from Abbot Hall were assigned to our ship but didn't stay long. Kepler wasn't among them, but he did request duty on the Rapidan; instead, they ordered him to our sister ship, the Sapelo.

Reykjavik began to remind me of what I had read about the Yukon during the Gold Rush days – wild and wooly. Several of our enlisted men got into trouble. A new Officers Club appeared right in the middle of town, with a rather weird Navy Chaplain in charge – Padre Tennyson. He drank a lot and the more he imbibed, the wilder his stories became. One night an Army officer claimed they were in Iceland before the Navy arrived. I heard the Padre tell him, "Not true. I, myself, was here ten years ago!" Then he went on to explain that he arrived after a solo flight from the States in a free balloon! (He was serious!)

One night Captain McIntosh and Joe Lykes won $150 in a crap game at the "O" Club and Joe got in a fistfight and sported a shiner for the next several days. The Captain was a great addition to our lives and times and I could fault him on two counts only: we sometimes had to take care of him when he had too much enjoyment involving alcohol, and since he had a daughter of marriageable age, he and his wife really tuned in on Joe Lykes as an extremely wealthy prospective son-in-law. Mundy and I called them The Odd Couple. Joe, by the way, turned out entirely differently than I thought he would, based on that one night at Miller Brothers in Baltimore. Among our officers, he became our resident cheapskate – the only one who argued about it, every time it was his turn to buy a round of drinks.

Skahill received orders to new duty – I don't remember where, and Mullen became our new Executive Officer! This was good news and bad news, all at the same time. Mullen was often referred to as "the terrible-tempered Mr. Bang." (This goes way back to a character in an ancient comic strip called "Toonerville Folks". Many of you won't remember that, but you get the idea. When Mundy and I were casting our movie about the Rapidan, we had Mullen played by an actor named Edgar Kennedy. You never heard of him either but he was famous for his personification of the "Slow Burn".

Anyway, almost everyone hated our duty in Iceland. We heard that Navy tankers were doing the same thing in Londonderry and in Recife, Brazil and we all prayed that we'd be switched with them. Meantime, it became obvious our enlisted men were slowly going crazy, so we got the Captain to approve a special outing for them. It was a several-hours deal, ashore, on an island with room for softball and football games, picnic food, burgers, etc., and all the beer they could drink.

MORE MULEDRIVER MULLEN MADNESS

When we brought them back aboard, need I tell you, we had a universally joyful and seriously drunk crew on our hands. Our job was to get them back in the crew's quarters, as rapidly and silently as possible. But we failed. Striding out onto the quarterdeck comes our new Exec, Muledriver Mullen, to take charge. (And screw things up.)

"Fall in!" he yelled. Then he confronted the officers: "Get them in line – for inspection! Right now!" The crew didn't fall in very well. Most were weaving, some giggling. This made him even madder. Then he began to walk slowly past them like some Commanding General at a major ceremony at West Point or Washington, D.C. In the line was a sailor named Joe Morosa, a tall, thin Sicilian who was in Mullen's crew when the Exec was the

First Lieutenant. Joe hated Mullen and when Mullen reached him, Joe said, "Quit strutting, you fat little turkey!" Mullen turned fire red. "What did you say?" Morosa repeated, word for word, only this time much louder. Mullen was livid. "Put that man in irons!"

So they did. Not really "in irons", but he was locked up in the Brig – which I don't think was ever used before. (Matter of fact, I didn't even know where it was!) And a Captain's Mast was scheduled for nine a.m. the next day. This procedure is where all or most disciplinary actions begin. The Captain can deal out some relatively minor punishment, or for more serious offenses, assign either a Summary Court Martial or a General Court Martial.

I was there at Captain's Mast. I'd never seen one. The Captain was seated at a table, Mullen standing alongside him. The Master-at-Arms. (Chief Petty Office – senior cop?) brought Morosa in. I think he was handcuffed. But that didn't stop him. In a flash he was all over Mullen, clubbing him with both hands! LICKETY WHOP! BANG! BANG! POW! He really got some good ones in! He was also swearing a blue streak. They pulled him off. This was a serious tactical error on Joe Morosa's part. (I did tell you he was Sicilian!) If he had gone to Hollywood he could have become famous in the movies and had a long career playing sinister Mafia hitman parts. He really looked the part. Mundy had worked with him for many months and said he never saw him smile. In short, Morosa was creepy looking. And now in big trouble. The Captain had to assign a General Court Martial so Joe was taken off the ship and we heard he was sentenced to eight or ten years in naval prison.

Another Mullen story. With his promotion, Mundy was now the First Lieutenant and in charge of fueling the ships that tied up alongside. Of course, Mullen couldn't resist spending time telling him how to do it. One day, Mundy and his crew were pumping oil into another ship – a tanker, I believe, because it had a steel deck with a lot of pipes, valves and other hard objects, and Mullen is looking down at the deck of the other ship, which was some 20 feet below, and suddenly he goes plummeting head first down onto the other ship's deck!

He was badly hurt. Lucky to be alive! He was rushed to a hospital. We heard he broke both arms and a lot of other stuff, and his condition was critical. Observing the scene, I would guess a crushed skull and a broken neck, but I guess that didn't happen. But we were sure we would never see Mullen again. This led to mixed emotions – by practically everyone on board. You don't want anyone to die or suffer permanent injuries – but life without Mullen was going to be a tremendous improvement for all of us.

The big question was, why did Mullen fall off our ship? Logical explanation: he was pushed. But who did it? Mundy swore he did not do it! But for several days, the enlisted men smiled and kept telling him, "Nice going, Mr. Mundy!"

A lot was going on in 1942, because of the war. The Japs were winning in the Pacific. They took Singapore and a lot of the islands, countries and cities in that part of the world. Our heavy cruiser, the Houston, a destroyer and several British and Dutch ships encountered a superior Jap force in Asiatic waters and all were destroyed. We had a lot of personnel changes. Joe Gillis was detached, Sam became Navigator and Acting Executive Officer. I became Gunnery Officer. Ensign Crawford made Lt. j.g. and was transferred. Tony Apuzzo, our doctor, was replaced by a Dr. Lovejoy, a rather "prissy" Park Avenue doctor who seemed totally out of place in the Navy, but turned out to be the best Navy doctor I ever met.

Forgot to mention Paul Pomeroy Stewart, another guy who didn't seem to fit. He was not a happy camper and had put in requests for transfer on several occasions – not only to other duties, but even for "out of the Navy". Last thing I remember about him is that he was Ship's Service Officer (a job no officer wanted) when the Ship's Barber was transferred. McGlohon told him a dozen or two of our sailors would rather cut hair than do the difficult work they'd have to do otherwise. So he should pass the word and have tryouts to see who would get the barber job. Officers and petty officers would serve as models and Stewart would pick the best haircutter to be our new Ship's Barber. After a few of us guinea pigs got really bad haircuts, Stewart got his, and returned to the wardroom and said, "I've got our man. I think Shepard did a great job on me. What do you think?" Mundy said, "Front looks good. Turn around." I'll never forget, when he did, the blood was running down his neck, all over his shirt collar! The kid had cut off all the moles on the back of Stewart's neck!

Among other events worthy of note, Mundy and I got into a bit of trouble – with Naval Intelligence! When we went to war all ships were told that all privately-owned photographic equipment was now forbidden and must be removed. One official Ship's Camera could remain on board, but never used without the Captain's approval, and only for "official business". Some officers had cameras but didn't take the new rule seriously. I think most of us forgot all about it.

So one day Mundy and I decided to get some "Men Against the Sea" snapshots, so we strapped on our Colt 45's, put on foul weather gear and went up to the Flying Bridge and pretended to (1) steer the ship, and (2) be firing one of our 20 mm guns at some imaginary attacking aircraft. Then we took the film into a photo shop in Reykjavik to be developed. Days later we returned for the pictures and were told they had been confiscated by British Army Intelligence! Apparently they turned them over to British Naval Intelligence, and they to U.S. Naval Intelligence. We were then ordered to report to them and explain ourselves. We did and that failed to end it. They came aboard to discuss the matter with Captain McIntosh who apparently convinced them the chances of our being Nazi (or Japanese?) spies were fairly slim. Also that we had used the official Ship's Camera with his approval. (We hadn't.) We got our snapshots back and heard no more about it.

Talk about mountains and molehills! All the photos showed was a 20mm Oerlekin AA gun of Swiss origin that almost every military in the world owned, and a ship's wheel you could find on every ship everywhere! Even more unbelievable, months later I was visiting in Waverly and stopped in the newspaper office to see Les Moeller. And he told me U.S. Naval Intelligence had come to see him (and) others in Waverly) to find out if I was a security risk or an O.K. patriotic American! (I still have the pictures. I'm the one with the Van Dyke beard!)

Man Against the Sea!
(That's me.) Iceland 1941.

Most of us worked pretty hard but weren't really getting the kind of exercise was needed to keep in shape. So Capt. McIntosh decided we needed some daily "mass calisthenics" and assigned me to take charge of the program. As I recall, it didn't last too long but I do remember getting everyone out on deck every morning, except Sundays, and putting them through their paces. Also, we were anchored in Hvalfiordur a lot and there was a nice island a mile away that looked appropriate for football and baseball. So one day some of us went over there to find out who owned it and if we could use it now and then.

A farmer owned it, but a unit of the Royal Artillery had set up anti-aircraft batteries there and we were told we should see them. So we contacted their CO, a Major, who said any time was OK, and when our games were over, our officers should stop by for a couple of drinks, and our enlisted would be welcomed for tea or beer (guess which?) at their enlisted men's mess. This blossomed into a beautiful friendship. They had booze and beer. We had much better food, so after a Happy Hour on the island, we'd take boatloads of them to the Rapidan to eat.

On April 4, we had our first football game. The most athletic of our officers and enlisted divided into two teams. My team won. I was the star, if I do say so myself. I passed for our first touchdown. I scored two more running the ball, and had another 80-yard touchdown run called back. It was a good morale-builder for me, and I needed it.

Today, I read a lot about Depression. A lot of people have it, it's serious, and I've been wondering why no one ever had it in my younger years. I knew I never was depressed, and was sure I never would be. Until right now. I'm reading my old diary, about Iceland in March 1942 and I suddenly realize that *I was in depression at that time!* I despised being on a tanker for months on end in dreary, drab, dull gray Iceland. I was in love with a beautiful girl thousands of miles away and I couldn't be with her. I seemed to work all the time, and never got enough sleep. I began to have problems with Joe Gillis (the navigator) who did something wrong (I can't remember what) and deliberately placed the blame on me. My mentor, Paul McGlohon, told me I was beginning to act like a grouchy old man.

It got so bad I put in an official request for a transfer – to PT boats. It was considered hazardous duty and the Navy was asking for volunteers. The Captain was required to forward my request, but he did so "Not Approved". He explained that I was a good officer and he needed me on the Rapidan. Probably the worst duty in the entire U.S. Naval Service was Underwater Demolition Teams. I even volunteered for that! I figured I could swim with the best. But again the Captain forwarded my request "Not Approved". Looking back, I now know I had that disease which is now called Depression.

Overton's Marine group got orders to leave and I said goodbye and that surely added to my unhappiness. But then the Sapelo arrived and Kepler and I were able to get together on numerous occasions. And we ran into Rolfe Christopherson, an Ensign I knew briefly when he came to Waverly for a job with Lutheran Mutual Life Insurance, about a year before I left.

Actually, the three of us were walking to the "O" Club in Reykjavik when a young man who looked like a "Fish Head" (Icelander) saw us and waved excitedly, yelling "Kepler, Kepler!" Turned out he was yet another Ensign, a classmate of Ed's at Abbott Hall, and he had quite a story. He'd been assigned to the Armed Guard, put on a cargo ship, on the (dreaded) Murmansk run, torpedoed, sunk, rescued and made it to Murmansk. Then he was put on another ship bound for Iceland and the States – but that was torpedoed, sunk, and again he was plucked from the icy waters and rescued! He lost everything (which explained his Icelandic civvies) but here was one happy camper! Quite a story.

This got me to thinking, to counting my blessings. I had chances to die at sea, being torpedoed, blown up, or in our "Perfect Storm". But I was alive, all in one piece and I should be grateful and happy. Good medicine for Depression.

The destroyer Meredith came alongside and I expected to see my Abbott Hall roommate, Mulcare, but they told me he had been reassigned to the Armed Guard. My diary said, "The Alexander Hamilton sank practically beside us, under strange circumstances." And I have no idea what that was all about. The destroyer Swanson came alongside and they had a whole shipload of survivors from a freighter torpedoed just south of Iceland.

Lots of things were happening. LIFE magazine ran a major story on the Flying Tigers and included a picture of Noel Bacon. Jack Althouse, my Waterloo friend, was shipwrecked when the Pollux ran into a rocky cliff in a storm and pea-soup fog in Newfoundland. He and many others survived by scaling a cliff onto high ground where some local farmers rescued them before they froze to death. Slater, our Coxswain, told me he had won $1300 in crap games since we arrived in Iceland. In another football game on "our island", my team won 18-12. I passed for one touchdown and ran 30 yards for the winning score. April 21, 1942 was my 26th birthday. It was 7 degrees below zero and I had the duty all day.

My birthday present happened the next day – we left Iceland, bound for the States. And I was standing top watches at sea. As usual, the trip was pretty hairy – a lot of U-boat activity, our escorts dashing around and through the convoy, dropping depth charges. One ship couldn't keep up, fell back and was torpedoed. Then we spent 36 hours in pea-soup fog, off the Grand Banks,

Boy, am I lucky!
(She said Yes!)

couldn't see even the adjacent ships for stretches of several hours at a time. In these cases ships try to keep station on whistle signals, each ship leading its column sounding off in rotation. But this is extremely difficult in every regard, and especially because you can't tell if you are dropping back on the ship astern or about to run over the ship ahead. Unlike Bunting, Captain Mac didn't live on the bridge. He trusted us to do the job, and this was more than a little bit scary.

I don't know who the Commodore of the convoy was, but he screwed up by trying to change course on whistle signals. Apparently some ships heard the signal and others did not. So the whole convoy pretty much scattered and went off on its own. I don't know about all the other ships but we arrived in Boston, O.K., on May 6. I went ashore as soon as I could and phoned Laura. I strongly suggested marriage, on my next leave, and was a bit surprised that she didn't enthusiastically agree. She felt we ought to wait awhile. Giving myself the benefit of the doubt, I believed she was reluctant to leave home and wait in some Atlantic Coast city until my ship came back to any of a dozen possible ports, after weeks or months somewhere outside the country. I knew she was aware of the possibility that I wouldn't come back at all. But I was at my persuasive best and she finally agreed to my suggestions.

It isn't easy planning a wedding when you have no idea as to WHEN. But she said she would try. When we finally completed our call on the pay phone, the Operator said the overtime charges were $4.75. But while I was fumbling for change, she interrupted and said, "Sir, forget the overtime. This one is on the house."

BACK IN THE STATES BUT NOT FOR LONG

Sutherland rushed to Washington, D.C. and got married. I took a 48-hour leave and went to New York City, saw some stage plays and just wandered around, getting better acquainted with Manhattan.

18 May we left for Portland. I went to Mass on the new battleship, North Carolina. Sat next to an Admiral. Have no idea who he was, and didn't much care. Then Halifax, and then Sydney, Nova Scotia, then convoy to Iceland. Same old, same old.

However (effective 4-15-42) Sam, Mundy and Wilbur all promoted to j.g.'s! This makes me "the Bull Ensign". But wait – on June 17, I make j.g.! And Cherry makes LT. Good news, but we found out the other U.S. services are promoting much faster than the Navy. An Officers Club here posted a large sign: "Intoxicating beverages will not be served to Marine Corps Majors, Army Lt. Colonels or Air Corps Colonels under 21, unless accompanied by parents."

In our previous times in Iceland, we never had much daylight. This time we had it 24 hours – around the clock. When I turned in at midnight, I had to cover the potholes in my cabin to keep the sun from shining right in my face.

2:30 a.m. 30 July we left Iceland (I hoped forever). Joined a huge convoy and survived another difficult passage, but arrived in Boston 15 August. Phoned Laura immediately. I didn't rate leave because our officers took turns and it wasn't my time. So Laura arrived from Chicago in record time. The ship stayed longer than we thought it would so we had 15 glorious days together and this was surely one of the most wonderful times of my life!

With Captain McIntosh and his wife leading the way, we had parties every night, mostly at the Copley Plaza, and every officer who didn't have to remain aboard, and every wife (there were many) attended. The Rapidan Gang had become a close-knit group. Usually everyone got drunk except for Laura and me and maybe one or two others, depending on which night it was.

I was so pleased that Laura immediately became one of the group and everyone told me how much they liked her – and how we should get married – not later, but right now! That became the theme of the first party Laura attended, on her first night in Boston. They ganged up on us, gave us the "hard sell." When we said we couldn't make arrangements in such a short time, Captain Mac demanded the floor and said, "We'll all leave now and go to the ship. We'll get her underway, and when we pass the 12-mile limit, I'm empowered to marry them at sea!"

Everyone cheered. But then Bos'n Mockbee emerged from the bedroom carrying The Gideon's Bible that all hotels provide. "No need to go to all that trouble," he announced with great solemnity. "I have the Bible and I've never told you, but I'm an ordained Minister. I'll handle it!"

There were only two sour notes in this glorious Boston adventure. (1) We ran out of money, partly because we didn't realize we'd have so much time in Boston, and because I spent $150 on a wedding ring! Laura didn't want the usual diamond solitaire engagement ring, because everyone had them and she had my jeweled Delta Chi pin and considered herself engaged. She preferred a wedding ring with diamonds all around. (On my salary the diamonds were awfully small, but she helped pick it out and she liked it.) So I borrowed some money – I don't remember where. (2) Mullen came back!

This Mullen was a piece of work. His wife was the only wife not with us in Boston. (I don't remember ever seeing her, and I'm sure he never asked her to come.) He had taken a room in the Copley Plaza and for some unknown reason had asked me to come there and get him when the party got started. When I knocked on his door, he wasn't fully dressed and he opened it just enough so I could see there was a woman in his room. He winked and grinned and I knew he set this up so I'd let the others know he was a "gay blade" with the ladies.

His reappearance was bad news. The ship was happier with Sam as Exec. Nothing we could do about this sad turn of events – except fantasize. Discussing possibilities, Mundy and I came up with the solutions, which we shared with our shipmates. Everyone enjoyed the idea, added suggestions and we all felt a little better, just thinking about it. Here's the plot: We'd get him drunk – not difficult to do. When he passed out, we'd remove all his identification and all his money, then smuggle him onto a train with a one-way ticket to Albuquerque, New Mexico. He'd probably wake up somewhere west of the Mississippi River, and by the time he could get back to the East Coast, the ship would be long gone. In wartime, it might take months for him to get back on board! Hopefully.

Laura's visit was surely one of the best things that happened to me in my life as a bachelor. But we had to get back to the war, Laura went home, and on 9 September we left in a fair-sized convoy. 11 September – 3:30 a.m. – on Mundy's watch, the General Quarters alarm and the collision siren woke me up. And then the ship rocked violently as an adjacent ship crashed into our starboard bow. The collision severed our anchor on that side and put a hole in our bow, fortunately above the water line. All this happened in a dense fog when the idiot Commodore tried to change the convoy's course 40 degrees to port on a whistle signal.

Mundy didn't hear the signal. The ship on our right did, and turned into us. We later heard that eight ships were involved in collisions on that same change of course! I took over the deck at 4 a.m. and it took the full four hours to catch up and regain our position in the convoy. We never heard what happened to the ship that hit us. But then we were ordered to leave the convoy and head to the closest port, Halifax.

WELCOME TO GREENLAND!

Had a couple days in Halifax, mostly at the Admiralty House and the Royal Canadian Navy Officers Club. Our collision damage was assessed and we were declared sea worthy, so we left for – of all places I thought I'd never see in my lifetime – Ivigtut, Greenland. I had mixed emotions: I knew this was one of the coldest places on earth and I was concerned with the combination of thick fog and icebergs which can be extremely dangerous. On the other hand, how many Iowa boys get to set foot on Greenland? Could be fun.

On our first day we nearly had another collision as the ship abeam missed a turn signal and nearly rammed us. But we arrived OK. Ivigtut is a long way up a fiord. It's surrounded by spectacular mountains and it's the site of the world's largest kryolite mine. (Kryolite is a vital strategic material, but that's all I know about it.) We were sent to provide diesel oil to the mine (and to fuel several Coast Guard cutters.) What a desolate place! I went ashore to pick up a Pilot and had a glass of port wine with a Danish mining engineer. I learned that laborers here earned $500 a month and some of our U.S. Army guarding the place make $50 a month. Also that hunting is pretty good – ptarmigan and snow rabbits (but watch out for polar bears!). Fishing is excellent. I saw men from a close-aboard Coast Guard cutter catching 30-lb. sea catfish.

A couple days later, we moved to Kingnat Bay and anchored beneath rugged rock mountains of huge size. Captain Mac, Lykes and I joined three officers from our Coast Guard escort on a hunting trip, but we didn't get anything except a couple of salmon trout, which we speared. Our next move was to "Bluie West One", near Julianahaab. Arrived in an ice-filled fiord, really an outpost, a couple of Eskimo villages nearby. Four miles away, the Greenland ice cap.

Army and Navy aviators, army troops, Coast Guard, and civilian workers were here. I have no idea what the enlisted men did to keep from going crazy but the officers spent all their off-duty time at the Officers Club – because there was nothing else. No women at all. And only one celebrity would be caught dead in Greenland: the legendary Norwegian aviator, Bernt Balchen. This man, you probably don't know, was the leading expert on polar aviation and the first ever to fly over both the North and the South Poles. *He did most of the heroic feats that made Admiral Richard E. Byrd famous.* Although not an American, he was (by a special act of Congress) granted honorary U.S. citizenship and given a commission as Colonel in our Army Air Corps. His job, at that time, was to rescue our pilots who had gone down on the ice cap, and he had done that, several times. So he was the number one local hero – and I was fortunate enough to meet him and talk with him, at the Officers Club, of course.

Mundy and I also met some Navy flyers and got ourselves invited to go with them on a 10-hour anti-submarine patrol in their PBY seaplane. With Captain Mac's O.K., we took off the following morning and headed out over the iceberg-laden North Atlantic. But a half-hour out we encountered pea-soup fog and spent the next 90 minutes trying to find better visibility and we couldn't. So the mission was aborted. However, we talked the crew into giving us a Cook's Tour of the ice cap, and that was a pretty awesome experience. Flew around and over for an hour, and I now have a memory few will ever have.

We anchored up a fiord, away from bases and Officers Clubs, and they seemed to leave us there forever. Our major recreation: every morning we went topside to watch an Eskimo paddle his kayak across the fiord and disappear. In the evening we went out to watch him paddle back. We told ourselves it was probably better than being torpedoed and sunk.

I never enjoyed fishing but I even came to that. I caught a good-sized fish that was the ugliest fish I ever saw. Nobody could identify it and even our Steward's Mates refused to eat it. Finally, I got the Captain to let me take practically everyone on board ashore (in shifts, of course) for target shooting – small arms qualification. Everyone enjoyed this. We used up a lot of ammunition, but it was "well spent". We built campfires and cooked stuff like Vienna sausages, hot dogs, and plenty of coffee and hot chocolate and made a party out of it. This was a good idea.

I was never a hunter, but as Gunnery Officer I set a good example, proving to be one of the best marksmen on the ship. I "qualified" with the 30 caliber rifle the first time I ever shot for a score. And according to my diary, I had eight straight bull's-eyes with the .45 automatic pistol. By the way, we received an Alnav outlawing diaries for the duration of the war. So mine went undercover: I couldn't believe the enemy getting hold of mine would give them a significantly better chance of winning the war.

THE FUR TRADERS. When not much of anything is happening, little things seem important. So we became curious and interested when another large ship sailed up our fiord and anchored near us. We learned it was a Hudson Bay Co.

ship returning from Baffinland where they had been buying furs from the Eskimos, and would join our convoy when we started back for the States. We also knew they would be carrying an ample supply of liquid refreshments and, of course, U.S. Navy ships were not allowed to do that.

I was never much of a drinker but some of our officers were, and they immediately began to signal our visitor with a message of welcome, hoping to be invited to join them for cocktails or whatever. It worked. At 1600 (4 p.m.) five of us were in a whaleboat, en route. We ended up in the merchant service's equivalent of a Navy wardroom, with several of their officers, getting acquainted, swapping sea stories and imbibing in something alcoholic – I forget what. They were mostly Canadians, good guys. They told us about their cargo, lots of different furs but mostly white arctic fox.

If we wanted a beautiful fur piece for our wives or girl friends we could buy the raw furs for bargain prices (20 or 25 dollars). I remember Sam bought a couple for Shortstop. I didn't want a smelly, salted raw animal skin in my room for who knows how long before we got back to civilization.

But then they brought in a huge polar bear skin – it would have made a 9 x 12 rug (or larger) and I fantasized about owning that as a conversation piece. But common sense prevailed – the huge pelt must have weighed 500 pounds (maybe much more), impossible to handle without a fork truck.

We were sitting around a very large round table and one of their officers kept thumping the tabletop with a club of some sort, about the size and shape of a baseball bat, only it was white and didn't seem to be made of wood. Finally, Mundy asked, "What is that thing?" The officer smiled and said, "Let me put it this way: the female walrus is probably one of the happiest of all female mammals on earth!" (If you can't figure it out, ask somebody.)

Mail from home finally caught up with us, and there was some very bad news: my close and longtime friend, Wayne Sparks, was killed in an accident during an Air Corps night training exercise. Wayne was an outstanding young man in every regard. He would have been a great lawyer and one of Waverly's leading citizens for his entire lifetime, had he lived. It was a real shocker for me. I immediately wrote his mother – one of the most difficult letters, ever.

This is what I hate about war: good people die. Surely, there must be a better way to solve the world's problems.

On a brighter note, Doc Lovejoy made Lt. CDR; Sam, Mundy and Wilbur promoted to LT, and Lykes and Sutherland made j.g. Also on a brighter note, we left for home on 31 October! Despite all the icebergs we encountered (I was thinking Titanic), for me, this was the Big, High, Hard One. We were slated for major repair work and would be at least three weeks in port – and I was now at the head of the officers list for 10 days leave. I would head for Chicago and Laura and I would be (as they say) united in Holy Matrimony.

BUT, HANG ON…A MAJOR CATASTROPHE! Halfway in the long voyage home, Mullen summoned me to his cabin and announced, "When we get to Boston, I've arranged for you to attend a three-weeks Gunnery School on the USS Wyoming, sailing out of Norfolk. So be prepared." Hearing this was unbelievable – I was stunned! Then, about as angry as I've ever been, I said, "Commander, you know I'm at the head of the line for leave. And you know about my wedding plans…" He interrupted me. "THAT'S IT! NO FUR-THER DISCUSSION!" I was dumbfounded. I stood there telling myself not to do myself any permanent damage. "Get out!" he bellowed.

I did, and I decided I would put up a fight. Ignoring the rules, I'd go over his head, direct to Captain McIntosh! As I stormed up the ladder to the Captain's cabin on the deck above, I realized this was sheer meanness: there was no reason for me to go to Gunnery School. With the limited armament we had, I knew everything there was to know, or ever needed to know. I tried to calm down as I stated my case to Captain Mac. He listened, then told me, "You'll get your leave. You can plan on that." Wow! What a turn of events! I was elated – with reservations: I knew Mullen would make my life hell because I'd gone over his head. As I was leaving, I heard the Captain tell his Stewards Mate to tell Mullen to come see him.

Sure enough, in five minutes I was summoned to Mullen's cabin. He was at his desk, writing something (my obituary?) with his back to me. Be cool, I told myself. Don't argue. Don't do anything foolish. "You sent for me, sir?" I asked. He didn't say anything, he just kept writing. His bald head and the back of his fat neck were almost cherry-red. If I could get a front view I'd guess he might even be frothing at the mouth. He said nothing, just kept me waiting and I waited in silence. Suddenly, in a fit of rage, he hurled his foun-tain pen up against the wall. It bounced off, broken into pieces, and ink splat-tered. He didn't turn to face me, he just said, *"I'll get you for this!"* And I was sure he would.

When we arrived in Boston and I knew my schedule, I called Laura and she said we'd be married on Sunday 15 November. All I had to do was get there – the Niewinski's would handle everything else. Except I would have to get a blood test, required by Illinois law. So Thursday evening I went to a hos-pital in Boston and got the blood test. Early Friday, I left on the train, bound for the Windy City, hoping nothing more would happen to louse up the most important day of my life.

If you stop to think about it, the three major events in our lives are birth, marriage and death – and marriage is the only one where we call the shot. It's a huge decision and may well determine whether you have a good life, or not. I was sure and very happy that I had made the right choice.

When I arrived in Chicago about 0930, Laura and all of my family was there to meet me. I was told everything was going well. The church was reserved for 4 p.m. Sunday and were specially honored in that a locally famous Polish Monsignor would marry us, and a locally famous budding opera star would sing at the ceremony. All the guests had been notified. Apparently, all bases were covered and there was nothing left to go wrong.

IF ANYTHING CAN POSSIBLY GO WRONG, IT PROBABLY WILL

We hurried to the City Hall to get the marriage license. There must have been more than a hundred standing in line! Mostly servicemen. And one window open, one clerk to serve all these people. Then we found out that since it was Saturday, this office would be closed at 12 noon! I wasn't sure I'd get to the head of the line by that time!

But not to worry – I made it with nearly 20 minutes to spare. Then, when nothing more could possibly go wrong, something did! The clerk looked at my blood test papers and said, "This is out-of-state. We can't accept it." That did it, I thought. Why is this happening to me? What do I do now? How do we tell everyone involved that the wedding is cancelled, at least for now? Then the clerk handed me a card and said, "Go to this address as fast as you can. It's just a block and a half. Tell them you need a blood test really quick. When you come back, don't get in line, come right up here."

I was totally confused, but didn't argue. I didn't even stop to explain to Laura and my family. "Wait here. I'll be right back!" I ran down the steps, out the door and up the street. Up a flight of stairs and into an office where at least a dozen people were ahead of me. I ignored them and went to the lady in charge. She looked at the card I'd been given, ushered me into the next room and a guy in a white coat drew a blood sample. I was sent back into the waiting room and I knew none of this would work, because in Boston I was told they had to put the blood into a machine and spin it for 20 minutes or so before testing it. I looked at my watch and I didn't have 20 minutes. Just then my name was called. I had my paper, paid $25 and ran back to City Hall, to the head of the line and got the wedding license with three minutes to spare!

(I'm sure you figured it out. I'd been taken for $25, which the City Hall clerk probably split with the testing lab. But who's complaining?)

OUR WARTIME WEDDING

Sunday was a remarkable day, a beautiful day. In Chicago, the middle of November should be cold, windy and gray. It was sunny and warm. The church was impressive and crowded – I wondered where all the people came from. (You would think we were famous.) My brother was Best Man; Josephine, Maid of Honor; Pat, Vi and Alvina, bridesmaids. Three young naval officers (Tex, Don and George) from my "alma mater", Abbott Hall, were ushers. Our mothers were in formal gowns, as were all the ladies in our wedding party. And Laura, of course, was the real star of the show. Laura's father died young, so Billy Jarvis, a longtime friend of the family, took his place.

We had all the trimmings – flower girl, orchids, Laura presenting her bouquet to the Blessed Virgin, rice, limousines, and even did the military thing with the two of us exiting the church under crossed swords!

The reception was huge. Dinner for sixty guests, bar, orchestra, dancing and attendant toasts and ceremonies (cutting the cake with my officer's sword) at the North Shore Hotel. It was a semi-Polish wedding – the real ones tend to get a bit rowdy and the Niewinskis didn't want that. It was a glorious day that could have been even more perfect by the presence of my old friends, but they were unavailable, all in uniform somewhere. Laura and I slipped away about 11:30, the party still going strong, and Billy drove us to the Edgewater Beach hotel where we spent our wedding night.

BRIEF HONEYMOON. We went to Waterloo and Waverly before heading back east. Saw Corporal Johnny Jones and wife Evelyn Moulton, Les Moeller, Fred Studier, Ed Engelbrecht, and Bob and Roberta Schulze. Jack and Barbara Wright had Bob Harris and us as dinner guests (roast pheasant). Dr. and Mrs. Grant (Ruby) took us out to dinner the next day in Waterloo. Had time with my family, and took the midnight train to Chicago and had another big party – a goodbye for Laura – on 11/20. In New York, we did the tourist thing – top of the Empire State building, etc. In Boston, Laura joined the Rapidan Wives Club by staying somewhere on the East Coast, ready to dash to any port when our ship came back from wherever – whenever.

New officers came aboard. Lt. Kurtnacher was older than most of us, and experienced. Ensigns Moriarty and Loiselle were bright and capable. Sutherland quickly named them "Curtain-Snatcher", "Candy Moe", and "Alfred" – Alfred being a funny-looking comic strip character of the time. Dr. Arida was our new ship's doctor, who Sutherland always referred to as "the cleanest Arab I ever met."

Tom Moriarity, from Birmingham, Alabama, was the son of a famous baseball umpire or pro football referee, I can't remember which. Soon after he met Laura, he told me that she was the most beautiful lady he had ever seen. (We've stayed in touch all these years through our Christmas letters, and now some 60 or more years later, he still mentions that occasionally.) Tom took over as Gunnery Officer after I left a few months later and stayed with the Rapidan until the end of the war, finally ending up as Captain of the ship!

A COUPLE OF VERY SPECIAL MUSTANGS

Wilbur Ulle and Boatswain Mockbee also received orders and left the ship. I was sorry to see them go, especially Mockbee: now I would have only Mundy and Sutherland to keep me laughing. And at this point I'm going to tell you more about two people who, by any standard, I'd consider of special interest. Both were "Mustangs": enlisted men who became officers – which is not an easy thing to do. Only the best make it. I served with two of them, enjoyed their friendship, and cherish their memories.

PAUL REVERE McGLOHON. Chief Engineer and my mentor – I've already told you some things about him. He had never gone to college, of course, but he read a lot and was a well-self-educated man. He also enjoyed fleecing his fellow officers at every possible opportunity. Here's how he would do it, and this is an actual case. He had read that a weather station on top of Mt. Washington in New Hampshire was, officially, the windiest place in the U.S. So he waits for a windy day, then joins the coffee drinkers in the wardroom and begins the conversation.

"Damn, it's windy out there today!" he would say. "Reminds me of one winter in North Dakota. Nearly blew me off my feet. And the people who lived there told me that happens much of the time!" Then he'd drink his coffee and the others would talk about windy places they had been. Finally, he'd say, "I guess North Dakota must be the windiest place in the whole country." Someone would argue, "No, that would have to be up on some mountain top – like one of the Rockies. Maybe Pike's Peak."

Discussion would ensue and eventually McGlohon would suggest a contest – involving a modest wager. The closest pick would win the pot. Several mountains were selected, then McGlohon would concede, "Maybe it's not North Dakota. Too flat. Oh, I have no idea. Maybe in the East. Wild guess, New Hampshire. What's up there? Oh, Mt. Washington." Then he'd pick Mt. Washington and after the answer was determined by consulting reference books, he would collect the money. He did this often, in many variations.

He loved the stories about Colin Glencannon, Chief Engineer of the fictional "Inchcliffe Castle", and to some degree he resembled him. Except for Muledriver Mullen, of course, everyone liked and admired McGlohon, including Captain Mac. So when our glorious leader was promoted and assigned as C.O. of a new, fast tanker, the Chikaskia, in the Pacific, he pulled strings and got McGlohon as his Chief Engineer. This didn't happen immediately, and the rest of the story didn't happen until a couple of years later, but my buddy Ed Kepler just happened to get ordered to that same ship – and of course became a friend and fan of Paul Revere McGlohon.

So late in the war, Kepler put in for Submarine School and was sent to New London, CT. Then Captain McIntosh was reassigned and left the ship. The war ended – VJ Day. *On the following day*, McGlohon was playing acey-deucy in the wardroom of the Chikaskia, and some Jap kamikaze pilot who didn't get the word (or didn't care) crashed the Chikaskia and killed this good man I so loved and admired.

BOATSWAIN JOHN MOCKBEE. Three and a half years after Mockbee left the Rapidan, the war had ended and I was taking post-graduate studies at Northwestern University. As a class assignment, I wrote about my old ship-mate and I called it, "FOREVER MOCKBEE". Here it is:

> Boatswain Mockbee was one of the few good things to happen to me in World War II. He came aboard our Navy tanker in Iceland. He walked into the wardroom and introduced himself, then sat down and started telling sea stories. He talked incessantly for the next nine months and he never told the same story twice.

> "Have a cup of coffee, Boats," someone said. "Don't mind if I do," said Mockbee. He leaned back and looked around the wardroom. "Nice place ya got here," he said. "More homelike than the Philadelphia. I just come off the Philly. Of course, I wasn't in the wardroom over there. I just made boatswain a week ago. Been a chief signalman for the past ten years."

> No one interrupted, so he just kept talking. He finished his coffee and the story of his life – first chapter – about the same time. I could see that everyone present had already decided that Boatswain Mockbee was just what the Rapidan needed. He got another cup of coffee and kept talking and laughing and from then on he was one of us.

He was an Irishman and a Texan. Take that combination and add salt – a great deal of salt – and you've got a big, seafaring man with curly hair, a rugged, weatherbeaten countenance, wrinkles in just the right places, and a loud laugh that made everything he said seem funny.

Somebody asked him, had the Philly been out long. "Well, not too long," said Mockbee. "Maybe two months, this last cruise." One of the ensigns was impressed. "Wow!" he said. "That's a really long patrol, isn't it?"

"Not for the Philly," Mockbee explained. "Let me tell you a story, son. Now you may not believe this, but so help me, it's the truth. One time I was at sea so long, rolling and pitching and bouncing all over the North Atlantic in stormy weather, that when I finally set foot on dry land, I was taken deathly ill. And would you believe it, the doctors in Boston swore up and down it was one of the worst cases of landsickness on record!"

Mockbee laughed and finished another cup of coffee. "Yes, sir, things was so rough we never knew where the next torpedo was coming from." He laughed again, in appreciation of his own jokes.

The new boatswain's good humor and high spirits, we soon found, were contagious. It wasn't long before the junior officers were kidding him like they'd known him all their lives, and he was handing it right back. I left the wardroom for awhile and when I got back they were razzing him about his twenty-odd years in the "old navy". One of them called him a "freshwater sailor", and said he probably served most of his time in a supply depot in Kentucky, or maybe an ammunition dump in Arizona.

"Well, I sure didn't get no eighteen years sea duty riding the Staten Island ferry," the boatswain growled, good-naturedly. He leaned forward and indicted the top of his head. "See that? You think that's dandruff, don't ya? Well it ain't. *It's salt!*"

He laughed and the ensigns ganged up on him. "Getting a little thin on top, old timer," said one of them. "'Thin?'" said Mockbee. "How d'ya like that! Me with a hairline like a gorilla!"

Another one told him that sailors in the pre-war navy were just a bunch of shipborne janitors – caretakers, who keep the rust off ships between the wars. And with that Mockbee chuckled and began agreeing with them.

"Sure," he said, "You taxpayers wouldn't give us enough money so's we could buy the fuel oil to cruise anyplace. We was so poverty-stricken, we couldn't afford to do nothing but sit around shining brightwork and drinking coffee. I remember the Pennsylvania – she was anchored in San Pedro harbor so long, when they finally got ordered to get underway, they had to spend two weeks dredging coffee grounds out from under her! She was practically hung up high and dry!"

Everything seemed to remind Mockbee of a story. Mostly, they were tall tales without a shred of truth, but always funny and appreciated in those days when most of us found little to laugh at. He talked about himself and his buddies in the old navy. Like "the time me and 'Foul Weather O'Toole' met them two White Russian girls in Singapore". Or, perhaps about "the time me and 'Bad Breath Flanagan' made a liberty in Shanghai and got tangled up with a couple of Limey sailors." He also had a number of good yarns about some guy he called "Detonator Benny."

And, of course, there was "Ernie", who turned out to be Admiral Ernest J. King. "Me and Ernie," the boatswain would say, "We used to run this navy. That was before he went to his desk job in Washington and left me out here, holding the bag. When Ernie had his flag on the Augusta, I used to be his flag chief signalman. He'd ask me for advice all the time. 'Mockbee,' he'd say – Mockbee, that's what he used to call me – 'Mockbee, what d'ya think I ought to do?' And I'd tell him. 'Ernie,' I'd say, 'If I was you, I'd hoist a Turn Five, and air bedding!' Yes sir, we ran the navy, Me and Ernie."

I was luckier than most of the Rapidan's officers: I got to know the boatswain better than anyone. That's because we were in the same liberty section and made our shore leaves together. When we were at sea, which was most of the time, we stood our bridge watches together. So for eight hours of every twenty-four, I was privileged to gather the pearls of wisdom that fell from his wind-chapped lips.

He was a good man to have around when I had the deck and things got sticky. OOD duty could be a tough job – especially in a large convoy in a dense fog and heavy seas, without the modern miracle of radar. Station-keeping was critical and most of the ships were 1916-model hulks that had been in mothballs since the end of World War I. Their engines would break down, they'd lose steering control and their officers weren't always experienced and competent. So it was some measure of comfort to have Mockbee's twenty years experience to back up my own judgment. And, equally important, was the way he made the tense moments seem considerably less tense.

One night the fog was so thick I had to feel my way up to the bridge, and when I got there I had difficulty in making out our own fore-mast. I located Mundy, the OOD, by hearing him swearing to him-self over in the corner. He was unhappy because I was three minutes late – he wanted to get rid of the responsibility before we had the collision he was expecting any minute. I relieved Mundy just as Mockbee came out on our wing of the bridge.

"Looks like California," he said, "or at least it probably would, if we could see it." He peered into the fog for a full minute. "I can't see a damn thing," he announced finally.

"No fooling," Mundy said. "What did you expect up here—a floor show?" Mockbee looked down his nose. "Ships," he declared. "I expected to see ships."

"Well, there's sixty-some of them out there – somewhere." Mock-bee raised his binoculars and examined the area ahead, where he assumed the horizon to be. "Can't see a blame thing," he reaf-firmed. "Might as well stayed in bed."

A moment later, he said, "Did I ever tell you about the time I was sailing up the coast of China and the Old Man anchored by getting a bearing on a barking dog?" He laughed heartily, and Mundy decided to stick around for the story.

"You guys think I'm kidding, don't ya? But I swear I ain't – it's the truth, so help me. We were probably the only ship in history that ever took an anchor bearing on the sound of a barking dog. It was the winter of '30, as I remember, and I was on this old tin can – four-piper, of course…"

"Steam or sail?" asked Mundy.

"Stop interrupting. Like I say, we was headed into this harbor – forget its name – and it was after midnight. There was a helluva fog, just like this one. Well, most skippers would of stayed outside 'til it lifted, but not this guy. 'Hell,' he said, 'I know this harbor like a book. I could go in blindfolded, with one hand tied behind my back.' So we started in, at standard speed, too. He never slacked off a single turn."

"After we been passing bell buoys for a half hour or so, and made a couple course changes, the Exec began to get uneasy. The Old Man just laughed and said it was O.K., we had a couple of miles of good water ahead of us. But, all of a sudden, the forward lookout reported he heard a dog barking. 'Dog barking?' yelled the skipper. 'Where away?' 'Dead ahead!' says the lookout. 'Back her down, full!' yells the Old Man. 'Let go the starboard anchor!'"

"Well, sir, the Old Man, stood there awhile then he went below without another word. And do you know, the next morning when the fog lifted, there was a big rocky cliff dead ahead of us, not more'n a hundred and fifty yards! Another half minute and we'd of been shipwrecked, high and dry – if it wasn't for that barking dog!"

Mockbee started chuckling and I thought it was funny but Mundy didn't say a word. "What's the matter," Mockbee said. "Don't you believe it?" Mundy laughed. "No."

"Would you like it better if I made it San Francisco?" asked the boatswain.

Well, that's the way Mockbee was, even in tense situations. Mundy layed below and the boatswain and I got back to worrying about the fog, the other ships, and collision. We still couldn't see a thing. Once in awhile the column leaders would sound off on their whistles and that helped some, but they didn't do it often enough to suit me. I was deeply concerned.

Then I noticed Mockbee had his nose in the air and he was sniffing. "You know something?" he ventured. "The wind is about two points on our port bow, ain't it? Do you smell that smoke?"

"Smell it?" I said, "I'm practically choking on it." "Well," said Mockbee, "that's that old coal-burning Limey freighter, over in column one, the second ship, remember? Hell's fire, it couldn't be anything else – she's always smoldering like a damn volcano. That means, according to her, we're right where we should be, right in position."

The more I thought about it, the more logical it seemed. At any rate I felt a bit better and we made it through our four-hour watch without a collision.

"Some seamanship," Mockbee remarked when we were back in the wardroom, drinking coffee. "Keeping station by the smell of smoke! The old guy with the barking dog ain't so hot, is he?" I told Mockbee here was a story he could add to his collection. "Oh no," he said, "this one is too far-fetched. Nobody'd believe me!"

Some day, I'd like to meet the long-suffering lady Mockbee married. She was the subject of many of his monologues. "The dumbest thing I ever did was to buy a house in Long Beach," he told us. "This house was on high ground and not far from the harbor. When we moved in, the little woman discovers that from our second floor bedroom, she can see right out to the fleet anchorage. So what happens? She takes up signaling! Buys herself a searchlight, binoculars, and a set of international signal flags. Then every time the fleet's in, she starts sending me messages."

The boatswain laughed. "I wouldn't have minded so much on account of I told our signalmen to ignore her signals. You know what happens? She starts *relaying* her messages through the Admiral's flagship and the whole damn fleet!"

Somebody asked him why his wife stayed in California when he was serving in the Atlantic. "I'm nobody's fool," Mockbee said, grinning. "If she came to the East coast, soon as I got in, she'd find out about me making boatswain. She knows about the Navy's pay grades and I'd have to increase the allotment that's paid direct to her! Nothing doing!"
"She still thinks you're a Chief?" I asked. "Chief?" he said. "Everytime I go home, I borrow some bell-bottom trousers and a white hat. She still thinks I'm a seaman second class!"

Mockbee sometimes referred to himself as a man of few words. But he laughed when he said it. He told us he seldom called his wife on the phone because she talked incessantly, for hours, and he "couldn't get a word in edge-wise – except hello, yes, and goodbye." But for some reason, none of us felt sorry for him.

He seemed especially to enjoy bantering with the ensigns. He called them "son" and constantly invited them to "feel free to draw on my wealth of experience." I remember the time in the wardroom when one of our newest ensigns picked up the boatswain's cap. Mockbee snorted. Then he said, "Put it down, son. Another minute with that thing in your hands and you'll be deathly seasick!"

And one day – I'll never forget this – our Communications Officer came into the wardroom and announced, "I have here in my hand, a message from the Bureau of Personnel – the one you've been waiting for – the latest promotion list. All you ensigns are now j.g.'s!"

Mockbee groaned. "Oh no!" he exclaimed. "Ye gods, what's this navy coming to?" The Communications Officer then interrupted the ensigns' cheering and celebrating. "But the BIG NEWS is…Mockbee, you've just made ensign!"

"Ensign!" Mockbee shouted. "Me, an ensign? Hell, I ain't no Johnny-Come-Lately! I'm the ship's boatswain!" Then Tom Moriarity, one of our brand-new j.g.'s, put his hand on Mockbee's shoulder and told him, "I realize this is all new to you, John. If there's anything you don't understand – at any time – don't hesitate to ask questions. You can always feel free to draw on my wealth of experience!"

That's my Mockbee story. I deeply regret two things: I wish he'd come to the Rapidan earlier and left later, and after he left, I never saw him or heard anything from, or about him, ever again.

HEY! THIS TIME WE SAIL AND NOT TO ICELAND!

We found Laura a room on Boston's Beacon Street, but a few days later the ship sailed to New York. Laura followed and moved into the Governor Clinton Hotel. Evelyn Mundy and Liz Sutherland took rooms there, too. 30 November to 6 December was a great week. The Rapidan anchored in the Hudson River off 79th Street. Very convenient! Our honeymoon continued – Stork Club, Waldorf Astoria (Xavier Cugat) and other big name clubs and restaurants. Laura came aboard for dinner when I had the duty. And I was promoted to Lieutenant!

In wartime, ship movements are SECRET, so I couldn't tell Laura where we were going, but my last night in NY I took her to see the movie, "Casablanca". Next morning, we sailed for that port in North Africa. Arrived there after some submarine scares involving emergency turns and general mismanagement by the Commodore of the Convoy. Arrived 12-30-42, anchored outside the breakwater – which was like anchoring in the open ocean.

GERMANS FROM GIBRALTAR, OUR WELCOMING COMMITTEE

On New Year's eve until 3 a.m. – I "enjoyed" my first-ever air attack. German bombers (believed from Gibraltar) hit the city and ships in the harbor. I never saw so many searchlights and the planes were clearly visible at 6000 feet. Three of them were hit and crashed. So much flak went up from shore batteries and the dozens of ships in port that I couldn't imagine how any of the enemy planes survived. And it took me about twenty seconds to realize the real danger wasn't the bombs but all the ack-ack coming back down! We could hear it "chunking" into the water all around us. We secured from General Quarters and got the hell below!

I had the 0800 to noon watch when morning arrived, and, as I said, it was like being anchored in the open sea. When I arrived on the bridge something didn't seem right and I soon discovered we were dragging anchor as the wind and the sea were moving us back toward the beach. I dropped our other anchor and called for the engine room to steam slowly forward so we could hold our position.

On the way over in the convoy we had followed a merchant ship I knew only as No. 54. I learned it also dragged anchor, went aground and the seas beat her up so badly that 17 men died, including all of the Navy's armed guard on board! And the U.S. destroyer Wainright lost three men in the rescue attempt!

After we moved inside the harbor and tied up to the dock, Mundy came and got me and said, "Come on. I want you to see something." We went topside and he pointed at the U.S. destroyer moored alongside. "See that guy taking a sun bath? Know who that is?" I looked and said, "I see him and have no idea who that is." Mundy said, "Look again. Doesn't he look familiar?" I said, "No." Mundy looked disgusted. *"That's FDR, Junior,"* he declared. I looked again. "Could be," I said. He shook his head. "Not 'could be' – *is.*"

FRANKLIN, WINSTON, CHARLES AND THE KING

Several days later we were in downtown Casablanca and suddenly the police and military, seemingly hundreds of them, descended on the center of the city and lined up to prevent anyone from crossing the main street. I wondered what was happening. There were no cars or camels or anything in the street. Then an open limousine went roaring by, maybe 60-70 mph! "Damn," I said. "That's Winston Churchill!" Then another car – with FDR! Another – General Charles De Gaulle! One more and I didn't recognize him (but found out later it was the King of Morocco). This was the day of the Casablanca Conference. And Mundy was right, it *was* FDR, Jr. – he was a junior officer in the Navy and was sent to be his father's aide at the Conference.

Casablanca was the best liberty port I ever visited. It was warm and pleasant – the opposite of Iceland and Greenland. And colorful: most of the buildings were in pastel colors. And interesting. We met a lot of people like the ones in the movie "Casablanca" – except we couldn't find Rick's Café and never saw Bergman or Bogart. (Or Sam.)

Until we invaded and took over, Morocco was held by the Vichy French. The harbor was littered with sunken or disabled ships, including the French battleship Jean Bart and the cruiser Primauget. Today, we know all about "suicide bombers" – they're all over the place, and mostly Islamic. But at that time I first learned about saboteurs smuggled into ports where at night they would swim underwater and attach explosives to the hulls of ships, then go aboard and surrender, just before the explosion would sink the ship.

I mention this mainly because a couple of times I had to patrol the harbor with armed sailors and a searchlight looking for these guys. It was an all night job, a bit eerie as we moved around and between the partially sunken ships and all the allied vessels we were protecting. We never encountered enemies, but always figured we might.

SHORE PATROL DUTY

Casablanca was still a bit dangerous with so many friends of the Germans and Vichy French around – and Moroccans and other North Africans who weren't all sympathetic to the Allied Forces – like us. Every ship there had to provide a Shore Patrol every day – one officer and two petty officers, armed with Colt .45's (the petty officers also carried "billy clubs") patrolling as a team. Shore Patrol HQ ashore was under the command of a former New York police captain who would assign the territory for each patrol. On his first S.P. duty, Kurtenacher found the body of a U.S. sailor who had been murdered.

All officers and men on Navy ships in port in wartime were divided into three Sections. One section could go on liberty, one stayed aboard to run the ship (the "duty") and one stayed aboard as "standby" – just in case. I found out that Shore Patrol duty came from the Standby section, so I volunteered and that way was able to go ashore two days out of three, instead of just one. And in deference to my newly acquired two full stripes, (when most SP officers were ensigns) the New York Cop didn't assign me a "beat" – he assigned "Roving Patrol" which meant a go-anywhere-patrol! This really came in handy.

Casablanca was originally a native Moroccan city on the coast, and walled in for protection from potential enemies. Later the French came in and built a modern city, pretty much surrounding the Moroccan city. The wall was breached in a number of places to allow easy passage between the two. Then the lure of trade and jobs brought more Moroccans – too many to fit in the original native quarters, so they built a new Moroccan city outside the French city. They then had the Ancienne Medina and the Nouvelle Medina and both of these were "off limits" to allied military on liberty.

So when I was assigned Roving Patrol, I immediately led my team into the native areas where we couldn't otherwise have gone. In the Old Medina we found an outdoor auction going on, where the desert Arabs were selling their handicrafts to the locals and it was fun to watch. We couldn't understand the language but the people were interesting, respectful and friendly.

Later, we took a horse-drawn carriage to the New Medina. It was 2 or 3 miles away and we went through an area outside the French city where camel caravans had come in from the desert and set up tent camps. Then we arrived at the main gate, which was guarded by several of the biggest, blackest Senegalese (members of the Foreign Legion) I've ever seen. As we approached, they eyed us and one hurried toward the gate. I figured he'd demand papers or summarily direct us to "get lost". So I told my guys to walk up like we owned the place. (I really wanted to get inside and find out why this was off limits to our troops.)

The guard and I got to the gate at the same time, and to my surprise, he opened the gate for me and saluted. There was another gate and another guard hurried over to open it for me. Inside, we walked down a wide street and into the Moroccan city. Most of the people we met just stared at us. This part of the city looked reasonably new but the architecture was old, traditionally North African. I remember stopping my companions and asking them to take a few minutes to examine our surroundings. "Look in all directions," I said. "Look carefully at everything, including the people." They were puzzled but did what I asked. A couple minutes later I said, "All right, now – did you see *anything* that you couldn't have seen in similar places a thousand years ago? Or even at the time of Christ?"

We stood there for several minutes. No clock tower. No traffic lights or street lights – no indications of electricity, anywhere. Nobody in any clothing (even shoes) that couldn't have been worn in biblical days. We even looked for wristwatches and found none except our own. I'm sure there were things relating to modern times, but we couldn't see them. At any rate, it was an interesting exercise.

Awhile later, we came upon a beautiful mosque surrounded by other buildings and in a large area, beautifully landscaped and with real grass lawns, a rare sight in this part of the world. A sidewalk led to a large door, which was open. I had never seen the inside of a mosque and wanted to. Nobody was in sight and I wondered if we could peak in – without getting stabbed or shot. We headed toward the door and suddenly a man emerged. I couldn't tell if he was the head man or what, but he looked at me, said something I couldn't understand and, with a smile, indicated the open door and apparently invited us to enter.

This took me by surprise. I hesitated, and I realized we were all carrying weapons, and also that I knew nothing about Islamic religion or whatever protocol would apply in the situation at hand. So I smiled and nodded (and tried to look as friendly as possible) and indicated, by body language, "Thanks, but no thanks." (Then and now, I consider this a reasonably good decision.)

In our walking tour we noticed there seemed to be a fairly large area surrounded by a high wall, and we didn't see any gates or entryways. In the next hour we pretty much walked around it and finally found one entry. Several Senegalese guarded it, but we headed in and they didn't stop us. We had no idea what it was. There were many two-story apartments and we saw several women in front of them washing their hair and washing their clothes.

Then we heard a lot of laughing and five girls – I'd guess about fifteen or sixteen years old – ran past us, apparently playing tag. Or so it seemed. Two of them were totally unclothed from the waist up! They looked at us and laughed. Suddenly four other girls walked up to us and said something in Arabic, then one of them grabbed the white hat off the head of one of the petty officers and they ran away, laughing. There was no way we could catch them.

Later, as we were leaving the high-walled area, we figured it out. It was about 2 p.m. and even in January it was a hot day with a dazzling sun. A middle-aged man, apparently intoxicated, came through the gate, and staggered down the street. I guessed him to be a merchant seaman. Then a woman of about thirty came up to him and they embraced and kissed and walked off like lovers, arm-in-arm.

I realized we had seen no men in this walled compound, except this one. Apparently, this was some kind of Moroccan-style minimum-security women's prison. And it seems that the ladies were able to practice their trade – prostitution – while serving their sentences. Prospective customers were allowed to come and go.

Shore Patrol in Casablanca was a lot of fun. I never encountered any problems I couldn't handle, but I do recall an incident between an English sailor and an Arab tradesman which I solved with the advice and counsel of some 100 curious onlookers who gathered to observe and tell me (in languages I couldn't understand) what they would do if they were me.

And I remember a pitiful, little, terribly deformed beggar that made me feel so sorry – until about "cocktail time" that afternoon when I found him in a bar, buying drinks for all his friends, and he wasn't deformed at all!

And I must tell you about one of our new ensigns, "Windy" Willrich. He was an engineering officer from someplace in Texas. A rather strange-looking fellow – or to put it more accurately – he was surely the unhandsomest officer on the Rapidan (probably in the entire history of the ship!) He was a good guy and fun to be with, but a bit weird. We immediately named him "Windy" because he hardly ever said anything! (Possibly the illegitimate son of Harpo Marx?) At any rate – guess what? I was told the first day he went ashore, he found a mistress! This was verified by another of our ship's officers. Asked for details, Windy would just grin. And say nothing at all.

FUN AND (GUESSING) GAMES IN SEVENTH HEAVEN

Mundy met a lady who lived in the "penthouse area" up on top of one of the many six-story (?) buildings in downtown Casablanca. In most places, "Penthouse" means the high-rent district. Just the opposite in Casablanca. The woman, Marie Jeanne Hubinet, was Corsican, divorced, with a ten-year-old son Robert – pronounced "Woe-bear". (He was one sharp kid.) Their "apartment" up on the roof was more than modest – it was pretty much "bottom of the barrel". Two rooms, one a combination living room and bedroom, the other a kitchen. Running water only in the sink. No bathroom. (That was a situation shared with tenants of other rooftop apartments.) We called her place "Seventh Heaven" after a movie made back in the Dark Ages starring Janet Gaynor and Charles Farrell. (I believe it won one of the first Academy Awards.)

Mundy and I, particularly, but our other officers as well, spent a lot of evenings there. We would take a few gifts – coffee, sugar – so we were welcome indeed. And Marie's friends, a motley crew if I ever saw one, assembled every evening to sit down and look at the Americans. Communication was primitive: none of them spoke English, except the Jewess from Gibraltar, and she wasn't there very often. None of us spoke any of the languages they spoke: with my one year of college French, I came the closest. I could read a little, but even then my vocabulary had rusted away from lack of use.

But we had a wonderful time trying to converse. It was like a guessing game – our main entertainment, every evening. Marie, by the way, was an attractive lady, although she did have a rather long nose – so Sutherland immediately dubbed her "Cyrano" (after Bergerac, of course). Regular visitors included a 17-year-old Spanish girl, Lusette ("Blondie Baby"); Angele Boustani (said to be "LIBAN", which stumped us as we didn't know if she was from Libya, Lebanon or wherever); Edith, an attractive Algerian widow; the Arab lady, "Fatima" (real name) who had a thin blue-black line tattooed right down the center of her face, from her hairline down to "out-of-sight"; the aforementioned Jewess from Gibraltor (a fairly hefty middle-aged lady); and the Corsican sisters.

The Corsican sisters, Anna and Marie, were interesting, especially Anna who had been a member of the Free French underground, involved in smuggling freedom fighters from Morocco (controlled by Vichy) to England to fight with DeGaulle. She had been captured, tried, convicted and sentenced to 10 years in a Moroccan prison – roughly equivalent to 20 or 30 in one of ours. Because of our invasion she had just been released.

Mundy and I were invited to have dinner with the Corsican family, the Paolantonaccis. They lived in the same building as Cyrano, but down on the fifth floor, in a much nicer apartment. It was a most pleasant evening. We ate sardines, bread, wine, omelet, wine, potatoes, wine, salad, wine, cheese, wine, oranges and tangerines, wine, French pastry – and then, of course, wine. And some of the coffee we had given them.

I also used my highly privileged Roving Patrol assignment to visit the Sultan's Palace. The Sultan wasn't there and the guards seemed to treat me like visiting royalty. My principal memory is an orange tree in the Sultan's garden that had the biggest, most beautiful oranges I had ever seen. I admired them, so the head guard, or whatever, he was, picked two from the tree, handed them to me and reached for more. I stopped him because I couldn't carry any more. When I returned to the ship and ate them, they were unbelievable! I couldn't imagine why anyone would ever raise any other kind. I have never again seen, or heard of, such magnificent fruit.

MORE CASABLANCA MEMORIES

Before we went ashore Captain Mac reminded us of the dangers of food poisoning and suggested it was always safe to eat hardboiled eggs. These were widely available in Morocco. "The hen has the perfect solution to the packaging problem," he told us. "There isn't much an Arab can do to contaminate a boiled egg that you peel yourself."

Our ship was moored at the Phosphate Jetty, an easy walk into town. The main drag was the "Boulevard des Quatre Zouaves", very Moroccan with palm trees and, often, native dancers, jugglers, acrobats, etc. Parallel and one block over was a street with a French name (I don't remember) and totally different atmosphere, totally French. We usually hung out at the Majestic Café.

They had strict curfews and blackouts during our stay. We ignored the former but a couple of times got lost in the latter. The police and military patrols treated us well and drove us back to the ship when we couldn't find it. Aboard ship at night, we could hear occasional explosions (sabotage?) and pistol and rifle fire. I heard Nazi spies and saboteurs, landed by gliders and parachutes, were captured and executed. This was confirmed in part by dispatches.

So – was my Casablanca anything like the famous movie? Yes, indeed. The film was about people who hated and feared the Nazis, became refugees to avoid them, and kept moving to other safe havens as Germany continued to advance throughout Europe and N. Africa. From France and Spain they fled to Morocco and then Vichy and the Germans took over there and these people were trapped, had to stay, and survive under difficult circumstances.

In our country there were shortages and rationing. In Morocco, no beef had been available for three months, no milk for two years, no sugar at all. I became acquainted with Silvio Levy, a Turkish rug dealer from Milan, Italy and his South African wife – wealthy, cultured people – who invited me to their home (85 Av. Moinier, Apt. 2A) and told me their story. They were bribing officials to be let alone, and they said the city was filled with people like themselves. But now that the Americans had taken over, they said, everything would change and the wealthy refugees would be able to leave for England and the United States.

THE LONG VOYAGE HOME

We sailed for home on January 20, and all I could think about was reunion with Laura. Fortunately, our destination was New York and that's where she was waiting. We anchored at 5 p.m. on February 7, and I went ashore and called her hotel and they told me she wasn't there and had left no forwarding address! So now I have a brand new wife, hopefully somewhere over there in a city of 6 million people, but I have no idea where!!!

Sam Houston suggested I go with him to his apartment in Manhattan and maybe Shortstop would know where she is. I was more than somewhat worried, but his suggestion made sense. When we got there, Shortstop said, "Yes, she lives right upstairs!" But she told me, "She's not home right now. She's having dinner and seeing a movie with a couple of girl friends." I knew Sam and his wife would appreciate my imminent departure and said I'd go somewhere and eat. Then Shortstop told me she had the key to Laura's apartment! Perfect solution. I'd wait there.

Coming from the sea into ports, harbors, restricted waters, Navy ships go from routine watches to "Special Sea Details". With the Rapidan, that meant every officer had an assignment and mine came on top of lengthy sea watches. I had not slept for some thirty hours and I was totally exhausted. I went to my wife's apartment, removed my coat and tie and lay down on the bed. The next thing I knew the door opened and I woke up and said, "Hi, Laurie." *Nearly scared her to death!* "It's me. Your husband."

MAN OVERBOARD! The next morning Sam and I took the subway and the Staten Island Ferry to the dock near our anchorage. We joined the Captain, the Exec (Mullen) and others in the Captain's Gig and as we drew near to our ship we could see that something important was happening. The entire crew was topside, looking over the stern of the ship. We all hurried aboard and found that a man had fallen overboard. A strong current had swept him downstream but he'd managed to grab onto a 30-foot launch we had tied to the stern of the ship. But he couldn't pull himself into the boat, and was having difficulty just hanging on.

Mundy was the senior officer on board and we watched him grab the rope holding the boat, go over the side, shinny down the rope, drop into the water, pull himself up into the boat, and then get to the sailor, grab his wrists and hold on. It was quite an athletic achievement that left Mundy pooped out. He lay there puffing, too tired to pull the man into the boat.

Meantime, "Muledriver" Mullen decided to take charge. He was leaning over the after rail and shouting orders to Mundy. "No, no," he yelled. "Let go with your left hand and reach around and grab his shirt from behind! No, no. Do this, do that. Now what you do…"

Mundy had been bullied by Mullen for two years and hated his guts. This was the final straw. He yelled back. "Listen, you goddam armchair coxswain – if you're so smart, *you* come down here and do it!" This, right in front of every officer and sailor on the ship! (*Not a good idea*.)

Mullen was livid. He didn't yell, "Put that man in irons!", but it pretty much amounted to that. Mundy was in big trouble. We all knew it. The Captain ordered him confined to his quarters, then ordered a boat to take him (the Captain) back ashore. Several hours later we learned that good old Captain Mac had called somebody in Naval Personnel in Washington and got Mundy orders to leave the ship effective immediately!

But the bad news was, we also learned that Captain Mac had been detached and ordered to a brand new, fast tanker, *and Mullen promoted to become the Captain of the Rapidan*! Naturally, I viewed these events with mixed emotions. Happy for Mundy – his life would have been hell, serving under Mullen. Unhappy for me: John was my best friend and the guy who kept me laughing in scary times. I would surely miss him and Capt. McIntosh. Worse yet, I was doomed to serve under this "Captain Bly" ("Queeg"?) *who just recently told me he would "get me!"*

OUR COSSACK FRIEND, THE STAR OF THE YAR

The night I returned from Morocco, Laura told me about her next-door neighbor. He was a huge man, Russian, and he spoke little English. But he seemed nice enough. We ran into him a day later. Wow! Was he big! I'd never seen anyone that size. (Wilt Chamberlain was just a kid and Yao Ming hadn't been born.) And not only tall, he must have weighed 330, and all bone and muscle! He told us he was an entertainer – at a well-known Russian restaurant, The Yar. He urged us to come see his act and gave us his card and said to show it and we would get a good table. So we did, and were seated right up front – ringside. After some preliminary entertainment, the feature act was introduced with great fanfare – and out he comes, in Cossack uniform and *ballet slippers!* He was a "toe-dancer"!

But he was remarkable – as graceful as you'd see in Swan Lake and he did all those great athletic Russian dance maneuvers. But that wasn't his whole act. He began (while dancing) *throwing knives – with his teeth!* He'd prance around with a knife in his mouth, flip his head, and spear a target ten feet away! As a finale, he folded a dollar bill into a 2" x 2" square, laid it on a table, danced, then flipped his head and pinned it, dead center!

He was given a standing ovation and I could see he was a star attraction. After his act, he came to our table and sat with us and had the waiter bring us a bottle of wine. I was flattered and I figured that it was mostly a gesture of friendship to Laura, his next-door neighbor, and (possibly) partly a "hands-across-the-sea" gesture since he was Russian and I was an American Naval officer. And, of course, we were now on the same side in the war.

THINGS, THEY ARE A-CHANGING FAST (OR SO IT SEEMS)

I suddenly realized that, in a relatively short time, many things had changed, and my life was crossing over from what it had been to something different, and hopefully better – except for my confrontation with Mullen, which I knew would someday come.

I was now a married man, and this was a wonderful experience. Pretty rough on Laura, having to live out of a couple of suitcases, in one of several East Coast ports and keeping ready to dash to one of the others when our ship arrived there, suddenly and unannounced. She handled this well and never complained. I was really proud of her.

Many of our officers had come and gone and now, except for the Captain and the Executive Officer, I was the senior officer on board – third in the chain of command. If anything ever happened to Mullen and Sam – highly unlikely – I felt I could take command at sea with no problems whatsoever. But I had never handled a big ship in crowded ports, like New York harbor, so I hoped that would never happen. But it did – sort of.

The Rapidan was anchored in the Hudson River and we were ordered to move to a new location, miles away, at 0700 the next day. An experienced harbor pilot came aboard to take us there. Mullen and Sam went on shore leave but were to get back aboard before we sailed. But they didn't. I was now C.O., underway, for the first time.

As we weaved our way among the hundreds of other ships in the crowded harbor, Paul McGlohon joined us on the bridge and began to make me as uncomfortable as he could. "Robert," he whispered, "I don't think this pilot knows what he's doing. I think you ought to take over. You're responsible, you know. Under Navy Regs, the pilot helps, but that doesn't relieve you of the command. Did you hear that last order he gave the helm? He's getting us into big trouble! You gotta take over now! If he hits anything or goes aground, you could be court-martialed!"

McGlohon kept up his dire warnings for the entire trip – about two hours, as I remember. And he enjoyed every minute of it. But I didn't.

On another occasion, also in New York with the ship anchored up the Hudson River, I returned from shore leave at 8 a.m. and Hal Sutherland welcomed me aboard. "Boy, am I glad to see you!" he said. "We have a BIG problem. Or rather, *you* have a big problem! Sam has the day off and Mullen was just carried aboard, dead drunk! That makes you the C.O. Lots'a luck!"

The problem was a strong tide coming into the harbor that had every ship hanging up-river from its anchor. In an hour or so, the tide would change and the outgoing tide and the river current would make every ship swing around 180 degrees to be down-river from its anchor. No big problem, except that a large merchant ship had anchored much too close to us. So when the tide changed we would collide, and with ships this size, serious damage could occur.

"A half hour ago," Hal told me, "I sent Ensign Moriarty and a boat crew over to tell their C.O. we were here first and they anchored much too close – and they'd have to move or we'll crash when the tide changes. But their C.O. wasn't there and the guy Moriarty talked to said he wasn't about to move the ship."

I wasn't sure what I should do. I never even heard of a situation like this. Damn Mullen, I thought. Why did he get so drunk at this particular time? I went to his cabin, figuring maybe I could slap him awake and get him to take over, or at least tell me what to do. No luck. He was like totally unconscious.

I decided to order the engine room to get up steam so that, in a half hour or so, we could move if we had to. I had no intention of moving very far, maybe just enough to avoid collision. I also decided to shorten up on the anchor chain. Anchors alone don't hold big ships. The anchor chain is very heavy and it provides much or most of the holding power. How much chain you lay out depends on the depth of the water, condition of the bottom, wind, currents, etc. By shortening up on the chain, I would reduce the radius of our swing and reduce the danger of collision. But I'd have to be careful – take in too much chain and we could drag anchor. But I began to feel this action, with some help from the engines, might help solve the problem.

Just before the tide changed, someone on the other ship began to shorten up chain, and I could see he overdid it. They began to drag anchor just as the tide changed. He tried to compensate by backing astern, upstream from us, and somehow ended up broadside to the current. And just when I thought he was going to hit us, he continued to back down, and this maneuver turned a serious collision into a relatively minor scraping of our paint job the full length of the Rapidan, but with no critical damage.

They cleared us but remained broadside, heading rapidly downstream. I rushed up to the bridge deck for a better view and grabbed binoculars in time to see them hit two other ships at the same moment, and all three went down river headed for another ship which I later learned was the Sapelo, with Ed Kepler on board watching the whole thing, and sweating it out! But suddenly the 3-ship pack broke up and all missed the Sapelo, the two ships stopped safely but our trouble-maker, still backing down, began to sink and ended up a mile downstream, near the west bank and on the bottom of the Hudson River, with only its masts and the bridge above water.

In retrospect, I think I handled matters quite well.

We were all surprised when the Rapidan was sent to the Brooklyn Navy Yard for major alterations. Someone apparently decided we had too much wood in our superstructure (especially in the wardroom and officers quarters) that had to be replaced with steel – so it wouldn't burn so fast when we got torpedoed. Actually, I figured, this was a stupid decision since that part of the ship was directly over the forward cargo tanks, usually filled with 325,000 gallons of highly explosive aviation gasoline, so if we were torpedoed, the whole area would be blown into little pieces!

But all of us were happy with the decision. An unexpected "vacation". We had to move off the ship and the officers were sent to live at the Pennsyl-vania hotel in mid-Manhattan, for about three weeks as I remember. With our wives! This was about as good as it gets in the wartime U.S. Navy!

It was pretty much a 9 to 5 job – like civilians! We did have to keep one officer on the ship at all times, but I caught this overnight duty only two or three times. So Laura and I were able to live it up, New York City style, with lots of Broadway theater and famous restaurants. We also got valuable dis-counts on all this, through the United Service Organization (USO) – much appreciated because it was the only time in my five years of service that I was able to participate in any of the great programs provided for the military in World War II.

The Sapelo spent time in New York, too, so we saw a lot of Ed Kepler.

When we did return to sea, we spent a few weeks up and down the Atlantic Coast in and out of several major ports, mostly from Charleston, S.C. to Argentia in Newfoundland. This duty became increasingly hazardous because the German U-boat Command discovered that our ships in this area were usually unescorted and easy prey, so they sent a lot of submarines and sank an awfully lot of our ships. But, fortunately, not us.

We were in and out of Portland, Maine – briefly – a couple of times. We were pumping our cargo into some very large storage tanks they had built there and they then supplied oil to Navy and merchant ships heading into the Atlantic or the Caribbean. Every time we were there, the loading and unload-ing operations were directed by a reasonably attractive young lady whom everyone called "The Oil Queen". She was fairly famous among the officers, many of whom tried to date her. On one of our visits I asked her about it. "Doesn't bother me a bit," she told me. "I have a special boyfriend so I don't go out with any of them." I asked her who the lucky guy was. "Some officer on one of the ships?"

"Yes, but we get a thousand officers a month. You wouldn't know him," she said. "If he's Navy, maybe I would," I told her. "I know a lot of Navy guys."

"His name is Kepler. Ed Kepler," she told me. "He's on the Sapelo."

RADAR COMES ABOARD. (NOT RADAR O'REILLY)

When we were in the Yard, they installed radar on the Rapidan. It was brand new at that time. We were told we got the fifth radar in the entire Atlantic fleet. Hard to believe, but it surely was not because we were considered important, we were just there when the first five radars became available. The first four were installed on a battleship.

Radar was a great invention and it made life a lot easier for line officers at sea. Radar could "see" in the dark. In wartime, all ships run dark – no lights of any kind, so you could hit a ship before you could see it. Now, radar could provide the bearing (direction) of anything within range, and very accurate readings of its distance. This was a wonderful aid to navigation.

On our first voyage with radar we went to Newfoundland. On the way back we were a one-ship convoy, so to speak; just us and one destroyer for an escort. I had the 4 to 8 a.m. watch. When I relieved Kurtenacher, he said radar had just picked up a suspicious "blip" that seemed to be following us, maybe a mile or so back, and traveling at the same speed we were. "Could be something worth watching."

Nothing much changed for the next hour. Whatever it was, it was acting like an enemy submarine, running on the surface, trailing us and staying far astern of our escort which was echo-ranging well out ahead of us. I told the Junior Officer of the Watch – I forgot who – that if it was a sub it would wait until it began to get light, then speed up, come abeam of us, maybe a mile away and on our starboard (west) side so just before sunrise we'd be visible against the eastern sky.

And as we got closer to sun-up, that's just what happened! I notified the Captain and he just said to keep him informed. I began to worry a bit, or maybe quite a bit. I decided to notify our escort... But all of a sudden I could see our escort, barely, well on our port side, against the Eastern sky. I asked radar where the sub was and he told me and it was now on our starboard beam, *exactly 180° opposite our escort*! Then I figured it out. We were getting a reciprocal bearing, and had been, all during my watch. In a few minutes it became a bit lighter and we could see there was no submarine or anything else in sight, but the blip continued to be exactly opposite our escort. Nothing in the radar manual warned us of reciprocal bearings and I don't recall it ever happening again.

HOW FANCY CAN YOU GET?

On my last trip to Argentia Bay, there was a surprising development and a very pleasant one. A year and a half earlier, I told you, the Officers Club was a Quonset hut where only one kind of drink was available on any particular day, and you sat on a felled log to drink it. And where I saw my first Malamute. This time we tied up to a dock and an officer arrived by Jeep and invited us to "be sure to use the cocktails and dining facilities of the finest Officers Club in the U.S. Navy!" He even stayed long enough to find out how many of us could attend and said he would make the required reservations. And when the time came, they even sent a couple of Jeeps to take us there!

It was hard to believe, but the Club was fabulous – even better than we'd been told. The building itself was remarkable. We had our cocktails in a beautiful lounge, and remember the limited selection eighteen months earlier? This time we were told we couldn't name a beverage they couldn't serve us!

When all the new ensigns had come aboard in recent months, John Benham, a young man from Texas was assigned as my principal assistant. John was bright and attractive – he could have passed for the twin brother of Tab Hunter, one of the Hollywood "heart-throbs" of those times. He was sitting beside me and when I ordered my usual Manhattan, he ordered "one of the same."

When we ordered a second round, John switched to a Martini. I questioned his choice – informing him I'd never seen anyone do that before. "I always do," John told me. "I like different things." Two drinks were enough for me and a couple others. But John kept going. The third round for him was a Scotch and soda. Since he was my guy, I felt responsible and I cautioned him again. "Don't worry, Boss," I was told, "I do this all the time."

The dinner was extra-special. We were told the food service was under the management of the former head chef of the Waldorf Astoria, now a member of the U.S. Navy! I could believe it because there seemed to be an unlimited choice and everything was perfect. Our group went back to the lounge and a few of us ordered after-dinner drinks including John – Bailey's Irish Cream, as I remember. This time, he assured me everything was O.K., even before I asked.

I left to wander around the Club by myself for awhile. Then Hal Sutherland joined me and said, "You better get back there and clamp down on your boy, Benham. He just studied the wine list and ordered a bottle of something I never heard of." When I got there, Benham seemed O.K. and he immediately assured me that he was.

It was only 8 o'clock but I decided to go back to the ship. It was only 150 yards away, directly across an empty field. And I decided to walk, despite the fact that it had been snowing pretty hard with nearly a foot of it already on the frozen ground. When I got up the next morning, everything was covered with a thick blanket of the white stuff.

When I went into the wardroom for breakfast, Sutherland had a big smile on his face. "You owe a big debt of thanks to McGlohon," he told me. "Of course, I do," I replied. "He's been my mentor for two years.." Hal said, "Not that. Last night he saved the life of your boy, Benham!"

He explained. "We didn't leave the Club until after midnight. Benham was drinking different stuff all evening, and he left about eleven o'clock. When we started home there must have been two or nearly three feet of snow on the ground. We could see the ship, and of course, we were pretty tanked up, so we started slogging through the drifts. McGlohon was out in front, when halfway there, he tripped and fell down in the snow." Hal laughed, then asked, "You know what he fell over? Your boy Benham! Passed out, and totally covered with snow! Would have frozen to death! You gotta put Mac up for a medal!"

THE MULEDRIVER'S REVENGE

You may remember, Mullen had promised, "I'll get you for this," and I was 100% sure that some day he would. This was one mean man. Almost everyone disliked him intensely and I felt my only hope was that somebody might kill him before he got around to doing something really bad to me. Joe Morosa was in Naval prison and Mundy and McGlohon could have been his cellmates if our good Captain McIntosh had not saved them.

Mullen was now the Captain and there was no McIntosh to save me. Navy and Merchant Marine regulations, probably created in the days of Captain Bligh and Mr. Christian, gave remarkable power to the Captains and Masters of seafaring vessels – probably because so many in their crews were bloodthirsty pirates and criminals.

I knew something bad was going to happen, I just didn't know when. I didn't worry on an everyday basis. I thought maybe the suspense was part of my punishment – waiting for the other shoe to drop. Or maybe it was just taking him awhile to think up something bad enough.

Then one night the Rapidan was standing down Long Island Sound and I had the deck, 8 o'clock 'til midnight. About 10:30, I'm aware that Mullen had come onto the Bridge, as he did quite often, to fire questions at the O.O.D., trying to find something to criticize. "Who's got the deck?" he snapped. "Lt. Zoller, sir!" "Course and speed?" "2 – 4 – 0, ten knots." He asked about the wind and the weather, the identity of the lighthouses we could see, the number of ships in sight and where they were. My answers were prompt and correct. Then he asked, "Who's the Junior Officer of the Watch?" "Ensign Moriarty, sir!" "Is he qualified for top watches?" "Yes, sir!" Then he said, "Turn it over to him and report to my cabin!"

This is it! I knew the time had come. Something unpleasant was going to happen, but I had no idea what it could be. I couldn't think of anything I had done wrong. He was sitting at his dining room table when I arrived. "Sit down," he said. I did – and wondered, "What horrors lay just ahead?"

What happened next was a surprising development. He looked at me – and I'll never forget this – he asked, "Do you like chicken sandwiches?" I nearly fell out of my chair. He rang for Bradley, the Captain's Steward, who appeared immediately. "Make us some nice chicken sandwiches, Bradley." I think he even asked me white meat or dark and if lettuce and mayo was O.K. And coffee, tea or Coke. (A well-known expression came to my mind: "the condemned ate a hearty meal.")

He leaned back and thought for a few seconds, then told me, "Being a Captain is a lonely job. Up here by myself. I really miss being in the Wardroom, especially at mealtimes, listening to all the small talk and the jokes and the arguments." He stared at the overhead for awhile and then said, "It's an awful lot of responsibility, being in command. It's 24-hours a day, seven days a week. You're never off-duty. I never knew how much you have to depend on your officers."

He looked at me and I think he actually smiled. "I remember when you – and that guy, Stewart – came aboard in Mobile. You were from Iowa and I don't think you had ever seen salt water before. I wondered what kind of guys are they sending us to run our ships."

Then he actually did smile. "But you surely learned fast. You turned into a damn good officer. Standing top watches at sea in just a few months. When I got to be a Commanding Officer I came to realize how much I depend on officers like you!"

I didn't say anything – but I did wonder if I was observing the early stages of Alzheimers disease. He continued to butter me up as we ate our sandwiches and then he sent for ice cream – with chocolate sauce! And I wouldn't believe this if I hadn't seen it, he left for a moment and came back with a small box full of insignia. "One of these days, you'll be a Lieutenant Commander," he said, "and you'll be able to use these." Then he gave me his shoulder boards and collar pins appropriate to that rank and said he'd be proud to have me wear them!

That was "Mullen's revenge". I'm sure there's a message in there somewhere. But I have no idea what it is.

A WONDERFUL BIRTHDAY PRESENT, ONE DAY EARLY!

April 20, 1943. It finally came! We were in Norfolk, Virginia, and *my orders arrived to tell me to prepare for a transfer!* There was no clue whatever to my next permanent assignment, but it didn't really matter: anything would be an improvement! I turned over all my responsibilities to Tom Moriarty, said my goodbyes (after 21 months on this ship) and departed on April 22. I went to the Fleet Air Base and tried to bum a ride to Washington. No luck, but I did run into Bill Green, the Newton and Hawkeye football hero who married Beth! So I caught a train, for the worst train ride of my life – I think they must have resurrected the passenger cars from Civil War mothballs: no A/C, stifling heat and not even an available seat! I sat on my suitcase from 7:20 p.m. until 3 a.m. when we arrived in Washington.

When it opened for business, I went to the Navy building and asked the Bureau of Personnel to transfer me from auxiliaries to the fighting Navy, and got nowhere. Caught another train to New York and rejoined my buddy Laura, late in the evening.

I still had no idea where my next duty would be, but as I thought about my two years on the Rapidan, I realized they were difficult but I survived and I learned a great deal in the process. I didn't know it at the time but after the war, I read about German submarine warfare in the Atlantic that killed tens of thousands of Navy and merchant seamen – like me!

And something else I never knew until long after it happened – *on its very first trip after I left it, the Rapidan was torpedoed in the Caribbean!* (But it didn't sink! The reason involved paravanes – "Rube Goldberg" devices so unwieldy and complicated that few ships ever used them, and I'm sure this was the first and only time the Rapidan ever did!)

BETTER DAYS AHEAD?

I was given a temporary assignment – until the Navy decided what to do with me: Anti-Submarine Warfare School on Staten Island. This lasted 19 days during which I discovered that, compared to sea duty, what an easy life the shore-duty boys had. Laura and I had a ball! We really "did the town". Saw a bunch of Broadway plays, hit a few of the fancy restaurants, visited Chinatown, the Bronx Zoo, museums, art galleries – and even joined 750,000 other people on 5th Avenue for the famous Easter Parade, after Mass at St. Patrick's Cathedral.

Meantime, the Big Wheels in Washington concluded that aircraft carriers were even more important than battleships if we were to win the critical sea war against Germany and Japan. And we had already lost several of our big Essex-class carriers, and it would take two or three years to build new ones. Henry Kaiser, a successful industrialist of those times, told the Navy he could build some "quick and dirty" small aircraft carriers a lot sooner, but they would be relatively slow and totally without armored protection. In short, they would be "expendable". The Brass decided they had no other choice, so they gave him the go-ahead to build fifty of them as rapidly as possible.

At first they were called Auxiliary Aircraft Carriers (ACVs) and since I was in the "auxiliary navy", I guess that's how I got assigned to the program. Kaiser had a shipyard near Portland, Oregon, on the Columbia River. As each ship was completed, it would be sailed down river to the Naval Station at Astoria, and turned over to the Navy who would then put on the finishing touches, load supplies and ammunition, bombs, torpedoes, etc. All this was to be handled by "pre-commissioning" officers and crews who would later man the ships and sail them off to war… assuming these rush-jobs could stay afloat.

Every third one of these ships, now called Escort Aircraft Carriers (CVEs), was to go to Britain's Royal Navy. Instead of being provisioned and commissioned by the crew that would serve on them, that job would be handled in Astoria by Ferry Crew No. 1 and Ferry Crew No. 2 – after which they would sail these ships out of the Columbia River and up to Victoria, B.C., and, in appropriate ceremonies with traditional British pomp and circumstance, turn them over to the Royal Navy.

On May 11 my orders arrived. I had been assigned to Ferry Crew No. 1 in Astoria. What a stroke of luck! *Shore duty!* Maybe some kind-hearted soul in the Bureau of Personnel figured more than two years at sea in the Atlantic had earned me an assignment that was easier and considerably less hazardous to health. At least for awhile. This was a 50-ship program and I felt sure by the time the last one was commissioned, the war might be over! So apparently I would survive after all.

We left New York later on the same day my new orders arrived. No small feat. You learn to move rapidly in wartime and Laura had adapted beautifully. She was never a problem. A very capable lady.

When we arrived in Chicago, my in-laws met us at the station. We grabbed a quick nap, and then Billy and Ann Jarvis, Pat, Vi and Alvina came over and we had a great Welcome Home party that lasted past midnight and on until 3:30 a.m. Then more tearful Niewinski goodbyes, another train ride to Waterloo to see my family and a couple side trips to Waverly to visit Aunt Gertrude and whatever friends were still there. (Jack Wright, Pete Cordt and others too old for war.)

May 18, at 2 a.m. we caught another train to Minneapolis, then switched to the Northern Pacific and headed west. It would be a couple of years before I ever got east of the West Coast again. Laura was a wonderful traveling companion and she made every moment I was with her a real joy. When we woke up on the morning of May 20, we were looking down on the Columbia River. As we passed Vancouver, we could see some of the Kaiser carriers being built.

I was beginning to get pretty excited about this new assignment. Astoria was a bit rainy, but it was lush and green with beautiful trees, and I had been pretty "treeless" for a long time. (None at all in Iceland, Greenland and the Atlantic Ocean, and even Casablanca was on the edge of the desert.) Delivering every third ship to the Royal Navy in Victoria, B.C., would be interesting and except for the few days I would be there, I'd be home every night! And the Pacific beaches were close aboard, for surf, sun and fun.

Alas! Almost before I got my sea-going posterior settled in my shore-duty swivel chair behind my shore-duty desk, the news came like a bombshell: *the Royal Navy took a closer look at Kaiser carriers and pronounced them "eminently sinkable". Thanks, but no thanks!* No valuable British seamen would be condemned to serve on a ship you could sink with small-arms fire! (Not in those exact words, of course, but you get the idea!)

The word spread rapidly and these fifty future (vulnerable) combat carriers were nicknamed "Kaiser Coffins". And the name stuck.

Because of the British decision, our Ferry Crew was disbanded. We'd all be ordered to new duties – aboard one of the Kaiser coffins! Officially, these 50 ships were the "Casablanca Class carriers" – named after the first of the fifty, the USS Casablanca. The Navy also numbers its ships, the first one of this class being CVE 55. (I have no idea why they didn't start with No. 1.) Officers and men assigned to the 55 were the lucky ones. It would never see combat, but remain based in Astoria as a training ship. The least fortunate were the crews of the 56 Liscome Bay, 57 Coral Sea, and 58 Corregidor – sent into combat ASAP to see if this class could be useful as operating carriers.

As soon as we arrived in Astoria for what we thought would be a couple of years of shore duty, Laura went up to Portland and got a license to work as a beauty operator, and a few days later she had a job. We had also decided life would be considerably better if we could somehow get an automobile – a project of real difficulty because none were being produced. (The auto companies were making military vehicles, tanks, bombs, airplanes, etc. for the war effort.) Harry O'Donnell, my sister's husband, worked for a finance company. On the outside chance they might repossess a decent car, I wrote Helen and offered to buy it and pay all expenses for Harry and my brother to drive it from Waterloo to Astoria and get a free vacation in the process. Surprisingly *they phoned and said they had a beautiful Lincoln convertible,* told me the price, and I said, "Let's do it."

By the time I found out my shore duty was a beautiful dream exploded by reality, my new car was halfway to Oregon. I didn't mind too much; I could probably sell it at a profit. My brother and Harry had a great trip through a part of America they had never seen. The car was quite spectacular – a cream-colored 4-door Lincoln convertible that you might expect to see Sinatra or Dean Martin driving down Hollywood Boulevard.

FATE STEPS IN AND DETERMINES THE NEXT TWO YEARS OF MY LIFE.

There were some pretty good guys in Ferry Crew No. 1 and until we all were ordered to new duties, we had some good times, mainly on the Pacific beaches near Seaside. Except for Ens. John Cronk, who ended up on the same ship I did, I never saw or heard of any of them afterward. I did get word that Wilbur Ulle had been assigned to Kaiser Coffin #60, but I forget its name, and I never ran across him until years after the war, at a Rapidan reunion.

Mostly, our crew just killed time in the Ferry Crew office, waiting for new orders. Couple days in a row, some red-haired Lt. Commander walked in, looked around for 10 minutes or so, and then left without a word to anyone. The third time he came in, he came to me, introduced himself and told me the Captain of the Corregidor would appreciate my coming to see him. So I did.

His name (the Captain's) was Roscoe L. Bowman. He was a good-size, nice-looking officer with a very pleasant smile. He waved me to a seat beside his desk, then told me they had been checking on my record and liked what they saw. "I have some good officers, but in some cases I'm not comfortable with their experience at sea. I'd like to have you come aboard as my Gunnery Officer and as my Senior Watch Officer."

I was surprised and, naturally, more than somewhat flattered. He told me he didn't need an immediate reply, but he'd like to know as soon as possible. I returned to my office and told my Ferry Crew shipmates what had happened. It was a major decision – possibly a life or death decision. The Corregidor, like any other Kaiser Coffin, could be extremely hazardous duty. (I kept thinking "expendable".) On the other hand, I had been invited by the man in command, and I knew this seldom happened. I found out his nickname was "Happy" Bowman. He had this wonderful smile, and I had observed a little sign on his desk that said, "Be Tolerant". It seemed to me this guy would be the ideal C.O.

What the hell! This wasn't a damn oil tanker. As an operational aircraft carrier, this was a combat ship! And the carrier war was where the action would be. Sounded like fun. Laura said O.K. So I said O.K.

The day after the day I accepted the offer, two things happened. First, I got orders from Washington to report for duty on a large troop transport, a converted passenger liner. I told Captain Bowman and he said, "No problem. I'll fix it." And he did.

Then some Warrant Officer I didn't know, came up to me in my office and said, "I heard you're going aboard the Corregidor." I said yes, I was. "Roscoe L. Bowman," he said, grinning, "is well known in the Navy – *Happy Bowman, the smiling son-of-a-bitch!*"

And he was.

Before the Corregidor was ready for sea, I made the most of my good life on the beach. The Ferry crew officers and wives became a close social group. Lots of parties, golf, picnics, and time at Seaside which was locally famous for its razor clams. (Laura became the champion clam-digger among us.) Unlike the East Coast beaches, you could drive cars on the Oregon sands and build driftwood fires. During workdays I spent a lot of time on the Casablanca, getting to know about Kaiser carriers and I even spent a day flying as a passenger in a torpedo bomber during the training exercises out over the ocean.

GUNNERY SCHOOL

One day, Capt. Bowman told me the several officers who would serve in my Gunnery Division were all attending Gunnery School in Seattle and asked if I wanted to join them. I suggested it might be better for me to attend the Gunnery School *in San Diego* – and somehow I slipped this one past him. My motivation, of course, was solely to see San Diego and get the opportunity to drive my new beautiful car all the way down the coastal highways in Oregon and California. I got away with it – despite the need for special orders to attend a facility in a different naval district, and get the gas coupons from the civilian Gas Rationing Board in Astoria.

The night before we left for San Diego, we had several friends in for drinks, and I was packing my white uniforms when one of them asked, "What in the world are you doing? They wear *blues* in San Diego!" That I did not know! I was going south, almost to Mexico – and it was late July! I didn't know about San Diego's perfect weather, year around.   (In life, you learn as you go.)

The trip and our time in San Diego was so good that it kind of made up for my rough times the previous two years. A couple of nights we just slept in the car. In San Francisco, we looked up my cousin, Sylvester Reith and had dinner and an evening with him. Passing through Salinas, I remembered that my Waverly buddy, Johnny Weires, lived there. We phoned and his wife said he was out driving his bread truck, making deliveries. An hour later we saw a bread truck, flagged it down, and it was Johnny! We hadn't seen each other for years. We parked on the shoulder and talked for an hour.

When we arrived in Los Angeles, I spent a few hours showing Laura the town. Driving down Hollywood Boulevard, we became aware of a lot of people staring at us. And we knew it was the car – they wondered if we were "anybody"!

Laura and I both fell in love with San Diego and neighboring La Jolla, and decided that's where we wanted to live after the war. At school, I met Lt. Robert McKenzie Ball. We became friends and he and his dates spent every evening with us until we left for our trip back.

August 11 to 25, Laura's mother came to San Diego and we had a good time, doing everything from the local beaches and restaurants to the bullfights in Tijuana. August 23 was Laura's birthday – the third I've now spent with her – and we made it an extra special day.

When we entered the packed stadium to see the bullfights – and cheer for the bulls to win – a loud voice shouted, "Bob Zoller, Bob Zoller!" It was Mary Ellen Stoeber from Chicago, who used to spend summers with relatives in Waverly – and occasionally go out smooching with me. She had married a naval officer, now stationed in San Diego. Later, we got together for dinner at famous Café La Maze outside of town – where great steaks were always available despite the meat rationing rules.

On the way back to Astoria, we finally located Aunt Rose in L.A. – she worked for the federal government in San Diego but was on temporary assignment – had dinner with her. (What a great old gal!)

BACK TO WORK, BACK TO SEA

On September 15, I reported aboard the Corregidor in Astoria, and the hard work began – getting ready for sea. Laura kept busy, too, winding up our affairs. Although she hadn't yet learned to drive, it was decided that four of the wives (three who drove) would take the car to our new home base, San Diego. On the 23rd we sailed out the mouth of the Columbia River and I never saw Astoria again.

Tom Talbot, the Communications Officer, and I were the most junior of all the ship's Department Heads, but we enjoyed certain perks. We were assigned as roommates in the "high rent district" – the deck just below the flight deck in an area shared by the Captain, the Exec, the Air Officer, the Navigator and the Squadron Commander (who was not yet on board). One major problem: our stateroom was directly below the catapult, and when a plane was revving up its engines, full power, prior to blast off, the noise and vibration would drive you crazy!

Tom was a Yankee, rich kid, Harvard, and a member of the Harvard racing crew. His folks owned the Boston and Maine railroad. As a friend of one of the Roosevelt boys, he had spent nights in the White House. But he was a good guy and a good, experienced officer. Before we left Astoria, the Captain called us to his cabin and told us how he planned to command his ship. "In the peacetime Navy you go by rank," he told us. "On this ship I plan to be a bit unorthodox: we'll go by what's best to get the job done. I've got several line officers senior to you two but none with your experience at sea. So I plan to spend 16 hours a day on the bridge – 0600 until 2200. That leaves eight hours (10 p.m. to 6 a.m.) which you two will split. We'll have regular Officers of the Deck but one of you will be there as an "assistant Captain" – to take over in any emergency. There's nothing like that in Navy Regs, but that's what we're going to do. We'll call you 'Duty Commanders'."

And that's what we did. Tom and I worked out our own schedules, four hours a night, every night at sea. We would sit in the Captain's chair and keep an eye on the OOD. Sometimes that would be a Lt. Commander and when that happened it made me feel like a big shot.

Our first stop was Puget Sound – Seattle – to load bombs and torpedoes and ammunition for the planes and the ship's guns. While there, I was able to locate Eddie and Ruth Harden and spent a full evening with them. I felt sorry for Eddie – as an athlete he was a real take-charge guy. As a patriot who couldn't pass the physical to serve his country like most of his Waverly buddies, he seemed embarrassed, beat down. Not the Eddie Harden I used to know.

Our squadron came aboard – a "composite" group – fighter planes, dive bombers, torpedo bombers and we spent a couple of weeks on a "shake-down cruise" in the San Diego area – practice gunfire, take-offs and landing planes – and all the other stuff that new ships do to make sure they are fully ready for the missions assigned. It's a hectic time and I don't think any civilian jobs compare in hours or effort to the demands on our military in time of war.

A lot of scary things happened to me in WW2, some because it seemed my demise might be imminent, and a few because they seemed to threaten my "career". One of the latter situations occurred on my very first night as Duty Commander, after we left Puget Sound. We were standing down the Oregon Coast, maybe 50 miles off shore, traveling alone, no escort, and totally blacked out, of course. It was just before midnight, there was a thick fog and you couldn't see anything! We were proceeding at about 18 knots and totally relying on radar. All of a sudden there was a flash of bright lights, almost like lightning except they didn't go off! *We were speeding right through a cluster of a dozen or more fishing boats, all lit up like Christmas trees, and too late to slow, stop or turn!* Before anyone on the bridge could react, it was all over – by some miracle we hadn't hit any of them, or get tangled in any nets (which I thought was a probability) and it was dark again, with zero visibility.

The radar had failed to give us any warning whatever, and I have no idea why. I never, ever again, saw any radar that didn't work at all. This was a major mystery and a once-in-a-lifetime experience! Again, I was unbelievably lucky. For sure, Bowman would have had me court-martialed.

We stopped in San Francisco to load something, but I don't remember what it was. Then to San Diego, our designated home base. Laura and her traveling companions had arrived safely. It was great being with Laura again, but I wasn't able to see her much, as our ship spent most of the time at sea, practicing and training prior to joining the fleet. In peacetime, this "getting ready" may take several months. We were ordered to do it in one week! We were more than somewhat disturbed by this seemingly impossible deadline but we tried to look on the bright side: *obviously the Navy was waiting for us to join the fleet* before proceeding with the war against Japan. (At least, that's what we liked to believe.)

Our squadron had come aboard in San Diego – fighter planes, dive-bombers, torpedo bombers. We practiced flyaways, catapults and carrier landings under various conditions. We fired the guns at surface and aircraft targets and practiced starshell illumination; held fire drills, boat drills, and abandon ship drills; simulated "man overboard" and steering casualties. No possible casualty was overlooked, and every contingency provided for. It kept us busy, night and day.

SOME OF MY NEW SHIPMATES: THE SURVIVORS

We had the makings of a very good crew. While many had never been to sea, we had a few really experienced petty officers, and I already had great pride in all the "90-day wonders", the college guys who became competent officers in remarkably short time. I knew many of them, and after all, I was one of them.

Two of my enlisted men had already survived two naval disasters each. Probst was on the Arizona, sunk at Pearl Harbor and Tonnisen went down with West Virginia, same time, same place (and obviously came up again). Both wound up on the Lexington, and swam away from her five months later in the Coral Sea.

Joe Quinn, boatswain's mate, was on the Pollux (along with my Waterloo buddy Jack Althouse) when it was shipwrecked on the rocky coast of Newfoundland. He was one of the twenty-some who swam ashore in frigid waters and made it, while more than ninety were frozen, drowned or pounded to death against the rocks in similar attempts! (Althouse made it, too.) Nearly frozen, Quinn, spent fifteen days in a hospital bed and when released, immediately requested duty in the south Pacific. "If they leave me in this warm climate," he told me, "I expect to be thawed out by 1952."

Arthur Elliot, who later became my Chief Gunners Mate, left the States in April 1940 and didn't get back until 1943, just in time for more sea duty on our ship. In five years, he hadn't had a single day's leave! His ship, the West Virginia, died at Pearl on 12/7, and then, as a master diver, he spent a lot of time underwater, burning open sealed compartments and bringing the waterlogged bodies of dead seamen to the surface. He was also the petty officer in charge of the firing squad that fired salutes at the military burials of 141 shipmates!

Ray Oddone, an officer in my Division who had served as an enlisted man for several years, told me about a friend of his on the Anderson, one of the hardworking, battled-scarred destroyers that saw a lot of action in the early war against Japan. Illustrious though it was, the Anderson's record was such that it was hardly comforting to the big aircraft carriers she was assigned to protect. The Anderson was with the Lexington when she went down in the Coral Sea – and with the Yorktown, sunk at Midway – and with the Wasp when it died at "Torpedo Junction". One day Oddone's friend told him, "The Anderson has been assigned to accompany your ship. So I'll expect to be fishing you out of the sea in the near future."

And he was right. As the exhausted and oil-soaked Oddone was hauled out of the water when the Hornet went down in the Battle of Santa Cruz, his friend was there to help him up over the side. "Hi, Ray," was all he said. "You all right?"

The toughest part of my short time in San Diego was saying goodbye to Laura. I had been increasingly aware that she was the perfect wife for a guy like me in the difficult years of wartime. I never had any doubts about my choice of a lifetime partner, but still she proved an extremely happy surprise. Already she had sold the car and had gotten herself a job – to start when I left town.

October 25 was our last night together. I had to stay on board but she came to the ship at 1630 and we had dinner in the wardroom and then just sat in my stateroom, being together for our last time in a long time. We never talked about it, but I was wondering if I would ever come back, and I knew she was thinking the same thing.

Visitors had to leave at 0200. We walked out onto the dock and I put her on the ferry to San Diego, and watched it sail quietly into the night.

ALOHA! As soon as I could get ashore in Pearl Harbor, I grabbed a bus for downtown Honolulu. I wanted to see the city and then head for Waikiki, rent a surfboard and see if I could do that fun thing on the big waves I'd seen in movies over a lot of years. As the bus drove through the streets downtown, I saw soldiers, sailors and marines lined up, four abreast, on a city street, for a distance of more than a hundred yards. "Wow!" I said. "That must be some movie!" An officer across from me laughed. "Not a movie," he told me. "*It's a whorehouse!*" (Equally surprising, it was about eleven o'clock in the morning!)

You won't believe this, but somebody wrote a novel based on this, called "The Revolt of Mamie Stover," and then Hollywood made it into a movie. But to show you how different things were in those days, Hollywood had the guys all lining up to *dance* with Mamie and the other girls!

Later that day at Waikiki, I came off again as pretty much a HAOLE – a Johnny-come-Lately. Catching a big wave and staying upright on a surfboard isn't as easy as it looks.

KAISER COFFINS: OUR ROLE IN A MAJOR INVASION

We didn't have to wait long for an assignment to an active role in the Pacific War. Joining up with the Liscome Bay and the Coral Sea, we formed a CVE Task Group as part of a major battle force. We even had our own Admiral! (He was based on the Liscome Bay.) And we were told we would soon get underway to challenge the Japanese fleet and support the invasion of a major enemy stronghold, which we guessed would be either the Marshall or Gilbert Islands. Ever since Pearl Harbor, our country had been on defense in the

Pacific. This would be our first offensive strike, and it was exciting to be part of it.

We were to sortie at 0700 on November 10. On the previous Sunday, I attended Mass on the Liscome Bay, where the priest gave all of us a general absolution – in case we didn't make it back. The day before we left, several of us visited the Submarine Base, went out on a sub during training exercises, then to the Officers Club where I drank somewhat more than usual. By 10 p.m., I had a throbbing headache and all I wanted to do was return to the ship and hit the sack.

Unfortunately, as I went aboard at 11 p.m., the Officer of the Deck told me, "The Captain said he wanted to see you the minute you return to the ship." (Wow! I had no idea why and all I knew was that this didn't sound good.) I went to his cabin and he said, "Big problem. We just got ordered to unload all armor-piercing bombs and replace them with 500-lb. general-purpose bombs. The exec is lining up working parties and we'll start unloading immediately. You've got to get to the Ammunition Depot and get the GP's heading this way. There's a car waiting. You'll have to hurry. There's not much time!"

Big job, little time. Tons to move up the elevators and unload, tons to bring aboard and send down into the magazines. Handling highly explosive materials is a bit touchy, you have to be careful. A job this size is an "All Hands Evolution" – every officer and man on the ship would have a part of the job. And we'd all be fighting the clock.

When I arrived at the Ammunition Depot, it was pretty much secured for the night. I got past the sentries and found that the officer on watch was a full Commander, two ranks higher than me. I told him what I wanted and he laughed in my face. "You crazy? It's nearly midnight," he said. "Maybe tomorrow. Where would I get all the trucks, all the working parties?"

"*Your problem*," I said. "I have my orders." I could see he wasn't about to budge. But two years in the Navy had taught me how to handle these situations. I reached over his desk and picked up the telephone. "I'll have to wake up your Commanding Officer – his number, please – I believe it was Admiral Nimitz who ordered this change of ordnance."

I lied about Nimitz, but it worked. He backed off. "We'll have to go like hell to make the deadline," I told him. It was a huge job – several hundred men and a couple dozen trucks, and all night long. We just made it. *The last truckload and I got aboard at 0700 just as the crew was casting off the last mooring lines!*

The three "Kaiser Coffin" carriers made up Task Group 52.3 under the command of Rear Admiral Henry Mullennix, aboard the Liscome Bay. His

Chief of Staff was Captain John Crommelin, who doubled in brass as the Division's Staff Gunnery Officer. Crommelin was an impressive man, one of six brothers from Alabama, all naval officers. He wasn't a likeable man, but the kind of guy you wanted on your side when the battles began. Before we left Pearl for the wars in the west, Crommelin assembled the Gunnery Officers from our three ships, to find out whether or not we knew our jobs. I was the lowest in rank. The other two were a Lt. Commander and a full Commander.

Crommelin fired tough questions at us for 20 minutes. Then he pointed at me and said, "You know your job. You others don't!" I'm not sure why, but I think it was because I stressed training my crews in sector responsibility (to make sure no attacking aircraft ever came in unopposed) and in technique for actually hitting fast moving targets.

Later, our carriers went to sea three times for gunnery practice and we got lucky: a shore-based plane would tow a target sleeve past the other two ships that would shoot at it, and then when it got into our range, *we'd shoot it down!* I expected Bowman to encourage (praise) our guys and he never did. When I did, he got sarcastic and said, "I thought it was pretty lousy!" Typical Bowman. I didn't dare tell him that Crommelin said I knew the job and the two senior guys didn't.

In port, after our crews kept shooting down the targets, one of the other ship's Gunnery Officers came up to me and asked if we had some new fire control director or "technical-whatever" that made our crews so accurate!

MEET MY OFFICERS AND SOME OTHERS

As we headed west out of Pearl, I began to get better acquainted with my Division officers. Lt. Elmer Fiorini, from the Boston area, was the most senior of the group and had sea duty experience – a very competent officer. John Cronk, my Ferry Command buddy, made Lt. (j.g.) and was next in line. The ensigns, all on their first sea duty, were Ripley, Jay, Cominos, Andrukitas, Smith, Flanagan, Rutherford and Prukop. A bit later, Bud Cox, a former football player from Ohio State, came aboard as "Athletic Officer" and was assigned to my Gunnery Division. His job was to help us stay in the best physical shape possible, but I don't remember ever having much time for jumping jacks and push-ups. We did have a basketball court on the hangar deck that we used quite a bit when the planes were parked somewhere else. (I shot baskets and played the game whenever I could.)

I was impressed with Prukop, Flanagan and Rutherford. Prukop was a handsome Polish young man from New Jersey who graduated from Middlebury College in Vermont, which he attended on a football scholarship. Married his college sweetheart, a beautiful English girl whose parents ran a missionary school on the island of Maui. John was bright, self-assured and positive, and I knew he would do well at anything and everything.

Flanagan was also a fine looking man – a New Englander, who had started studying to become a Catholic priest. He had the look of a scholar, perhaps a poet. Quiet, smart, capable and admirable in many ways.

Rutherford came aboard as a Bomb Disposal officer. Unlike the other two, "Scoop" looked like a young Abraham Lincoln, totally beaten-up by life. From a poor family. Worked his way through Oregon State U., became a forest ranger. When I got to know him, I discovered one of the most intelligent men I ever knew. (As I write this in 2006, Scoop is close to death in Oregon. We've been friends ever since 1943. More on him later.

Fiorini, from the Boston area, was experienced and competent; Cronk was all-around O.K. Jay was a short, quiet guy I didn't pay much attention to, until one day I realized he did well at almost everything. George Cominos – Greek, obviously – was a journalist from St. Louis – balding, bright. Great sense of humor. He kept all of us laughing. Smith was unobtrusive. Never stood out – he was just there.

Andrukitas was something else. (I'm not sure what.) At our first Gunnery Division officers muster in Pearl, he arrived with a black eye and a beat-up face. In a lame attempt at humor, I said, "I hope the other guy looks even worse!" Everyone laughed – except Andrukitis. He got mad – at all of us! And he stayed angry. Never became one of us. I could see I had a problem. I found out his father had become a wealthy owner of a beer distributor business. So Andy lived like a rich kid, attended a rich kid's school (I forgot which) where he became an all-American (or All-East?) lacrosse player. But apparently he was never accepted by the other rich kids – possibly due to his ethnic background or his family lacking blue blood, or both. After we returned to Pearl from our first great adventure, Andy got into a fight in downtown Honolulu, resisted arrest by the Military Police, ended up on top of a three-story building, threatening to jump. Of course, that terminated his duty on the Corregidor.

I also had two Chief Warrant Officers and was grateful for their long experience. Joe Proctor, for years a Chief Gunners Mate, really looked the part. Talked loud, out of the side of his mouth, with a Boston accent. In front of the ensigns, I asked him to help educate them and he used this to lord over them like he was the Admiral commanding our Carrier Division. It was obvious that he resented these green college guys outranking him. But they all listened and learned and I was proud of the way they treated Proctor.

Ray Oddone, an Italian from Milwaukee, was younger than Joe and totally different. Just easy-going and competent. Had spent most of his Navy

time as a Chief Boatswain's Mate. I assigned him as Battery Officer of the 5"
38 cal. big gun on the stern of our ship. (We also had eight director-controlled
Bofors twin 40 mm and twenty 20 mm Oerlekins.)

When our squadron (pilots) were on board, which was most of the
time, we had close to 100 officers on the Corregidor. I'll mention only a few.
Regular Navy (Annapolis) were Bowman; Lex Black, the Exec.; Marcus
Williamson, Air Officer; and Russ Wilkinson, Navigator. I didn't care much
for the Exec, nor he for me. His ambition was to gain a rank and get command
of a carrier. But Bowman trusted me and Tom Talbot to be Duty Commanders
at sea, not Lex, and he needed the experience to achieve his career goal. I
know he resented this – we were two-stripers and he was a full Commander.
Williamson, the Air Officer, and I had the two largest divisions on the ship and
often disagreed on how our enlisted personnel were assigned and treated. Clifford, the Squadron Commander, was a good guy, later became Air Officer and
still later, Exec. We got to be very good friends and several times he invited
me to join him when he had to fly to keep getting his flight pay.

Wilkinson was the oldest officer on board. Graduated from the Naval
Academy in 1923, the year of the great Naval Disarmament Conference. The
major naval powers agreed to cut back the size of their navies, so that class of
Annapolis graduates was encouraged to forego military careers and return to
civilian life. Russ went home to Memphis and became a successful realtor.
When the war came along years later, he was recalled to teach navigation, and
later sent to our ship as the navigator. Russ was a Southern Gentleman type.
We became good friends.

WE ATTACK, THE JAPS RESPOND. MAJOR CASUALTIES RESULT

As our Task Force assembled outside of Pearl Harbor and headed west,
I was impressed by its size and power. Our target was Makin Island in the
Gilberts. The mission: to take it over. It was a major Japanese base, so we
knew a major battle would take place. Lives would be lost, many I feared, on
both sides. We hoped they would be mostly Japanese.

On our way to and back from the target, we crossed the equator six
times and the International Dateline twice. Going west, Thursday immediately
became Friday. But we got our lost day back when we returned to Pearl. It was
suggested that all on board prepare an "abandon ship kit" and a letter "To Be
Opened in Case…" On Nov. 17, we were less than 700 miles from Makin and
within range of enemy air attacks, in case they would call for reinforcements

from Japanese bases farther west.

November 20 was D-Day. Fortunately, the Jap fleet failed to show up. Reveille at 0245. Soon after, our battlewagons shelled the beach and Task Force aircraft (including ours) bombed and strafed. We were close aboard when the battleships were firing and it was an impressive sight. When they let go a salvo, we could see these huge ships blown backwards from the concussion. We heard a turret on the Mississippi had a powder fire – 31 casualties! Our troops went ashore, established a beachhead and reported "The going is tough." We received word it was even worse at Tarawa where Jap planes attacked and the fast aircraft carrier, Independence, was torpedoed, but didn't sink.

The next day, two of our Corregidor pilots were shot down by enemy fire, Bermingham and Jones – but two crewmen on one of the torpedo planes were rescued. We buried Bermingham at sea at 1830. We never found Jones.

THE SAD STORY OF BRIAN FLANAGAN

Two days after that, Nov. 23, (a day I'll never forget) one of our planes had its tail hook pull out when landing. It sailed into the cable barrier, then whipped around, off the flight deck, into the gun gallery where the whirling propeller hit my battery officer, Brian Flanagan, and one of my gunners, a sailor named Trainor. I ran to the scene as they were hoisting the plane, knelt down by Flanagan and saw he was horribly wounded. I leaned closer as he tried to talk, and then I heard him say, "I'll never see home again." Padre Hoffman administered the Last Rites of our church on the spot. *Flanagan died a little later and I'll never, ever forget it!*

We buried him at sea in the early evening. I was so affected by the loss and the scene as the crew assembled on the fantail of our ship, that I wrote about it shortly thereafter. It occurred to me then, and frequently ever since, that so many good people like Flanagan die – by the millions throughout history – that war is an unbelievably stupid method of solving problems. And it *must* be avoided whenever possible.

My war, I'm sure, was a just war – for the United States and our allies. The "bad guys" had become extremely powerful and made clear their intentions to take over and change the world. We were attacked. We had to respond. But in too many cases, "fools rush in" – and war becomes an unnecessary choice. As I write this, more than 3000 young Americans have died in Iraq and surely many more will, before this totally unnecessary war is over. And that's only a part of the story. Maybe ten times that number were gravely wounded. We went (we were told) to *help* the Iraqi people: *many thousands* of them have been killed! And it's still going on!

With so many countries now having, or getting close to having, nuclear weapons… Think about it! Whatever became of common sense? Yes, I'm anti-war. "Blessed are the peacemakers…"

I have no idea how many died in the battles of Makin and Tarawa. I know Tarawa was considered one of the bloodiest invasions of the Pacific War. I suspect that *thousands* died – Makin, Tarawa, Japanese, Americans. Most were unknown to me – all but Flanagan, Jones and Bermingham. Trainor, my gunner, was badly hurt but he survived – after many painful months in a naval hospital. Doc said he would lose one of his legs.

ONE OF THE WORST DISASTERS IN OUR NAVY'S HISTORY!

The next day was even worse. Thanksgiving eve, along with the other two carriers of our division, we were steaming off Makin Island with two battleships, a cruiser and seven destroyers. In war zones, all Navy ships go to General Quarters (battle stations) an hour before sunrise. I woke up, looked at my watch, decided it was time to go. *At that moment there was a huge explosion!* The ship shook violently and I was certain we had been torpedoed! I ran up to the flight deck, on my way to Gunnery Control on the bridge. It was still dark and I saw two tremendous fires – and then I realized we had not been torpedoed, but apparently two other ships had been!

As soon as I arrived on the bridge, two of the lookouts told me, with great excitement, "Mr. Zoller, we saw the torpedo! We saw the wake! It was aimed at us! It just missed, astern!"

"Are you sure?" I said. "You're goddam right!" one of them answered. "We both saw it!"

As I learned what happened then and later by reading the investigative reports, I discovered that only the Liscome Bay had been hit – what I saw burning was two pieces of the same ship! That "Kaiser Coffins" and "expendable" were appropriate terms. That I had witnessed (and come close to being a part of) the greatest single-ship loss of life in our Navy's history! (Until the big carrier Franklin and the cruiser Indianapolis near and at the war's end.)

In 26 minutes, 646 of the Liscome Bay's officers and men were dead!

Putting together my vivid memory of those moments with official reports released later, I know for sure our lookouts were right. The torpedo had been intended for the Corregidor and I am mighty lucky to be alive. This diagram proves the point. It agrees with what our lookouts told me and exactly with what I saw. Liscome Bay survivors also reported seeing the wake as shown above, and this is where the torpedo hit, and where I saw the Liscome Bay in flames.

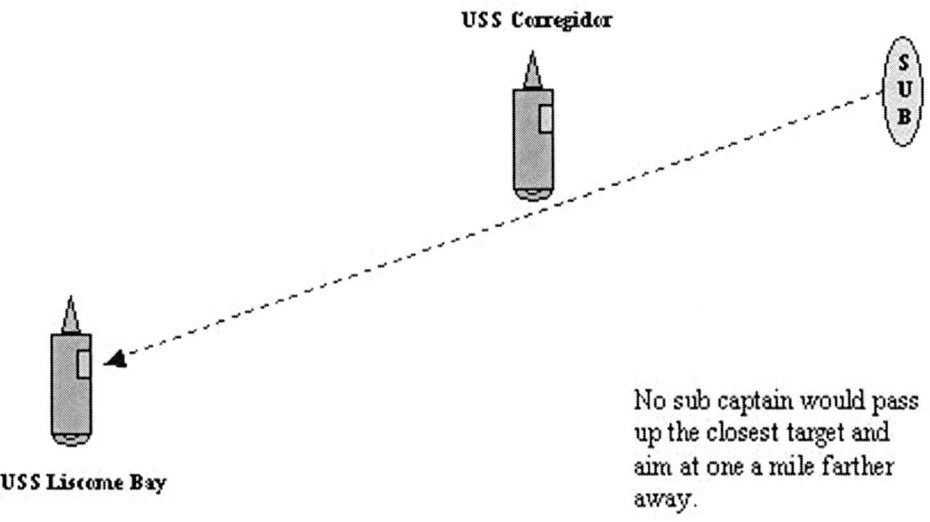

The rest of our task group was over here.

USS Corregidor

S
U
B

USS Liscome Bay

No sub captain would pass up the closest target and aim at one a mile farther away.

One thing I wondered about: where was the destroyer usually abeam of us, on our starboard side? Why didn't it detect the enemy submarine? Later I found out.

Two of our destroyers normally patrolled in that area, but the USS Hull was detached and sent to Makin; then 35 minutes before the torpedoes were fired, the USS Franks reported seeing a dim light in the distance and was sent to investigate. With both DD's gone, Rear Admiral Robert Griffin ordered the remaining destroyers to reorient toward the gap left by the two escorts, but they didn't get there in time to discover the sub and save the Liscome Bay.

Many years later William T. Y'Blood researched the role played by CVEs in the war against Japan and called his book THE LITTLE GIANTS. In his account of this event, he wrote:

"A huge column of bright orange flame, flecked with white-hot pieces of metal, shot a thousand feet into the air. Immediately following, another explosion, hurling fragments of the ship and clearly discernable planes 200 feet in the air. Debris from the Liscome Bay rained down on the other ships. Fifteen hundred yards away, the New Mexico was showered from the forecastle to quarterdeck with particles of oil, fragments of decking up to three feet long (some still burning) molten drops of metal, bits of clothing, *and pieces of human flesh!* Even the Maury, three miles distant, was splattered by pieces of the carrier."

Admiral Mullennix and Irving Wiltsie, Captain of the Liscome Bay, died. William T'Blood produced a lengthy account of this disaster and concludes with these words:

> "Many survivors were badly injured…shattered limbs, frightful burns. The men on the Morris, who had rescued survivors from the Lexington, Yorktown, and Hornet, felt unanimously that the condition of these survivors constituted the most heart-rending disaster yet seen. And that it was a miracle that anyone managed to escape such a roaring inferno."

> "Silently watching the hideous death of the Liscome Bay and the abrupt snuffing-out of the lives of many men they had known, were the crews of the Corregidor and Coral Sea. Suddenly and forcibly, the horrors of war had been brought to their attention, and they thought about their own ships, sisters to the Liscome Bay. If the Liscome Bay could blow up like that… They remembered with dread the mocking words that other sailors had hurled at them – *'CVE means combustible, vulnerable, expendable!'*"

The next day we learned that five pilots from the Liscome Bay on air patrol got lost the day before the torpedo hit their ship. They wandered around until after dark then stumbled onto the Lexington 50 miles away and landed successfully in the night! And thereby missed out on a great chance to die for their country!

We also heard the Lex shot down 31 Jap planes in two days, only 50 miles from us.

JAP TORPEDO PLANES – NIGHT ATTACK

Thanksgiving night we went to General Quarters and spotted a Jap "Betty", a torpedo plane on the horizon, low over the water. Betty must have gotten on the party line because it didn't take long before she had a lot of company. While it was still light enough to see, we could tell they were surrounding us. Nothing happened until it got dark and we couldn't see them at all. We started to zigzag and they dropped float lights that bobbed around us like lighted buoys that mark the entrance to a harbor.

Then they began to drop high-intensity magnesium flares on parachutes – lots of them. They turned nighttime into daylight and seemed to burn forever. Our radar told us they were coming in on us but we couldn't see them, so I ordered my crews to hold their fire. A few ships, particularly our screening destroyers, cut loose with heavy AA, but I figured that was a waste of good ammunition, and besides it would give away our position.

We stood by our guns, watching, waiting, sweating and praying. Exactly what happened that night I'll never know. The whole Task Group maneuvered to avoid the torpedoes we couldn't see, but felt sure were coming. But none of our ships were hit. The enemy planes withdrew shortly before midnight. We'd played this game for nearly three hours and I was deadly tired. It had been another 20-hour day and I had to go back on the Duty Commander watch at 0230.

I didn't mind, actually. It was Thanksgiving Day, and I had a lot of reasons to be thankful.

Somebody with super-high authority may have taken pity on us: they ordered us back to Pearl. Maybe just to catch our breath and reload for the next invasion, which we knew was coming. Our recent fun-and-games in the Gilberts had been successful: we now occupied Makin and Tarawa, and important territory far west of Pearl was in our control.

Two other things happened on our way back. First, we heard that LCDR Eddie O'Hare, one of the early war's outstanding heroes, had lost his life in a volunteer night fighter attempt to stop the Jap Betty's, just a few miles away from us. Next, our Captain announced that we ought to square ourselves with King Neptune for crossing his line – the equator – without properly observing the occasion en route to our recent invasion.

So the shellbacks made sure the lowly pollywogs were properly initiated into the Solemn Mysteries of the Ancient Order of the Deep. On civilian cruises, this is a somewhat genteel, fun thing, followed by cocktails. In the Navy, it involves a ridiculous degree of gross unpleasantness and considerable pain. I ran a full-length-of-the-flight-deck gauntlet, swatted by a hundred or more leather belts (the only restriction being "Not with the buckle end"; dunked (totally) into a tank of noxious, foul-smelling gunk; was made to kiss the Royal Baby's posterior (fattest sailor on board, in diapers smeared with some concoction – heavy on the mustard – that looked and smelled like "the real thing" (only worse!). And John Cronk, one my own officers, teed off on me with a semi-lethal paddle, several times, in such manner that I was happy to *stand* watches the next few days – because I couldn't sit down.

Before we arrived in Pearl Harbor on December 6, we heard the enemy had sunk the two great battleships of the Royal Navy – the Prince of Wales and the Repulse – in the far western Pacific. *I noticed the combined loss of life was less than that of our sister ship, the Liscome Bay!*

Every time we went in or out of Pearl Harbor, someone sent an airplane towing a sleeve for our anti-aircraft target practice. And almost every time it was my gun crews that shot it down. And never once did "The Smiling Son of a Bitch" say anything nice to me or to our gun crews as a result. You wonder what makes some people tick. However, I forgot to mention that before we left on our Gilbert Islands adventure, every line officer was required to take an Officer of the Deck exam. To my surprise, the Captain did tell me, on our way back, that my score of 3.9 out of a possible 4.0 was the best on our ship. (*No surprise that I did, big surprise that he did!*)

SOME GOOD NEWS, SOME BAD NEWS

The good news, we were ordered back to San Diego. The bad news, Laura wasn't there. She had no way of knowing when we'd get back (or *if* we would) so she decided to go back to Chicago for Christmas with her family. I really missed her, but I knew it was the thing for her to do.

We talked on the phone and she said she'd leave for San Diego immediately and stay there for ten years if necessary. It was my sincerest hope that that would not be necessary. I told her "Don't come," as we might leave before she could get there. We did leave abruptly – I'm not sure why our trip back from Pearl even happened. Another Christmas at sea. I didn't even get to the Christmas Party: during the day, Bowman was sick and he asked me to take over for him on the bridge.

During our stay in the States I received some late intelligence on the tactics used by Japanese aircraft attacking U.S. ships. So I decided to assemble my gun crews for a briefing session, as soon as we left the harbor and were well out to sea. We met on the fantail where I spoke for sometime. When I finished, I heard someone behind me say, "That was an excellent presentation, Mr. Zoller." I turned to see who it was. It was one of our 400 Marine Corps passengers – Jack Marion, one of my assistant lifeguards in Newton, five years before!

It was a great reunion. Jack was a PFC. He told me he had been a Corporal, but had been in a fight and was demoted. During the trip I had him come to my cabin as often as possible, to talk over old times. He told me the other lifeguard, Jack Nichols, became a pilot but was killed early in the war.

And that Peanut Niebur, a marine, was at Tarawa. (62 years later – just last year – I heard that Marion and Niebur also died in combat. All three of my assistant guards in the summer of '38 had volunteered to fight for their country, and all had given their lives.

In San Diego I ran into Hal Sutherland, now the navigator of the USS Elmore, and can't remember what kind of ship it was. We were able to spend time together and he gave me all the late-breaking news about Sam (now LCDR and exec of the Sapelo), Mundy (C.O. of an LST), Cherry, Mullen, et al.

When we got to Pearl, it was like Old Home Week – I was able to spend time with Bill Green (Beth's husband and now Asst. Landing Signal Officer on a CVE); Fred Joyce, Waterloo – my roommate at Tower Hall, a fly-boy on the Yorktown; good friends, Paul McGlohon and Ed Kepler – both now on Capt. McIntosh's fast tanker, Chikaskia, as Chief Engineer and Cargo Officer, respectively.

NEW YEAR'S EVE 1943. I spent the day window-shopping in Honolulu, hanging out at the Royal Hawaiian hotel, swimming at Waikiki, and having dinner at P.Y.Chong's – all with various shipmates. Then, CDR Gray (who I don't remember at all) took us to his home, up on a mountain, a picturesque abode, in a lush tropical setting. And that's where I spent the last moments of an interesting and eventful 1943.

THE MARSHALL ISLANDS CAMPAIGN

Our main objective this time was Kwajelein Atoll, in the heart of the Marshalls, protected on all sides by powerful island airbases – Wotje, Mille, Jaluit and Maloelap. This was also a major submarine base. It wouldn't be easy. *On the positive side, we were now part of the most powerful invasion fleet in the history of mankind!*

Admiral Kelly Turner (his flag aboard the battleship Pennsylvania) was in command. I later heard our Task Force consisted of 1600 aircraft, 16 battleships and 20 aircraft carriers. Of course, there were cruisers, troop ships, supply ships, ammunition ships, oil tankers, hospital ships, and a huge number of landing craft of all types. I have no idea how many destroyers, but a lot. I didn't write it down, but I seem to remember a total of 300 ships were involved. (On D-day +2, the world press reported, "World's greatest naval armada attacks Marshalls – 136 Jap planes destroyed.")

Before the actual invasion we were, of course, discovered by the Japanese air patrols. And they sent their torpedo planes to stop us. I remember every detail of that night attack on our fleet with great clarity, because the enemy picked a time too dark for us to see aircraft, but they could dimly make out large hulls of our big ships; they tried to come in on us from abeam, to get the biggest targets for their torpedoes; and Kelly Turner (with radar) knew when they were nearing launching ranges and (with voice radio) ordered all ships to turn at the same time, directly toward or away, to present the smallest targets possible. So the aircraft would pull away, change course, and try to come from a better direction.

The Admiral used the "Shackle Code" to order which way to turn and how far to turn. Decoded, most orders were "TURN NINE" or "NINE TURN" meaning Turn Right 90 degrees or Turn Left 90 degrees – or whatever was necessary to present the smallest target. It was a pretty hairy experience for the tens of thousands of us aboard our ships.

Russ Wilkinson and I were on the bridge with Captain Bowman. We could hear the radio signals and his orders to the helm. When he ordered, "Come left to course (whatever it was)", I grabbed the Navigator's arm and said, "He's turning the wrong way!" Russ calmly answered, "Let the son of a bitch hang himself." We did. And he did.

There was, of course, a huge chance of collision. I had more than a hundred men at their guns, fore and aft and down both sides. Immediately, I warned all battery officers of the situation and told them to have their crews watch for other ships and report any one getting close. Within ten seconds, I would guess, the radio proclaimed, for all ships to hear, "Zanzibar, Zanzibar. Where the hell do you think you're going?" (Zanzibar was our code name.) The Admiral watching his radarscope had seen one ship turning the wrong way. Bowman then realized his mistake, got us back in position. *But I'm sure every C.O. on every ship in our fleet looked to find out who Zanzibar was, and what C.O. had just ruined his professional career!*

The deadly game continued for quite a long time, then the enemy departed and no ships were torpedoed. We couldn't tell if the Japs were running low on fuel, were frustrated by inability to get high-percentage shots, or whether they did actually fire their torpedoes and missed. We do know that Kelly Turner's handling of the matter was written up as one of the classics of naval warfare. And people who know ships marvel that so many ships of different sizes and types, with different turning circles and handling characteristics could do all those maneuvers in close formation without numerous collisions.

After the war I heard that our illustrious C.O. never made Admiral. *And I'm sure he would have, if not for his error – which could have led to disaster.* And now, if you are paying attention, you are wondering why two officers who caught the mistake, didn't immediately tell the Captain. The answer is, that without either of us mentioning it at the time, *we both knew, with 100% certainty, that it wouldn't have done any good!*

We had lived with this man, in close proximity, for months. In his own mind he was a superior naval officer, one step away from Admiral (and vastly superior to the Admirals he was temporarily forced to serve under!) *He just did not make mistakes!* And there was no way he would stand to be corrected by a 90-day wonder and an officer just called out of a 20-year retirement, and recently selling real estate.

We had learned a lot at Tarawa: at Kwajelein our battleships, cruisers and destroyers virtually pulverized every square yard of island soil before our troops went ashore. In addition, our carrier aircraft dumped tons of bombs on them, just for good measure. On D-day +3, reports said 1200 Japanese had died, 43 captured; 26 Americans dead. We were just getting started.

As expected, the enemy resisted with fanatical fury, but the battles were short and decisive. The major Jap fleet decided not to get involved. Within a few days our ship was anchored in the largest atoll in the world, and I went swimming. I was impressed by our apparent contempt for the enemy threat. At night our ships were "lit up like Christmas trees" – necessary, of course, in order to rearm, refuel and reprovision the fleet. All these lights twinkling merrily like the skyline of a great peacetime city, while Hawaii, two thousand miles to the east, was still under a rigid blackout!

A couple of intelligence officers came aboard to barter: a good stock of bloody battle stories in exchange for a warm shower and a decent meal. We learned a lot from these men. A Jap admiral walked out of his pillbox to certain death in a full dress uniform, with white gloves, epaulets and all his medals and decorations. About the young prisoner who stated, arrogantly, "You may have taken this island, but you won't hold it. And you'll never get the Hawaiian Islands back either!" And it seems that the enemy leaders told their troops that the Japanese had taken all of California, Washington and Oregon and were advancing eastward across the Rocky Mountains according to schedule!

Later in the war I talked to Marines who interrogated prisoners captured on Guadalcanal. The prisoners thought they had actually been fighting on the mainland of the United States, because their leaders told them so. (The moral of this story is, don't believe everything people tell you!)

WHAT I LEARNED ON BURTON ISLAND, ABOUT THEM AND US

I'm sure you know by now, my war experiences included many events burned so deeply in my mind that I will never forget. I was one of a couple of officers who convinced our Captain that when we were anchored in the lagoon we should give our people the opportunity to go ashore and see what it looked like after the battle was over. I was the senior officer of the first "inspection party" of about sixty officers and men who visited Burton Island. It was a hot, sunny day. The island was total rubble – not a single palm tree was still standing, and there had been hundreds. I have no idea how many Japanese died there – surely hundreds, maybe a lot more. The SeaBees had been there, digging mass graves, bulldozing the dead and covering them up. When we arrived, we were the only living things there, except for a few surviving lizards, about 200 billion flies, and a scrawny little shell-shocked pig that nearly scared me to death when I suddenly discovered him. I thought for a moment I had stumbled into a booby trap!

I told the officers and men in my party they could go their own way, but the boat would leave in two hours, with or without them. (I even used that stupid order, "Synchronize your watches!") Then I went my own way and discovered there were dozens of pillboxes, mostly under the sand that the bulldozers couldn't cover up, so they left them alone. I went down into one – interesting, but uncomfortable. The stench was awful. There were five mangled corpses, an unexploded thousand-pound bomb and no less than ten thousand flies. I beat a hasty retreat.

Then I decided I needed to see more – that's why I had come. I wrapped my tee shirt over my mouth and nose and went down into several other pillboxes. All were filled with the dead and most of them had been burned to death by flamethrowers. The more I saw, the more I began to feel sorry for the dead. I knew they weren't there because they hated Americans. Like most of us, they fought because it was expected of them. They were told when and where. Some of us on both sides were lucky, and a lot of us were not.

This feeling grew as I found a few souvenirs: diaries (which I couldn't read), pictures of their families – which I could. It became an emotional experience, one I will never forget.

I got back to where we'd beached our motor launch and everyone made it on time. But I couldn't believe what I was seeing: Lt. Ivan Washburn was proudly displaying a Japanese head on a stick! I really got mad and lit into him (verbally) right in front of all the officers and men. "What the hell do you think you're doing?" I yelled. He looked surprised. "It's my souvenir," he explained. "When I get back to the ship, I'll clean off the flesh, and then I'll have a Jap skull as a trophy."

"Not on my watch," I said. "You take it right back where you got it, and leave it there. You've got five minutes. Miss the boat and you may spend the rest of your life on this island."

Then he got mad. "I just spent a half hour prying this off the body!" he yelled. "You now have four minutes," I said. He glared at me, but did what I ordered. I couldn't believe any of my shipmates would pull a stunt like this. Especially Washburn! I didn't know him well. Never spent any time with him. He was the quiet type and obviously well-educated: his job was to repair any highly technical electric or electronic equipment that needed fixing – radar, loran, computers, directors, all the sophisticated equipment in our Combat Information Center. And he's the guy who pries the head off a dead enemy soldier?

SPEAKING OF WARTIME SOUVENIRS....

Based on personal observation, I became convinced our souvenir-hunting American soldiers and marines became the world's best combat troops (at least in WW2) because they were in such a hurry to beat each other to enemy souvenirs. Jap officer's hara-kiri knives were bringing $500. Their fancy swords, even more. When a Jap bank on Kwajelein was blown up, our soldiers found crisp new paper money, both U.S. currency and Jap Marshall Island "invasion money", similar to the legal tender we were using in occupied territories. Allowed to keep the worthless (?) Jap money, our savvy GI's set up in business and sold reams of the stuff to sailors for souvenirs at $1 per piece!

HOW DID THAT TURKEY EVER MAKE ADMIRAL?

One of the good things about writing about people at this stage of my life is that I can. I can tell all the bad things and name names, because they're all dead! After Admiral Mullennix died at sea during the Makin Island campaign, Admiral Davison replaced him as the head of Carrier Division 24, with his flag on the CVE61, the Manila Bay, which had joined my ship and the Coral Sea after the Liscome Bay disaster.

Davison got off to a great start. On his first night aboard, we were running darkened ship, as every ship does in wartime, and he stands on the bridge at General Quarters, and gets out his trusty Ronson lighter and fires up a cigarette! It was a dark night and you could see flame for ten or twelve miles! I saw it from a mile or so away, and I could hear a few hundred officers and sailors cussing him out, both from that ship and ours.

Of course, he learned from that. Or did he? The next day he walked out on the flight deck where the crew is gassing up the dive-bombers and torpedo planes – *where no smoking is ever allowed* — and immediately lights up a cigarette!

I heard he came from a desk job in Washington and I suppose he may have been good at paperwork. But he soon proved that, at least to some degree, he had not kept up with how to command a Carrier Division in wartime 1944.

Back in World War I (the Battle of Jutland era), the big guns of battleships would pretty much define naval power. Their mission was to find the enemy battleships and destroy them. They traveled one after the other in a straight line. When changing course, the lead ship would turn, the others keep straight ahead until reaching the point where the lead ship turned, then turn to follow it, and so on down the line. If your ship was first in line, it *always* was first in line, no matter what direction the fleet was heading. Same with all the others. In those days, the Big Idea was to get the enemy ships on your beam, so every big gun in the battle line could get a clean shot. The maneuver was called "Crossing the T."

In World War 2, aircraft carriers became most important. Maybe due to that, or for whatever reason, combat vessels abandoned the "battle line" and traveled in a circular disposition. The point in the middle was the "fleet center", around which were imaginary concentric circles. On the inner circle, the carriers (for maximum protection), then on the next circles, whatever other ships you had – troop ships, tankers, battleships, cruisers, whatever. Destroyers patrolled the area around the outer circle. When the disposition changed course, every ship turned at the same time. This was easier and safer, especially during low visibility. But with every course change, every ship's position *relative to the others* also changed. But that made no difference whatever.

Except to our Glorious Leader on the Manila Bay. He adopted the idea of a circular disposition and simultaneous turns, but for some reason unknown to anyone else, he insisted on being "out front", maintaining his position as the lead ship of the three aircraft carriers. This narration may not be of much interest to you readers (if any) but it was really a big deal to the few of us who had to cope with the bad things that happened because of it.

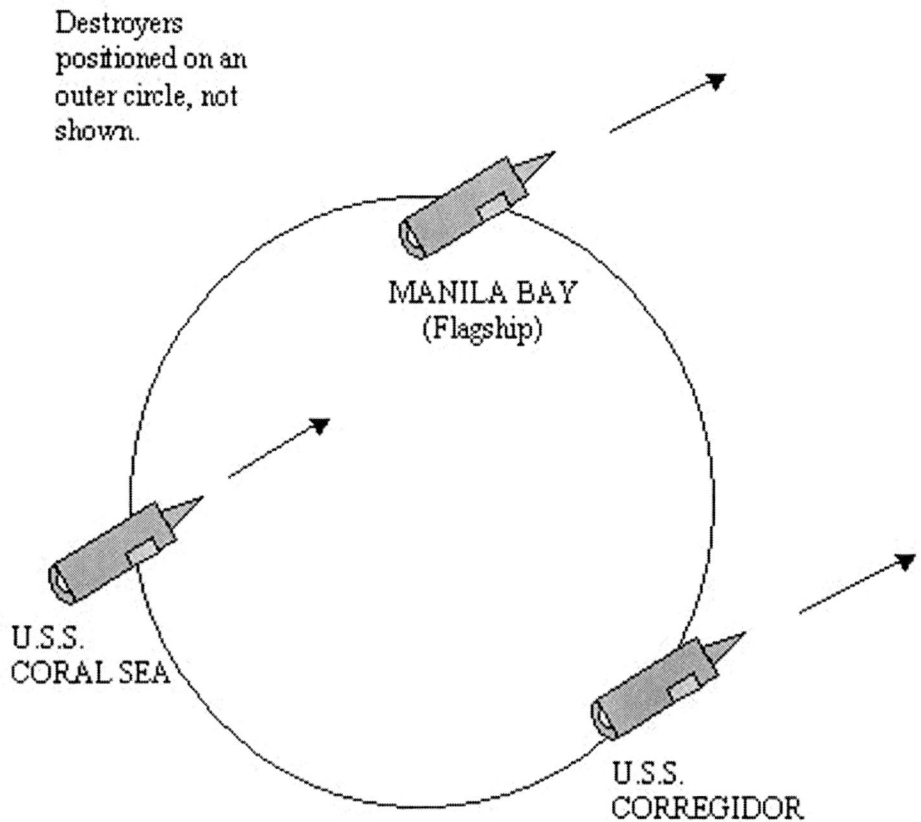

Destroyers positioned on an outer circle, not shown.

MANILA BAY
(Flagship)

U.S.S.
CORAL SEA

U.S.S.
CORREGIDOR

You can see, after this 60-degree turn, the Corregidor would be out front, and to drop back behind the Manila Bay, we'd have to slow down and it might take a few hours to resume our previous position. The first time it happened – on my watch – the Admiral (or his rep) gave me a POSIT, meaning "Get back there, now!" I couldn't slow down any more than I did, without losing steering control.

The next night Tom was in charge and it happened again, only this time (don't ask me how) the flagship turned into the Corregidor and nearly rammed us. Next day, Bowman blamed Tom and removed him as a Duty Commander, and gave the job to Fiorini. And a night or two after that, I tried to anticipate the need and began slowing drastically, before the scheduled course change; and after the course change, the flagship headed for me on a collision course! I called the Captain and he got there in a hurry, but then told me, "You handle it. I can't see yet." This time I swear our ships came so close, a good athlete could have jumped from our flight deck to the other!"

Strangely, Bowman didn't blame me, and was really teed-off at the Admiral. I suspect he discussed it with Mr. Davison – to no avail, since the Admiral didn't change his procedures. We started calling the night watches "Dodge-em Time". And Bowman reinstated Talbot and let Fiorini continue, so now my time as Duty Commander was somewhat lessened.

With these thin-skinned Kaiser carriers, collisions could have been fatal. We used to say you could sink them with a rifle. Now, we agreed, you could sink them with a can-opener! Especially if the can-opener was another ship.

We spent a couple of weeks patrolling at sea and then we anchored in the lagoon at Kwajelein. I played basketball with officers younger and better than I – one, Davis from San Diego State, an almost-all-American – and a couple others from college teams. But I discovered I still could sink a high percentage of my shots.

We swam. Diving (twenty or thirty feet) from the hangar deck or the flight deck was fun, but it has hard work getting back up again. The waves were pretty high, the current strong and you worried some about sharks. We always had a "shark watch" – two or three marksmen with 30 caliber rifles.

I've always been something of a PR man and I got the Captain's approval to produce a "Plank Owner's Certificate", which I designed and wrote, to provide all of us on board with something to hang on our walls after the war, to prove we had some part in its final outcome. The certificate says: "To all sailors and aviators wherever ye may be – Greetings: Know ye by these presents that (name) was a member of the original crew which commissioned the USS Corregidor and, and having sailed in her a total of 35,000 miles during the first six months of her gallant career, engaging in two successful campaigns against the enemies of the United States, is therefore entitled to all the honor, distinction, rights and privileges of a Plank Owner on said ship, including a clear and unencumbered title to one plank in the flight deck."

We got them printed when we returned to Honolulu. Everyone was delighted. Mine has been displayed in my study ever since. 62 years, and counting.

Before we left for Pearl, I visited the new battleship, New Jersey, had an excellent tour and was much impressed. I haven't mentioned it, but WW2 gave me a lot of time for reading and I went through a lot of novels, something I haven't had much time for, since. While reading Eric Ambler's "A Coffin for Dimitrios" it struck me funny; in a combat zone in the middle of the greatest war in human history, I'm reading spy stories for excitement!

On February 17, I received ten letters from Laura, dated from 8 January to the 22nd. All our ensigns with more than fifteen months duty were promote to j.g.'s . Somebody with adequate gold braid in Washington (or maybe Pearl Harbor) decided to give us a breather and ordered us back to Pearl. We arrived on March 4. George Clifford gave me an aerial tour of the Islands. Naval aviators, with passengers who aren't, always try to scare them as much as possible. So we went up way over the clouds, to more than 10,000 feet, then roared almost straight down, playing divebomber, pulled out and leveled off about twenty feet above the water. It was better than anything the amusement parks can offer today.

THE SOLOMON ISLANDS: GUADALCANAL AND TULAGI

Underway 11 March: Corregidor, Coral Sea and 3 DDs. Target practice on sortie, my guys shot down five sleeves – and still no "Well done" from Bowman. Crossed the equator for the seventh time – this time as a shellback. St. Patrick's Day – 17 March – did not exist: we crossed the International Dateline. We must be considered somewhat important: we now have an Associated Press war correspondent on board! Al Dopking, Kansas City Star. He bunks close to the Zoller-Talbot stateroom so we became friends almost immediately.

One day, Dopking wrote a feature story about the officers of the Corregidor – how the Captain, Exec and Air Officer were career officers, but all the rest of us were 'civilians", doing a great job at sea – the Navigator, a Memphis real estate man; the First Lt, a college math professor, the Gunnery Officer, a former Chamber of Commerce executive – and so on. (I told him at my former salary I was surely no executive!) I guess the story was widely published by the AP – months later the Waverly papers ran a story: "Local Man Mentioned in Associated Press Story".

The Solomons were about as I expected – hot, humid, mosquitoes, malaria and mud. Not the place to build your dream house and settle down. Couldn't even go swimming, due to fungus in the water. We anchored in Tulagi harbor. Our squadron had flown off the ship ahead of our arrival and landed at Henderson field. They returned the next day with glowing tales of how the army pilots had mistaken our new FM-2 fighter planes for our old F4F's and when they started to "dogfight", were dismayed to find their P-38's, P-40's and P-47's coming out second-best in almost all cases. Our boys are mighty proud of their little FM2's.

REUNION WITH PEP. All during the war, I'd been getting the Waverly newspapers – sometimes many weeks late. Carl Grawe, Pep's father, who couldn't tell us where Pep was, frequently published hints, and I had an idea that he was somewhere in the Guadalcanal area. So when Dopking talked me into going to the big island with him, I agreed, on my belief that maybe some of his war correspondent buddies could help find my Waverly friend and fraternity brother.

It was an all-day trip, 20 miles (more than two hours) each way by boat. We went to the Camp Crocodile Press Club – interesting, because I met Verne Haugland, Don Casswell and John Henry, all well-known war correspondents. I presented my case and all agreed to the detective work necessary. This took some time due to a primitive jungle telephone set up. But it worked. I found Pep and we arranged to meet at his encampment a couple days later.

Pep was a Marine Captain, the C.O. of an AA battery (8 officers, 300 men) living in the jungle. I stayed overnight – under mosquito netting, ate what they ate (pretty lousy), took a cold water shower. In short, like a marine, for about 24 hours.

A couple of days later, we met again when Pep visited me on the Corregidor, ate a real dinner (with three dishes of ice cream), watched a movie and slept in a real bed, under clean sheets. I took him down to Ship's Store before he left and he took a bunch of candybars and three boxes of cigars back to his camp. He agreed I had it much better than he did – until I told him I stood middle-of-the night watches almost every night at sea, and had been doing it for many months, so he said he'd rather stay a marine – we worked too hard. We agreed it would be nice to eat like the navy, work like the marines.

Our next assignment was to assist and support the invasion at Emirau, in the Admiralty Islands, near the Bismarck Archipelago, and not far from major Jap bases at Kavieng and Rabaul. We did, and strangely I can't remember much about that and my diary notes don't help. Lots of take-offs and landings and bombing and strafing, I presume.

Now that we were winning the war in this part of the world, the enemy started getting their key people moved out of the bases they thought would be our next targets. We had sea and air power near Rabaul and Kavieng so they began to evacuate these strongholds, sending a lot of people to Truk. So our ship was stationed in between, our mission to prevent any daytime traffic and force them to evacuate only by aircraft, and at night. Nobody flew off carriers at night in those days so we couldn't stop them, but it was hazardous for them to find tiny islands in thousands of square miles of empty ocean, by operating in the dark.

This was an extremely uncomfortable assignment, for several reasons. (1) The Japs might send a few submarines out to take care of us so they could go back to operating ships, boats and aircraft in this area in the daylight. (2) We were patrolling right on the equator, we had no air conditioning and the ship was an uninsulated steel oven. The wardroom, where officers ate their meals, was right above the engine room. Our clothes were saturated all the time. At dinner if you said, "Pass the butter," you got more flying sweat than butter! (3) All U.S. aircraft had IFF equipment. This was an electronic Identification Friend or Foe gadget – so we could tell if planes on our radar were ours or theirs. If the latter, we had to dash to our battle stations. So we would work all day, stand watches half the night and then spend the rest of the night going to GQ because there were planes overhead with no I.D. as being ours. Before firing up at aircraft we couldn't see anyway, we learned to send a radio message: "Turn on your goddam lights!" (which meant, "Turn on your IFF!") Then they would, and most of us would go back to bed. One night it happened three times, and during the third, my battery officers begged me, "Let's shoot 'em down, anyway!"

These were always formations of our Army Air Corps long-range bombers. And a lot of us on carriers weren't quite sure if they really were on our side!

GUADAL, HOTEL DE GINK AND THE HOW-BOAT

We received information that some fuses we had on our ammo were probably defective, should be replaced, and would be available on Guadalcanal. So when our patrol finally ended and I heard the squadron would fly back to Henderson Field ahead of us, I went with them. Talbot also discovered some communication problem that could be solved only on Guadalcanal, so the next morning found us doubling for the turret gunner and radioman in the rear of George Clifford's torpedo bomber. We were catapulted off the Big C and flew south over Choisel, New Georgia, the Russells, Santa Isabella and Savo Island. It was fun just to get off the ship. Even Guadal's famous Hotel de Gink, which is just one step better than a foxhole, is preferable for a night or two. Lukewarm water was available, but you couldn't get a small glass of ice water on that island for $50. But around sunset, Sullivan, our new First Lieutenant, suddenly appeared in a Jeep with a huge tub full of cracked ice and two cases of beer! And a couple fifths of rye whiskey! (He could have sold it all for $1,000 in cash, not including the Jeep!) When asked "HOW?" he just smiled and wouldn't answer. Somehow I think it had something to do with an Admiral's Mess – and possibly a war crime!

For reasons just explained, then and there I had the first beer of my lifetime. (Now, some 61 years later, my total is two – but I don't remember any details about the second one.)

The next day Tom and I were faced with a problem: how to get ourselves and the fuses back to the ship which was due to arrive in Purvis Bay, Florida Island, about noon. The Army controlled the transportation so I got on the phone, located the Colonel in charge and explained my problem. "We have a How-boat available. Would that be O.K.?" he asked. "Yes, that would do nicely," I told him, wondering what in the devil a How-boat was. Being a navy officer, I couldn't admit I didn't know. Especially not to an army man!

So he told me where it would be. Joe Cooper, one of our pilots, had a Jeep and drove us down to the dock. "I don't see it," I said. "Maybe it isn't here yet." Tom pointed. "Don't tell me it's that!" Sure enough, there was our How-boat, 136-ft long, manned by thirty-seven officers and men. All for Talbot, the fuses and me!

A lot of things were happening. I joined the Iron Bottom Bay Club on Guadalcanal and ran into old Newton and ISTC friend, Dale Gidley, Capt. USMC. We decided to visit a jungle mission up in the hills. Talking to the natives was interesting – they were extremely intelligent. I ended up buying a Solomon Islands war club. (Still have it.)

March 1944 was a month long remembered by those of us who have been fighting the Pacific War. It was the month white women arrived in the Solomons! And we got them first! Fifteen accepted our invitation. Dinner, of course, and my diary says "Happy Hour – our first ever." But I have no idea what that means as I'm unaware of anything alcoholic aboard the Big C – ever.

WAYLAND D. SEARS

The feature attraction, other than the ladies themselves, was our local talent prizefights. I must tell you about Wayland D. Sears – a remarkable young man. He was a Steward's Mate (a nicer name than Officer's Servant, which they really were, and at the time the only Navy job available to anyone the Navy considered non-white.) Sears was a black lad, slim, trim and handsome. I told you how everyone on board perspired something awful in the tropics. That wasn't quite true: everyone but Sears. He didn't sweat at all. And he meticulously ironed everything that he wore. He was the neatest dude we'd ever seen, and he made everyone else on the ship look like slobs. We had a Ship's Laundry, but "perma-press" hadn't been invented and nothing was ever ironed. Officers, in rumpled sweat-stained khakis, never looked neat. So we all found Sears to be an enviable phenomenon.

About the prizefights. A couple months before, our athletic officer, Bud Cox, decided to develop a boxing team, and maybe fifty or sixty of our enlisted men signed up. They would meet, train, get into condition, hone their skills and eventually there would be matches, and our Corregidor champions decided in each weight class. Maybe we'd challenge other ships.

Most of our officers were there to watch the first day the training began. All these guys in swim trunks and tennis shoes. And Wayland D. Sears – body beautiful, in professional silk boxing trunks and real leather boxing shoes! About 150 pounds and looking like *really somebody*!

We pieced together the story. He started fighting at 14 and (at his mother's insistence) retired at 18, winner of 53 of 55 fights. One of his victims was well-known Beau Jack, who later became the welterweight champion of the world! Sears joined the navy, and in peacetime fought a lot and was undefeated three straight years. The war came and he was at sea, unable to fight, but then got shore duty long enough to win not just the All-Navy, but the *All Services championship* in November 1942.

That was his last boxing until Bud Cox started his program in early 1944. When the matches started, Cox tried to even things up a bit, matching 150-lb. Sears with the heavy weights, some of them 100 lbs. bigger. But it was no contest – nobody could hit Sears and he administered boxing lessons that were a pleasure to watch. He was such a nice guy, he was sure never to hurt the big guys. And – he never sweat! Not even a bit!

OUR NEW BOSS: GENERAL DOUGLAS MacARTHUR

We had been under the command of Admiral Spruance (Fifth Fleet) and Bull Halsey (Third Fleet). But now we were on loan to MacArthur for a big show on New Guinea. We got Al Dopking back from Guadal, just in time to join us, and (aren't we getting famous?) we were assigned another observer, "LCDR Ronald Brooke of the Royal Navy, dispatched to the Big C by none other than Admiral Lord Louis Montbatten, Commander, Allied Forces Southwest Asia – for the express purpose of watching us in action! It turned out that "Brooksey" was a good guy, and he fit in well.

On April 21, I "celebrated" my 28th birthday off the coast of New Guinea. Exactly 2 years ago, I was sailing out of Iceland. These two places are almost exactly halfway around the world apart. Off hand, I can't think of any worse places to celebrate anything.

This year I had the Duty Command watch in the middle of the night, which is a lousy birthday present in any locality. *It didn't make it any better that I hadn't seen my wife in six months!* The following day was D-Day. Our troops were landed at Aitape and Hollandia, in the strategic Humboldt Bay area. Our planes covered the troop landings and some of them came back pretty well shot up. But none of our guys were hurt. When the newspapers reported the event, they said this had cut off and isolated 140,000 Jap troops, rendering them ineffective. MacArthur, watching from the bridge of a cruiser, pronounced the operation "a great victory!"

We patrolled the area for several days and Bowman finally took pity on Tom, Fiorini and me and our constant schedule of night watches, by promoting Prukop and Rivel (both good officers) to join us in our "assistant captain's duty."

Two Australian cruisers, the HMAS Australia and HMAS Shropshire, joined our disposition. We had a bad General Quarters the evening of April 26 with three successive barrier crashes as our fighter planes landed just at darkness. Four of our torpedo planes had to land in the dark, but all made it O.K.

War is, among its many disadvantages, extremely expensive. Ensign Perry has the dubious distinction of being tied with "Crash" Caravacci, another fighter pilot, for having the most crashes to his discredit. (Some of these can be repaired; if too damaged, we just push them off the flight deck for "a decent burial at sea".) Perry also has had to swim away from his sinking airplane on two occasions. (Probably not his fault.) However, Lt (j.g.) Truesdale got his feet wet when he was in the landing circle, low over the water, and *he just forgot* to switch gas tanks so his engine konked out and he dropped into the sea. One of our destroyers rescued him and his crewmen, but the Air Officer was really sore. "We'll take it out of your salary," he growled. "Fifty dollars a month for the rest of your life."

Not all flight operations that go awry are costly. Believe it or not, we had an Ensign Duck in our squadron – "Donald", of course. On patrol, he ran into a bit of engine trouble and had to make a forced landing on the beach. He was lucky enough to find a landing strip that our troops had just taken from the Japanese. He spent the night and returned aboard the next day, loaded with Jap souvenirs and an impressive amount of cash. It seems he found a bunch of soldiers who thought he was kidding them when he said, all airplanes aboard carriers had folding wings. "After all the bets were placed, I took them out and showed them. I flapped them back and forth a few times just to rub it in."

The next day the following notice was posted on the Ready Room bulletin board: "Any pilot who knowingly and with malice aforethought, simulates engine trouble and a forced landing in order to take advantage of innocent and naïve army personnel will be fined the sum of one dollar ($1.00) to be donated to the Army Relief Fund, and also will be compelled to split the take with me on a 50-50 basis." (Signed) G. M. Clifford, Squadron Commander.

DEATH SOMETIMES HAPPENS. It's not all fun and games. The guys who fly earn an extra 50% for "hazardous duty". Fair enough. I had seen this happen on several occasions, but during the New Guinea campaign it was so close aboard, the explosion made my teeth hurt. A bomber from another carrier in our formation was just completing an antisubmarine patrol, low over the water, preparing to land on his ship. Right alongside us, his engine sputtered, stopped and he settled into the sea. His depth charges went off immediately and blew the plane and all its crewmen into a thousand small pieces. Even seeing a thing like this makes a defense job back in the States definitely preferable when it comes to the matter of storing up pleasant wartime memories.

A SEA-GOING SON-OF-A-GUN. Right now (2006) everyone in the U.S.A. is concerned with the price of gasoline. Fuel was a lot cheaper 62 years ago. But the Chief Engineer (Yukon Jake Le Vake) told me that, except for 30 hours last month, the Corregidor was at sea, steaming nearly at full speed every minute of the 30 days! That's a lot of Bunker C. Add all the high octane avgas we used to keep out aircraft airborne for almost all the daylight hours, and you're talking some real money!

Finally, we did drop anchor in Seeadler Harbor in the Admiralty Islands. Rearm, refuel, reprovision. Liberty parties were not allowed – too many Japs still up in the hills. (Poor losers!) Sometimes they'd sneak down on a Commando-type raid for the glory of the Emperor, and also for the more practical purpose of their own reprovisioning. Our first night in port they wrecked a radio station and killed a dozen or more American soldiers. Several of our men came to me and (seriously) requested we pack a few box lunches and send out a hunting party. I said no.

The good news was, the Chikaskia was in. I had the duty and McGlohon had the duty, so Kepler got a boat and came over for dinner. He was now a full Lieutenant and had just put in for submarine duty, and expected to get it. That would involve lengthy shore duty, at the sub school in New London, CT. I told him, "I hope you get it. You go and have a nice time. I'll stay out here and take care of the war in this part of the world."

ESPIRITU SANTO. COINCIDENCE IN THE NEW HEBRIDES.

Being here was great. No enemy troops, ships, or aircraft. Maybe some subs, but we didn't see any. A lot of mail, probably chasing us for months, caught up with us. Lex Black got his orders to shore duty in the States and in my opinion that probably made the Western Pacific safer for the United States Armed Forces, and especially me. So Williamson moved up to Exec and

George Clifford, now a full Commander, to Air Officer – the latter being good news for me because now I have one good friend among our ship's "Big Three".

Padre Hoffman, who just made LCDR, came up to me and asked if I had plans about going ashore our first day in Espiritu. I didn't, so he invited me to join him. "I'm going to meet the Catholic chaplain here. He has a Jeep and he'll show us around this part of the island. Matter of fact, we're going to meet with the French Archbishop who heads our church in this part of the world."

We rode the boat ashore and Padre's friend was there, waiting for us. Padre introduced us. I climbed into the back seat and we started down the road. The priest in the driver's seat looked over his shoulder and told me, "Sorry. I didn't really catch your name." "Zoller. Bob Zoller," I replied. He immediately stopped the car. "Hell," he said (*really*), "I know you! I'm Father Minster. I was chaplain at Mercy Hospital in Waverly, and your sister Helen talked about you all the time! Your high school sports. Lifeguarding. President of your fraternity at Iowa. The Chamber of Commerce thing. I know all about you, and I can't believe we never actually met in Waverly!"

So we met in the New Hebrides, a few years later, halfway around the world from Waverly, Iowa! We spent a great day there, talking about all of his friends and my friends – who, of course, were the same people. War does often produce some strange by-products.

UP THE RIVER: FUN, GAMES AND A HOMEMADE TRAPEZE

Due mainly to George Clifford, as I remember, a bunch of us spent a glorious day on what we planned as a fishing party. We borrowed a fast, flat-bottomed "rearming barge" and started up a little river, switched into bathing trunks and Frank Buck hats and cruised up this jungle river for several hours, trying to kid ourselves into believing we were explorers.

This was a tropical paradise. Dense foliage lined the riverbanks and we passed by cocoanut palm groves and bamboo thickets. It lacked only the beating of war drums and Dorothy Lamour. After ensuring the absence of alligators and/or crocodiles, we swam in the crystal-clear waters and aquaplaned without aquaplanes – that was, towing each other at high speed on fifty-foot ropes. (I believe they called this "keel-hauling" in the days of sailing ships.)

Several times that day we beached our boat on a sandbar and sent an "expeditionary force" into the jungle – war-whooping in true American Indian fashion. Had we encountered a war party of aborigines, I truly believe they would have dropped their spears and fled back into the jungle. (Some of our ex-football players were very scary – and hairy.)

Our big discovery was a trapeze arrangement someone had rigged near an especially deep spot at the bend of our river. Here, the bank rose high above the water and a substantial tree limb hung out in just the right place. A sturdy line, a triangular iron bar and a high take-off platform completed the device.

Someone called for a test pilot and when nobody stepped forward, it was somehow decided (by majority vote) that I had volunteered. It was quite a climb, just to get there, and a long way down. Most of our party were Airedales (flyers, Air Dept.) – so I had to uphold the reputation of the Gunnery Division. I took a deep breath, and swung out and up, and let go. The best I can claim is survival, for it certainly wasn't pretty. Others then followed. And I advised all of them to decide "head-first or feet-first" before reaching the release point some forty feet over the water, because you will surely have other things to do on the way down!

This was a day when grown men acted like 14-year-olds and had a wonderful time. I was happy it happened: because I was sure that at least a couple of us might be dead in the very near future.

And I did meet the Bishop. New Hebrides is (or was) a French Protectorate so he was very French. He was a white-haired old gentleman with a white beard, a keen mind and a good sense of humor. Fun to be with.

Kepler's ship came in but stayed only a day or two – just long enough for a short visit in which I said goodbye. He had his orders to Submarine duty at New London, and I wouldn't see him again until a couple of years after the war ended. It was also great to see old friend and mentor, Paul Revere McGlohon – for the last time ever.

QUEENIE. It was here in Espiritu that Queenie came aboard. Somebody saw her wandering around the island with a couple of sailors – which is not quite proper behavior for a young lady, even in the New Hebrides. Queenie is a small mongrel, resembling a police dog, but not much. I have no idea who named her Queenie. Or why. Few dogs anywhere were given a better home – with a couple hundred "owners" who considered her special. She had the run of the ship, but the forecastle was her particular domain, which she ruled with an iron paw. She went to all the movies, helped launch and land aircraft upon occasion, and faithfully reported her presence at Quarters where she mustered with my First Division, of which she was a member. Her primary duty, of course, was serving as our morale officer. Welcome aboard, Queenie.

HEADING FOR THE MARIANAS

June 2, 1944, back to serious business. We sailed north (and later, west) en route to what we all knew would be our greatest adventure and our greatest risk. We were going right past the Jap-held Caroline Islands with its great naval and air base at Truk. With Tokyo only 1200 miles from our objective – the Marianas – the enemy would have to come out and fight, probably with their main fleet, which we correctly evaluated as a situation extremely hazardous to our health.

I knew our gun crews were pretty damn good, but I felt our key to survival was my making sure they would be fully alert and not caught off-guard in those critical moments when all hell breaks loose. I talked to the battery officers, gun captains, gun crews and ammunition handlers almost every day. "Many of you," I told them, "will be fighting for your lives for the very first time. I can tell you now, it's going to be a spectacular show – and I'm scared to death you'll be watching the fireworks and forgetting to guard your assigned sectors. Your job is not to cheer when one enemy plane goes down. If you do, another one will park a thousand-pounder in your back pocket – or strafe your head off with his fifty calibers!"

"The Japs will be attacking from all directions and all angles of elevation at the same time. You'll think the divebombers are coming straight down – you'll have to practically lie on your backs to track them. And all of them will be coming in three times faster than the target sleeves you've been shooting down. Their job is to catch us by surprise. Your job is to make sure they don't."

THE SAGA OF SPONSON JOHN

We stopped at Roi in the Marshall Islands to top off with fuel and supplies. Before we proceed to our rendezvous with whatever adventures lie ahead, let me tell you a story about one of the many "unforgettable characters" I encountered during my lengthy stay on this planet. His name was John Glenn. Not the famous astronaut, the Senator from Ohio. He was a businessman in Beardstown, Illinois, a Naval Reserve officer who pulled strings and got a safe and easy shore duty job at nearby Glenview Naval Air Station, but he got somebody mad and ended up at sea on the Corregidor. And now he was the officer in charge of the hangar deck of our ship. Kind of like a parking attendant, getting the planes in their proper position. Older than most of us of similar rank, something of a philosopher who seemed to feel it was part of his job to educate or "square away" the younger officers and enlisted men.

Glenn was the Officer on the Deck who had given me a severe reprimand for wearing the wrong uniform when I returned to Astoria from Gunnery School in San Diego. I thought the guy was an old sea dog (maybe a Mustang) and later found he'd never been to sea.

Well, John became a master storyteller and held daily court while sitting comfortably in his easy chair on the starboard sponson. Dispensing wisdom, as it were. The sponsons, one on each side of the hangar deck, were like little balconies in the large openings used for loading and unloading operations. At sea, they were the best place to be, with wonderful breezes and the pleasant sound of our ship slicing through the tropical sea. John Glenn owned the sponsons – or thought he did. I was his shipmate for many months and don't remember ever seeing him any place except the starboard sponson. Hence the name, "Sponson John". Scandalmonger that he was, it was only natural that he should end up writing a column for our ship's paper, the Corregidor Boomerang. It was a pretty good column and John had the foresight to enlist Murphy, our disbursing officer (who was a Harvard man) to help with the spelling.

In his very first column, John published his unforgettable words of wisdom: "I guess I'll move over to the port sponson once in awhile. I don't want to get a one-sided view of the war." It was inevitable that Sponson John, who was surely not the most likeable officer on board, would nevertheless become a minor legend. I was impressed enough to immortalize him in verse. And here it is, with appropriate apologies both to Rudyard Kipling and Gunga Din:

The Saga of Sponson John.

"You may talk of famous men
But I sing of one named Glenn,
A modern hero – (boys, remove your hats).
He was Illinois-born
But he left the land of corn
To make the world safe for Democrats.

Someone named him Sponson John
When his ice-plant days were done
When he'd left his home to fight for liberty.
The name's phonetic quality
Engraves it in my memory,
It was destined to go down in history.

While a-roaming on the foam,
The starboard sponson was his home,
Where he preached and lived a really easy life.
He would sit there in the sun
Till the longest day was done,
And chill your bones with tales of blood and strife.

Oh, I'll not forget the night
When the moon was shining bright,
'Lamplighter Charlie' started in, a-dropping flares.
Then they started in their runs,
But we were ready by our guns
We were bound they wouldn't catch us unawares.

Then we filled the air with flak
But they kept a-coming back,
And they hit the 'Mighty C' but couldn't stop her.
Though they had a score before,
Tojo sent a thousand more
And they really nailed us this time, good and proper.

Well, they hit us aft and fore
At least a hundred times or more
And they slowed us down to barely thirty knots.
We had started in to bail
When we heard the power fail.
They had blown to pieces all our amps and watts.

But we still were full of fight
When we saw the gruesome sight,
(A Betty did the job as I recall)
With delicate precision,
Tojo laid one on the sponson…
It disintegrated – Sponson John and all!

Sailor men like me and you
When our earthly span is through,
And reluctantly the cloak of death we don,
We will journey without fear
For we'll soon be drinkin' beer
In the realm of Davy Jones – and Sponson John.

—- (REFRAIN) —-

For it was John, John, John –
Where the devil has he gone?
For I've looked both high and low,
    and I've looked well.
Sponson John's no longer here.
He's been sittin' many a year
On the sponson, on the starboard side of hell!"

Admiral Felix J. Stump relieved Admiral Davison as ComCarDiv 24 and moved his flag aboard the Corregidor. His staff took over a lot of the best space, but Tom and I were lucky enough to hang onto our stateroom. I considered Stump a major improvement, having had no respect for his predecessor. He had been the C.O. of the new carrier, Lexington, and they had seen action and that always helps.

10 June 1944. We headed west out of Roi, bound for Saipan, with the battleship Pennsylvania, six cruisers, five other CVEs and a bunch of destroyers, forming a formidable Saipan Bombardment Group. We knew our main Battle Fleet (fast battleships, big carriers, cruisers, destroyers) were already in the Marianas area, as were all the troop ships, landing craft, supply ships, oilers and other auxiliaries we needed to invade and conquer Saipan, which was defended by 82,000 Jap troops. And there were thousands more on nearby Tinian, Guam and Rota. It would be one of the greatest operations of the Pacific War, and we expected it would be costly to both sides and possibly one of the major factors determining the outcome of the entire war.

On June 11, the destroyer, Talbot, collided with the Pennsylvania during my watch and we nearly ran into her, too. June 12, I don't know why, but I figured out that in a bit over three years, I had now sailed 111,000 miles – 56,000 in the Rapidan, 55,000 to date in the Big C.

On June 14, our battleships and cruisers bombarded Saipan and Tinian and we provided combat air patrols (to engage enemy aircraft if they attacked) and anti-submarine patrols. Nearby, another Division of CVEs shot down a Jap Betty.

15 June was D-Day – our troop landings began. One of our fighter pilots, Ensign Glen L. Collins, was last seen diving into heavy AA fire on Saipan, never returned and was presumed dead. About 6 p.m., shore-based Japanese aircraft attacked us. We put up so much AA, it was difficult to see through all the smoke and tracers, but we got lucky – none of our CVEs or

destroyers were damaged. Fighter planes from another CVE division shot down four or five Jap planes, in sight of our ship, but well out of our range. We stayed at General Quarters until dark – about 8 p.m. Then I had the Duty Commander watch until midnight; then we went back to GQ three times during the midwatch, and finally just stayed at our battle stations until 7 a.m. For me, no sleep at all.

That same night something noteworthy happened – not spectacular, I guess, but I believe it was a Navy "first" – during the night, a whole group of U.S. Navy oil tankers came and fueled at sea several dozen of our major ships, to ensure they could chase the Jap fleet all the way back to Tokyo if given the opportunity. Fueling ships while underway at sea had been perfected only a couple of years before – quite an accomplishment in daylight. But now we did it in the dark of night, and without any collisions or damage.

It was still Top Secret that we had broken the Jap code, so I didn't know how, but we all heard the main Jap battle fleet had been located, so all of the big ships of our main battle force dashed off to engage them. Our three little Kaiser coffins and our destroyers were left alone to "hold the fort" off Saipan.

On June 16, we sent Red Goss and Wilkes, Chief Photographer, on a photo mission. When they returned, the plane was riddled with enemy AA fire, neither of the men wounded, but the Chief was missed by only three inches!

ALL HELL BREAKS LOOSE!

The next day, June 17, was unquestionably the most exciting day of my entire life. But I must explain something else first: PROXIMITY FUSES. Just prior to our sailing to the Marianas Operation, a messenger came to my stateroom and said a visitor wanted to see the Gunnery Officer. The visitor then told me he had brought me ordnance materials that were TOP SECRET – (and he said those words in all caps!) Before explaining what it was, he warned me, "You have to account for each of these. If you lose just one, you will spend the rest of your life in Naval prison!" So now he had my full attention.

He turned over to me – I had to sign several official documents – fifty top-secret "proximity fuses" – and I was delighted to have them. I knew immediately these were a godsend. Here's why. The big 5-inch cannon on the fantail of our ship was a pretty good weapon against surface targets on land or sea. But I considered it nearly worthless as an anti-aircraft weapon. Your chances of actually hitting a 300 mph airplane with the projectile itself were almost zero! So there was a timing device in a fuse on the nose of the projectile, so you could set it to explode in 3.5 seconds, or 5, or whatever. Then it would spray shrapnel over an area you hoped would be close enough to the enemy plane to bring it down.

Fat chance! So radar gives you the distance to the target, or you esti-
mate it. Take into consideration whether the plane is coming in on you (at 300
mph), going away, or crossing in some direction. Then, since you know the
speed at which your projectile travels, you figure how much time it will take
for the shell to get to where the plane is (or will be), and then you set the fuse
accordingly. (Actually, you don't set it, you got a guy with a tool that does
that. You tell him. He sets it.) Your crew loads the projectile and the powder
bags, closes the breech, your pointer and trainer aims the gun, you yell, "Fire!"
and the projectile goes for X-number of seconds, explodes – and usually
misses by a mile or so because the target has been moving rapidly all the time
during the process.

But now the new invention. No fuse-setting. You just aim and fire. If
the shell ever gets near enough to the target to bring it down, it *automatically*
explodes and you and your gun crew can all yell, "Splash one meatball!"

O.K. Back to the fireworks of June 17. We were alone, the Corregidor, the Coral Sea and newcomer Gambier Bay, plus our escort of five destroyers. Late afternoon, our radar told us a large number of enemy aircraft were
taking off from the airfields on Saipan and Tinian and heading toward us. We
immediately launched our fighter planes and went to our battle stations.

I was at Gunnery Control, sharing a relatively small area on the bridge
with Admiral Stump, Captain Bowman, Russ Wilkinson, Ray Hilding (Aircraft Recognition Officer), Rivel (Signal Officer), the helmsman and my telephone talker who kept me in touch with all my gun crews.

Looking south, I could see the fighters from our three carriers engage
the incoming enemy planes. Couldn't see much at that distance, but I could
tell generally what was happening. I warned our gun crews to stay alert. In
just a couple of minutes we all saw the divebombers high overhead and
screaming down on us at steep angles. The first one had targeted the Gambier
Bay and I could see him drop the big bomb and then pull up steeply. Our big
5"/38 on the fantail fired its first shot with sound and fury, fire and smoke, and
I could actually see the projectile spinning like a football toward the enemy
plane and in about three seconds there was a huge puff of black smoke and a
thousand small pieces of the attacking plane dropping down into the sea! As
I knew it would, a great cheer erupted from all over our ship. On our very first
shot, the proximity fuse had worked perfectly. The bomb had narrowly missed
the Gambier Bay, and our big gun was now batting 1000!

All this happened in seconds. Other divebombers were coming down,
two of them seemed focused on us, and every gun on our ship was blasting
away, rapid fire. It was pandemonium. The noise was awful and the air so full
of bullets and tracers and smoke from the guns, and from a couple of the

attacking planes burning and crashing and exploding, that daylight almost disappeared. I thought, this is like a movie – and surely the most exciting time of my life! I knew of the danger but somehow I was enjoying being involved in this remarkable event. Words fail me: *you had to be there* to fully understand what this was like!

I watched everything through binoculars much of the time, while frequently scanning the entire scene to make sure no attacking aircraft got in on us unopposed. My gunners were great. I remember how cool Hilding was. He and I and Rivel, I think, were the only ones on the bridge who were standing up and watching the battle raging around us. I don't remember Wilkinson, but I did notice that Admiral Stump and Captain Bowman both were down on the deck behind the protective steel shield around the bridge, not even peeking up to see what was happening.

Ray Hilding was a tall man, a forest ranger from Montana – we all called him "Trapper". He was trained to identify enemy aircraft by type. I remember him watching the battle through binoculars, talking to himself. "Those dive bombers are Judy's," he said. "And that one is a Lily. But that one...Damn, I've never seen that one before. I'd say it's a modified Nick. Must be something new." One cool cookie, Hilding.

CLOSE CALL: TORPEDO BOMBER COMING IN!

My gun crews were all business. Almost the same time that "Fantail Fannie" (Big Bertha's kid sister on our fantail) got the Jap divebomber with its very first shot, our 40mm crews hammered two of the planes coming down on us and both crashed into the sea close aboard. About the time I was beginning to feel lucky, I saw a torpedo bomber coming in at tremendous speed, only a few feet over the water, only a mile or so away and *directly abeam with a shot at us so easy they call it a "slam dunk" in basketball!* I immediately remembered the Liscome Bay – what a torpedo did to her – and I wondered if maybe this would be the final moments of my life! Before I could cry out to my gun crews, every 20mm and 40mm gun on that side of the ship let loose with everything we had. I could see shells exploding on the front of this plane. It burst into flames, and suddenly rolled over and arced way high into the sky and then, burning furiously, it started down. *Instead of breathing easily, I now was convinced it was coming right down on top of me!*

Being lucky is better than almost anything else I can think of: it missed me! But not by much. It came so close the flames streaming out behind felt like a blast furnace! When he plunged into the sea, I was splashed by salt water! That's about as close as you can get.

But all of us survived. And I knew this was a great victory. I felt proud, and exceedingly grateful!

FAMOUS FIERY FAILURE PHOTO

Next time we got ashore, I learned the photographer on the Coral Sea had gotten a great picture of this particular kill. So I went there and persuaded the good guys on our sister ship to run off 800 - 900 copies, so every officer and man on the Big C would have one to hang on his wall for the rest of his life. My framed copy has been on display for more than sixty years.

Also, this photo is considered one of the best combat pictures of the Pacific War. It has been used in several war anthologies. And fifty years later, TIME Magazine devoted an entire issue to The War Against Japan and our famous photo was included. The caption said, "FIERY FAILURE. A kamikaze goes down, stopped by U.S. anti-aircraft guns." I clipped the picture, framed it and it's now on my Study wall, alongside the one I got from the Coral Sea.

FIERY FAILURE A kamikaze goes down, stopped by U.S. antiaircraft guns

I thought this one would kill the Corregidor and almost everyone on it. But my gun crews got him first.

KAMIKAZE? I hope you noticed that TIME called it a kamikaze. I wrote them and said, "On 17 June 1944, we had never heard of kamikazes. But as the Corregidor's Gunnery Officer, I had to submit a Battle Report to Naval Intelligence, and in it I emphasized that after dropping their bombs or torpedoes, these aircraft took no evasive action whatever. They seemingly tried to fly right into our ship." I also said that a month or two later we heard all about these suicide planes and *then knew we had probably seen the first kamikazes of the war!* TIME thanked me, said my letter was scheduled to be published, but got bounced due to some other late-breaking news. (You can't win 'em all.)

ENCORE? The morning after the Big One, the bad guys came out to take another crack at us, but we put up so much AA fire they seemed a bit discouraged. Dropped a few bombs, but didn't scare us all that much. We did have to go to GQ six times that day, and we'd rather have been shooting baskets.

It seems everyone on our ship was ecstatic about the performance of our ship's gunners and our combat pilots. Everyone but Roscoe L. Bowman. He never even said "Well done"' to me, or to anyone else that I knew of. (Of course, it's possible he never actually *saw* what happened!)

Admiral Stump seemed pretty proud of us. On several occasions he watched us operate and said he had never seen anything better on the big carriers. He gave us a "Well Done" for our battles off Saipan, and he convinced me he meant it.

Later, on shore, an officer from one of our destroyers sought me out to tell me, "Your guys can really put out the AA. I couldn't even see the Corregidor for all the smoke and flames coming out of your gun barrels. You had those Jap planes dropping like flies!"

Most surprising of all, on August 6, we received this message from Admiral Nimitz: "CINCPAC SENDS CONGRATULATIONS TO THE CORREGIDOR ON COMPLETING A FINE TOUR OF COMBAT DUTY X WELL DONE." As Commander-in-Chief, Pacific Operations, Nimitz was the second highest officer in the Navy – only the Chief of Naval Operations in Washington outranked him. I'm amazed he'd even heard of our Kaiser Coffins!

Best of all, our entire Division – three carriers and five destroyers – emerged from the battles totally untouched. Our ship did lose another pilot, Ensign Billy Hudson. He peeled off from the formation and dived to attack some target our other pilots didn't see. He was never seen again. Another of our guys lucked out: the Japs shot him down in the big dogfight when our fighters went out to break up the enemy attack on June 17. Johnny Guzzino survived both the barrage of machine gun bullets that tore his little FM-2 fighter to pieces, and the crash into the sea, which is usually fatal from high altitudes at high speed. He was rescued by a destroyer and was completely uninjured.

YOU DOWN 16 PLANES AND WHAT DO YOU GET?

After the battles, post-mortems. What really happened? So much happening, so fast, and all the noise and smoke and fire, and everyone well aware that thousands of lives were in great danger, that I'm sure nobody saw everything. Pandemonium is a good word which the dictionary defines as tumult, a wild uproar, violence and hell! At any rate, the Big C ended up getting *official* credit for downing sixteen enemy planes – eight by our squadron, eight by my gun crews. We claimed several more but they won't count any unless they are certain kills, and witnesses agree that nobody else was shooting at them. (I'm not sure about the other ships in our Division. I know the Coral Sea shot down at least a couple. And somewhere I read the Kalinan Bay shot down and killed its own Squadron Commander!)

One of my major worries was our guys tracking enemy planes and shooting right into one of our sister carriers! I kept warning, but it nearly happened. Almost, not quite. Lucky for me. Bowman would have had me "hanging from the highest yardarm in the U.S. Navy". According to my Personal Log ("diary" sounds prissy), I had spent most of my time in 1944 not getting along with Bowman, Lex Black and Marcus Williamson, the three top officers on the Big C. I was well aware that "buttering up the brass" is a valuable procedure both in military and civilian life, but I just couldn't seem to connect with these guys. But about that time all of us were given our periodic Fitness Reports and *I was really surprised to find I had been rated exceptionally well!* Go figure!

MY OWN PERSONAL EVALUATION

I'm not sure how many people do this – a few, a lot, or most. But right in the midst of surely one of the worst times of my life, when the sky was full of airplanes whose pilots were determined to kill me and as many of my friends as possible – and I was convinced they might – I found myself watching the battle and, at the same time, watching myself. In time of war, I believe many servicemen spend some time thinking about how they will react to the danger of dying. When all hell broke loose on June 17, I first thought, *"Damn, this is it, the real thing – and I'm in it!"* Then I tended to business, and while all this was happening, I (mentally) looked at myself to see how I was doing, and I felt good with what I saw. I was not afraid, I was doing what I'd been trained to do, and was doing it well. And I never forgot this. I don't remember ever being afraid of anything or anybody since.

But don't misunderstand. Bad things can happen suddenly and change one's life or end it. In wartime, in combat, the danger is much greater. I never tried to avoid it, but I surely tried to be ready if it happened. I attended Mass and received Communion at every opportunity. I mention this not to seek your approval; in view of my faith, it was just the sensible thing to do.

One of our pilots, Gordon Love, came in for a landing and our Landing Signal Officer noticed his tail hook was missing – and you can't make a carrier landing without one! So he waved him off, and now what do we do? While the pilot flew in circles and our senior officers tried to figure it out, a radioman interrupted them, but was told, "Not now. We're trying to rescue Gordon Love!" The radioman said, *"I thought you'd want to know, we just took the airfield on Tinian!"* So Love was saved and became the first U.S. pilot to land ashore on Tinian!

Unfortunately, Gordon Love died shortly thereafter. He was coming in for a landing when his engine sputtered and died, and the torpedo bomber tumbled into the sea. His three crewmen bobbed up to the surface and were rescued. Gordon didn't, and wasn't. He was a handsome young pilot and popular with all of us and his loss was a major one.

THE BATTLE OF THE PHILIPPINE SEA. TURNING POINT?

It was quite natural that we thought our encounters off the Marianas and re-taking these islands from major Japanese forces was the biggest news happening. But it wasn't. Task Force 58, our main battle fleet of fast battleships, big carriers and other combat ships – cruisers, destroyers – had located the enemy's major Task Force and sailed west to meet them. This resulted in a huge conflict in which our side won and probably determined to final winner of the entire Pacific War.

On 20 June we heard that 500 enemy aircraft attacked our battle fleet and 300 of them were shot down, and the rest landed in Guam. And that one of our submarines torpedoed and sank a big Jap carrier. The next day, enemy aircraft losses were boosted to 395! Three large Jap carriers and two fast tankers had been lost and six other enemy ships badly damaged. Much of Japan's formidable naval air power was destroyed! *This battle was noteworthy because U.S. and Japanese ships never saw each other.* Except for submarines, the battle was entirely waged with aircraft!

SO MUCH HAPPENING, SO FAST. Surviving enemy aircraft were landing on the Mariana's airstrips and U.S. pilots went after them, destroying so many, they called it "The Marianas Turkey Shoot". Here, another 300 enemy aircraft were said to be destroyed!

The Coral Sea – never more than a four miles away from us since leaving the States – had serious engine troubles and was sent back home for repairs. This made "The Big C" the "senior carrier" of the entire Kaiser fleet! Most of the 50, we found out, had never heard a shot fired in anger, had spent their time at sea ferrying aircraft from the States to Pacific bases where they were transferred to the big carriers as replacements. The few who had sailed with us served short tours of combat duty and returned to safe havens. The Kitkun Bay and Gambier Bay were detached and replaced by our new partners, the White Plains and the Midway. When the battle-hardened old Corregidor was ordered to join the invasion fleet scheduled for Guam, our new partners were left out of it, and former partners Kalinan Bay, Nautoma Bay, Manila Bay and Fanshaw Bay were assigned to ferrying replacement planes. I don't know whether our ship was being honored or punished.

THE BATTLE FOR GUAM. We heard there were thousands of enemy troops and hundreds of airplanes on Guam. Our mission was to protect our invasion fleet and landing forces from air and submarine attacks and bomb all targets assigned. D-Day was 21 July. Our forces retook the island and the Corregidor was lucky not to lose any more pilots or planes. On August 1, we were detached with another "Well Done."

Before we left, we heard an amazing story about a navy radioman named Tweed who had evaded capture when the Japs took Guam from us in 1941, and somehow survived, hiding in the hills until we invaded and found him in late July 1944! He was healthy, and he had kept a diary full of important and useful military information.

GREAT NEWS: BOWMAN ORDERED TO NEW DUTY!

I'd say this was one of the best things that happened to me in World War 2. He didn't leave until his replacement came aboard, but that was O.K. Cronk, Rivel, Howe, Warren Smith, Fiorini, Ripley, Doc Payne, Padre Hoffman and a few other ship's officers were also reassigned, and the entire squadron of our airman will be leaving when we get back to the States.

SPONSON JOHN ORDERED … TO WASHINGTON! Also getting orders, the Legend of the Starboard Sponson, "Honest John Glenn". This became a major source of shipboard discussion – because there were rumors that nobody on board had seen The Great Warrior during the big battle off Saipan, and many suspected he had gone into hiding when everyone else was fighting the ship. (Since he was one of the older officers on board, I just figured this was not all that unusual.)

When we got to know him, few of us on board ever believed anything he told us. But now we realized we were wrong. He always bragged about his political pull, and on this he must have told the truth: nobody else on this ship could ever have gotten shore duty in Washington!

At any rate, some said this transfer was good for the country: he was likely to "straighten out" all members of the Senate and key members of the Administration – at least until they had him figured out.

One thing is for sure: the several thousand naval officers fighting the war from desk jobs in Washington would be taking a verbal beating from the salty old pirate.

Lt. Murphy, our Phi Beta Kappa Harvard grad, took over the "On the Sponson" column in our Boomerang and devoted the first issue to predictions about the forthcoming "March on Washington". The vast intellectual desert that had been our starboard sponson would now be transplanted, probably to a park bench somewhere in the vicinity of the immortal Bernard Baruch. And John would descend on the bureaucrats like a swarm of locusts.

"After the war," said Murphy, "I plan to stop in Glenn's hometown in Illinois to get the true picture of wartime Washington from our old patriarch of the sponson. The story of his visits to the White House, and so on." Someone asked, "How will you go about finding him?" Murphy smiled. "Easy. He'll be sitting in a comfortable chair in the middle of Main Street under a tremendous neon sign with six-foot letters that say, "I SERVED – DID YOU?"

THE PAINFUL ORDEAL OF SEAMAN JOHN TRAINOR

We finally heard what happened to the lad who was so badly injured in the flight deck crash that killed Bryan Flanagan in November 1943. A woman newspaper reporter heard about him and published his story. She described the accident. "The whirling propeller caught the back of his leg and tore away all of the skin and most of his flesh, splintering the tibia and fibula and left the leg almost amputated. It hung by a few shreds of muscle and nerve. The hospital ship, "Solace", brought him, gaunt and emaciated, from the Central Pacific, his body wracked in agony, his mind tortured by an incessant, menacing voice that shouted in his brain, "They're going to cut off my leg!"

He had weighed 140 pounds when injured. When admitted to the Naval Hospital in San Diego, he weighed 89 pounds! It was nearly six months after the injury before Trainer (finally) was told the leg could be saved and that someday he would walk again – with two real legs, and no crutches!

War is not fun and games, waving flags, ticker tape parades and heroic deeds. (That's what they'd like to have you to believe!) War is blood and pain, death, and sacrifice. If mankind had more common sense, we'd have fewer wars. Maybe none at all.

CRIME REARS ITS UGLY HEAD, RIGHT AT MY DOORSTEP

August 9, en route to Pearl, I was told an investigating officer would need my stateroom, or part of it, on a certain night at 2 a.m. to spring a trap on suspected wrongdoers. I was not on night watch (at 2 a.m.) so I was in my bunk, awake, as a silent observer. Three radiomen had threatened to charge an aerologist with being homosexual if he didn't pay them in cash. They were meeting in the middle of the night outside the aerology office which was also just outside my room. Ensign Hofman hid behind the curtain in my room, eavesdropped and recorded the conversations. The bad guys were arrested and confined in the brig – a place on Navy ships where you don't want to be.

August 11, arrived in Pearl Harbor. I ran into John Benham, the Tab Hunter look-alike with the strange drinking habits, who was my assistant on the Rapidan. Hawaii was our return to civilization so we started wearing neckties again, our first time in many months. It made everyone look uncomfortable and it occurred to me that Admiral Halsey should be nominated for sainthood for deciding that naval officers didn't need neckties in combat areas during the war against Japan.

My buddy Tom Talbot got royally screwed. Admiral Stump's staff communications officer developed a medical condition requiring his transfer, so Stump arranged with Bowman to take Tom as replacement. After so many months of hazardous duty at sea, Tom deserved time stateside, but now he had to go west to the wars again. He was a good guy. I'll miss him.

FLYING INSIDE VOLCANOES, AND GOING INTO TAILSPINS

Commander Clifford, our Air Officer, had become one of my best friends in the Pacific War, and he talked me into flying with him, down to Hilo (on the "Big Island"). We made a full day of it and George made it a memorable day for me. As we flew over the island of Molokai, George pointed out the village of Kaunakekai, where, according to a popular Hawaiian song of those days, the "Cockeyed Mayor" did several things, but I forgot just what. In those days, Molokai was known mainly as a leper colony, and we flew low to get a good look. Know what they were doing? A big crowd of them were packed in a stadium watching horse races! And we flew really low for a good look at the tombstones of the many lepers who died there in years gone by.

We flew low over the village of Lahaina on Maui where Prukop's wife, Pat, lived with her parents while John was with us at sea. We gained altitude, up to 15,000 feet to clear the top of the crater at famed Mauna Loa. Then

George did something I never thought possible: he flew down *into* the crater of the volcano! He flew in tight circles, necessary because the crater isn't all that big. So we were banking steeply – when I looked left, I was looking straight down at the steam and smoke, fire and bubbling lava! Quite a thrill.

Then he climbed out of the crater and headed for the Kilauea fire pit and flew down into that for another close-up look. Back up then, and down the mountain right over the huge wasteland caused by the lava flow from the great volcanoes, all the way into the sea.

We stopped in Hilo for a couple of hours involving cocktails at the beautiful Hilo Hotel, and kingsize steaks at the Officers Club. On the way back, we flew fairly low up the northeastern sides of Hawaii and Maui and it was spectacular: sheer cliffs ranging from fifty to well over a thousand feet above the pounding surf, and everything unbelievably green, even the perpendicular sides of cliffs and mountains. I kept wondering how the greenery could stick to the jagged peaks. It looked like they were covered with green pool-table cloth!

We passed myriads of magnificent waterfalls, spaced a few hundreds of yards apart. Many tumbled for hundreds of feet. Some started as waterfalls but halfway down they'd give up the struggle and the wind would whip them into misty rainbows. I've never seen anything like it, anyplace else in the world.

George gave me a bit of a flying lesson and turned the controls over to me. I did pretty well. But after awhile he said I was ready for Lesson #2. "You're in a dogfight with a Japanese pilot in a Zero. He's on your tail and you're trying to get away. But you climb too fast, stall, and go into a tailspin. You have to know how to get out of that." So he told me to climb and watch the rate of climb, air speed and a couple of other things, and we did stall and went down tail first for a bit, then just fluttered and dropped, and the joy-stick went limp, and I was aware how nice it was to have George on board. He gave me directions which didn't work so well for me so he finally decided it was time to take back the controls and, of course, he got the plane back under control. Then he said, "Check the altimeter." I did. We had dropped nearly 5000 feet.

En route, Pearl to San Diego, I was appointed to serve on the Court Martial Board trying the case of our three blackmailers. We found them guilty and sentenced them to receive bad conduct discharges. Also worth noting: we had spent so much time in our sea-going "hot box" in tropical weather, that in the milder climate from Hawaii to S. California we got so cold we stood our watches in sheepskin overcoats! (The "thin blood" thing, I guess.)

CAPTAIN BOWMAN'S FAMOUS FAREWELL ADDRESS

Aware that he would leave the ship in San Diego, Captain Roscoe L. Bowman – on the day before our arrival – assembled the entire crew for his "farewell address". The officers and men of the Corregidor had served this man admirably, virtually every moment since we left Astoria, surviving great dangers, winning "Well Dones" from senior fleet commanders, *and even years later a book written about the Kaiser carriers commented several times about the accuracy of our gunfire in all the attacks at Saipan!* I was sure he would offer thanks and praise to everyone on board.

I was astonished at what he said. I don't remember exactly, after all these years, but it was something like this: "When you get ashore, many of you are going to act like idiots, get drunk and disorderly and end up in serious trouble. That's stupid! The local police and the Shore Patrol won't stand for that, and you will disgrace the Navy and yourselves. If any of you can stay sober, I hope you'll have the good sense to take care of the others. Keep them out of trouble!"

That was pretty much it. This guy just didn't get it. Boy, were we lucky to get rid of him!

Changes were happening, fast. A lot of mail that had been chasing us, finally caught up after we left Saipan. 25 letters from Laura! News from my family – weddings in Waverly, babies born, Aunt Rose sent to Washington. A $107 income tax refund from IRS. A year-old letter from me to Overton, returned, undelivered. Another letter from Cathy Dickinson, Mary's sister, now an Army nurse in England. (Cathy wrote to me off and on through all of WW2.) The bad news: old Wartburg friend, Paul Scharf, was shot down over Germany and presumed dead.

22 August – the day before Laura's birthday – we arrived in San Diego and I was able to get off the ship at 4:30 p.m. but had to be back at midnight: I had the Duty Command for all of the following (24 hour) day. *When I saw Laura again, it was for the first time in 10 months!* She was doing fine – had a job she liked, with co-workers she liked, at Auguste's Beauty Parlor. A wonderful French couple owned the establishment and Laura said they were the best people she ever worked for. She had a nice apartment on Howard Street, just north of Balboa Park. When I arrived, guess what? John Cronk was there, talking to Laura and drinking my beer! (More accurately, Laura's beer.)

We didn't ask him to stay. We let him finish his beer, mainly because his glass was almost empty. Quiet evening, but really great to be back. She took me back to the ship just before midnight, in time for me to serve as Senior Officer on Board all day on her birthday.

Times like these made me wish to be Secretary of the Navy someday. The first thing I'd do is have a rule that when a ship like ours spends many months at war and finally gets home, everyone on board would immediately leave and a whole contingent of shore-duty guys would take over and give the war-weary crew some real time off – until the ship was scheduled to sail again. Present system: every other day I couldn't leave the ship at all. And every other day, I'd have to stay on board until 16:30, then finally I would get off until midnight. So of every 48 hours, I got off 7 1/2 hours, and the Navy kept me on board 40 1/2 hours. Civilians normally work a 40-hour week. *I was on duty 141 hours a week! In port! And this after many months of very little or no time off at all!* War is hell, even if you don't get killed or wounded!

Cupid worked overtime when we got back to San Diego – 37 enlisted men and two officers committed Holy Matrimony!

SEPTEMBER 8 – LEAVE! TEN DAYS! I couldn't get government approval for Laura to fly, so a train ride back home (hers and mine) would take all the time just going and coming back. So we just phoned everyone back there and planned a more local vacation. Mr. Auguste drove us to the station for a train ride to L.A. and a bus ride to Lake Arrowhead. Rented a cabin a mile-and-a-half uphill and camped there in the deep woods. The next day we went horseback riding, swam in the lake, rented a canoe and paddled around, ate dinner, played miniature golf, were too tired to dance and hiked back to the cabin by moonlight. Had a good time in a beautiful place but decided we'd done everything there was to do. So the next day we caught a bus to L.A. and got a suite at the Hollywood Knickerbocker.

WE VISIT WARNER BROTHERS

The Chief Photographer on the Corregidor had been a big wheel photographer at Warner Brothers studio before the war. On a previous trip to San Diego he had arranged for several of our officers to visit the studio and they had a wonderful time. So before we left the ship on this little vacation, I had asked him if he could get Laura and me visitors' passes. He said probably not – all the studios were processing combat footage and had been closed to the public for the duration. But he said he'd try and I should give him a phone call. I did, and he said the next day a bunch of Admirals and Generals were reviewing footage taken at Saipan and Guam and he told the powers that be that I had been there, and he got me in as a technical expert and eye-witness to this particular campaign! He said to be there at 10 a.m. and take Laura with me. A PR representative met us and became our guide.

We sat in a small theater with about 35 top military brass and a dozen studio executives and watched nearly two hours of film. Then the PR guy introduced us to the President of Warner Bros. who treated me like visiting royalty because of my combat experience. He told the PR guy to take the day off and give us the VIP tour of the studio.

It was a great experience. We watched "God is My Co-Pilot" being made, were introduced to Raymond Massey, Dennis Morgan, Ida Lupino and a bunch of other actors and directors I can't remember. Watched Ida Lupino doing movie scenes. Saw the set for Bette Davis making "The Corn is Green", but the lady never let any visitors watch her work. We liked the prop department and the street sets best. We spent the rest of the day, and before we left, the PR guy invited us to be guests at the upcoming big Warner Bros. Party – said it would be lavish: cocktails, dinner, dancing, special entertainment. "All the stars will be there," he said. "It's virtually a command performance. It's an annual event, one of the biggest bashes in Hollywood!"

Unfortunately, it was scheduled for two days after our ship was leaving San Diego! But it was fun just knowing we'd been asked.

We had a great ten days. Dinner at the Brown Derby (famous in those times as a movie-people hangout. Saw minor stars Joan Davis, Rags Ragland, William Frawley and others you wouldn't remember. Sat beside Frawley who later became semi-famous playing "Fred Mertz", one of the main characters in "I Love Lucy" which ran on TV for years. At "Slapsie Maxie's" night club, we ate, drank, watched the Ted Lewis stage show and danced along with Ben Blue, Joan Davis, Harry Ritz, Eddie Cantor and wife Ida and George Burns and Gracie Allen. Great Chinese food at Don the Beachcomber. A couple of stage plays. Bussed to Compton and had dinner with longtime Waverly friend, Carol Jane Osterholm and her parents, Pike and Myrtle. CJ is now Mrs. Brown – he's 10 years older, a Captain in the Army, *and she hasn't seen him in 2 years!* She believes he's in Italy.

Returning to San Diego by train proved something of an adventure. Trains were crowded. Service men got on first, wives later. I got on to get us seats, as half the passengers would have to stand up all the way. When the train left, I walked about 15 cars looking for Laura – and learned she was among many not allowed on. I got off in Santa Ana, caught another train back, and hoped I would find her: *I was carrying all the money – she had none at all!* But Travelers Aid was taking good care of her when I got back to L.A. and found her.

My remaining days in San Diego were very good ones. The Augustes invited us for a great dinner and a Sunday afternoon tour of the area, and on another occasion, let us borrow their car. I got acquainted with Laura's best friend and co-worker, Brownie. Got her a date with LCDR Wiley, our Supply Officer and took them (in Augustes' car) to famous Café La Maze in National City for steaks.

George Clifford threw a cocktail party for the two Captains – new and departing – at his house with all officers attending. It was my first meeting with our new C.O., Wade McClusky, and I was favorably impressed. Wiley had a date with a gal named Shirley: we went in style as he rented a car and after the party we went out for dinner and dancing. We even saw my first football game in years, Army vs. San Diego Bombers. Lots of former college All-Americans.

I think I made a good impression on Mr. and Mrs. Auguste. They gave us a chocolate pie and a bottle of wine from their collection, advised us to see Europe while we are young, and told me Laura was the best employee and most popular person who ever worked for them!

I truly savored every minute of my time with Laura and being back in civilization. But as repairs were completed and we loaded all our ammunition and bombs back onto the ship, I knew we'd soon be headed back to sea. I could only hope my luck would hold out so I'd eventually return all in one piece.

As we loaded all our ammo back on the ship, we set a new record for CVEs and got a "Well Done" from the Naval Air Station Command. When I had the Duty Command, Laura came aboard for dinner and evening and told me how proud and impressed she was when, as Senior Officer on Board, I headed the Wardroom Mess! She also got acquainted with my good friend Clarence "Scoop" Rutherford, and agreed he was a very special young officer.

The night before we sailed, I was the Standby Duty Commander and slated to stay on board. I was surprised when the Exec, Red Williamson, let me go home and report back at 6 a.m. Even so, saying goodbye was more difficult than ever.

We sailed at 1300 (1 p.m.). *Thirty-two of our enlisted men failed to show up – Absent Over Leave.* I wondered what would happen to them.

As we stood out of San Diego harbor, heading west, I was thinking about an ALNAV announcing a new School of Military Government, requesting officers to train for duty in formerly enemy countries where we expected to take over and run things after the war. It sounded interesting. I had discussed it with Laura and she gave me the go-ahead. I felt I had a chance to be selected – my Political Science major, a college course in Municipal Government, Chamber of Commerce experience, good war record, and I hoped to be promoted to LCDR soon. If a lot of exams were involved, I knew I'd do extremely well. On the other hand, with my experience and good record, they might want to keep me at sea.

At any rate, I applied and the new C.O. and Williamson forwarded my request, approved.

As we got out to sea, we fired AA gunnery practice and even with so many replacements in my gun crews, we shot down five sleeves. And guess what? McClusky gave us the "Well Done" Bowman never did!

CAPTAIN CLARENCE WADE MCCLUSKY

As I look back on my years in our wartime Navy, I realize that the three greatest things that happened to me were: (1) I survived; (2) Laura; (3) Wade McClusky. I learned our new C.O. was one of the pioneers of naval aviation, had been a member of the famous Saratoga "High Hat" Squadron, was considered to be the hero of the Battle of Midway, and Admiral Spruance had labeled him as "The Outstanding Naval Hero of World War 2"!

Quite a record, I'd say. As a very young flyer, he helped prove that aircraft carriers were feasible and could become a major military weapon. His High Hat Squadron was the earliest version of the famous Blue Angels aerobatics team. These guys, flying old bi-planes, would tie three of them together with 50 feet of rope between the planes, then take off, do spectacular aerial stunts and land – all roped together. They were so good, they made the Army Air Corps look bad, and were finally ordered to stop!

THE BATTLE OF MIDWAY

In World War 2, we had broken the Jap code in time to know a huge enemy task force had left Japan, heading in the general direction of Pearl Harbor. Their Dec. 7, 1941 attack on Pearl had damaged our Pacific fleet and Japan was then considered to have the superior naval power. On June 3, 1942, our long-range patrol planes discovered a Japanese force of 80 ships, including troop transports, believed planning to attack, or more likely invade, either Midway or the Hawaiian Islands. Our carrier force went out to meet them, arriving in the general area a few days later but unable to find them. CDR McClusky was in command of the planes of the USS Enterprise, searching vast areas of the Pacific. Back on the ship, the Combat Information Center

(CIC) was monitoring the air time of the planes to assure getting them all safely back. Then all of the pilots were ordered to abort the search mission and return (before they ran out of gas).

McClusky had been recording data on areas searched and felt sure that with some additional time he could find the enemy fleet. So, he feigned radio malfunction, ignored orders to call off the search, and a few minutes later, found the Jap fleet. Flying a divebomber, he attacked a large carrier and put his bombs "right down the stack". His wingmen also hit the ship and it exploded, burned and later was seen to go under the sea. Others in his squadron bombed, strafed and scored. Planes from other U.S. carriers joined in; the result was an overwhelming victory. The invasion never occurred. In three days running battle, the Japanese lost four large aircraft carriers and two heavy cruisers, and three battleships and ten other vessels sank or were badly damaged. Our side lost the carrier Yorktown and one destroyer. We lost 92 officers and 215 men; the Japanese casualties were estimated at 4,800!

McClusky had been an expert fighter pilot and soon found himself fighting for his life as carrier-based Zeroes arrived. Several went after him. His plane was hit and McClusky was badly wounded. By skimming the waves, he made it back to the closest of our carriers, landed safely, then immediately lost consciousness. The doctors in Sick Bay fought to save his life as the carrier fought off attacking enemy divebombers. The Battle of Midway was a major victory for us and the turning point of the Pacific War.

The more I learned about Wade McClusky the more I liked and admired him. He was so badly shot up at Midway, he had to put in lengthy hospital time, then was given a desk job in Washington to regain his health. When fully recovered, he was given command of the Corregidor.

Where Bowman constantly criticized and belittled, I never heard McClusky criticize anyone. Our new C.O. was "one of us". A lot of ship captains, when off the ship, seek out old Annapolis classmates. McClusky (like Captain MacIntosh) spent his Officers Club time with his officers. We came into Eniwetok and he asked all of us to join him at the "O" Club, at "cocktail time". I and a few others went swimming first, and were a bit late in joining the party. As we arrived, Bud Cox was telling McClusky, "With all due respect, sir, I know damn well, you can't do it". The reply came: "Tell you what, Bud. If I can't, I'll buy the drinks for every one of our officers. If I *can*, you buy!"

I had no idea what they were talking about, but as soon as Cox agreed, the Captain set his "usual" – a Gibson – on the floor, then got down on his stomach, wiggled a bit, *then did seven push-ups with one arm!* And then he downed his drink. He was, I'd guess, in his late 30's or maybe 40 at the time and not too long from being badly wounded in combat. We probably had 80-some young officers on board, most in great shape, and I knew not a one of us could do what he just did!

Sometimes in port, I played badminton when space was available on the hangar deck. I got pretty good at it. One day, McClusky challenged me and totally humiliated me – 21 to nothing, as I remember! Then I heard he was, at one time, the Pacific Fleet tennis champion, and just before the war often played with famous Bobby Riggs.

THE GUY WHO SLEPT WITH GARY COOPER'S WIFE ????

As we headed back to the war, I was extremely busy, standing middle-of-the-night watches again and training gun crews. So I didn't get the big news until my fourth or fifth day underway. I finally sat in a bull session when someone began to talk about "the guy who slept with Gary Cooper's wife." Obviously, some kind of a joke. Or was it?

As I mentioned, we had a brand new squadron of flyers on board. They had previously been on a Kaiser carrier in the Atlantic, but were detached months before and given some R. and R. time and retraining in Southern California. It seems that all Navy squadrons had a couple of fairly-senior non-flying officers serving as Intelligence Officers, Personnel Officers, Fighter Directors, etc. who manned stations in CIC whenever our planes were in the air. These men were usually a bit older than the flyers, men who had been successful lawyers, business executives, stockbrokers, college professors, etc.

In VC-42 (our new group) one of these was a Hollywood talent agent who told the flyboys if they got anywhere near Los Angeles he would throw a big party "with a lot of movie stars". He had never talked much about his civilian life, so nobody in the squadron really believed that would ever happen.

But it did, and it was a fabulous affair, with more of the agent's clients attending than the number of officers in the squadron. And some of them were famous movie stars, not just movie actors. The flyers were treated as heroes. Dinner, dancing, speeches – and unlimited alcoholic beverages. A number of the officers woke up the next day in strange surroundings – *one in the bed of Gary Cooper's wife!* When he found out where he was, he couldn't get away fast enough – scared to death! According to the story, she phoned him the following day – and the day after that. He was flattered – who wouldn't be – but had the good sense to resist the temptation. (At least for awhile.) The squadron then moved from somewhere south of L.A. to somewhere north of L.A. and he felt safer. But she found him and drove up to see him. I was told human nature took over, and you know what happens when that happens! At least that's the story. But I remained skeptical.

But I knew Gary Cooper, rich and famous, was middle-aged and some of the WW2 flyboys were young, dashing, handsome. I suppose it could have happened. At any rate, I saw one member of our new squadron who looked familiar. I introduced myself and found out he was Scotty Oleson from Cedar Falls. We found out we had many mutual friends, we talked a lot and finally figured out I had seen him play high school basketball against Waverly in 1939 and most likely had never seen him after that! (What a memory!) At any rate, we hit it off and Scotty assured me the Gary Cooper story was true.

What do you think? By the way, the fly-boy involved was definitely *not* tall, dark and handsome. She could have done much better!

Guess who I ran into in Pearl? Paul Pomeroy Stewart. We agreed to meet for dinner but he never showed up. For which I was thankful. (What was I thinking?)

NEW DEAL? Russ Wilkinson came to see me and said, "Robert, I'm too damn old for this war business. I have connections in high places that can get me shore duty, but first I have to get someone to navigate this ship. It's the best job on this ship – or any ship – and I think you should have it."

"Now I know how you made a million selling real estate," I told him. "You're a super salesman." But the navigator does have the best job, and one of the most responsible. It would be a good change of pace. I was inclined to accept the invitation – except I knew that if I became navigator I'd probably be condemned to sea duty for as long as the war went on.

Two things bothered me greatly: I had been at sea too long, and too long without another promotion. Bowman had given me two jobs – Gunnery Officer and "Duty Commander" – without giving me the rank that either of them deserved. I surely rated a "spot promotion" but Bowman would never think of that. (Maybe I should have asked – I knew I was a better Gun Boss than the higher-ranking guys on the Coral Sea and Liscome Bay, and neither of them stood night watches at sea as "Assistant Captains".)

A NEW RANK? LIEUTENANT SUPER-GRADE?

Adding considerably to my problem, the Navy fell way behind the other services in promoting its officers. My friend, Pep Grawe, joined the Marines more than a year after I was commissioned and sent to sea; he was a good officer and had some hazardous duty, but he never came close to my combat experience and he made Major while I still remained at a lower rank in the Navy. Without a spot promotion I couldn't move up faster than my class – and we were delayed so long, some wag, somewhere, "invented" a new rank, "Lieutenant Super Grade". This was for guys like me, and it stated that if Congress couldn't authorize the promotions and pay increases we deserved, they should (at least) bestow appropriate privileges, and it listed them. I can't remember them all but one was we would be the only rank authorized to wear neon stripes! And our only duty would be as members of Station Wagon Crash Investigation Boards. This made its way throughout the entire Navy.

Anyway, I told Russ Wilkinson I'd start training for the navigation job and began to get up early and take star sights with him. Also, I was spending a fair amount of time writing the story of the Corregidor. Early in the war some guy got drafted and wrote a book called, "See Here, Private Hargrove". It wasn't very good – full of old military clichés. But his timing was great: it sold like crazy and even got made into a movie! I thought: I can write better than that! I was in the Atlantic, pretty busy at the time, and never got started. Later, a war correspondent, Ernie Pyle, became famous – embedded with army combat troops and writing about it. My Corregidor story was Ernie Pyle style, real events, real people, real names. I finally completed it and got it to Fleet Censorship in Pearl in December 1944. My timing was bad, actually fatal. By the time it got through Fleet Censorship – many months later – book publishers figured the war was almost over and no longer had any interest in books like mine.

Actually, it was a pretty good book. One of the officers at Fleet Censorship was a successful writer: he thought it was good and suggested I send it to his literary agent in New York. But as months went by and the manuscript was still in Hawaii, he began to warn me that time was working against me and my prospects were fading. I finally ended up with several complimentary rejection slips from major publishers, but no sale. (A couple suggested I get started writing about a serviceman's return to civilian life, post-war.)

One of the Navy's most famous aircraft carriers, the Enterprise, was nicknamed "The Big E". So, tongue-in-cheek, I called my Corregidor story, "The Big C". The manuscript is around here somewhere. The censors actually scissored out what they didn't want published, so some pages look like lace.

NEW JOB, THE BEST JOB ON THE SHIP

McClusky drank a lot, but never showed it. He especially enjoyed time ashore with Russ Wilkinson – they wore roughly the same age – and they always ended up with Russ totally inebriated and the Captain taking care of him. This amused the Captain immensely.

So, one day Russ told me, "Robert, you're ready. Let's go talk to the Captain." Russ then told McClusky I could navigate and suggested he ask the Bureau in Washington to cut orders assigning the two of us to new duties, accordingly. (Navigators had to be assigned by BUPERS in Washington.) McClusky asked, "Is he fully qualified?" Russ said, "Oh, yes. He's been navigating right along with me…" McClusky interrupted. "Russ, *I know he can navigate.* But is he *fully* qualified?" Then, with a straight face, he added, "Can he drink with me? Some of these young guys can't hold their liquor like you and me! You're the only one who can keep up with me. Can Bob do that?"

Washington responded in a hurry and I became the Navigator – the best job on the ship. I got a new larger stateroom, all to myself. Also, I got a "sea cabin", a small "bedroom" just below the bridge, with a voice tube so the Officer of the Deck could call me in the night if he felt I was needed. (The Captain also had a similar "sea cabin".) I was taken, of course, off the watch list – I didn't have to do anything but navigate.

What I didn't get was a spot promotion. I continued to be the senior "Lieutenant Super-Grade" on the Corregidor.

NEW DUTY FOR "THE BIG C" – ANTI-SUBMARINE WARFARE

Someone in Washington apparently decided we needed a respite from the hazards of supporting our invasions of Japanese bases: we were assigned to test a new idea in Anti-Submarine Warfare. We became the first aircraft carrier to head up a "Hunter-Killer Task Unit". But first we had to go to school – in Hawaii.

So a bunch of us – Captain, Exec, Air Officer, yours truly and a couple others – spent a couple of weeks at Anti-Submarine Warfare school at DesPac (Destroyers, Pacific) and even at sea on a destroyer, training with a live sub – one of ours, of course.

We also had to keep training our new squadron. In this regard we encountered more casualties than expected. On 15 October, a barrier crash badly damaged a plane. That night one of our pilots got lost and had to make a night landing – dangerous on a small CVE in those days – but made it OK. Next day, we catapulted a torpedo bomber that tried to go straight up and, of

NAVIGATOR – the best job on the ship. And important: he decides where we are, and how to get where we're going.

course, plunged into the sea, crew rescued, plane lost. And the day after that, another TBM wrapped itself around a smokestack and broke into pieces. The radioman escaped, miraculously. No other injuries.

POSTSCRIPT. Sometimes it takes awhile for battle statistics to be refined and published. I had just heard that in our invasion of Saipan, the island was defended by 32,000 enemy troops, and after the action ended, we counted 28,811 of them dead! We had 3,426 killed and 16,000 casualties. That's just Saipan – not Guam, Tinian or Rota – nor any who died on both sides at sea.

THE BATTLE OF LEYTE GULF

On 23 October, we heard about another huge naval battle, this one without us! We were landing a large invasion force in the Philippines, in Leyte Gulf. The Japanese knew about it. The senior Jap admiral divided his total remaining naval power into three forces. The Northern Force would let itself be discovered and lure Admiral Halsey and our entire major naval Task Force to come after it, believing it to be the entire Japanese fleet. Then the enemy's Southern Force – would sail virtually unopposed into Leyte Gulf and totally annihilate our invasion force, which was almost totally non-combatant ships. Halsey took the bait. When the enemy's huge Southern Force arrived, at the site of our invasion, only eighteen "eminently sinkable" Kaiser carriers and a few destroyers were there to confront them. (A couple of the CVEs weren't Kaisers.)

This was so one-sided it would be like shooting fish in a barrel. Our CVEs couldn't outrun the enemy, couldn't survive the 8-inch, 14 and 16-inch gunfire. This powerful Jap force could destroy all our CVEs and DDs in a very few hours and then totally destroy all our troop transports, landing ships and landing forces!

But something important happened. The CVEs launched their aircraft and attacked the superior enemy forces. Our destroyers and destroyer escorts attacked. Suicide missions, but it was all they could do. The boldness and fury of our attacks caught the enemy by surprise and the Jap Admiral began to believe his Southern Force had been lured into a trap, and the main U.S. battle fleet would suddenly appear. After a bloody battle that sank two of our CVEs and three destroyers and downed many of our aircraft, he decided to leave! Broke it off, turned around and got the hell out of there!

So, did our forces thank God and get the hell out of there? No, they rearmed and went back attacking the retreating enemy forces!

Incredible mistakes were made on both sides. The greatest, of course, was by the Japanese Admiral Kurita whose powerful 30-knot battle force was closing in on our 17 1/2-knot vulnerable CVE's and could have annihilated all 18 of them (15,000 of our men, plus possibly another 10,000 on our destroyers) – and then annihilate our landing forces which involved some 700 non-combatant ships and many thousands of men! Talk about shooting fish in a barrel! This could have been an unprecedented disaster!

Kinkaid's CVE's were taken by surprise and their confused response could have been comical if not so tragic. There was no time to remove 100-pound bombs and other light-weight explosives and load torpedoes, so many of these flyers attacked the armored Jap battleships with weapons that only succeeded in messing up their paint jobs! One CVE even catapulted a torpedo bomber with no pilot or crew in it!

And the Japs made mistakes. Their battleships and cruisers were using armor-piercing shells, and several cases were reported of these hitting our flimsy "coffins" *and going right in, through, and out the other side without even exploding!*

The two Kaiser CVE's sunk were former members of our little three-carrier division at Saipan and elsewhere: the Gambier Bay, and the St. Lo (named the "Midway" when it sailed with us – the name changed because the Navy wanted Midway for a new super-carrier).

But far to the north, Halsey's powerful 3rd Fleet caught up with the enemy's Northern Force and scored a major victory, sinking four of their carriers and a cruiser. *Japan's naval power was finally and irreparably crushed!*

A lot of us on "The Big C" felt left out, not being in the Leyte Gulf action. You have to be a total idiot to feel that way, but I'm sure we all felt we would have survived, and until this happened, we knew we were (or had been) the King of the CVE's.

THE HUNTING PARTY

As the war against Japan moved ever westward, the Pacific from Hawaii to our west coast became ever safer. But all of a sudden an enemy submarine popped up between Hawaii and California, torpedoed and sank two ships, then rammed and strafed the survivors. The Corregidor was ordered to go hunting.

We had trained for this – but not much. We'd try out the new ASW (Antisubmarine Warfare) system and see what happened. We sailed in company with five destroyers – maybe they were DE's – I forget. The Big Idea was to launch three aircraft, one to search an area up to 100 miles ahead of us, the others 75 miles out on each side of us. This would cover a huge expanse of ocean and we hoped they would spot an enemy sub on the surface.

Seeing our aircraft, the sub would dive. Our plane would dash to the area and drop a dozen or so "Sonobuoys" in a big circle around where the sub had been seen. These gadgets would transmit sound or radio signals that would tell the pilot where the submerged sub was heading. Then the pilot would drop a new device called "FIDO". It was like a small torpedo that would "listen" for the sub, chase it and explode on contact. Hopefully. All super-secret at the time.

As we left Pearl, the Captain and I and the Communications' Officer, Paul Phillips, were on the bridge. One of our escorts was skippered by no less than *Franklin D. Roosevelt, Jr.* During the war, every ship was assigned a code name (changed with every operation), so TBS (Talk Between Ships) radio transmissions, if overheard, would not reveal what ships they really were.

Phillips was there to tell McClusky what the code names were for our escorts. We all knew FDR, Jr., was C.O. of the Moore and Phillips said the code name for Moore was "Eleanor". Our Captain laughed and said, "O.K., Paul, what is it really?" It took some time for Phillips to convince McClusky that it really was "Eleanor". (In case you are reading this many years from now and don't get it, *Eleanor* Roosevelt was his mother, FDR's famous wife.)

On November 2, we thought we got the sub – or a sub. Our search plane got a radar contact, went there, the pip disappeared, we dropped sonobuoys, regained contact, attacked with three FIDOs. One exploded. But, we could never verify the kill!

On November 14, we received word that a destroyer got him (or one of his buddies) about 200 miles from us, a hundred miles from where it had sunk the Johnson. And this kill was confirmed.

Also on the 14th, we began to have an unusual run of accidents – a lot of crashes. Two planes went into the sea and one, on landing, got tangled in the barrier cables, whipped around and knocked Leo McCarty, the man in the asbestos suit, right off the flight deck and into the sea. He never came up.

November 15 was the second anniversary of my wedding. I last saw Laura *many months* ago.

On November 16, another of our planes crashed into the sea. Our trailing destroyer picked up all the crewmembers – but S.J. Pakulski, the tail gunner, died aboard the destroyer.

On November 18, we had another landing go badly, the plane crashing into the gun gallery where a similar accident killed Brian Flanagan and horribly injured seaman John Trainor. This one nearly ended the life of Petty Officer Whitmore, ship's photographer. When he saw the airplane veering toward him, he dived over the side and grabbed the railing, hung on for dear life, yelled for help to get the plane lifted enough for him to be pulled back on board! A less athletic person would never have been able to escape, or hang on that long with his body and legs dangling over the sea 30 feet below. Label him lucky!

November 7 was Election Day; FDR won and became the only President in U.S. history elected to four terms. Arrived in Pearl on the 19th. Bud Cox and Slim Coffman (Flight Deck Officer) were passed over for LCDR. Lots of mail. Bad news: my sister, Helen had her first child, a boy, but he didn't survive. Back to sea on the 21st. This time we sighted a sub on the surface, attacked, but he got away. Played a lot of basketball. I can still score – high point man with 21 in a short, 20-minute game. Returned to Pearl Harbor on Dec. 6 – what if this were three years ago? (I'm sure you remember, Dec. 7 was "the day that lived in infamy.")

At sea again, 14 December. Then another Christmas at sea, my 3rd in a row. Back in port, 12/26. Aunt Gertrude sent me subscriptions to Readers

Digest and Coronet and said my (older) cousins, Charlie Shepard and Ralph Jurgensen, were in Hawaii. Letters from Laura, home, Fred Studier, Pete Cordt and Overton, who just became a father for the first time (of many!).

New Year's Eve at the Tennis Club in Pearl with the Captain, Exec, and our Chief Engineer. It had been quite a year. I have been on sea duty now for 45 months. I am very tired. Some things bother me greatly, but all in all, I'm happy: we are now winning the war, both in Europe and in the Pacific. Equally important, I'm still alive.

1945, HERE WE COME!

At this stage of the war, I was spending much of my "leisure" time with Clarence "Scoop" Rutherford and Atwood Ely. These two were roommates and surely an "Odd Couple". Scoop came from a "dirt poor" background, and he looked it. Atwood was every inch the "rich kid" – *really* rich: prep school, Yale, summers on a dude ranch, the works. Strangely, they were best friends.

Rutherford was one of the most intellectual guys I ever knew, and perhaps a bit on the weird side, constantly pondering the meaning of life (and death), wondering "Is there a God?" and "What exactly is a soul?" He must have read everything ever published as he seemed to know everything about everything. We had spent a lot of night watches together and we talked about important things on all of them. Scoop became my best friend of the Pacific War.

Atwood looked like a sissy but he sure as hell wasn't. He was on the Yale wrestling team and, I think, Ivy League champion in his weight class. One day he saw me do a half gainer at an Officers Club pool in Pearl, was impressed and wanted me to teach him how. He couldn't get it and lit flat so many times, and took such a beating, I finally made him quit. He was ready to die trying. And I thought it was funny to find out Atwood had spent so much time with rich friends that he thought everyone who had ever attended college was also rich. He watched me navigate one time, opined that I seemed to enjoy it, then suggested, "After the war, Bob, you should buy a yacht!"

We talked about the stock market and he told me he had done "a bit of investing" on his own. It seems he had four siblings, but his father had adopted and raised five others, nieces and nephews orphaned when they lost both parents in an auto accident. "I grew up with nine other kids and we were all like one family." When the ten were teenagers, the father gave each one of them $10,000 and told them, "Use this to learn about the stock market."

$10,000 then was like $50,000 or much more (as I write this) and maybe considerably more when you read it – depending on when that is. 10 kids. You do the arithmetic. Until Atwood told me the story – which he didn't consider at

all unusual – I never knew anyone was that wealthy.

In 1945, we continued to spend a lot of time at sea in the central Pacific, logging a lot of nautical miles and continuing to have more barrier crashes and landing accidents than we ought to. In "Queen of the Flat-tops", the author pointed out, with some amazement, that the famed Lexington had steamed a total of 43,311 miles during the busiest five months of her career, December 7, 1941 until May 8, 1942 when she met her glorious end in the Coral Sea. The Corregidor has been keeping up about the same average ever since our commissioning! 85,000 nautical miles in our first ten months out of Astoria. And the Lex cruised at least 30% faster, so we had to put in 30% more time at sea to match the mileage!

By Christmas '44, we had logged 100,000 nautical miles. A nautical mile is longer than our statutory miles, so this amounts to more than 113,000 of those.

SOME ODDS AND ENDS: officially, in the United States Navy there is no such things as seasickness! During the war, Annapolis graduates were called "the Trade School Boys", and reserve officers, "Feather Merchants". Officers like me maintained that we "Volunteers" served only in hazardous wartime, while "the regular navy" guys were "glorified caretakers" who simply kept the equipment from getting rusty between wars. And someone (obviously regular navy) claimed that Academy men were officers and gentlemen, and the Merchant Marines (Mundy, Houston) were officers trying to be gentlemen, and the rest of us were gentlemen trying to be officers.

One day when mail arrived, Scoop came to tell me that he and Alice had produced the first of a new generation of Rutherfords. It was a boy, and this cost me $5 because I had called it wrong. I paid up and was told the money would be used to buy Robin Lee a present, in my name, and I should designate the item. Of course, I thought of a football, but I recalled my many discussions with Rutherford, Sr., so I suggested books. Not kid books, but some tailored to the Rutherford I.Q. "Meditations of Marcus Aurelius" and Spengler's "Decline of the West" immediately came to mind. But: "Like father, like son," so I rather expected a letter from Robin Lee saying, "Thanks, but I've already read both in their original languages!"

LUCKY DOG TAGS! We all wore "dog tags" during the war – metal I.D.'s on a chain, in case we got killed. J.W. Randle, photograph's mate, put in for a new one, but said he'd like to keep the old one as a souvenir. When a fighter plane crashed into the catwalk, its whirling propeller sheared a piece of metal from the catwalk and hurled it toward him with bullet-like speed. It hit him in the chest, but the dog tag got in the way. Casualties: badly bent dog tag, badly bruised chest. *Doc said the dog tag saved his life!* Randle claims he saw he couldn't get out of the way so he used the dog tag as a shield. Shipmates say he is now eligible for membership in the politically powerful Corregidor Liars Club.

Another item worth mentioning. Ensign Forehand came in for a landing, much too low, pulled up steeply, cleared the flight deck, but his tail hook caught the rear edge of said flight deck. So, the after half of the torpedo bomber stopped right there, and the front end kept on going! Nobody was hurt, including C.Q. Rappold, the radioman, who found himself on his seat, alone, on the flight deck, with some of the plane well behind him and the rest of it way out ahead! None of us had ever seen anything like this before – or since!

Sometimes I think about all the mangled aircraft we pushed off the ship for "burial at sea", and wish I could inherit all the millions of dollars they cost and spend the rest of my life being rich.

OUR SEARCH FOR GENERAL HARMON, DOWN IN THE PACIFIC

Next to General "Hap" Arnold who ran the Army Air Corps from a desk job in Washington, the senior officer of all Air Corps operations in the Pacific was General Millard Harmon. While flying base to base in the Central Pacific, his plane suddenly disappeared. The Corregidor was sent out to find him, using the same technique we employed searching for enemy submarines. For several days, we searched, our aircraft covering a huge expanse of the largest ocean on earth. We never found him. I never expected we would.

TYPHOON!

But we did find something: ourselves, in the middle of a dangerous typhoon! All we could do was head into the wind and ride it out, the Corregidor and our five destroyers. All of us were deeply concerned, wondering if our "quick and dirty" Kaiser Coffin could stand the high winds and heavy seas.

We rode it out for three full days, with no opportunity for me to get a sun line or star sight, and in those days, in that part of the world, there was no other way to navigate, except for dead reckoning. Whenever we could, we would use celestial navigation to "fix" our position and we'd expect that to be accurate. Then we'd use dead reckoning to approximate our position between "fixes", and usually that's close enough. (If you travel from fix A on course 270° (due west) at speed 15 knots for eight hours, you can assume you end up 120 nautical miles due west of A at that time.)

But in a typhoon, hurricane or whatever, celestial navigation is impossible and dead reckoning doesn't work very well either. The navigator has to play a guessing game. This because, heading into the wind and sea at 15 knots (or whatever), you know you *may* be progressing at that speed *through the water, but not over the land under the water* – and that's what determines where you are. Whatever speed we were using (for maximum safety) – probably 8 or 10 knots – I had to guess whether the wind and sea were allowing us to edge forward a bit, just hold our own, or maybe actually setting us back – and in any case, how much?

After three days, the winds died down, the weather cleared, and our escorts regained their proper stations. Now we were all (practically) in the same place, so we asked each of our new escorts to report their positions, and we plotted theirs and mine on a chart. These were, of course, our dead reckoning positions. At evening twilight, good visibility allowed us to shoot the stars and get a good fix.

Turned out, I was the best navigator—18 miles off with my dead reckoning. Not bad for three days in a typhoon. The best of our escorts was off by 36 miles – the worst by 110! But we never had to be concerned with running aground: the closest shallow water was two or three hundred miles away.

Typhoons may be said to be nature's warfare against the human race – especially those of us at sea. We got lucky – no loss of life, and even our flimsy Kaiser Coffin survived, although we did sustain structural damage serious enough to alter our assignments for the rest of the war.

HOWEVER…much later we discovered just how fortunate we were: *the same hurricane, just west of us, totally devastated a larger naval task force!* I'll tell you more about this later on, but consider this: *three destroyers capsized, with no survivors!* And this is just part of the story!

Obviously, we just missed the worst of it – saved by geography? (As they say, *location* is everything!)

IN WHICH I GET JUST A BIT TOO COCKY

We were ordered to abandon the search for General Harmon – he was never found. (We had searched half a million square miles of the Pacific Ocean!) Our escorts were detached, except one assigned to protect us on the way back to Pearl Harbor. En route, I did something stupid, on purpose. It was after midnight. I was asleep in my sea cabin when the OOD called me. It was Rutherford. He had a problem, needed my advice, and asked me to come to the bridge.

Our escort, on our left, reported an enemy submarine contact. Scoop acted properly – he turned to starboard, away from the contact. Unfortunately, there was a low-lying atoll close on our right. It showed up on our radar but the atolls are so low, you can't depend on radar to accurately measure the distance. In addition, coral reefs extend outward from several yards to a mile or more. Question 1: turn back toward the sub contact? (Better that than going aground!) Question 2: call the Captain? (Of course – according to Navy Regs, you have to.)

McClusky had stayed awake, on duty day and night, throughout the raging typhoon. He was totally out of it. I said, "Let him sleep, Scoop. We can handle this." I ordered a zigzag course and we changed as often as I thought necessary to avoid "Scylla and Charybdis" – the enemy sub on the one side and the coral reef on the other. And I got away with it.

I knew my decision to go it alone was totally stupid, but somehow I was proud of being so sure I could make the right decisions. The next morning, the Captain sent for me. He'd been checking the Dead Reckoning Tracer that records all course changes, and he asked, "What the hell was happening last night?" I told him the story. He thought for a minute, then laughed. "Next time," he said, "maybe you better call me."

"I will," I told him. "Next time you probably won't be going three days without any sleep." (Happy Bowman would have had me court-martialed. But then, I wouldn't have done it for him.)

ORDERS TO SHORE DUTY? YOU'VE GOT TO BE KIDDING!

I hate to keep repeating myself but, except for that Polish girl I met in Chicago, Wade McClusky was the best thing that happened to me in WW2. He gave me my best Fitness Report ever. And one day the Captain called me in and said, "I'm looking at your records and it says here you've been on sea duty for 46 months." He looked up and I said, "That's right." He said, "No, that may be *true* but it's not *right*! That's much too long. You should have been rotated ashore." I totally agreed. He said, "There are a few others out here too long. None as long as you. I'll ask the Bureau to send all of you ashore." (Now *that's* an A-1 C.O.!) Not too long after that, we all got orders – back to the States for further assignment. In a few weeks the other officers – I forget just who they were – began to pack up and check out. But as navigator, I couldn't leave until I was replaced by another navigator assigned by the Bureau of Personnel. His name was included in my orders.

So I waited. Meanwhile, Scoop and a couple of others who left us wrote me the good news: "When you get back, you won't believe how things have changed! They treat you royally. You'll get 30 days leave, and they'll ask what part of the U.S. you'd prefer for your next duty! (*Shore duty*, that is!) This was hard to believe! Really?

Didn't make any difference to me. Someone who knew my replacement told me the guy had been on duty in the Pacific early in the war and he'd never go back. After quite a long time, the Bureau notified me that the guy was in a Navy Hospital in Seattle with a bad back and should be relieving me shortly. But he stalled with great success. I met him many months later, *after the war was over,* and he was reporting aboard the Corregidor just as I was leaving the Navy on my accumulated point totals! (He didn't stay long. He was an old-timer like me and he left on points the day after I did.)

SOMETHING TO THINK ABOUT. Strange things happen in our lives. This reluctant officer, I'm sure, changed my life from that time on. In the last months of the war, the Navy realized it needed a number of its reserve officers to stay in the service. They asked for those interested to apply and they would pick the best qualified and offer Regular Navy commissions. Surprise! *Practically nobody applied!* (Embarrassed, they kept the rejections SECRET!) Then they sent another Secret message to the Commanding Officers of all ships and stations, directing them to select their very best and sell them on making the Navy a career – and give this program high priority. McClusky showed me the messages and said I was the one he wanted especially. He gave me the hard sell, emphasizing the peacetime Navy being a whole different (and better) world for its people than the way it was in a difficult, global war.

I know that if my relief had come when ordered, and I had those several months on shore duty, I would surely have accepted the Navy's offer. For one reason, I still had no idea what else I could do for a living. I had a fine war record, a lot of sea experience and Lt. Commanders made a great deal more money than what I expected to make at that time in civilian life. But when my relief didn't show up, and I was so fed up with my (finally) *54 months of sea duty*, I went out of the Navy on the point system – just to get home as soon as possible.

I have no idea whether my life would have been better or worse. It surely would have been different. (As it turned out, it has been very good, and hard to beat!)

EMERGENCY LEAVE: A GREAT INVENTION

The typhoon had damaged the Corregidor, enough that the powers that be wouldn't include us as part of the final assault on Japan. To patch us up, they put us in drydock in Pearl. About that time, I learned (from her friends in San Diego) that Laura was ill – depression, overwork, what-have-you – a source of great worry for me. Scoop was still on board at that time. He told me I should apply for emergency leave and get to San Diego. I had no idea how long it would be before we were ordered to sail and as the navigator, I'd have to be aboard when it did. While I was deciding what to do, I encountered Lt. Sullivan leaving the ship, carrying a suitcase. "Hey, where you going?" I asked. "Emergency leave," he replied. "Gotta go to Seattle." I knew what this was. Everyone on board knew Sully was a "Big Time Operator" and he had impregnated an Army nurse – whom he couldn't marry because he already was. She lived in Seattle. I guess he was going there for discussions with her family.

I felt I deserved Emergency Leave one helluva lot more than he did, so I headed for the Captain's stateroom and in very few minutes I had orders for 10 days leave in the States! McClusky was totally supportive, and Scoop and Atwood pitched in getting a Jeep, driving me to COMAIRPAC and to the Airport. It was a major rush job and by 1800 (6 p.m.) I was airborne on a PB2Y flying boat. At the airport, I ran into Tom Talbot, headed stateside. He told me one brother, Dudley, fell out of a coconut tree on Guam, and brother Fred had won two Navy Crosses!

Lots of officer-passengers on the PB2Y, but I was senior enough to get one of the few bunks. The flight to San Francisco took 17 hours. (No jets then.)

18 – 27 MAY 1945. Ten glorious days. I was the medicine Laura needed. She had lost weight, but perked up, and I realized that down deep she worried more than I had imagined – about the long separations and my chances of never coming back.

I made some phone calls: to Scoop's wife in Oregon; T.M. Clevenger, retired Waverly High School Superintendent in Burbank; Nip Blake's folks in Glendale, who said Nip was in Czechoslovakia, and Tuck in Saipan; and Carol Jane (Osterholm) Brown, but she wasn't home.

All good things end – the bad ones, too, I guess – so it was another goodbye, but I felt better now. Reported in on time in San Francisco and was told I had to wait for a flight back to Pearl. Had to wait three days. Spent time with cousin Sylvester Reith and Helen and Mildred, ran into Herbie Heist from Waverly, and Commander Neil Kingsley, one of Waverly's "famous" sons (our first ever to attend and graduate from any of our military academies). He invited me to his hotel room for a drink while he changed for an evening dinner-date. His roommate was another full commander, George Earnshaw, famous Major League baseball pitcher. I noticed Earnshaw had some fairly impressive military decorations and asked about them. Turns out he was the Gunnery Officer of one of our Essex-class (big, fast) carriers. Under attack, his ship's gunners downed four Jap planes – and he was awarded a medal! I didn't mention that *with less than a tenth of the firepower, my own crews killed eight* – and my C.O. didn't even say, "Well done!"

THE REST OF THE WAR wasn't bad at all. I made Lt. Commander (although to this day, I'm deeply resentful that my class of naval officers waited 2 1/2 years with no promotion eligibility, while the Army, Marines, and Air Corps had two – sometimes even three – promotions in that time).

FDR died on 13 April (age 63) only a few months after being elected to his 4th term. The war in Europe was winding down and ended on May 8, 1945.

We were still doing some ASW patrols in the Wotje and Maloelap areas and now we were routinely flying at night. In and out of Pearl a lot, and then assigned to train various Navy squadrons for night takeoffs and landings. Hawaii became like Old Home Week: I ran into Dick Westerfield, all-American swimmer, SUI, who owns a smalltown newspaper near Waverly; Cronk, now C.O. of an LCI (Landing Craft, Infantry); Andy Cumming, Newton buddy, with a great job as a Naval Air Transport Service pilot. He just ferries 4-engine aircraft, draws flight pay and spends 6 days of every 21 at home in Oakland, CA! (He married Ann Rash, the Newton gal who used to take swim lessons from me – with a bit of extra-curricular underwater smooching on the side.)

Also, I ran across Jack Althouse, Waterloo (whom I saw in Newfoundland in 1943). He was the Captain of a Sub Chaser, I believe. We got together a few times and had dinner on his ship so he could show me all the perks that go with being "The Old Man". I also met and went out a few times with Max Hawkins from SUI, the guy who married my one-time college girl-friend, Dolores Helmer. Also spent a few Officers Club hours with Hal Sutherland, and reestablished contact with good buddy Robert McKenzie Ball – "Powder River Mac" from San Diego Gunnery School. Mac had shore duty, in Pearl Harbor. And a Jeep! So we spent a lot of time together. He introduced me to a couple of civilians, Don Burum and his buddy Stan, bachelors who had a nice home near Waikiki Beach. Don was a Californian, a journalism guy, Editor of the Hawaiian Farm and Home magazine. We hit it off, became friends. Don and Stan were generous hosts. We kind of made their place our Honolulu headquarters, drank their booze, ate Chinese food nearby and walked to Waikiki to sun, surf and swim. Don was interested in my post-war plans and wrote a former journalism professor of his for a list of the best colleges for me to attend (post-grad) after I left the service.

A MIGHTY BUSY ROUTINE

I was having a good time but still working long hours. Navigation was easy – ashore. But they kept us training various squadrons for night takeoffs and landings, in Hawaiian waters which were fairly crowded, so I got a lot of wake-ups at night when the new OOD's got worried. I was Senior member of the Summary Court Martial Board and we seemed to be trying cases all the time. Violating censorship rules, AOL's and AWOL's, getting drunk, fighting, resisting arrest, etc. In my "spare time" on board I was trying to write saleable short stories (without success). Lots of basketball (still a high scorer), volleyball, and badminton in which I thought I was good except when playing McClusky!

Accidents kept happening. Two of our flight deck crew drove the tractor (used for moving aircraft) off the flight deck and down to the forecastle about 22 feet below. Both badly hurt.

In late May I saw a member of our flight deck crew killed in a freak accident. In a flyaway takeoff (no catapult) a plane went into the catwalk, its whirling propeller hitting something hard which broke the prop and its airstream blew a piece of steel back to where two or three of the flight deck crew were standing. It hit one of them, Carlson, and killed him. Doc said he was dead before he hit the deck.

On July 6, a miraculous escape from death! One of our planes landed successfully and was taxied forward of the cable barrier, the barrier raised and another plane immediately landed – badly. It went bouncing down the flight deck, jumped the barrier but the tail hook caught the top cable of the barrier, so the plane landed piggyback on top of the previous plane, where the pilot was still sitting, buckled into his seat. One wheel of the top plane pierced the body of the bottom plane and wedged there. The prop of the top plane, still revving up on maximum power, threatened to decapitate the pilot in the bottom plane! Strapped in, all he could do was move his head as far forward as possible – an inch or two! Lucky for him, the wedged wheel of the top plane kept it from moving forward – even a fraction of an inch! Before the spinning prop was stopped, it wiped out the headrest normally used by the pilot – who survived by no more than a single inch!

Except for McClusky, the best fighter pilot I ever knew was a guy named Knudsen. He was the acknowledged hottest fighter in VC41, our first squadron, and the one credited with two Jap kills in our very first battle at Saipan. He was a handsome guy but he looked somewhat lethal, like a fighter pilot should. Late in the war, Knudsen reappeared on our ship, training for night takeoffs and landings. One day he was flying over Pearl and got involved in some simulated air combat with Army or Marine Corps flyers. One accidentally flew into him and Knudsen was killed.

DON'T BELIEVE EVERYTHING THEY TELL YOU!

I LEARNED A LOT DURING THE WAR. One of the most important is what I just put in the headline above. I've been pretty suspicious of so-called "conventional wisdom" all my life so I wasn't too surprised. There are millions of people in this world who work hard to mislead you – for purposes of their own. And not just in war, but always. Some facts are facts, but many are just "spin" or propaganda. You have to be careful. *Think for yourself!*

In wartime, all sides claim their cause is just and their people are the good guys, and enemies are almost 100% bloodthirsty monsters. The U.S. and Japan played that game all through WW2. I told you about Lt. Ivan Washburn and the head-on-a-stick story. Not a nice picture of a well-educated young American officer. Then, reading SECRET messages late in the war, I came across one ordering all commanding officers to take immediate steps to stop the massive flow of Japanese "body parts" being mailed home by our boys for souvenirs of their Pacific War! The dispatch also said this traffic was so bad it was considered a matter of public health!

We were also told horror stories of the brutality of Japanese soldiers and their hatred of Americans. The SECRET messages I read said many, if not most, of the enemy prisoners of war admired our country and our people *and were so anxious to cooperate when captured, they willingly told us everything they could. But be careful – if they don't think it's enough, they may make up something just to be friendly!* Later on, I had a post-war reunion with George Petriz, my friend on the Arkansas. He was a Jap prisoner (and involved in the notorious Bataan Death March) and he told me much of the same thing. In short, both sides did some bad things (e.g. the Japanese Rape of Nanking, before we got into the war). War itself is inherently violent and brutal, but people everywhere are mostly decent people. In all my postwar travels, I never visited any country with more genuinely friendly people than in Japan.

WADE MCCLUSKY LEAVES, REPLACED BY PAT MITCHELL

Our new C.O. – Pat Mitchell – was a four-striper and, of course, a naval aviator – which he proved by reporting aboard by landing his plane on our flight deck while we were at sea. I learned his last command was a training carrier, the Wolverine, based in Chicago, and he had no wartime command at sea. He seemed OK. No McClusky, but OK.

After he took over officially a week or two later, we went out to train aircraft takeoffs and landings, and on the way back into Pearl Harbor I could see he was pretty nervous taking the ship back in through the crowded waters. He stood near the helmsman and began to wonder out loud. "Let's see. We've got those two cruisers on our starboard bow…" I stood at the back of the bridge with our new Quartermaster and, pretending to talk to him, I'd say (quietly, but loud enough), "I'd come left to 050." Mitchell would hear this and say, "Come left to 050." This way, I'd give him a hand, kind of "under the table", and he seemed to like the idea. This went on for nearly an hour and he took my advice every time.

Of course, all this time I was doing the navigator's job, taking bearings on all the available navigational aids and keeping the Captain informed on the courses to steer to stay in the proper channels and avoid trouble.

I think I got off to a good start with my new CO, but a lot more important to me, I figured I had really piloted a big ship into the entrance to Pearl all by myself, and this made me feel good.

V-J DAY

When we first heard the Japanese had surrendered, all hell broke loose! This is the other thing I remember most about Captain Mitchell. It was a nice night and we were anchored in Pearl Harbor. Most of the crew and officers were in chairs on the flight deck watching a movie. I was sitting beside the Captain, when all of a sudden a whole bunch of ships began firing their guns up into the air, and one of our radiomen yelled from the bridge, "Japan surrenders! The war is over!" Like I said, all hell broke loose! Everyone cheered and screamed and yelled and danced with the next guy. Then someone started shooting *our* guns into the air. This was sheer stupidity! Everything going up had to come back down, and all I could think of was, are we going to kill a few hundred of us NOW?

Mitchell yelled at me, *"Get this stopped!"* Wondering how, I ran to the bridge as there was a P.A. system there. Some other officer beat me to it and ordered the shooting stopped. It stopped on our ship and in a few minutes got stopped on a couple hundred other ships in the harbor, as wiser heads took over.

Up to then, Mitchell's reaction was proper and normal. But as I rejoined him I could see he was devastated by the news. There were several hundred of us on the Corregidor and Pat was the only one not ecstatic about the end of the war. And I knew why: he was a career officer, just got his first wartime command, and the war ended before he could get combat command experience. Four-stripers want to be Admirals, and combat experience is a great help. But for him, that possibility ended on V-J Day.

WRAPPING UP ODDS AND ENDS OF MY WORLD WAR II

Official V-J Day, a couple of days later. I was in downtown Honolulu, had Atwood's camera and took a few pictures. I got one of sailors climbing the statue of King Kamehameha and one of Japanese-American kids waving U.S. flags. Mac and I swam at Waikiki and ate steaks at Don and Stan's. In the evening we all ended up in a fabulous home up on the mountain overlooking all of Honolulu. The place was owned by somebody named "Bill". He wasn't there, but I'd guess fifty or sixty people were, and it was a big party. Liquid refreshments, of course, food, music and we could look down at the city and enjoy the almost endless display of fireworks and searchlights. Mac and I didn't leave until after 2 a.m. – "Bill" finally arrived – then we went to some-body's house for "breakfast". I got back to the ship at 4 a.m.

The atom bomb was really big news – as it should have been: it changed the world!

When McClusky departed, the officers wanted to express our appreci-ation and finally decided to give him silver candlesticks from (famous) Gumps. They were pedigreed stuff – 16th century. (Came with a certificate of authenticity.) When I made Lt. Commander, I found out Paul Pomeroy Stew-art didn't. We still kept training aircraft and had one more major accident totally demolishing a brand new late-model fighter, but no one got hurt. I let my assistant, Atwood, do most of the navigating. The Navy announced a point system that would determine the order for releasing officers to civilian life. Only Le Vake, Bolton, Sullivan and I had enough service and combat service to qualify for immediate release.

MY SERVICE WAS MORE THAN MOST. At war's end, I had more consecutive months of sea duty – 54 – than any officer or man who ever served on the Corregidor. You're allowed 30 days leave per year, but the Navy never made that possible for me. *So they owed me 105 days!* That's 3 1/2 years worth of leave I was too busy to take! But they counted that as "Terminal Leave" and kept me on full salary for 105 days after I was released from active duty. Fair enough. I'm fully satisfied that I served my country well in the greatest war the world has ever seen. (I hope we never have another war like it.)

August 31, a disturbing letter from home. Good friend Pete Cordt – who gave me a "going away party" my last day in Waverly in December 1940, was arrested, tried, and found guilty of sodomy. Sentenced to 10 years in prison! I never knew Pete was homosexual (although I guess the signs were there) because I never knew a homosexual person and surely couldn't believe there was one in Waverly and even in my circle of friends! I guess Claude was his special friend and when Claude was drafted, things changed and this led to Pete's arrest. Can you imagine 10 years in prison for that? I learned the Sheriff, Harley Ehlert, a good friend, drove Pete to the Iowa State Penitentiary in Ft. Madison and told the warden that Pete was a great guy respected by everyone in Waverly, so take it easy on him and treat him well. I'm sure this was the most surprising news in Waverly in many years and I surely felt badly to hear it.

September 4 was the day I ran into Noel Bacon at the "O" Club. He was the guy planning to marry Loraine Scherf until I guess I screwed it up for him. I mentioned this earlier. I'm sorry it happened – he was a really nice person and I got the impression he was still a bit sweet on Loraine, after all this time, even though he was married and had a couple of children.

14 September, I left the Corregidor and on the 16th it sailed off on another training exercise without me – *it's first sailing ever without me!* Atwood was the navigator. I moved into the BOQ – along with, I guess, a thousand other officers leaving the Navy. We all awaited transportation to the States. Don Burum gave me his favorite Aloha shirt as a going-away present.

24 September, Sutherland and I were assigned to the Hornet for the trip to San Francisco. I wrote Laura to pack up, leave San Diego and get to San Francisco ASAP. On the next day, we left Hawaii, arrived SF on 30 September.

And I finally got my
"scrambled eggs"
(on my cap!)

PART 3. CAREER, FAMILY, MALAMUTES

A WHOLE NEW LIFE. I couldn't believe all the freedom I now had! Not a lot of rules to follow and no watches to stand. I could sleep all night! But to some degree, I was right back where I was years before – pre-Navy. That is, *I still had no idea what I could or should do to earn a living.* Laura was now involved. I was concerned but not worried: whatever I decided, I could handle it.

I still thought I might do well as a free-lance writer but Laura, being more practical, thought I should get a regular job. We compromised: I would go back to college – graduate studies – under the GI Bill of Rights, study creative writing, but also some writing-related courses like Advertising, send out some short stories, work on a novel, and see what happens. The GI Bill would pay my tuition and $90 a month – if I remember correctly.

First decision: what college? Don Burum's list included Stanford, Columbia, NYU, Northwestern, Iowa and Missouri. Stanford was rated best. We wanted to live in California and college contacts could lead to job offers, most likely in that area or state. So I applied for post-graduate studies at Stanford. Their reply: "If you are married, don't come! Not even a doghouse available for married students!" So we decided to check out Columbia and NYU.

But first, we agreed we deserved a vacation, so we moved into the Mark Hopkins Hotel in San Francisco and stayed a week. All three of cousin Louie's offspring were in town – Helen, Mildred and Leo, who just left the Navy after two years on one of our top submarines. (They sank more Japanese tonnage than any sub in our Navy! Leo had been in a lot of combat action and earned a medal, but I don't remember what it was. The gang of us did a bit of night-clubbing, including the famous Top of the Mark, and cousin Sylvester and his wife Jean sometimes joined us.

We got train tickets through the Navy and left on October 6, sharing a lower berth. With so many service people heading home – including WACS, WAVES and nurses – the trip was a three-day party. I tried to call Mooney in Salt Lake City and Overton in Ottumwa, but no luck. Laura's mom and sister Jo met us at the station in Chicago. I had to check in at Great Lakes to check out of the Navy. Andy Cumming was there, and Laurel Bentley, my classmate at WHS. Laurel said Les Moeller had been there yesterday.

The Niewinski dog, Tippy, was older but no smarter. I had my first hay fever in more than five years. Les and Dorothy Moeller were on the train when we embarked for Waterloo – very bright people – we talked all the way.

It was good being with my family and friends. We were in Waterloo and Waverly three weeks. On Navy Day, I was the speaker at the Waverly Rotary Club. A lot of the old gang just came home (John Meyer, Johnny Jones). Pep Grawe and Junior Strotman were en route. We saw my brother's magic show and ran into the Dana Shepherds at the Colony Club. Dinner and evening with Fred Joyce and wife. An evening with Jack Wright and Barbara, of course.

Surprise: Scoop Rutherford stopped to see us, en route from East Coast duty to Alice, Robin and Oregon. Driving a rather decrepit 1930 Model A roadster I didn't figure would ever make it. Scoop looked underfed, as usual, so we took him out for a big steak dinner. Offered him lodging for the night, but he was in too much hurry to get home.

We returned to Chicago to spend time with Laura's family. I switched totally to civilian clothes. Bob Harris (Waverly) is attending Northwestern – we had a get-together.

21 November, we left for New York. Checked NYU and Columbia. Picked Columbia, submitted my credentials and they said I was welcome. Then we started to look for a place to live. This turned out to be an unhappy experience. Five years of war, no new construction (anywhere). Millions of service personnel, home from the war – in need of places to live. *Every hotel in Manhattan had a three-day limit!* After that, get out and give somebody

else a chance! Habitable apartments were not available. I finally remembered Atwood's father, supposedly No. 1 in NYC real estate. His office gave me a few leads. All were unfit for human habitation. Then I remembered Prof. John Chellevold, Waverly, was a Navy math instructor at Columbia Midshipman School, which would be shutting down and a hundred or so officers reassigned. Chellevold gave us a list of all their apartments. We started checking and when the first ten or so laughed *and said they had waiting lists of dozens*, we knew we were headed back to Chicago, the Niewinski's and Northwestern U.

Laura's family welcomed us, but Billy Jarvis, who owned several properties, found us a place shortly thereafter. Great location, just a block from Lakeshore Drive, near to Lincoln Park and Lake Michigan. It was a big stone mansion, once owned by a wealthy meatpacking family. Divided into apartments. Ours was the basement apartment, once the Billiard Room. One big room, plus small kitchen, bath, closets. All oak-paneled. A fireplace (never used). A huge old roll-top desk came with it; we used this as a divider between living and dining areas. In Hawaii, I'd seen how almost everyone stacked mattresses, upholstered them, threw on a bunch of pillows and had furniture that doubled as beds called hikias and punies (although I have no idea about the proper spelling). We did that. It worked out very well.

A NEW KIND OF LIFE AND WE BOTH WORKED HARD AT IT

Laura got a job right away. I signed up for a full schedule of courses in N.U.'s College of Commerce, and the Medill School of Journalism. My classmates weren't regular college students seeking degrees: most were working people, some college graduates, attending to develop skills leading to new jobs or better jobs. All these classes were night classes, none in Evanston, all in buildings of the "downtown" campus, right where I had attended Midshipman School.

Besides my classes and assignments, I spent all my time writing. Started a novel, "The Hypocritic Days" (after the poem, "Days" by Emerson), the story of a veteran, returning to his hometown after the war. And a lot of articles and short stories that I kept mailing to various publications on a regular basis.

I didn't sell anything – which was discouraging. But things kept happening to make me feel I really could write and that in due time, I'd sell a few things and be on my way. A lot of the rejection slips were encouraging, many saying I "showed real promise". Some asked me to continue sending them my stuff. My Professional Fiction Writing course was taught by the Chicago rep of a New York Literary Agency. Don Wilcox. He came to believe I was the best of his classroom-full of aspiring authors – he told me so. He read a few chapters of my novel and had me submit them for a Twentieth Century Fox writing fellowship, kind of a shot in the dark because big money was involved. My Nonfiction Article Writing course was taught by a well-known pro, Elmo Scott Watson. He criticized my first submission, but after that, everything I sent him was marked "A – Excellent!" and he kept reading my stuff to all his classes.

Someone – I have no idea who – found me and I was invited to join a group of young writers who were going to Boston and start, for that area, a New Yorker-type magazine.

Ray Weber, Assistant Ad Manager of Swift & Co. (the meat packers) taught my classes in National Advertising and Radio Advertising – no TV at that time. He said I was the best student he ever had, and there was a job for me in Swift's ad department anytime I wanted it! He gave me A's in both courses and told me I didn't even need to take the final exams.

He asked me to visit Swift's and said I would start as a product manager. He also said if I'd rather have an advertising agency job, he'd recommend me to Swift's agency and arrange an interview, which he did.

Several things were happening. I decided I did not want to spend the rest of my life in Chicago. And I was learning a lot about freelance writing: mainly that it took much more than good writing to succeed. You had to know *which* publications bought *what kind of writing*. "A" would accept stories and articles only between 1500 and 2500 words; "B", only if the protagonist (hero) was a well-educated man, 25–40 years old, from a good family. Etc. Also, any writer's hardest sell was his first, and those who made good money were usually on some publication's "team". Once you were on their "team", they knew what you could do, and they preferred you to "unknowns". Some would ask those on their "authors team" for stories especially on certain subjects. More than writing, you had to know the publications.

I also learned you had to want to write so badly you'd stick with it, whether you sold or not. One of the great American writers, Booth Tarkington, wrote constantly for 14 years before selling his first word! When I heard that, it occurred to me I wasn't "temperamentally suited for starving in a garret".

THE FINAL STRAW: "A WHOLE HALF DOLLAR"

In Professional Fiction Writing, one class assignment was to write a short, short story, and Don Wilcox started reading three or four of these in every class. And then we'd all critique them. I kept wondering why it took so long for him to get to mine.

Then one night he told the class, "I have a special treat for you. Listen to this!" Then he read mine, which I had titled "A Whole Half Dollar". I couldn't believe it. Wilcox seemed to be savoring every word. Sometimes he'd stop and say, "Isn't that great?" or "See how skillfully that was done?" When he finished, all I heard was "Wonderful!" "Outstanding!" They almost cheered. Someone then asked, "Who wrote it?" When Wilcox told them, the whole class gathered around me, asking questions like I was some oracle, some wanting to know what magazine would be lucky enough for me to let publish it.

Ah, my breakthrough! Now, I'd be on my way. Or so I thought. *When I couldn't sell it* – because it was always too long, too short, had old people as the protagonists, or whatever – I decided freelancing was not for me. I would do what Laura suggested: get a job – hopefully one where the ability to write might be especially helpful.

COLLEGE REVISITED. BETTER THIS TIME.

Last time I was so broke it was a struggle. This time, money was not a problem and besides, the Niewinskis kept us overeating on a regular basis. This part of my education took about a year. Much happened; here are the highlights:

THE GEORGE PETRITZ STORY. My first class at N.U. The prof was making sure he had our names right. When he called "Petritz", I figured it couldn't be – but it was. Notre Dame George. Hadn't seen him or heard about him for five full years! "Tell me about your war," I said. "Prisoner of war," he told me. "Early on. In the Philippines. Bataan Death March." He told me it wasn't all that bad. "Worst part was being a big American trying to survive on what they fed the little Jap soldiers. I found most Japs liked Americans. I acted friendly as hell and mostly they treated me that way."

George remained a prisoner in the Philippines for three years. Just before we retook these islands, the Japs decided to send all prisoners to Japan. But as his ship left port, U.S. forces attacked and sank the ship he was on. All survivors swam to the closest land and remained prisoners. *George swam in the other direction* and eventually got ashore on another island and met friendly Filipinos! Then after the war, George, like me, decided to return to Chicago for a bit more college before getting a real life.

BACK TO MY OLD LIFEGUARD DAYS? Summer school classes were all in Evanston. On a hot summer afternoon, I decided to walk from our apartment over to Lake Michigan and do my studying there, to take advantage of the cool breezes. There's no beach there, just huge rocks lining the lake, about 8-10 feet above the water line, then deep water. I perched on a rock observing the arrival of eight or nine boys, 13-15 years old, who came to swim. They had fun diving off the boulders and all seemed to be good swimmers, except one kid who, despite the urging of the others, declined to join the party.

I immediately decided the kid couldn't swim, so I watched awhile to make sure the others didn't change his mind. He continued to refuse, so I decided all was OK and went back to studying. They were making a lot of noise and suddenly I realized all was totally quiet – *the kid was in the water, just the top of his head showing and all the others just standing there, looking!*

I was in midair instantly, trying to remove my new prescription sunglasses and toss them back on the grass beyond the rocks while I was halfway to the water. I saved the kid but my glasses went into the water. I made sure the kid was OK, then I dived for the glasses and I couldn't find them. So I scolded the kid and asked why he would go into deep water when he couldn't swim. I got his name and phone number so I could talk to his parents. They lived nearby so I called and then went to see them. They had recently moved from Oelwein, near Waverly, so we got along well. I made them promise to get their 14-year-old swimming lessons immediately, and I also suggested they might buy me a new pair of prescription sunglasses!

Before summer school began, we went back to Waverly to see my family – and sister Helen's new baby girl, Vicki. Surprised to learn most of my old buddies came back to Waverly and Waterloo when the war ended. Bob Schulze and Fred Joyce settled in Waterloo, Overton in Cedar Falls. Spent time in Waverly with Jack Wright, Fred Studier, Pep Grawe, Bill Leary, Jim and Bill Clark, Max Eggleston, Les Moeller, Marj Moodie, and many others. We took Ruby Grant to lunch.

My mother came to Chicago and I took a week to show her around. I discovered Benadryl and it really helped my hay fever. Lots of letters: Sam Houston in Tsingtao, China! [Did I tell you Shortstop divorced him and later served on the White House staff (Protocol) in the Reagan Administration?] Don Burum wrote: he's getting married. Pep bought out Les Moeller's share of the Waverly newspapers; Les is going to become Dean of the Journalism School at the University of Iowa! Letters from Jack Wright and Ed Kepler. George Cominos of my Gunnery Division, Corregidor, dropped in for a surprise visit.

MY VERY OWN PHILADELPHIA STORY

One of my classes was Advertising Design and Layout. One night the instructor said, "I have a job opportunity for one of you. It has two drawbacks: it's a copy job, not design. And it's not here in Chicago." *To me, these were advantages!* Short version of a long story – I got the job. Burpee Seed Company, Philadelphia.

Moral to this story: if you're having trouble making good things happen to you, be patient – things will happen. Good things, if you're lucky. Keep in mind: *LIFE IS WHAT HAPPENS TO YOU WHEN YOU'RE NOT LOOKING!*

The Big Boss, David Burpee, hired me. Told me he had bought out a smaller competitor, the William Henry Maule Co. Like Burpee, a mail order seed company. I would write and produce the Maule catalog and manage all their advertising. The only problem I had was finding a place to live. Housing was still in short supply, everywhere. I left Laura in Chicago until I could find us a place to live.

My best friend, John Mundy, had left the Navy and returned to the Merchant Service. With his wife, Evelyn, he now had two small children. On his first voyage, the ship left the States and didn't get back for nearly a year! So he decided to hell with the sea and began looking for a 9-5 job in Philadelphia. They lived in Yeadon, a suburb. When I got in touch, they moved me in with them until I could find something.

A Jewish girl named Marge lived alone in a beautiful home in a high-rent district. Her father had skipped; her mother died. She found another Jewish girl, Trudy, a refugee who just arrived in this country and moved her in. They decided to find a young couple to live with them, eat with them, share expenses. I decided this was the best I could do, moved in, sent for Laura. Nice place, but not a good situation.

Then one day, Mr. Burpee – "DB" – called me in and said he'd heard I needed a place to live. There was a vacant apartment on his famous Fordhook Farms in Doylestown. I could have it. It would be *rent-free* and I'd have company transportation, to and from, everyday, also at no cost. This was like a major pay-raise almost immediately!

Burpee's was the largest mail-order seed company in the world – and DB, in some ways, I thought, was a very bad business manager. But he surely treated me well, and he did *some* things extremely well. He had a staff of plant scientists who developed new, improved varieties of flowers and vegetables. He was a nice-looking man and an excellent speaker. Every year, during the big Flower Show in New York City, he would have a Burpee exhibit and hire Powers Models to man the booth. He'd book the Main Ballroom of the Waldorf Astoria to "unveil" the newest Burpee flower variety and invite all of the horticultural press, and key members of the garden clubs in the Greater New York area.

Laura and I would go to New York with him. We'd stay at the Waldorf-Astoria and have dinner there with DB and the Burpee group on the Sunday before the show opened, man the Burpee exhibit with the models, and I'd help where needed at the big DB speech and new product introduction.

One time, at the big cocktail party at this event someone came to me with a problem. A lady had shown up, uninvited, somewhat inebriated, insisting to see Mr. Burpee – *now*! DB was closeted with the Press and did not want to be disturbed. Would I handle it? The lady was Osa Johnson, celebrity, big game hunter. Mr. Burpee had named a marigold after her a few years before. She and her husband (recently deceased) had written a best-seller about their adventures: they would throw stones at a lion, get him to charge while Martin took movies, then Osa would drop him dead at Martin's feet with one well-placed shot in the brain!

I handled the problem. Since Osa was well-lubricated, Laura and I took her to the bar and added fuel to the fire! She passed out, we got her room number and took her there and put her to bed. Problem solved.

A couple of times, DB invited me to fly with him in his private plane, "The Marigold", to his Midwest distribution center in Clinton, Iowa. (He was so polite, always asked if "it would be convenient" for me.) In Clinton, he'd tell me he would be there a few days, so I should take a couple of days and go and visit my family.

Then we flew to Chicago to attend a Seed Trade Convention. I had a great room at the Palmer House and time off to spend two evenings with the Niewinskis.

The Burpee Advertising Manager was in his mid- or late 50's, and their agency was in Buffalo. DB sent for me and handed me some proposed ads, told me to come back the next day with my critique. I didn't want to step on any toes, but I thought they were easily improved and I rewrote them to show how. My version was used.

I had been working on the Maule catalog for some time, but it wouldn't go to press for a few more months. Then to my utter surprise, DB called me in and said they had a change of heart. "Trying to make the Maule Co. profitable," he explained, "is like giving blood transfusions to a dead horse." Instead, they would announce that Burpee bought it and ask all of its customers to buy their seeds from Burpee. And we'd mail Burpee catalogs to all of them.

"I guess I no longer have a job," I said. DB smiled and said, "We like your work and we'd like to have you stay." Quite a surprise. "What would I do?" I asked. "Look around," he suggested. "You'll find something."

Quite an assignment! I was comfortable there, so I looked around. So much was badly handled, it wasn't hard to find something in dire need of improvement. Employee relations were bottom of the barrel, because the pay for most of the office workers was bottom of the barrel. But I didn't want to get into that, then. I found the Complaint Department a bad situation, easily fixed. I researched and found: Burpee business was unique, *the major part of it their catalog sales, where hundreds of thousands of individual orders averaged less than $15 each*, and we received thousands of complaints – and handled them badly. They would complain that our seeds were no good and we'd just send them their money back – with no argument about the quality of our products.

I also found that it wasn't the seeds – thousands of orders of the same seeds, same crop, grew perfectly. (Maybe Kentucky had torrential rains at planting time?) but if they thought we sold bad products, they did business with some other company the next year – or maybe for the next ten or twenty years!

I revised the entire system. Composed several form letters, made them look like personal letters, and I found a bright girl who assured the right ones were sent in response to the right situations. If any complaint didn't fit one of our forms, I'd answer it myself. We defended our quality but always said we valued their business and would send a prompt replacement if it wasn't too late, or a credit slip, or cash. *I knew the new system salvaged thousands of customers we had been losing. DB agreed.*

Bucks County was beautiful and interesting – lots of New York literary and theatre people lived there – Pearl Buck, Moss Hart, Oscar Hammerstein, Kitty Carlisle, Walter Slezak and many others. We enjoyed famous Bucks County Playhouse in New Hope, and went there often. It was almost impossible to buy a car so soon after the war, but I got a new Ford convertible through Burpees!

Maybe 30 or 35 of us "Burpee people" lived on the several farms that made up Fordhook, and we socialized a great deal. Frank and Beatrice Mar were Chinese – he a Canadian national, she Costa Rican. Frank's father was head chef at one of the major hotels in Canada. Beatrice was a dietician. These two taught the rest of us how to cook Chinese. Laura became excellent in this regard.

Then I was asked to take the farm payroll from the Burpee office in Philadelphia to Fordhook every Friday noon. So every week my weekend began before 1 p.m. Friday! (A dirty job, but somebody has to do it!) But I did wonder if it wasn't all too easy and maybe not much future.

I started reading the Help Wanted ads. Sun Oil was seeking a writer for their PR department, and mentioned that a background in economics would be helpful. I could handle it – but it seemed perfect for my buddy, Ed Kepler. After the war, he had attended U. of Arizona and received a Master's Degree in Economics, and was awarded a Roberts Fellowship to study for a Ph.D. at Columbia University! They lived in Shanks Village, N.Y., on the western side of the Hudson River where Columbia placed all of its married students. We visited and kept in touch, and Ed told me he'd leave the program for a good job offer. So I called him, and he got the Sun Oil job. (He did an excellent job for Sun and as a result, he got an even better job with General Electric in their corporate headquarters in New York City!)

On my vacation, Laura and I drove to upstate New York and then to Montreal and Quebec, back down to New Hampshire and Vermont, arrived with *just two* suggestions by the American Kennel Club where we might be able to purchase an Alaskan Malamute puppy. Kayak of Brookside joined our family – but I'm going to tell about that later on.

LAURA, ON OUR VACATION. Right now you are probably wondering, how did that guy ever manage to get such a beautiful wife? (Answer: "Boy, am I ever lucky!")

My time at Burpees was time well spent. It was there I realized fully that I could handle almost any challenge and do well. We both had a lot of fun there. From that location we were able to visit New York City often, and Atlantic City and the Jersey shore, and all of New England.

Both our families came to visit and we took them to all the places just mentioned. Everyone at Burpee treated us well, and we became full-fledged members of the "Fordhook Gang". A surprising number of old friends wrote to me – many from Waverly: George Clifford (from Peru!), Don Wilcox and Ray Weber from Northwestern, Prukop, Overton, Carol Jane Osterholm, et al. Jerry Carney and his brand-new bride came to visit. (He stayed in the Navy.)

We got together with our wonderful friends, the Keplers and the Mundys, frequently.

One other fringe benefit. When I moved to Fordhook, Vic Hollar, the farm manager and soon-to-be good friend, came and said, "Where do you want your garden?" We picked the site and he had his crew plow it up, ready for planting. Laura and I planted a bunch of vegetables and it was a learning experience. Vic said, "The secret is *fresh*! Your garden must be close to the house. At mealtimes, you get everything ready. If you have kids, get them sitting at the table. Go pick the vegetables, *then run, don't walk* – and if you stub your toe and break your stride…throw away the vegetables and go back and get some fresh ones!"

(Once picked, the vegetables' sugar begins to turn to starch, and the difference in taste is surprising. So – the vegetables (especially corn) that you buy in a store are *not really* fresh. You have to grow them yourself.)

Laura and I, at the Burpee booth at the New York Flower show, met and talked with several of the famous ladies who had new flower varieties named for them: Helen Hayes, the "grand dame of American theatre; June Lockhart, the lead on long-running TV show, "Lassie"; Shirley Booth, "I Remember Momma" and "Come Back, Little Sheba"; Mrs. Charles Dana Gibson, the original "Gibson Girl"; and quite a few others I can't remember. All of them were surprisingly nice.

One girl working our booth, was "head writer" with the (really big in those days) radio show, "True or False" – one of those where contestants try to win big money. She came to me and asked me to be a part of the show. She could get me on, and then *hinted* she could even tip me off to the answers! That scared me, but I figured I could win important cash on my own. I was told to go to the back alley door of the theatre – a couple thousand were lined up at the front door. She'd open the door for me – I should come in, cross the stage and sit in a front row. However, due to the flood of eager humanity pouring in at full speed, I ended up way in back, way off to the side.

But "the fix" was in. After selecting 8 of the 10 contestants, the MC asked, "Anyone here from the Flower Show?" He took me up on the stage. I was No. 9, but then he moved me up to No. 5! I answered the first five questions correctly, then: "The Anti-Saloon League and the Temperance Union are the same organization – True or False?" I hadn't even looked at the list of answers she had given me (that would be cheating). And she had told me, if I was stumped, to look at her – she was on stage – if it were True, she'd look at me; False, she'd be looking away. But I wouldn't do that. I could figure this out: Anti-Saloon League seemed violent, Temperance Union sounded more tolerant, reasonable, low-key. I said "False" and *immediately* I realized I was wrong – *I had just read about the name change in that week's TIME!*

There were no huge jackpots in those days but seven correct answers involved a couple thousand dollars. The writer was really angry with me, but I'm glad I didn't win. It was too much of a set-up.

GREENER PASTURES?

The employment agency who conducted the search for Sun Oil told me they had several job possibilities for me and I began to think about leaving Burpee. I realized that I could do great things for this company – *if* I could sell DB on giving me a major promotion (with a lot more money) and a great deal of authority to put my ideas into practice. And I was loaded with ideas I knew would work.

I prepared a detailed 25-page, *brutally frank* memorandum on everything being done wrong by the company, and how we could fix them, with considerably increased profitability for the company. I started by telling DB, "You may remember asking me to think about an acute company problem – why three million Burpee catalogs are ignored annually by those who receive them, and why more than half of the people who buy from us one year take their seed orders to a competitor the next year!"

As I said, I gave him 25 pages of answers, too long to report here. In short, we lost so many customers because our service was poor. It was poor because our hourly employees were underpaid and cared for nothing except putting in their time. Managers were *company-oriented* and we would have to change this to *customer-oriented*. Except DB himself (I told him that, but didn't mean it), nobody at Burpees knew anything about Public Relations, Customer Relations and Employee Relations – except me. (Brutal, self-serving, but true.)

We had a gold mine not being used, in the Garden Clubs all over America, where every program chairman had to come up with something to do at the next meeting. I proposed we prepare a whole series of color films on various aspects of flower gardening and offer to lend them to the Garden Clubs all over America. With a bit of subtle "advertising" included, this could boom our sales as much as 50% in the first few years.

I told him our direct mail piece on hybrid vegetables, sent to market growers was particularly bad. "An advertising piece prepared by a plant scientist and checked by an office manager is likely to be no more skillfully executed than my work would be, if you assigned me to develop a new petunia and gave me six weeks to do it!"

I told him about all the good things a Philadelphia neighbor, Sun Oil, was doing to keep good employees happy – cost-of-living pay increases, a major program of social activities (dances, picnics, bowling leagues, etc.), formal, *published*, pay and pension systems, even a stock-sharing program to make employees part-owners of the company – to build esprit de corps, morale, a sense of "what happens to my company happens to me".

And so much more – no holds barred. I said I was sure he must have asked his senior managers for their opinions on the 50% loss of customers. *"And I firmly believe you received only the answers they thought you wanted to hear.* But 'yes men' do not solve problems."

I made it clear that I was the man for the job. And I would accept it only on the following conditions: 1. Title: Director of Public Relations (to include senior responsibility for all customer and employee relations). 2. Work personally under you, the Company President. 3. Verbal promise of a two-year tryout. 4. All backing necessary – financial and otherwise – to ensure success of programs designed to increase profits by holding our old customers and gaining new ones. 5. Encouragement to accumulate PR material and join Marketing, Advertising and PR organizations, attend seminars and conventions and do all possible to borrow useful ideas and learn what other companies have used, and are using, successfully. 6. Added incentive in the form of an appropriate increase in salary – to one commensurate with the job.

I closed by assuring him I appreciated the courtesy he had always shown me personally and expressed my gratitude for making me a member of the "Fordhook Family". *Then I said, "This is the best way I can think of to show my appreciation: to call your attention to a large number of things that should have been pointed out by someone else a long time ago."*

SO WHAT HAPPENED? As I rather expected, it was a bit too much for DB to accept, fully. He owned the company 100%, ran it as he pleased, was a multimillionaire who, in addition to the Burpee business, probably owned a huge fortune in real estate in many different parts of the country where Burpee seeds were produced on Burpee property.

His rejection, also, was as expected: courteous and complimentary. He recognized my proposal as a thoughtful piece of work, but told me he was set in his ways and major changes would be difficult for him to accept. He would keep it as a guide for possible future actions. He said I was an outstanding young man – "too good, really, for this small company" and I would surely succeed elsewhere. He wished me the best and (although I hadn't been there very long) he said he'd keep my salary going for another three months. And, "Stay at Fordhook as long as you like, until you are ready to move elsewhere."

LOOKING FOR "ELSEWHERE"

Several companies expressed interest and asked me to interview – Hammermill Paper Co., B. F. Goodrich, Gulf Oil, and Pangborn Corporation. I had never heard of Pangborn, but the agency told me the company was a major exhibitor at the Foundry Show in Philadelphia that week. So Laura and I went there and met Les Gardner, the Ad Manager, who was looking for an Assistant to write and produce their quarterly external house magazine.

Mr. Gardner was obviously interested and urged me to come to Hagerstown, MD. I agreed. Hammermill offered me the job, but I wasn't interested. At Gulf Oil, the job was Assistant to the Director of Public Relations. Not the next in line – they had a whole staff of PR people. But more like a "Chief of Staff", working directly with him on everything. The job paid extremely well and Gulf Oil, in one of the biggest buildings in downtown Pittsburgh, was impressive. The PR department was on one of the top floors, with a magnificent view of the entire city. The Director was on sick leave, due back in September, so no final decision could be made until then. I spent the whole day meeting and talking with all the other PR managers, and the Personnel Manager told me I had been "unanimously approved" by all the PR people, and there was no doubt the job would be mine if I wanted it. He scheduled me for a return visit in early September.

I went to Pangborn, and, after I talked with Vic Stine, the Vice-President, I was offered the job. Actually, I liked Hagerstown better than Pittsburgh and was impressed when Les urged me to look around in Blue Ridge Summit, where he lived. We really liked this mountain village and decided to take the Pangborn job. The Gulf thing wasn't 100% sure – but if Gulf made me an offer, I could then decide.

In September, the people at Gulf Oil asked me to come to Pittsburgh, but I told them I was no longer available. So the three of us – Laura, Kayak (our 'teenager" Malamute) and me – became Marylanders, and I became part of Pangborn for quite a few years. It was a pretty good life.

PUTTING UP WITH PANGBORN, THE GOOD AND THE BAD

One of the first things I learned: this was a screwball company. Mainly because Thomas W. Pangborn, who started the business when he was very young, still ran it. He was now in his 70's, wealthy, and he hadn't learned much about modern business management in all those years. It might be hard for me to live with some of their old-fashioned ideas, but maybe – hopefully – I could drag them into the twentieth century. (I considered this an interesting challenge!)

It didn't take me long to discover Les Gardner was a bit behind the times, as well. But I noticed that he seemed to "live rich" and played a lot of golf.

I didn't think much of the Pangborn Magazine. I could do a lot better. It was totally about how great Pangborn products were – and I could see a lot of copies going straight into wastebaskets. So I would give them a reason to open the envelope and take a look.

Everyone came to call my innovation "the green sheet". Business Week and some other publications had just started one sheet (front and back, on tinted paper) in each issue, sort of a quick review of late news items. Everyone read them, usually the first thing, and they were very popular. Mine was a take-off, not real news but humor – titled: **"If you haven't heard it…. IT'S NEWS!"**

It really worked. Our district managers thought it was great and told me so. When my first issue was produced, Tom Pangborn called me in and said I had done a great job on my stories about our machines, but he wondered "why I wasted two whole pages on that other stuff." I told him it was bait, to make sure our publication was opened and looked at – and I would poll our district offices and see if they could report any customer comments. The district managers gave it a glowing report, I reported this to "The Chief", and I never produced an issue without it.

ABOUT THE COMPANY AND ITS PRODUCTS

Almost everything made of metal is formed by some process that leaves a surface condition requiring further treatment before it can be machined, painted, coated or whatever. At one time this was often done by sandblasting.

Two companies – Pangborn and Wheelabrator – developed wheel-like mechanisms that hurled steel shot or grit with great centrifugal force – a major step forward. We called ours "Rotoblast". These "wheels" were used in dozens of machines designed for specific tasks. They all included systems for "dust" removal (minute particles of whatever was blasted off the metal) and systems for reclaiming and reusing the shot or grit used in the process.

The two companies shared nearly 98% of the world market and were fierce competitors. Each provided the dust collectors for their machines and both were major providers of dust collectors – air pollution control – for hundreds of other industrial processes.

What I enjoyed most was visiting customer companies to see our products in action and get photos and "case histories" of the benefits. I would use this information in Pangborn Magazine, and our agency would use it in our advertising. In my years at Pangborn I visited foundries, forges, automotive plants, shipbuilders, steel mills, "bathtub makers" and a hundred other metal processing plants. In dust control, dozens, maybe hundreds: Kelloggs in Battle Creek where we collected the fine particles of Corn Flakes (so they wouldn't be soggy) and used them as ingredients in their lucrative dog food business. Tire makers, leather plants, woodworking, etc. I enjoyed seeing much of America's manufacturing in action.

MY RELATIONS WITH "THE CHIEF"

Tom Pangborn was a big Catholic – really big – "Knights of Malta" big. Pangborn Halls at Notre Dame and Mount Saint Mary's in nearby Emmitsburg. Personal friend of Cardinal Spellman. Laura and I are Catholics and maybe that's the reason "The Chief" seemed to treat me better than he treated my boss and a few other managers.

And this in spite of my giving him a lot of reasons not to like me. One day I told Les Gardner I planned to take my vacation the first two weeks in September. He looked upset and *then told me I didn't get two weeks vacation until I'd been there five years!* I told him I wouldn't work for a company that far behind the times.

Les was apologetic. Said he'd talk to Vic Stine. Ten minutes later Mr. Stine came to me and said I'd have two weeks vacation. That was my first rebellion. There were others. Many others.

THE PIPE THING

The first day I was there, observing that Les smoked cigars at his desk, I lit up my pipe. Les quickly told me: "Get rid of the pipe – The Chief hates pipes!" I was surprised. "Cigars O.K., pipes not allowed?" Les said that was the rule; and I said most people found cigars more offensive than pipes.

Les persisted, almost in a state of alarm. I told him it was a dumb rule and if the Chief objected to my pipe, I'd wait until he told me himself – and then I'd decide to forego the pipe, or forego the job. (I'm sure Les Gardner had never met anyone like me. Everyone at Pangborn seemed to live in fear of "The Chief".)

A few days later, I found out that the Chief told both Les and Vic Stine to tell me to get rid of the pipe. They did and *I didn't*. From my first day on the job until many years later when the company was sold, I continued with the pipe and the Chief never said a word about it directly to me!

THE ADVISORY COUNCIL

Like most of us, Tom Pangborn yearned for the approval of his fellow man. He had risen from nothing to great wealth and had given much to charities. He wanted most of all to have his story told in FORTUNE magazine. He told Les to arrange this: FORTUNE told Les that Pangborn was too far behind the times. Pangborn began to advertise, full pages, in FORTUNE to butter them up. (This was not a good place to advertise our products!) FORTUNE did a great feature on Charles McCormick, founder and Big Kahuna of McCormick Spice Co, another Maryland company. Tom Pangborn read about their Advisory Council of managers who studied problems and opportunities and advised senior management. So Pangborn established an Advisory Council. Les Gardner was on it, with about twenty others of that rank.

After every meeting, Les would tell me what happened. I quickly learned it was a total waste of time – they were all old timers who knew nothing about modern business management, and too scared of the Chief to suggest any changes – because that would be considered critical of his present practices!

After a wasted year, the next echelon of management was assigned to take over. That was me and Jack Wiles and 16 old timers like the guys on the first Board. Wiles was a new kid in town, a scientist or advanced engineering type, in the Dust Control division. We took over, met privately and decided on changes that would benefit Pangborn in major ways.

A PROPOSAL FOR IMPROVEMENT OF COMPANY OPERATIONS

I wrote the document. Many pages. Reorganization of the company. The Chief pretty much served as Chairman of the Board, President, and Executive Vice President. Two VPs handled everything else – marketing, finance and manufacturing. We suggested the Chief stop being President and Exec. V.P. – just be Chairman, and hire or promote others for the vacancies. My job was to write this and all the other stuff in a way that would not offend him, but make sense.

Wiles was a tower of strength. We suggested many changes. It took us nearly a year to sell others on the Board to do the job we were appointed to do. ("We'll all be fired!") Lloyd Stauffer, VP, had become my good friend. After we sent our Proposal to "The Cabinet", I asked Lloyd about the reaction. Frank Kaiss, the General Superintendent, immediately had said, "They all should be fired!" But the Chief said, "There's a lot in here we ought to think about."

PLAUDITS

Almost a year after that, Lloyd asked me to drop by and said, "You can take a bow." Then he told me the Chief had promoted Vic Stine to be President and was bringing in Ralph Trent, our West Coast District Manager, to be Executive V.P. And a bunch of our other suggestions were being put into effect!

I was able to get a number of things changed. I couldn't believe they had no soft drink machines. I got them put in – over Frank Kaiss' vigorous opposition. I had smoked my pipe (and Les, his cigars) while twenty Sales Correspondents (all men) at desks right outside my office weren't allowed to smoke. Most of them went to the Men's Room every hour or so, smoked a cigarette, got into a conversation, then had another. Maybe three. The waste of time was huge. I got the rule changed. They could then smoke at their desks. It saved a lot of company time and it improved morale – they could see me smoke at my desk from Day One: they hadn't been allowed to. Some had been there nearly twenty years. I was a Johnny-Come-Lately. How do you think they felt?

ON LETTER WRITING

These same men dictated letters to customers about their orders and contracts all day, every day. I took a look at their letters and almost fainted. They were pre-historic! The way business letters were written in Benjamin Franklin's time! I told Vic Stine this painted our company as "old-fogey" at the time we were advertising our company and its products as modern, "state of the art". He gave me the green light and I "taught classes" – which made me pretty unpopular with the Sales Correspondents who had come to Pangborn right out of high school, many years before. But it got the job done.

I never got a growl out of "Mr. Thomas" – as he was also referred to. Matter of fact, after every issue of Pangborn News, he would call me and tell me how good it was. And Laura and I were always included in his Christmas parties and other social functions usually limited to the senior managers. When the new Thomas W. Pangborn bell tower and men's dormitory at Mount Saint Mary's were dedicated, I think we may have been the only Pangborn people invited to attend. (Except for his Secretary and "Special Friend", Helen Fisher.)

MY MAILING LIST CAPER

Actually, Les Gardner wasn't very good at his job, but I was careful not to rock the boat. The mailing list for Pangborn News and other direct mail advertising was huge for our size and situation – 25,000 or more. It had been established mostly by Direct Mail Service, a company in Pittsburgh. They maintained the list, adding and subtracting names as required, and we kept a copy in our mailroom. Ike Bloom, owner and manager of the Service, a friend of Les Gardner, would visit two or three times a year, butter up Les, take him to a 2-hour lunch, and leave him a couple boxes of very expensive Cuban cigars. Les bragged how great this mailing list service was.

I paid little attention until I was visiting a customer company with one of our District Managers. We were with the superintendent who had picked our equipment over Wheelabrator's. He was the "principal buying influence" in that company. I was introduced as "the guy who writes the green sheet". The customer looked blank. *This important customer had never seen a copy of Pangborn News!*

The District Manager was dumbfounded. When I told Les Gardner, he said, "Must be a rare exception. Ike Bloom is the best in the business."

The Foundry Show was scheduled a couple weeks later, and the entire field sales staff would be there. I phoned every District Manager and asked for the names of the five most important customer companies in his district. These were the big ones – Ford, GM, GE, DuPont. Then I asked Chuck Ford in our mailroom to give me a list of all names and titles in these companies. "Then you select, at random, five other companies in each district, and give me those names and titles." (Our entire 25,000 list was personalized; people names and titles, not just company names.)

With this information, I sat down with each District Manager and his salesmen at the Foundry Show, named a plant and asked, "Who do you have to sell to get the order?" They would give me three or four names, I'd show them the card and say, "None of them are on the list." They couldn't believe me! When I showed them who was on, they were amazed – seven names, maybe – two retired years ago, one deceased, *the others they never heard of!*

Long story short: much of the same for every company in every district! Our mailing list was a disaster! More than 80% obsolete! Ike Bloom hadn't kept it updated. Les and the District Managers didn't, because they thought Ike was doing it. I even found dozens of ferry boats and cruise ships on the list: Ike had added them under the heading "Ship Building"!

Les Gardner wasn't at all happy with my research and discovery. It made him look bad. I knew he surely did not want Management to know. I never told them. But I used my leverage to get the Bloom Agency fired (not easy) and Les to let me visit every district office, to sit down with the field sales staff and build a totally new list of key buying influences in every prospective customer company in America and Canada.

I learned a great deal. Big money was involved – printing, postage and the Bloom Agency fees for a huge number of mailings several times each year to people and companies of no importance to us! And nobody paying any attention. Who knows how many potential customers never heard a peep from us?

I learned a lot at Burpee's and Pangborn. Both were successful companies – with dozens of opportunities for major improvements. Their "people policies" especially were out-dated.

At Pangborn, for managers, the work week was 5 1/2 days. Everyone had to be there on Saturday mornings. By the end of my first one, I found that practically no useful work was done on Saturdays. It seemed that everyone played golf, and replayed every round, every hole and every shot in their Saturday bull sessions. In my lengthy 'Proposal for Improvement of Company Operations" I tried to solve this problem by suggesting a change in management philosophy. "Managers should be told their job is to manage, and that promotions and compensation will be based on successful innovations and improvements in their areas of our company's business. They will be judged on results obtained, and not on how much time they spend on the job."

I'm not sure the Chief bought into this one, but I know Vic Stine, Lloyd Stauffer and Ralph Trent got the message. Quietly, without fanfare, things got better over time.

ALL WORK AND NO PLAY? HARDLY.

Change happens. Everywhere. You can't stop it. One of the changes: Les did less. He spent most of his time talking to the salesmen who called on him – about golf, vacations, anything but business. Two-hour lunches, always. When he got into his seventies, with no intention of ever retiring, Ralph Trent made him. I became Ad Manager.

BLUE RIDGE SUMMIT, PENNSYLVANIA

This residential community was located right on the Pennsylvania-Maryland state line – in the Catoctin Mountains, a few miles north of Camp David. Years before, wealthy families from Baltimore and Washington built large homes and spent summers there to escape the city heat. Wallis Warfield Simpson (who seduced England's King Edward VIII to give up the throne) had been our most famous citizen.

It was nicely forested, a good place to live, and quite a few managers who worked in Hagerstown and Waynesboro lived there. Fort Ritchie was there – great for me, as I immediately joined their Officers Club. Laura and I attended their parties and sunned and swam at their lakeside beach. It was a focal point of our social life – one of them, the other being an organization of people our age called "The Hilltoppers".

A guy named Charlie Gardner ran the place – owned most of the real estate, the realty office, the bank and provided all kinds of insurance. We didn't have much net worth, so he showed us a small summer cottage and got a contractor to tell us how to fix it up, winterize, and what it would cost. We gave the go-ahead and Charlie even had his bank give us a lower rate on our mortgage than we could get anywhere else. Charlie and his wife, "Tish", became our good friends.

We had all the social activities we could handle. Most of our friends were older than we were, and "well-heeled". But nobody paid attention to that. We fixed up our little cottage – the first real estate we ever owned – and fenced in the yard for Kayak. This dog was a ball of fire, always raring to go, and he kept us exhausted, trying to keep up with him. We decided he needed a girl friend, to take some of the pressure off us.

ALASKAN MALAMUTES: LITTLE KNOWN, BUT IMPORTANT

There are only two kinds of dogs – Alaskan Malamutes and "the other kind". That's what everyone who owns one firmly believes. Over time, I became "the foremost authority" on these remarkable dogs and I wrote: "They can do anything any dog can do, and most things better. They are special dogs for special people." One time a bunch of owners brought their dogs to the Mason-Dixon Kennel Club show in Hagerstown, and we had them all for cocktails and dinner at "Husky-Pak". Soon the guys were showing pictures of their dogs, and one of the wives said, "I'll bet all they carry in their wallets is dog pictures, and none of their children!" She was right, not a single kid picture in any billfold! But lots of dogs. Malamutes.

I put a lot of time into research. The breed was rare and virtually unknown – even by the American Kennel Club! I found a female in Seguin, TX, same age as Kayak, had her flown up and named her Mikya of Seguin. Kayak fell in love with her immediately.

Mikya and Laura enjoyed being together. Mikya, our only M'Loot, looked much like a wolf. Had a great body and movement and became a champion.

A woman named Hazel Wilton in Great Barrington, MA, had saved her best two puppies for someone who would show them. Pictures of their parents sold us – the sire had been Best of Breed at Westminster – the big one in Madison Square Garden. We named the male, Great Barrington Geronimo, and his sister, Wilton's Black Takoma. AKC made us change their names when they earned registration. Geronimo became Apache Chief of Husky-Pak, and Takoma, Arctic Storm.

These two became the biggest winners of their time and were milestones of progress in our breed. We took them to the big Westminster Show in New York City and they literally "stopped traffic" as we walked them from our hotel to Madison Square Garden.

Ch. Apache Chief of Husky-Pak ("Geronimo"). A spectacular fellow and the best of his time. His size, power and personality helped popularize the Malamute breed.

THE STATE OF THE BREED, AS I FOUND IT

There were a few Malamutes around. Not many. Paul Voelker, a somewhat weird lumberjack-type in Marquette, MI, produced and sold more Malamutes than anyone at that time. He called his kennel "M'Loot". Ralph and Marcheta Schmitt, ("Silver Sled") outside of Milwaukee, bought M'Loot dogs and eventually became even bigger than Voelker.

I wrote to and received many letters from Voelker. I found some things I didn't like about his M'Loot dogs, visited the Schmitts and found their dogs, all M'Loots, to be much the same. None were registered with AKC. (Few Malamutes were.) The real pioneers in our breed were Milton and Eva Seeley, Chinook Kennels, in Wonalancet, N.H. They had assembled dogs they declared to be Malamutes, produced a few litters (not many) and got AKC to recognize this breed as distinctive from the Eskimo, where they'd been included previously. The Seeleys wrote the original Standard, based on their dogs. Chinook Kennels became the place where sled dogs were assembled and trained for various expeditions to Antarctica.

I found things I liked and things I didn't like in both strains, and other dogs I liked better. In Vermont, I was greatly impressed by Irwin's Gemo, Kayak's grandsire, once owned by Lowell Thomas, famous explorer and news-caster. And his son, "Hinman's Alaska," looked much the same. I saw "Alaska", sire of my Geronimo and Takoma, and later, two of his litter brothers, "Chisholm's Viking" and "Duke" – and I thought all of these were better than Seeley's Kotzebues or the M'Loot dogs.

An arctic explorer, Dave Irwin had brought some dogs from Alaska to the States and these were in the background of the dogs I liked. I called these the "Hinman-Irwin Strain" – or "third strain" (although there weren't really enough of them to be called a "strain"). I knew that by using these dogs I could produce better Malamutes than the pure M'Loots and Kotzebues.

And I did. Geronimo and Takoma were of this ancestry and they quickly became a major step forward in quality. They won everything, even beating their sire "Alaska" who had won at Westminster twice. Mikya was pure M'Loot, but one of the best – sired by Moosecat M'Loot, one of the best-ever M'Loots.

Kayak didn't turn out so well and sadly, he encountered some strange disease and died young. But he sired litters with Mikya and Takoma resulting in several champions. We surely missed our "first born". He was a fun dog and a "hell-raiser". Whatever killed him took a long time. Our vet tried hard, and even our family doctor brought specialists to our house to see if they could help.

THE HUSKY-PAK "C" LITTER MADE MALAMUTE HISTORY

With Geronimo and Takoma, I became the biggest frog in the Malamute pond – which was a pretty small body of water at the time. But I knew I could do better. I wanted to add some Kotzebue good points, if I could find a really good Kotzebue. Eva Seeley would be no help. By beating her dogs, I wound up No. 1 on her list of Mortal Enemies. Apart from that, she had the only registered Malamutes and was determined to create a monopoly, selling pups on contract that they could be bred only with her approval – to her bloodline.

She and her small circle of Kotzebue owners weren't very active. So AKC did something unprecedented: because many of the registered Kotzebues were destroyed in Antarctica, they reopened registration to any "proven" purebred Malamutes who could accumulate 10 championship points in AKC show competition. Immediately, all my dogs and the pups I sold became AKC registered. And Seeley went ballistic!

The Standard for our breed was based on the Seeley dogs which were smaller than mine or the M'Loots. So she tried to get AKC to "outlaw" any Malamutes larger than hers, and AKC wouldn't do it!

There was an Alaskan Malamute Club in New England, all Seeley customers. She tried to get AKC to recognize them as the official breed club, but they told her that club was local and it would have to become national. So two "outsiders" were allowed to join – me and Jean Lane, a rich lady who had a good M'Loot named Master Otter that she had been showing at dozens of dog shows all around the country. Long story short: I was able to outmaneuver Seeley and her club and ended up getting most of them and most of the Schmitt customers and mine into *The Alaskan Malamute Club of America*, which was then approved as the official breed club.

But I was explaining the Husky-Pak "C" litter. I had received an envelope full of 8 x 10 photos of Kotzebue dogs, 12 or more, from a sportsman's camp in Canada. These were two full litters of Kotzebues that Dick Moulton had produced when, in Seeley's absence, he was in charge of Chinook Kennels. They had been used as dog teams at the resort but now were for sale and I was the first person they contacted. I loved the lead dog, Toro. Best Kotzebue I ever saw. I wanted to buy him, but Laura said no. I had no idea where these dogs ended up. Then a couple of years later, Bob Spawn phoned me. "That Kotzebue you're looking for, just won at Westminster!" And he gave the information I needed.

The dog was Toro! Owned by Earl and Natalie Norris of Anchorage, Alaska. He was in the States, being shown by a professional handler. They agreed to send him to us for stud service. He stayed with us for a month and what a wonderful guest he was! I used him with Takoma (whom I now know was probably the best female Malamute ever). The "C" litter, Cherokee, et al, were results. And I'm convinced this one event changed and substantially improved our breed – forever.

My "C" litter was widely recognized as the best Malamute litter ever. All became champions except one whose owner hated dog shows and wouldn't show him. Cherokee won everything – three consecutive Best of Breed at National Specialty Shows, and three consecutive Dog of the Year awards.

CHEROKEE. Three times winner of the National, three times Dog of the Year. Maybe the best Malamute ever!

SEELEY VS. ZOLLER:
THE MAJOR EVENT IN MALAMUTE HISTORY.

"Hell hath no fury like a woman scorned." Mrs. Seeley had lost her total control of registered Malamutes, and the Club. She tried to change the Standard to disqualify all Malamutes larger than hers, and failed. She couldn't win in the ring. She was totally frustrated. So she trumped up charges that my dogs weren't purebred Malamutes and should be "outlawed" accordingly. I was provided with her specific charges and told to appear before the Trial Board at AKC headquarters in New York on a given date.

I knew I had "Truth, Justice and the American Way" on my side. But I was worried: I was nobody – Seeley was well-known at AKC, had written the Standard, had the first-ever registered Malamutes, and provided sled dogs for early Byrd expeditions in Antarctica. Also, our breed was new (in the world of purebred dogs) and even AKC didn't know much about them. If Seeley's charges were sustained, all "Third Strain" dogs would become worthless – and that meant all of my Husky-Pak dogs and practically all of the best Malamutes in our breed.

Before the Trial, I wrote and submitted a lengthy, detailed history of the breed – my first attempt to level the playing field. And along with a number of wild-eyed accusations, her big, high, hard one involved one Dr. Gibson Perry. The name was familiar – she had quoted him many times as an authority, and I came to believe he was a close personal friend of hers, or a relative. According to the charges, Seeley and her husband had sold several dogs to Dr. Perry, years before – and some of these dogs were in the pedigree of our Husky-Pak (and most other "third strain") dogs. *Dr. Perry had verified, she said, that they were NOT Alaskan Malamutes!*

So there goes my case???

I was able to locate Dr. Perry, retired and living in his cabin in the deep woods in Vermont, near the Canadian border. Good friend Jim Lynn had said, "Take a week off. I'll drive you there and we'll check it out." So Jim and Connie, his wife, and I set out on a long trip, one that had to be made.

We arrived at the Perry cabin late afternoon, getting dark, and beginning to snow. I was nervous and well-aware that several years of hard work and great success could vanish completely in the next few minutes.

We knocked on the door. A man in his 80's opened it and said, "Yes?" I said, "Dr. Perry, we came to talk to you about Eva Seeley." He held up his hand to stop me, but waved us in, looked at us and then proceeded to light his pipe. He puffed a few times, then without anything further from me, he said, "Has it ever occurred to you, that woman is either an alcoholic, a drug addict, or the victim of a mental aberration?"

Wow! Thirty seconds with Dr. Perry and we hit the jackpot! He told us she had arrived unexpectedly one day a few months before. He was outside and when she drove up; he told her, "I don't want to see you. Stop bothering me." She said, "All I want is for you to sign a simple pedigree – of the dogs Milton and I sold you ten years ago." Dr. Perry didn't have his glasses and told her so. "It's just a pedigree," Seeley said. "Here, sign it, and I'll be on my way." So he signed, he told us, to get rid of her.

I told him about the charges against me at AKC and her claim the dogs the Seeleys sold him were not Malamutes. "Of course they were Malamutes," he said. And he sat down at his desk and wrote a letter to AKC to that effect, signed, and gave it to me, and said, "If you have any problems, let me know. I'll go down there and tell AKC that the Seeleys sold them as Malamutes, I bought them as Malamutes, and they were never considered anything but Malamutes!"

GUESS WHAT HAPPENED AT THE TRIAL???

Jim Lynn went with me to the Trial – so I could call him as a witness. *Seeley arrived with a high-powered Boston lawyer!* Not just a lawyer, but a man who had been on AKC's Board of Directors for a number of years! And currently, President of the Great Dane Club of America! Jim and I saw them arrive – Seeley, the lawyer (Ken Tiffin) and several big wheels of the AKC, all greeting each other like long-lost family members!

So it was me – one year of law school (years before) vs. the Boston lawyer, and maybe his AKC buddies.

Talk about "dirty pool!" I won't blame you if you don't believe this:

1. Seeley showed up with a guy named John Hofft, who had bought a pup from my "B" litter. I had thought of him as a friend, but before the Trial, I had received a letter from Dave Irwin's wife – the Irwins didn't know me at all, or even where I lived. (They sent the letter to me c/o AKC!) They had befriended Hofft, gave him a job at their mink farm – and learned Seeley had bribed him with a promise to get him on the next Byrd expedition to Antarctica! After Hofft (who probably had an I.Q. of about six) left the Irwins, he wrote them threatening letters under an assumed name (John B. Roth) and demanded they sign letters to AKC denouncing me as a terrible person who "controlled" the Malamute breed and wouldn't let AKC register any Malamutes

without my approval! I had old letters from Hofft and took them to the Trial to prove that Hofft was "John B. Roth". *The idiot had done everything in his own handwriting!*

2. In regard to the Dr. Perry thing, Seeley's lawyer then introduced into evidence the pedigree the old doctor had signed – and this included a statement, *"These dogs are not purebred Alaskan Malamutes."* So I immediately countered with my Dr. Perry written statement that indeed they were! And I told the Trial Board, "This should be no problem: phone Dr. Perry. He assured me if there was any problem, he'd be happy to come to New York and state the truth in person!"

The lawyer and Seeley whispered to each other. And in a minute or two, the lawyer told the Trial Board, *"Mrs. Seeley added that statement."* In plainer language, she tried to win her case by forgery!

The Trial Board found in my favor, of course. It was a great victory for a magnificent breed that could have been terribly diminished – virtually destroyed – if Seeley had won. This case, the decision, and my part in it, is why today I am said to be "the father of the modern Malamute".

UNBELIEVABLE INCOMPETENCE. It was an easy victory – not because of brilliance on my part (although I poured a lot of time and effort into it), but I couldn't believe how badly Seeley and her lawyer botched their case. They had made literally dozens of charges and in almost all cases they offered no evidence or proof whatever! Bringing Hofft and having him there for my cross-examination was incredibly stupid. How they expected to get away with the forgery was even worse! Lowell Thomas' dog, Gemo, was in my dogs' background: they claimed he was shown at Westminster *as an Eskimo dog in 1935*. I pointed out that that was somewhat difficult to believe, since Gemo wasn't born until several years later! And AKC records could easily verify that he was entered in Westminster K.C. shows twice in the 1940s – and was the winning Alaskan Malamute at both!

I even learned that their Appeal stated, as their reason for reversal, that "It was apparent that Zoller was lying and Mrs. Seeley was telling the truth!" How silly can you get, saying that, in view of her forgery! (High-powered Boston lawyer?)

At any rate, my winning the trial at AKC made our beautiful breed what it is today.

Our dogs were always part of our family. That's Sioux asleep and the puppy is Hunter. (See photo below.)

BEST FRIENDS: Hunter, Kris, Greg and Cherokee. And Merry Christmas!

LIVING WITH MALAMUTES –
THE GOOD, THE BAD, AND THE UGLY

These dogs were a very important part of my life – so beautiful that it made me feel good just to look at them. Laura loved them as much as I did. They became members of our family. This is the good.

Malamutes are a product of evolution in the arctic. Associated with man longer than anyone knows for sure. Possibly, *the* oldest breed. They are the power dogs, not the smaller, faster Iditarod dogs. Said to have descended from arctic wolves. Some resemble wolves so much that Hollywood often has them playing wolves in the movies.

Some are so powerful they could kill you. Fortunately, they are characteristically endowed with love and/or respect for humankind. Early arctic explorers wrote of seeing Indian babies nursed by "mother Malamutes"! In World War II, the army tried to train them as attack dogs, but had to give up. Malamutes, ordered to attack, usually signaled, "Why? He's not bothering either of us." (This maybe related to their refusal to cross frozen rivers when ordered, when they sense that the ice is too thin for safety.) Sometimes they seem to think they know better than you do.

Some claim the Malamute, pound for pound, is the most powerful draft animal in the world. I don't know for sure. I do know their biggest fault was their penchant for fighting. (This is the bad, and often the ugly.) In my day, every male thought he was the Alpha male, and most females, the same. We had elaborate security measures, but we lived in fear. Wolves don't fight to the death – when one gets the upper hand, the other gives up, and lives to stay in line, or fight another day. Not Malamutes!

Nobody's perfect – including these beautiful, people-loving, almost perfect companions. Always ready, willing and extremely able to tangle. Hair-trigger tempers – especially with other Malamutes. We tried hard to prevent fighting, but accidents happen; blood was spilled (including mine) but we lucked out – our dogs never did serious damage to each other or to anyone else's dogs. We soon learned there were several degrees of fighting – squabbles, bloody squabbles and deadly serious dogfights that I don't even want to think about. The Kotzebues were not nearly as aggressive as the Husky-Pak or M'Loot dogs. At the 1953 Specialty in Rye, NY, two litter brothers (Schmidt M'Loots) – ninety-pounders, fully mature – got into it and it took a half dozen men swinging heavy maple folding chairs to break them apart so they could be physically separated. One was badly torn up. The worst dogfight I ever saw!

Females would fight each other and even the males, if something set them off. Eagle and Cherokee were mortal enemies, and so were Mikya and Takoma. In these cases, we couldn't even have them in adjacent runs – they would try to get at each other through the chain link fence! Kayak would try to kill anything canine, except the girls, whom he dearly loved. We even had seven-week-old puppies fighting each other!

Even in the heat of battle, Laura and I could wade in, grab tails and pull, and none of our dogs would ever turn on us! Unlike pit bulls, Malamutes aren't grippers; they chomp, then chomp down again. So pulling tails could get them parted – between chomps, so to speak – until you could get a door or fence gate in between.

THE CLASSIC ALMOST-DISASTER

We lived in fear that a big fight would happen without both of us there to stop it. And it did! Laura had taken the kids to Chicago for a couple of weeks. I was alone, switching dogs before going to work. A door I thought was tightly shut, wasn't. All of a sudden, I'm in a small bedroom with four Malamutes – and two of them were Cherokee and Eagle! The two big males attacked in a flash and I was scared to death as I had no idea how I could stop it. They were standing on their back legs, going at each other's faces and throats – eye-level with me! Fortunately, the bedroom had one door leading to our basement, and even better, it was open! So, in desperation, I put a head-on tackle on Cherokee and we went sailing head-first down the wooden stairs onto the concrete basement floor. How I ever was able to think that fast, I'll never know, but I did: surely Eagle would sail right down after us, Cherokee was probably injured – I had gone all the way down right on top of him – but miraculously, on the way down, I was able to hook the open door with my toe and pull it shut!

Cherokee wasn't hurt. I got him out of the way and went back up to the bedroom, totally shook up. I put Eagle out. The girls, Sioux and Kelerak, who had quietly observed this entire event, apparently fascinated by it, decided they should fight! I was so angry that these dogs I loved and cared for as my own children, *would do this to me* that I doubled up my fists and belted them both right on their noses and jaws! Boy, were they surprised! I had never hit any of my dogs. They stopped and looked at me and I got one of them through a door and into another room.

Then I sat on the floor for a long time, catching my breath and thanking God for what I figured had to be some kind of miracle.

ENTER ROBERT GREGORY "DOGFIGHT" ZOLLER

We woke up early on the Big Day and Laura said I wouldn't have to go to the office. "How much time do we have?" I asked. (Expectant fathers want to get there on time.) "No big hurry," she said. "But you should call Joe and Sara to come here now." (They were good neighbors, the Bocks.)

Off the kitchen was an alcove leading to the fenced back yard where Geronimo and Mikya were living. Mikya was coming into season, Geronimo was pestering her, but she wasn't ready for romance. She had retreated into the alcove and was up against the kitchen door. When the big guy became too insistent, she lost her temper and bit him in the face. Much too hard, he figured, and the Alpha male doesn't have to put up with it. *Dogfight!*

"I have it!" I yelled. This couldn't be too serious – one male, one female – and I surely didn't want my really pregnant wife involved. But she came running – along with Takoma and Cherokee who had spent the night in our bedroom. Laura opened the door and Takoma saw the hated Mikya lying there, pinned down by Geronimo. She rammed her head through the opening and grabbed a leg, and now we have big trouble! If we can't get Takoma off quickly, we'll soon have a three-legged Mikya!

Laura was beating Takoma over the head with something. My job was to keep Mikya from chomping on Takoma. So I grabbed Mikya with both hands between her upper and lower jaws. In the melee, all three dogs and yours truly were all down in a pile. Mikya pulled her leg – the one being bitten – up until her nose was against some part of Takoma and she struck! My hands – both of them – were inside Mikya's jaws. She chomped and I screamed so loud the sound must have echoed through the hills! Startled, all the dogs stopped. We got the door closed between them, Joe and Sara arrived (to take care of Kris), and I bled all over the kitchen floor.

"I'll call the doctor," Sara said. "Don't call Keifer," Joe told her. "Keifer doesn't like the sight of blood. Call Doc Youngs!" Joe drove me and Youngs met us at his office. Both hands were crushed near the base of my thumbs. "Can't get in there to clean them out," Doc explained. "But dogs' mouths are pretty clean. I'll bandage them loosely and let 'em bleed." He gave me shots – tetanus and penicillin and sent me on my way. I had so much gauze on my hands they looked like I was wearing boxing gloves.

Laura drove me to the hospital. While she was in the delivery room, I sat outside. Nurses kept telling me, "Emergency is at the other end of the hall!" I kept bleeding. They changed the bandages several times. When Greg arrived, Laura sent me home – an adventure getting there, steering with my elbows! I couldn't go to work for several days – you need at least one hand to function in this world and both of mine were unavailable. Sara lived nearby and came over several times a day to help. On top of everything, I had a severe allergic reaction to one of my two shots – glands swelled like baseballs in both armpits. Damn the dogfights!

Malamutes were like that, in those days. (Where in hell was "the Dog Whisperer" when I really needed him?) Most owners worked hard to avoid trouble but a few like Voelker and the Schmitts seemed to enjoy proving their dogs could lick all the other breeds.

But Malamutes weren't always to blame. Our first show ever was at Fredericksburg, VA. Kayak was a youngster, not quite fully mature and less than 80 lbs. I was walking him near the benched dogs and a St. Bernard, twice that size, lunged at Kayak, snapped his chain and attacked. I saw him coming and dragged Kayak as fast as I could but the Saint caught up and grabbed Kayak by a back leg. I let Kayak loose to defend himself and like a flash he was on top of the Saint, sinking his teeth in the back of the big dog's neck. I pulled Kayak off, but the Saint caught up with me again, and again Kayak ended up on top. Then, a half dozen men grabbed and held the Saint. I hate any and all dogfights, but I declared Kayak the winner – and was mighty proud of him.

A GIANT LEAP FORWARD. Flash forward forty or fifty years, to the National Specialty at Sturbridge, MA, in 2003: more than 240 Malamutes in crowded areas for 3 or 4 days, and not a single fight, bared fang, or even a growl! I couldn't believe it – but it was a wonderful surprise! Their one really bad habit bred out!

THE DOG AT THE "O" CLUB, NEWFOUNDLAND 1941

I told you about the dog that got me interested in Malamutes. Years later, a salesman called on me at Pangborn and saw the picture of Geronimo on my desk. "Great looking Malamute!" he said. I was surprised – nobody knew our breed in those days. "How did you get interested in Malamutes?" he asked. I told him and he laughed. *"I saw that same dog in 1941!* And I took a picture of him. I'll send you a copy." He did, and I was surprised all over again: the dog was a lousy specimen! Come to think of it, I'm now pretty sure he wasn't really a purebred Malamute at all!

Several years after that, a young artist called from New York City about a puppy. "No offense," I told him, "I would never place a Malamute puppy in a big city apartment." But he said he just bought a ranch in California and was moving there in the next few weeks. And that his mother

SIOUX. Never beaten by any female, she defeated every male in the breed except Cherokee. After Takoma died, she was the very best of those years.

"Howdy there, big fellow!" Greg tells Geronimo, "Let's go play – or maybe snuggle up and take a nap."

lived in Waynesboro, about six miles from us*! It turned out that Laura knew her!* She was a rich lady, also an artist. When Alva Haywood, the son, came to get his puppy, I asked how he knew about Malamutes. His father, he said, was a naval architect and, for some reason, went to Newfoundland in 1941, and took his young son with him. Alva had seen the same dog at the same place as I had!

One Sunday, several years later, a car pulled into our driveway and I went to see who it was. An elderly man got out. "This the place with the Malamutes?" I invited them in – man, wife, son-in-law (my age) and his wife. "Guess what?" the old man said. "My son-in-law is a naval officer – in Antarctica just a couple days ago! He was in charge of the sled dogs there. I kept that article about you that ran in the Baltimore Sun. When he saw it, he said he would like to drive up. We live in Virginia."

I brought a couple dogs in and eventually the son-in-law asked how I got interested. I told him about Newfoundland. He looked surprised, then laughed and said, *"That was my dog!"*

(The article in the Baltimore Sun was pretty big in our lives in those days. "MALAMUTES IN MARYLAND." Feature story in their Sunday rotogravure section – the front cover and three full pages inside.

A GOOD WAY TO MEET GOOD PEOPLE

A lot of the "good" in our Malamute years were the people we met and came to know. I've never met AMCA member DOROTHY L. W. REDDING, but she is a Husky-Pak fan, an artist who produced (from photos) an oil painting of me and four of our dogs. Recently she offered the painting to the American Kennel Club for permanent display in their art gallery at AKC's New York City headquarters and they have accepted! It is now there on exhibit! This is a singular honor for Dorothy – and for me, Geronimo, Takoma, Sioux and Cherokee. She also wrote A PORTRAIT OF ROBERT ZOLLER for the 1995 Alaskan Malamute Annual (a commercial publication based in Colorado) that summarizes my contributions many years after they happened.

JUDY PAULE lives in Australia and heads up my one-person Fan Club, down under. She phones me fairly often – and sometimes after Florida hurricanes, just to see if I'm O.K.

WESSON SEYBURN bought Attila from my "A" litter. In Detroit on business, I gave him a call and ended up being chauffer-driven to his "farm" for cocktails, dinner and a wonderful evening. He was elderly, rich, on the Boards of several major industrial companies, married into the Dodge family (autos), home on Grosse Pointe, owner of a huge residential complex on the

The painting is now on permanent display at AKC's Headquarters in New York City.

Detroit River, nextdoor "farm" neighbor of Charles E. Wilson (then CEO of General Motors). His wife had something to do with horseracing's The Widener Cup, and Mr. Seyburn told me that he had brought the first German Shepherds to America at the end of WWI. (His friend, the famous dancer, Vernon Castle, had called from Europe to tell him about the wonderful Alsatian dogs of Germany.) Because of Attila, Mr. Seyburn did many nice things for me (including The Wesson Seyburn Trophy for Dog-of-the-Year) for years, until his death.

JIM LYNN drove a taxi in 1941. Got a job producing war materials and at war's end, bought surplus Swiss screw machines, got General Motors contracts and became wealthy. He bought our Buccaneer – and a "farm" in Bucks County (for the dog), and installed a 6-foot chain-link fence around a couple of acres so Bucky could run and play safely. Then they bought Eska, a female puppy, from us so Bucky would have a playmate. The fenced property had no trees, and they felt Bucky needed a tree. So no saplings for Buck – the Lynns undoubtedly broke the Pennsylvania State record for size of tree transplanted – a forty-footer with a 12-inch diameter trunk! (Must have cost a fortune.) First time the dogs were let out, Eska raced to the new tree, Buck in full pursuit; Eska dodged, Buck didn't and rammed the tree head-on and went down for the count. He was O.K.—but Jim had the tree cut into firewood later that day!

DAVID AND CHRISSIE FOURIE, Pretoria, South Africa, "discovered" Malamutes and came to the States to visit Husky-Pak for a week, went through every photo and scrap of Malamute paper we owned, spent a small fortune for photo-copies and wondered how they'd get all that paper back to South Africa.

BOB AND ELIZABETH ANINGER. Cliquot of Husky-Pak became the light of their lives. They made him our breed's first Champion CDX. Bob bought a Royal Canadian Mountie uniform and (as Sgt. Preston and his dog, Yukon King) put on obedience exhibitions. When they visited the famous painter, Norman Rockwell, Cliquot and his daughter ended up on a SATURDAY EVENING POST cover, part of a picture of a guy trying to sell an electric refrigerator to an Eskimo family. I'm happy that Rockwell painted Cliquot, but he made him much too small! Bob died and Cliquot died. When Elizabeth died, a neighbor of hers phoned me and told me Elizabeth had visited the editor of the Hartford newspaper and made him promise that her obituary would include: "Proud owner of the famous Alaskan Malamute, Ch. Cliquot of Husky-Pak, CDX." Drew Drasher's drawing of Cliquot's head has graced the official symbol of the Alaskan Malamute Club of America for many years, and still does. And I hope this goes on forever.

HAL AND DOT PEARSON. Hal was a colorful character who had a great way with animals. Dot became active in AMCA. Their Redhorse kennels near Chattanooga was sometimes called "Husky-Pak South", because they bought Banshee, Durango, Ginoko, Kiowa and Morning Star from us. Banshee was National Specialty Best-Opposite at nine years old! (Her son was Best of Breed at the same show.) Durango was almost a year old when we sold him. Many years later, I visited Pearsons; they let Durango in and he greeted everyone in the room. Then a few seconds later he did a "double-take", whirled and was all over me, ecstatic at seeing his old friend! All of us were amazed at his memory and reaction.

Many other friends and followers helped me get the Alaskan Malamute situation sorted out and headed in the proper direction. Bob and Martha Gormley of Barberton, OH; Bob and Alice Spawn, Newark Valley NY; Dick Tobey, Bedminster NJ; Bill and Lois Dawson, Manassas VA; Penny Devaney, Cedar Crest NM and others too numerous to mention.

Our dog hobby had become a source of lifetime friendships. Frosting on the cake!

THE 1953 NATIONAL SPECIALTY: RYE, NY

Big day for Husky-Pak. In the largest entry of Malamutes ever in our breed (to that date), Takoma was Best of Breed, Geronimo BOS, and Takoma's kids Cliquot, Cheyenne and Comanche were WD, WB, RWB and Best of Winners – a total family affair. After that, everyone, it seemed, wanted to get in line for puppies from Takoma's next litters.

AND TRAGEDY. Two months later, Takoma picked up a virus at the Philadelphia Show and died shortly thereafter. Dr. Lower, our vet, and we tried desperately to save her. Gormley's Comanche also caught it and died. Laura and I were devastated and never fully recovered. *Worse, we thought we might lose all of our dogs at the same time!*

We went on for a few more years with Cherokee and Sioux dominating the breed, but it was never the same. We came to realize every crisis in our lives had been dog-related. We had watched too many approach death and had to have them put to sleep: *they never just died.* We agreed to phase out, and waited until our last two grew old and departed, and then it was over.

We loved our dogs too much to be good at this. But we have great memories, and no dogs anywhere had it better than the Malamutes of Husky-Pak. And they surely did great things for the breed, forever after.

AMONG THE MEMORIES. Our dogs wanted to be with us all the time, but because of the fighting, we had to bring them in the house in shifts – two at a time. The oldest dog got to sleep in our bedroom – with a compatible companion. This worked out well until one night when Geronimo was old and accidentally stepped on Sioux in the dark. (She of the short fuse.) You haven't lived until you wake at 3 a.m. with two big Malamutes fighting in your small, dark bedroom!

Ch. Arctic Storm of Husky-Pak ("Takoma"). Big, powerful, maybe the best female ever! She was the dam of the famous Husky-Pak "C" litter and Best of Breed at the big National Specialty Show in 1953.

When Laura became pregnant, it made me angry when people asked, "So now, what are you going to do with your dogs?" I came up with this answer: "Laura and I decided if the baby doesn't interfere with the dogs, the kid can stay!" That worked pretty well.

Christmas Morning at Husky-Pak **MERRY CHRISTMAS**

The Zoller family ★ Laura, Bob, Greg and Kris....

AT THE U.N. WITH VON BRAUN'S BROTHER

Wernher Von Braun was the world's leading authority on rocket technology. In Germany he developed V-2 rockets that bombed the hell out of Britain in WW2. After the war, important buddies of Hitler were imprisoned and tried at Nuremburg. Not Wernher. Everybody wanted him – we got him. He was invited to head up research and development of advanced weapons technology and our space program. He was the major factor in the success of our moon landings, became an American citizen and an American hero.

Laura and I were in New York, being seated in a Times Square restaurant, when a man at the next table saw me and said, "Hey, Bob Zoller!" It was Bob Lesher, husband of my secretary, Helen, at Pangborn. He was with the Washington County Board of Education, in charge of a new program involving closed circuit television in the teaching process.

He told us he had brought students and technical people to videotape interviews with U.N. delegates on the following day. We said we planned to visit the U.N., so Bob invited us to become part of his team. "You'll avoid standing in line and you'll get a better behind-the-scenes view of the United Nations."

We met him and his troops the next morning and were ushered into the U.N. through the delegates' door. We sat in (and were invited to participate in) interviews with ambassadors from Norway, Pakistan and West Germany. All were interesting, but the German – Wernher Von Braun's brother, Sigismund – was a man of exceptional charm and considerably more fun than the other two.

After the taping, he stayed and talked with us for quite some time. As I remember, he and I did most of the talking, and I thought we rather hit it off, maybe because of my Teutonic background, or more likely just because he made everybody feel that way.

Years later, a major scandal rocked Great Britain and rippled through the civilized world: a member said to be of the Royal family – the Duke of Argyle – was divorcing the Duchess, having found her in bed… with Wernher Von Braun's brother!

STAR OF THE FAMILY: F. C. REITH, JR.

I hadn't seen my Whiz Kid cousin for many years, but our Aunt Rose had kept me informed. General Electric had recruited him for their management-training program, but the war came along, and he enlisted in the Army. Meantime, Washington was feverishly engaged in growing all branches of our military to meet the needs of the new world situation. The generals in charge of our Air Corps were old-time flyers who knew everything about aviation but were ill-equipped to manage the billions of dollars involved in the build-up. So someone got an idea: get some young geniuses from the business world and assign one to each general. Jack was selected, commissioned and sent to Harvard for indoctrination.

There, his instructor was a man named Robert McNamara. They became friends. Jack was assigned to the Commanding General of the Air Material Command at Wright-Patterson in Dayton, Ohio.

A couple of years later, the General was assigned elsewhere. He told the top brass not to send another General. "I've got an officer here that can handle this job better than anyone in the Air Corps." So they promoted Jack from Lieutenant to Lt. Colonel and put him in charge of "The Statistical Control Office" with its 5,600 employees. He developed a new system that substantially reduced the time required to get emergency replacement parts and supplies wherever needed, worldwide. At the end of the war, he was sent to Washington to receive The Legion of Merit from "Hap" Arnold, Commanding General of the Air Corps. When I visited Jack in Detroit, I saw his citation that specifically mentioned, among other things, "saving our government one billion dollars."

(That was in June 1945. I suspect it would be "many billions" in today's money.)

THE FIRST OF THE WHIZ KIDS

Right after the war, young Henry Ford took over the Ford Motor Company. Looking for help, he contacted General Knudson, former President of General Motors, who headed our nation's War Manpower Board. Ford told Knudson he had a good staff of auto industry people, but now he wanted "some bright young men with new ideas." Knudson told him about Jack.

Henry made my cousin an offer he could not refuse. But Jack asked, "What if I bring some friends with me?" Young Henry said yes, he wanted more – and Jack contacted Robert McNamara, who joined the party. Tex Thornton was the oldest and best known of the group (that soon became famous as "The Whiz Kids"), but he left shortly to start his own company, Texas Instruments. Lee Iacocca, later the "Mustang Man", and still later, CEO and savior of the Chrysler Corp., was also one of the original Whiz Kids.

On my first business trip to Detroit, after the war, I gave Jack a call and was surprised that he really seemed interested in seeing me. I was invited for dinner and he sent a chauffeur to pick me up at my hotel.

I met his wife, Maxine, and Donna and "Fritz", his kids. They lived in Bloomfield Hills. Had servants. Every room in the house had a built-in sound system that would play their choice of music. Jack told me that "John" had arranged for its design and installation. When he told me about John, I was duly impressed. John was a lawyer and CPA about Jack's age (30's) whom Ford assigned to handle all of my cousin's personal matters like investments, taxes, shopping, travel arrangements, dinner reservations, etc. – so Jack would not be distracted from Ford business. (Each of the company's top brass had a "John".)

I was also impressed with Maxine. She could have made me feel like "the poor country cousin", but she didn't. She was an Oklahoma gal and really "down to earth" – no airs. I liked her immediately. Jack even talked me into staying overnight: he wanted me to ride in with him on the next day, to show me his office. Then he'd get me back to my hotel, as I had work to do.

Next morning, when we walked out to his six-car garage, I noticed a car I didn't recognize and asked about it. Jack smiled and said, *"That's next year's Ford."* He was chairman of Ford's Design Board.

He had a top of the line Lincoln for personal use. On the way into Detroit, I learned he was a speed freak. He put the car up to 105 mph on the six-lane highway, then told me, "Next year, we're adding another 100 horse-power to this model." I asked, "Why?"

After my first visit, Jack told me whenever I was coming to Detroit, let him know and he would have a company car sent to my hotel. I could use it as long as I was in town, drive it to their house for dinner, and just leave the keys at the hotel desk when I left Detroit.

The car he sent was his new "invention", a high horsepower Mercury "Turnpike Cruiser". I had a lot of fun beating everyone out of the stoplights.

Cousin Jack and Robert McNamara were the first of the Whiz Kids promoted to Vice Presidents at Ford. (McNamara, of course, was later U.S. Secretary of Defense and famous for his role in managing, or mismanaging, the Viet Nam War.) I visited Jack on several occasions. When he became a V.P., he moved to a new office. It was the one formerly occupied by old Henry, the founder. He was eccentric and had that office designed with a back door opening into an area totally hidden by bushes and trees. That's where he parked his car, so no one could know if he was in, or not in. Jack told me, "Now nobody can tell if I'm here or not."

Francis "Jack" Reith was a nice looking man who always seemed to be smiling. Tall, 6'3" or 6'4", and the only relative on either side of my family that to my knowledge, ever topped 6 feet. (Emma, his mother was Swedish.) I was pleased that he seemed interested in my life – my family, my job, my dogs, my wartime experiences. One time, I spent a weekend at his home. We were in his Study when someone came to talk to him. He said, "I'll only be 10 minutes. Take a look at those papers on my desk – a proposal I'm making to the Board on Monday. You're a writer. Tell me what you think." When he returned, I suggested a rewording of one paragraph. He said, "You're right, I agree, that's better." And he made the changes on the spot.

He is the only person in the history of the Indianapolis 500 who served as the Grand Marshall and drove the pace car at the same event! (A Turnpike Cruiser, of course.)

DIRECTOR GENERAL, FORD OF FRANCE

One day, young Henry summoned him and said, "As of now there is only one major component of our company that continues to operate at a loss – Ford of France. I want you to go over, study the situation, tell me why – and what we can do about it. He also said, "Take your wife along. Paris is a great city. Have some fun. Stay as long as you feel you need to!" So they went to Paris. Stayed a few months. Went back to Detroit and Jack submitted his situation report and recommendations. Then Henry said, "Great. As of now, you are the new Director General of Ford of France."

Jack became something of a celebrity in France – at least in the Business Press, mainly because he was in his 30's and over there most of the heads of major industries were in their 80's. Aunt Rose told me he got a lot of publicity as "the young American". And after he got things going his way, his love of golf kicked in, and for reasons I don't know and never asked, he occasionally would fly to *Egypt* to play golf! Probably because North Africa was Ford of France territory.

There was a man in Morocco who became filthy rich by owning the Ford franchise for all of that country. With new management in Paris, he lost no time getting up there to cement relations with his new boss. Jack and Maxine were invited to be his guest in Morocco, to see what a great job he was doing for Ford, but mostly to be guests of honor at a party he promised they would never forget.

"All the really important people of Morocco will be there," he said. And it seems that he was right.

THE SULTAN OF MOROCCO AND HIS HAREM

Not long before that, they had an unusually benign revolution in that country. The King of Morocco was forced to step down and the senior religious leader of the country was given full control of the government. His name was El Glaoui. I remember reading about it in TIME magazine.

El Glaoui, the Sultan of Morocco, was at the party and he and Jack hit it off, as the saying goes. Near the end of the evening, El Glaoui asked how long Jack and Maxine would remain in Morocco and then said he wanted to have a party for them. Who could refuse? On the evening of the party at the Royal Palace, Maxine found out that El Glaoui had a harem and she was curious.

It turned out the old guy had, I don't know, 40 or 60 wives, most of which – maybe all but one – never left the harem. The one who did was a gracious lady, highly educated, who spoke many languages. She was the "ceremonial" wife, or head wife, who attended affairs of state and diplomatic and social functions.

"What goes on in those harems?" Oklahoma-born Maxine asked the head wife. "Would you like to go there and see?" was the surprising response. "I surely would," said good old Maxine. And away they went.

En route, the head wife told Maxine that no "Western woman" had ever been allowed to visit the harem. She was the first. On arrival, Maxine told me, they were immediately surrounded by the wives, all talking excitedly in languages Maxine could not understand. They were attractive, as one might expect, but varied in their ages and in their nationalities. Most had been *bought* and brought there as small children or teenagers, from many different countries – apparently on the theory that "Variety is the spice of life," (as I suspect is true).

As a result, their education was pretty much limited to becoming good at the main purpose of their being there. They were excitedly firing questions at the head wife, who finally turned to Maxine and explained, "I'm having difficulty telling them who you are… *because, you see, they do not know there is a place called America!"*

Wow! This was in 1953 or 1954! And we were unquestionably the most powerful and important country in the world! And they never heard of us! (Aren't you surprised? I'm amazed!)

Next Maxine realized that another major discussion was going on – this time with a lot of giggling among the harem wives. The head wife was smiling, too. "They've never seen a Western woman before," she explained, "and they are curious as to what you are wearing under your dress – your undergarments."

"Good question," said Maxine, lifting her dress up high. "Let them look!"

Much excitement! More questions. Lots of laughing. Maxine told me she felt a bit like an alien from outer space. One very pretty young wife had tried hard to get the head wife's attention, and finally did. They talked. Then the head wife told Maxine, "She wants me to tell you that of all the wives here, she is El Glaoui's favorite. She has so pleased the master that he has arranged that *when he dies, she will be free and allowed to return home to the family she left a long time ago."*

"The one so favored?" Maxine asked. "Yes, the only one." "The others?" "Some perhaps will be given to friends or relatives. Most will stay for whoever succeeds El Glaoui."

Property. Chattel. Like his horses. Cars. Like furniture. Not people. Things. This is what a harem is. Still. Even today, as I write this in 2006. Undoubtedly, it will still be much the same when you read this.

I visited Jack again in Detroit after they returned from Ford of France (which Jack had reorganized, made profitable and later sold – to Renault, I believe). They brought with them a French couple to be their butler and maid, and an English governess for their children. If I'm right, they produced an additional offspring – Charles – while they still lived in Paris.

Sometime later (I'm not good on dates), Jack left Ford. A new big wheel in American business was a man named Victor Emanuel. He had bought a number of companies and formed a conglomerate that was into many businesses and very successful. I remember reading about him in TIME and FORTUNE. His empire was growing rapidly, he needed help, he heard about Jack and hired him as his next-in-command and as President of his largest company.

Jack told me he made the move because this company was planning to become a major factor in aerospace, the only industry he thought was more exciting than the auto business.

Headquarters was Cincinnati. I visited Jack and Maxine after they settled in. Before Jack left Ford, he planned to launch the most powerful production car in the industry: 500 horsepower (in the early 1950's!) He had built 5 of them. When he left, Henry Ford gave Jack one of them, along with a hefty pension-for-life (in return for agreeing never to work for any other automotive company). Jack had his chauffeur pick me up in the super-car. When I asked how hot it was, the driver said, "Hang on!" and the acceleration made me feel like I was going through the back of my seat!"

(These cars were never mass-produced for sale to the public. About that time, gas prices went up and buyers turned to economy models. That may have been when Americans began buying Japanese cars.)

Jack and Maxine had a beautiful home in the "high-rent" section of Cincinnati. John (remember him?) had spent some time in Cincinnati, screening new home possibilities and arranging private schools for Donna and Fritz, and had handled most details of the move – and then left Ford and accompanied Jack to his new company. "I couldn't live without John," Jack told me.

Then – brace yourself – a shocking event and a mystery I could never solve. On a 4th of July morning, Jack was found dead with a gun in his hand. I was told he bought the handgun for protection and little son Fritz wanted him to shoot it, and Jack promised they would do it on the 4th of July. Suicide? Sure seemed like it. But I could never believe it! Over several years, I had come to know this man. He was about as successful as one can get. He loved his work. He loved life. He loved his wife and kids. I thought Maxine was great, and I never saw any evidence they weren't one of the best-matched, most perfect married couples on earth. I believe he was a good Catholic. Most of all, he was one of the easiest-going guys I ever met. I never knew anyone less likely to take his own life – with the possible exception of me, and maybe the Pope!

Anyway, the police and the Catholic Church both conducted investigations and both declared it an accident. Maxine and the children returned to Detroit. I think Maxine remarried, a few years later. When she was 15 or 16 years old, Donna became a skilled horsewoman, one of the best in that part of the country. At the big annual Detroit Horse Show, her horse failed a jump, fell, and Donna was killed.

To me, this sudden turn of events was a major tragedy. I'm about as far as you can get from being a hero-worshipper: most I have met got that way by luck or family, not talent or intellect. I could cite many examples; I'll mention two: David Burpee and Thomas W. Pangborn, my former bosses. Both were extremely rich and therefore much honored and kow-towed to. But in both cases, I hadn't worked for either of them for six months before I felt I could run their companies better than they. And not because of brilliance on my part – it's just that both were terrible managers.

Francis Reith, my cousin, never made me feel he was lucky; he was just plain, unquestionably, smarter than most people. And, as I mentioned before, one of the nicest guys I ever knew.

Life is strange. Jack was much more talented than I, but as it turned out, I was much luckier.

COCKTAIL HOUR, MIDWESTERN STYLE

My brother, Ed, was a salesman for Raleigh Tobacco when I visited him in Waterloo, I'm not sure when. I rode with him on his route and about 4 p.m. he said, "That's it for today. Let's go have a drink." I thought he was headed for home, but he stopped the car and said, "Come on."

For years, Iowa never permitted the sale of liquor "by the drink". You had to get a permit, then purchase your bottle from a State Liquor Store, take it home and drink it there. Unknown to me, they finally allowed exceptions for private clubs, properly licensed.

We had stopped at the Knights of Columbus. Ed ordered "the usual". When the bartender looked at me, Ed said, "This is my kid brother. He lives in the East and he probably wants some fancy drink."

"No," I said, "I'll keep it simple." But the bartender told me, "Order anything. We can handle it." So I didn't get really fancy – I ordered a martini. "One martini, coming up," the bartender said.

He turned away from me, but I could see that he got out the Bartender's Guide, flipped pages, found the recipe, then fished around in the storage area underneath the bar, picked out a few bottles (wiping off dust to check the labels) and finally located what he was looking for. Then he mixed the drink (double-checking the Guide to make sure he was doing it right) and proudly set it before me. "There," he said. "Give it a try."

"Looks fine," I said. But as I reached for it, he grabbed it before I could. "Oops!" he said. "*I forgot the cherry!*"

A couple of years later, I had another trip to Iowa. In Waverly, I invited Pep and Ruth Grawe to join me for dinner and found that Iowa again had changed its law. (Both ordered cocktails I never heard of, and the waiter never batted an eye. I call that progress!)

BUILDING THE BEST HOUSE ON THE MOUNTAIN

Both our kids turned out well. Kris was especially bright and cooperative. Greg became the youngest Eagle Scout in the area. This triggered a search by Scouting officials and they discovered he was the youngest in the Eastern U.S.A. (No data available for the U.S. as a whole.)

GREG, the youngest Eagle Scout in the East.

I had come to believe that Blue Ridge was a great place to live and Pangborn was a bit of OK, so we decided to build our dream house. (Doesn't everybody?) I often walked our dogs up in the woods, an area with magnificent trees, including very large dogwoods that flowered to create a veritable fairyland every Spring.

Charlie Gardner owned that property, so I asked him, "What's in it for me if I'm the first to build there, and I build the best house on the mountain?" Charlie smiled and told me it was already laid out in large lots. He agreed to get me water, electricity and extend the road, and gave me two lots for the price of one. 400 ft. frontage and 285 ft. deep. I'd design the house myself and put it right in the middle of the property.

But first, I'd have to do a lot of clearing. Get rid of dead wood and grapevine, and make space for the house and lawn.

I hired Bruce McCleaf, who worked on the railroad section gang, to help me every Saturday, weather permitting. (Laura gave me a double-bladed axe for Christmas that year.) Bruce had a chain saw and most always would bring another worker, sometimes his 14-year-old son who could climb tall trees like an orangutan. The clearing took many months, but it was a labor of love.

I completed the design. We hired the best builder in the area, and we did build "the best house on the mountain". 20 x 30 foot living room with a cathedral ceiling 22 ft. high; "the largest privately-owned stone fireplace in Maryland" (my description) with a raised hearth and room for five-foot logs; eighteen feet of floor-to-ceiling picture windows on one side with a mountain view; a lot of wood paneling and built-ins; a very large Study (also with large picture windows); screened porch and an open deck; thermopane in every window; and special flooring to withstand 100-pound dogs with toenails.

And floodlights around the entire house with a "panic button" in our bedroom: one touch and the entire property would light up.

The kennel was worthy of "the World's Greatest Dogs". All varnished wood inside. Concrete runs with chainlink fencing. A fenced exercise yard, nearly half of an acre, with grass and trees.

It was a place to be proud of. We expected to live there the rest of our lives.

TALK ABOUT TRUST. After Charlie and I agreed on the sale, I had the property cleaned up and was starting to build *before* I paid Charlie and officially owned the place. I'd remind him once in awhile and he'd say, "No hurry." Of course, this would be totally stupid, except I knew Charlie and he knew me.

ABOUT JOHN BIRNLEY

Father Daniel Mahoney, pastor of St. Rita's in Blue Ridge Summit, was a triple-threat priest – also pastor of the church in Fairfield, and Catholic Chaplain at Fort Ritchie. He was great with kids, and one day he told Bob Gorman and me he wanted to have his altar boys form a basketball team because they had no organized sports in their Junior High.

He could get the gym at Fort Ritchie but the fathers who had played basketball would have to coach them, scrimmage with them, and drive them to games he would schedule with Catholic schools in the area.

Good idea. One of the soldiers at Fort Ritchie – a black man named John Birnley – had been a big star at Gonzaga, one of the top basketball colleges in our country. Father Mahoney signed him up as head coach, everyone had a great time, and this turned into a wonderful experience for all of us.

As I recall, Bob Gorman's son, Robert, and our son Greg were the best players and this is probably why the Gormans and the Zollers were the biggest supporters of the whole idea.

On Sunday afternoons, we'd load up our station wagons and drive to schools in Harrisburg, or Gettysburg, or York, et al, to play their Junior High teams – kids roughly the same age.

John Birnley fit in beautifully. All the kids and parents thought he was great. He always rode with me and we became good friends. One day I asked him where he was from. He said Louisville. "By any chance," I asked, "did you ever run across Cassius Clay – Muhammad Ali?"

"Cassius was the best friend I ever had," John replied. "We lived next door to each other. Grew up together. Inseparable. We had sleepovers and always ate our meals at whose house was having the best food that day!"

We didn't win any basketball games, but John Birnley became like a member of our families. We apparently made a good impression on him as well, because after the season, John took the instructions and became a Catholic!

We all took a day off work to attend the ceremony and afterwards had a big party for him.

MUHAMMAD ALI AND ME

One evening after dinner, Laura and I were walking the boardwalk in Atlantic City when it began to rain. We ducked into a very large souvenir store to keep dry, and a few minutes later we heard a lot of yelling and we went to see what was happening. And there was Muhammad Ali, ranting and raving, doing his thing, surrounded by a crowd of more than 100 people, all cheering him on.

This was just after Ali refused to be drafted into the Army and had his World Heavyweight Championship taken away. Now he was shouting about Joe Frazier, the current titleholder. "That phony champion thinks he's a song and dance man, putting on a show right here in Atlantic City – at some night-club right here tonight! I'll be there in the front row, and I'll be yelling, "You aren't the champ! I'm the champ! Besides, you're ugly and I'm beautiful!" He embellished his message in various ways and the whole crowd kept cheering him on.

When he finished, he raised his hand and dismissed the crowd. Quite a show!

It stopped raining. Everyone left the store. I followed Ali out onto the boardwalk, went up to him and said, "Do you remember John Birnley?"

Wow! You should have seen the man change. He immediately became quiet and respectful. "How do you know John Birnley?" he asked, almost in a whisper. I told him the story. He was impressed. "John Birnley was the best friend I ever had. Lived right next door. We were brothers!"

He told me the same story John had told me, and he wanted to know where he was now. I couldn't tell him: John had been sent to new duties and I never knew where.

A crowd had reassembled and started shouting. Ali scowled and held up his hand to quiet them. (They responded – immediately.) He wanted to talk to me.

We chatted for some time. I was impressed with how friendly he had become. I introduced Laura and he shook her hand. She asked for his autograph. Ali snapped his fingers and one of his entourage produced a pen and a piece of paper. He smiled at Laura and she became an Ali fan forever after.

When we parted, he shook my hand and said, "Thank you."

I'm no hero-worshipper, but I admit I was impressed. Up close, Ali at that age was one of the most beautiful people I'd ever seen. Impeccably groomed and perfectly tailored. I'm sure the suit he was wearing was the most expensive one I'd ever seen and everything about him was in perfect taste. He was so nice to me that I've cherished this memory ever since.

Maybe you know, not long after this, TIME or some other authority reported a survey showing that Ali was the most famous, best known person in the entire world!

MEANWHILE, BACK AT THE PLANT

When I became Ad Manager, I hired Bob Benner from Philadelphia, quite a guy, one of the smartest young men I ever met, especially on technical subjects. He arrived for an interview when I was tied up, so I had Red Hensel show him through our plant. Red told me later that Benner watched several processes and, in every case, suggested ways they could be done better, faster, or at less cost! I think he was a better engineer than our engineers!

For technical publicity, Les Gardner used a New York agency. But I decided to hire a writer, supervise him, and produce more publicity at less cost. I found Rufe Jones, a writer, also in Philadelphia. Benner, Rufe and I became good friends and a very good deal for Pangborn. After a couple of years, Benner left to become Ad Manager of a company in Reading, PA. And later, he hired Rufe as his assistant; and still later, left to join General Electric, so Rufe became Ad Manager of the Reading company.

And after I went to Carborundum in Niagara Falls, I hired Rufe to work for me up there.

REUNION WITH THE HERO OF MIDWAY

In my final days in Blue Ridge Summit, I discovered that Wade McClusky was living near Baltimore. I got in touch, invited him to spend a Sunday with us, and was happy that he agreed to come. "The outstanding naval hero of WW2" was now an Admiral, in his 80's. Son Greg was nine or ten. I had told him about McClusky so it was essential to warn him, "He's a very old man now. Don't ask him to do his seven pushups with one hand!"

You guessed it. We just got settled and Greg asked exactly what I told him not to. The Admiral laughed and said, "Oh, I don't do that anymore!" His wife said, "Wade, tell them." He protested, "No, no, I don't do that anymore." His wife looked at me, laughed, and announced, "Not since last Saturday at the Country Club dance! He was showing off and tore up his shoulder!"

MEMPHIS SURPRISE

I had a business trip to Memphis and looked up Russ Wilkinson, our first navigator on the Corregidor. Russ still headed a large real estate business. We had lunch, and since my plane didn't leave until late that night, decided we'd hoist a few to honor our departed shipmates, and have dinner at his home. It was a great reunion: we had been close through some hairy adventures in the Pacific War. When we left for the airport, his wife said, "Russ, show him you-know-what." We drove out of his driveway, turned right for a half block, then right again. He stopped the car, pointed to the left and told me, "I sold it to him." *It was Graceland. Elvis Pressley's Graceland.*

ANOTHER "BOY, AM I EVER LUCKY!" NOTE

Strangely – or more likely due to genes from Laura – both Kris and Greg ended up much taller and stronger than I am. And Greg looks nothing like me; for him, a major advantage in several ways. When he got into his twenties and thirties, he sometimes sported a moustache and I began to claim he wasn't my kid, but looked suspiciously like the illegitimate son of Mike Ditka! (Of the Chicago Bears.)

A GUY NAMED MATTISON. WASHINGTON SURVIVOR.

The land we owned in Blue Ridge Summit was level, but south of us, there was a steep slope downward and at the bottom, a spring-fed pond and a modest cottage. Nobody lived there, but one day I heard some activity and went to take a look. Workmen told me some Washington big wheel bought the property to fix up for weekend getaways. Later, I heard sounds of bulldozing and asked Charlie Gardner about it.

Son Greg on his birthday. I don't know which one!

He said the new owner was remodeling the cottage, cementing around the pond to make it a swimming pool, would be adding tennis courts, and was removing trees for a short ski run! Eventually, a small chalet was built at the top of the ski run. It had a large deck with comfortable chairs, so I'd sit there when I let my dogs loose and watch them in comfort.

One day I saw a lady walking uphill toward me. She would be the new owner. I introduced myself. We talked and I invited her and her husband for cocktails. When they arrived, quite a surprise: *the guy was dressed in the official uniform of a Nazi Storm Trooper!*

He told us his name was Mattison and when we were comfortable, he said, "I guess I should explain the uniform." He was in Berlin recently and had seen a store selling such memorabilia and bought the outfit just for fun. Then his wife said, "Tell them what you were doing in Berlin."

We got the whole story. President Kennedy was to make a major speech at the U.N. and wanted a number of world leaders to receive in-depth briefings ahead of time. Mattison, a member of the White House staff, was given the assignment. He was flown around the world to notify heads of state accordingly. (Obviously, our new neighbor was a pretty important dude.)

He was from Minnesota (explains the ski run), had gone to Washington with Harold Stassen, a three-term Minnesota governor who ran for President (several times), never made it, but had important jobs in the Eisenhower administration. When Stassen fell out of favor, Mattison found other jobs in the federal government – CIA, State Department, White House staff – becoming a successful survivor.

I told him a buddy of mine had gone to Carleton College and became captain of the basketball team. "Wayne Sparks," Mattison said. "I was a year ahead of him, and I was captain of the football team. I knew Wayne very well!" (Small world.)

Several weeks later, the Mattisons invited us to a party – informal, al fresco, drinks and hot dogs, etc. around the campfire. We were the only locals there. All the others were White House staffers and their wives. (Unfortunately, at that time in my life I no longer kept a diary and sadly, I've forgotten most of the names. Seven or eight couples, all familiar names at the time. I should have written them down, but didn't: I had no idea I'd be writing about it, many years later.)

I felt privileged to be there. Mattison apparently told them I was a Kennedy fan and of the same political persuasion, because they talked business (and government gossip) openly, with much mention of important Washington people. I felt like an "insider", fortunate to have spent several hours with bright young people JFK had picked to help him run the country. (Again, I simply got lucky!)

ENTER CARBORUNDUM

We were all surprised when Tom Pangborn agreed to sell his company to The Carborundum Company of Niagara Falls. Nothing much changed for awhile. I worked with DeNatale, their Graphic Design Manager, to integrate the "look" of our advertising and sales literature for compatibility with other Carborundum companies and divisions. And I made a couple of presentations to their senior management in Niagara Falls.

Jim McConnell, Pangborn's President after the acquisition, came into my office one day and said Frank Massard, Carbo's Ad Manager had a heart attack and they wanted me to go up there and fill in for him until he was able to return. I did, for a couple of months, and it became apparent that Massard wasn't coming back.

So they reorganized and asked me to move there and become a Group Advertising Manager. I would still handle Pangborn plus two other divisions of the company. I had an assistant at Pangborn – Jim Coe – and I could bring him along with me.

It was a whole new life. We hated to leave our beautiful home on the mountain, but our phase-out of dogs was timely: the last of our gang, Hunter, died just before we had to move. In all, this was an excellent move for me. Pangborn was behind the times; Carbo was a vast improvement. Just before Massard became ill, he was the (national) "Industrial Ad Manager of the Year". Soon after I joined Carbo, Bill Wendel was voted Business Week's "Industrial Chief Executive of the Year". Joe Forness, one of my fellow Group Ad Managers and I had been assigned to getting Wendel nominated and elected – over the top guys at General Motors, GE, DuPont, etc. – and we succeeded. Actually, Joe did most of the work. I just wrote the final draft.

More important, Carbo had a "Management Incentive Plan" which treated me quite generously for all the years I worked there. When I retired, I had these accumulated funds to invest – and this became the principal source of my later affluence.

Daughter Kris enrolled at Niagara University. Greg attended brand new Lewiston-Porter H.S. and became a member of the wrestling team. We bought a "modern" home in Lewiston – with a swimming pool – about a quarter mile from the lower Niagara River and four or so from Lake Ontario. When I drove home from work, I could see downtown Toronto in the distance.

My job was fun. I worked for the VP of Marketing, Bob Quayle. He had been VP at Montgomery Ward and some other major U.S. company (I forget which). He respected my abilities and used me in many different ways. Carbo was acquisition-minded and when we bought a company, Quayle would appoint me their Ad Manager, just long enough to get them properly integrated with us and our systems. I had Pangborn (and their Pollution Control Division when it was split off), Commercial Filters in Lebanon, IN, Lockport Felt (nearby), Spode China (NYC), Irrigation Systems (Waycross, GA) and Lortone, a lapidary equipment company in Seattle.

In Seattle, I contacted Malamute owner, Diana Ross, who insisted I take a couple days off – and she drove me up in the Cascade Mountains to visit her Totem Kennels. Later she wrote a book on the breed and asked me to rewrite any errors I could find (which I did – and there were many).

Bill Wendel, our President, and Bob Quayle became deeply involved in an ambitious renovation program for downtown Niagara Falls. Over time, Quayle began to spend almost all his time on programs for redoing the city and I ended up doing much of the managing of the Marketing Division – Business Planning, Zero-Based budgeting, Financial Controls, Salary Administration, MIP AWARDS. I was the only manager not a Vice President who developed Staff Division plans, objectives and budgets, and presented them to Senior Management for approval.

Quayle rewarded me in several ways. MIP awards, of course, and he sent me out on fun trips, usually with Laura included – association get-togethers that were 5% business, 95% social – at places like The Cloisters in Sea Island, Georgia.

THE O. J. CONNECTION

When Pangborn had a seminar on vibrating finishing for a large group of potential buyers in Los Angeles, I was sent "to supervise". I found things well under control, including the hiring of several very beautiful young "Beach Bunnies" (to give our guests something unusually pleasant to look at.) One was a rather large, solid, athletic-looking gal who told me she recently graduated from Southern Cal. "Ever run across O.J. there?" I asked. (I didn't have to explain I meant Simpson, not orange juice.) "Every day," she said. "Al Cowling is my husband."

I was intrigued. I knew Al Cowling was O.J.'s best friend. Inseparable. Both men were black. I knew Simpson married a white gal. Cowling was black; this lady was white. O.J. was the most famous football player of his time. When his wife was murdered and O.J. was charged with the crime, the world watched as O.J. was driven down the expressway in a Ford Bronco with his buddy Al Cowling at the wheel (and five or six police cars going along with them). Then I remembered the pretty blonde lady with the beautiful tan I'd talked to at the seminar. The one who said she'd "hung out" with O.J. at USC.

During the murder coverage, the networks ran a photo of Cowling with his wife – a black lady. Obviously, the first marriage didn't last.

Greg graduated from Lew-Port High and enrolled at a college I never heard of – Michigan Tech, on the upper peninsula of Michigan, about as isolated as you can get. He figured on being an engineer and this was the school where the auto industry did its hiring. Besides, his best friend was going there. With both kids in college and no dogs to worry about, we decided it was time to do some serious traveling. We took several trips to Europe and N. Africa, visiting practically every must-see city, country and tourist attraction, having a great time and storing up memories for future enjoyment. I'll tell you about only our super-tour of Asia. Several days in Japan, where our former enemies were the friendliest people we ever encountered. Tokyo and the mountains of Japan, to Beijing *on Air Iran during the hostage crisis*, sitting alongside a villainous-looking Irani who I thought might cut my throat, but turned out to hate the Ayatollah Khomeni! He offered me a drink and candy, and turned out to be something of a "fun guy". He even wrote to me after we both returned home!

In Beijing, we stayed at the State Guest House (for VIPs). The Foreign Minister of Japan and our Vice President, George H.W. Bush were there when we were. We visited the Great Wall and ate at Maxims de Paris. We did Shanghai and cruised the Yangtze River; flew to Singapore and drank Singapore Slings at Raffles Hotel, then to India; Kathmandu in Nepal; Bangkok in Thailand (the palace of "The King and I"); and then back to Hong Kong.

The trip was super-deluxe. We could go out on our own, to the best restaurants in any city, order anything (including drinks) and the tour would pay the check. No limit. In Kathmandu, we flew alongside Mt. Everest in a special aircraft, and stayed at the Soalti Oberoi where former President Jimmy and Mrs. Carter were staying as guests of the King of Nepal.

India – Taj Mahal, New Delhi, and bus tours of many areas. At dawn, in Varanasi (Benares) we went to "Mother Ganges", the sacred river, and witnessed the bathing of the faithful and cremation of the dead on the burning ghats. A memorable event for me.

OUR GREATEST NIGHT? THE HINDU WEDDING

How lucky can you get? Laura and I agreed that maybe this was one of the best nights of our life together. Surely, of our later years. The Taj Mahal Hotel in New Delhi was crowded; our dinner reservations were for 9 p.m. At 7, we decided to go down to the main lounge, have a cocktail, and watch all the

interesting people. Our elevator stopped one floor below us and four beautiful young ladies got on, wearing gold lame and so bedecked in diamonds,
rubies, emeralds, pearls and sapphires that we couldn't imagine who they were
or where they were going.

I asked at the desk and learned that a wedding of national importance
would take place that evening. "That was the bride and her attendants," we
were told. "Go down that marble staircase, turn right and you'll see the main
ballroom. Go in and see what's going on. It's OK."

So we did. Maybe a hundred people in the huge hall. The bride and
her attendants were sitting right near the entrance. One of the attendants
smiled at us, then came and said, "If you're interested, go back out and follow
the oriental rugs. That's where it's happening now." We were surprised at her
suggestion, feeling somewhat like intruders. But we saw that oriental rugs had
been laid on the grass, from the hall to where we could now see lights and hear
Indian music, more than a hundred yards away.

Laura was somewhat reluctant, but I said nothing too bad was likely to
happen. As we moved closer we could see the bridegroom *sitting on a white
stallion, dressed like a maharaja!* Still closer, he looked self-important,
almost silly I thought. The horse was magnificent, and the saddle and bridle
was adorned with more precious jewels than we had seen at the Topkapi
Museum in Istanbul! (O.K., so maybe not quite that many.)

A couple hundred people – all Indians – were watching the ceremony.
On each side, the land rose up and there were trees. We moved up, to be less
noticeable. Soon, I heard a lady's voice behind me. "Are you Americans?" she
asked. (I felt we would be invited to leave.) I turned to face her. She was a
handsome Indian lady, about sixty. Again, I marveled at her beautiful gown
and all the diamonds, rubies, emeralds and pearls. "Yes," I said. She spoke
perfect English and seemed friendly. "Where in America?" I figured she
probably didn't know much about the U.S., so I spoke clearly, "Flo-ri-da."
"Where in Florida?" she asked. "Sarasota." She smiled. "I own property on
Longboat Key!"

Shortly after, a fine looking man, impeccably attired in obviously
expensive western clothing, came up to us and introduced himself. Again, I
expected a courteous invitation to "get lost". He was very friendly and after
learning we were Americans, he began to explain what was going on. This was
an "arranged wedding" – the bride and groom had never met. Their families
lived in different parts of India: they had never met. They were two of the
"most important" families in India. Right now, they would meet.

We watched it happen. First, the two fathers, shaking hands, embrac-
ing. Talking. Bowing. More talking. This went on for ten or fifteen minutes.

Then the oldest brothers, much the same, then other brothers. The nice man explaining all this, then said, "This will go on for another half hour. Uncles, cousins, mothers, sisters, and so on." He suggested we go back to the Main Ballroom and he would tell us more of what would happen that night.

I was overwhelmed by the friendly reception. We just barged in and everyone treated us with great courtesy! He also told us that he and the lady we had talked to were members of the wedding party!

Outside the Main Ballroom was a portico, forty feet wide and sixty yards long. All marble. The roof was held up by huge marble columns. He took us to where four large oriental rugs were positioned to surround a large rectangular area where nothing covered the floor. "Here is where the actual marriage will take place. Just the bride, the groom and the holy men. A fire will be built. I can't tell you the exact time of the ceremony – that will be determined by the planets and the stars. Holy men are watching the skies. They will tell us when. Probably in the next two hours."

He took us back into the Ballroom, now filling rapidly with people. We were standing right up front, by the stage. The bride was now on the stage, waiting to meet her soon-to-be husband, who we heard was on his way. It was a long wait, but finally he rode onto the stage, dismounted and faced the audience who now applauded. Again, I felt he looked a bit silly, and that the bride, who was truly beautiful, wasn't getting a very good deal.

I was beginning to feel a bit overwhelmed by all of this. More gold and precious jewels than I had ever seen before. It was like a scene out of "Arabian Nights" – a fairly tale with us in the middle of it. How we had been welcomed. The tinkling Indian music and the perfumed air of the warm New Delhi night. I wanted to memorize it all and never forget.

The popping of flashbulbs sort of woke me up. I looked around and saw a dozen television cameraman, news photographers and large professional movie cameras. Then I realized we were among two hundred wedding guests, every one with brown skins and coal-black hair – and right up front by the stage, about as conspicuous as we could be – *two obvious strangers, one with a lot of very blonde hair!*

I struck me funny. I whispered to Laura, "Look at all the cameras. Tomorrow morning, 200 million Indians are going to watch this on TV and ask, "Who the hell is that blonde up front?"

We watched awhile longer – not as part of the crowd, but right up front. Then I made a huge mistake which I wish I hadn't. Our host told us, "I'm a member of the wedding party and I would like to have you attend the wedding banquet as my guests." This took me by surprise but I did a lot of thinking in a very few seconds – mostly on the idea that this was a religious ceremony, and I knew practically nothing about the protocol involved. Would we make a major mistake and offend two of the "most important" families in India? Create an international incident? I chickened out – while also thinking how lucky we were to have had the wonderful two-plus hours few Americans will ever experience. I made some lame excuse, but was lavish in expressing our gratitude. (What a magnificent adventure!)

Next day, I couldn't wait to tell everyone in our tour group. The Hindu lady who was our guide explained about Hindu marriages. "The young couple will now go to live with the bridegroom's family. There may be a dozen or more women – mother, grandmother, sisters, aunts, even cousins – in that household, and the bride will be the most lowly of them all. Her life will not be easy. Some of these new wives are beaten – in some cases, even killed! It has happened so often, India now has laws to stop it. But they're not always enforced.

Hard to believe. Live and learn.

EASING INTO THE GOOD LIFE CALLED RETIREMENT

Kris got married – to her Niagara U. boyfriend, Bill Haile. Greg graduated from Michigan Tech – not in Engineering, he switched to Commerce – and returned home just as the Niagara Frontier slipped into a deep recession with major unemployment. Bad time for job hunting.

LAURA AND KRISTIN: the most important ladies in my life! (Shown here at Kris's wedding 1972.)

Carborundum was courted as a possible acquisition by several companies and finally was bought by Kennecott Copper Co. of New York. This was said to be a most unusual situation: all of our top brass moved to New York City and took over the management of Kennecott! Kennecott management, for the most part, reported to them.

For some time I had been contemplating an early retirement. Our net worth had grown to where we could afford it – and I always believed that retiring early was a symbol of success. (And I'd be able to sleep late!) So, where would we go? One thing was for sure: it would be someplace totally without ice and snow and New York State taxes.

We loved San Diego and had visited Tucson and Scottsdale in Arizona. We checked the Carolinas, the Gulf Coast, and all of Florida. We figured our kids would end up in the East, and California was a long trip. Property was much more expensive there. Our Blue Ridge Summit friends were all living in Sarasota. We considered Naples and Clearwater, but decided on Sarasota – and ever since moving here, I'm certain this was the perfect choice.

Bob Quayle arranged a beautiful retirement party for us – the entire Corporate Marketing Division (and spouses) at the Niagara Falls Country Club – everything first class and in perfect taste. We were pleased.

A couple days later, Rufe Jones told me I had done him a lot of favors and he and June wanted to take us out for dinner before we left – at some new restaurant in Buffalo that was supposed to be especially good. It was late January and snowing on the agreed date, so I suggested we just go somewhere in Niagara Falls. Rufe insisted on the Buffalo place, and when we got to Buffalo we ended up in an area that didn't look promising. Down near the waterfront, but eventually we went through a large building that looked like a warehouse, came out the other side, and there it was: the navy cruiser, USS Little Rock!

A bunch of the people who worked for me or with me, had not been satisfied with my Country Club retirement party. They wanted to do one their way – *a roast* and more of a fun thing. Because of my Navy background, they searched for an appropriate venue. The Little Rock was a tourist attraction in the summer, closed for the winter. They had to contact the Navy Department in Washington to get it opened up, electricity and other facilities restored, and the Admirals' Quarters heated, for just the one evening, for my party.

I was told the Navy was reluctant to go to all that trouble. So they represented me as a naval hero! (Apparently, repeating my favorite war stories!)

They roasted me and I replied – in spades. They didn't miss a trick. Open bar and a catered banquet. Even a shapely model in a teeny bikini who presented me with a new bicycle and other stuff appropriate to retirement in sunny climes. And many photos of the occasion, of course. It was a great night for Laura and for me. A perfect send-off from a large group of very nice people. I'm very proud of their doing all of this for me.

I was told that nothing like this had ever been done for anyone at Carborundum before.

PART 4. THE GOLDEN YEARS

BIG LIFE CHANGES COMING UP

We had gone to Sarasota a couple times before moving there, looked at many possibilities, bought a lot in Center Gate, decided on the house we wanted and hired a contractor to start building. It was all ready for us when we arrived.

I retired on the last day of January 1980. At 8 a.m. the next day, we were heading out of Niagara Falls *forever*. Never went back.

We encountered a heavy snowstorm just east of Cleveland and icy highways in Kentucky, Tennessee and Georgia. When we hit the Florida state line, everything changed to summer! Warm, green and fragrant. An omen? I told Laura, "This will be a whole new life for us, and I know we are going to love it!"

RETIREMENT: THE GREATEST INVENTION OF MODERN MAN

We did have a great retirement – and I still am! Our kids were on their own. Kris and Bill graduated and moved to Philadelphia. Greg moved to Texas where jobs were more plentiful, got into the homebuilding business, worked hard and became a success. My mother died. Helen's husband, Harry, died so Helen moved from Waterloo to live with her daughter, Vicki, in Arizona. My brother died – and his wife, Olive, immediately changed their wills and screwed Helen and me out of a lot of money – as we discovered after Olive died. (I'm told these things happen in a lot of families.)

But life in Sarasota and Center Gate was very good. I decided to do my own landscaping, so for several months I did a lot of "pick and shovel work", planting trees and shrubs. The manual labor (and swimming laps in our pool every day) got me into better shape than I had been in for years.

Almost immediately, I was drafted to serve on the Center Gate Board of Directors and soon noticed that First Communities, the developer, had done a terrible job on the By-Laws and Maintenance Covenants. So I rewrote everything our members really needed to know. (A couple of years later my friends, the McGilvrays, moved to Sherwood Forest and found their documents needed improvement, so I rewrote those as well.)

ED AND ANN MCGILVRAY. Ed was a retired Air Force Colonel, Ann a former nurse and one of the most capable and generous ladies I ever knew. It seems she spends her time looking for neighbors who need help and then provides it. Their daughter, Patty, married the oldest grandson of the famous Connie Mack (of baseball fame), a wealthy banker from Fort Myers who had political ambitions. But he died suddenly and his younger brother changed his name from McGillicuddy to Connie Mack and became a nationally known U.S. Senator. (He almost became Vice President: Bush, Sr. had him in the final phase of running mate selection, but Dan Quayle was finally chosen.)

STAN AND KAY CHICHESTER. Stan is a retired Air Corps pilot who I enjoy referring to as "America's Greatest Flying Ace of WW2". Then I explain that actually he was one of the worst investments our government ever made: we spent a million dollars teaching him to fly, and another million (or so) for the bomber; then sent him to bomb Germany – and he gets shot down en route, over France! (Mostly True but not entirely. I changed it to make it a better story.)

Stan is the poster boy for Nice Guys (and Kay is easy-going, just like him), so he takes my kidding good-naturedly. He survived the crash, but the Germans started looking for him immediately. He hid until French farmers found him, hid him, and took care of him for months. The Underground finally smuggled him right into Paris, under the noses of the Gestapo, and in time, on to the channel coast and back to England. Quite an adventure for one more of our many thousands of unsung heroes of WW2. Movie material.

The McGilvrays and the Chichesters are as conservative as I am liberal, but we manage to stay totally true to our political beliefs and remain best of friends anyway. Too bad the Shiites and the Sunnis and others like them can't come here and take lessons from us.

JIM AND FLORENCE MEIGHAN, South Dakotans. Jim, a former mayor of Cedar Rapids, Iowa, started out like I did, as Secretary of a Chamber of Commerce. The Meighans knew everybody famous in South Dakota including Joe Foss, the Air Corps flying ace who became Governor, and Joe Robbie, who owned the Miami Dolphins. I was "drafted" to write and deliver a "Roast" for Meighans' Golden Anniversary party.

Jim died, Florence moved to Peoria to be near her daughter, then she died. So did Ed McGilvray. Ann, the Chichesters and I remain close friends and see each other frequently.

Laura and I met often with our Blue Ridge Summit friends, Bocks, Kerleys, Annises, and Tish Gardner (Charlie's wife) and her new husband. (Charlie got caught cheating.) Soon as we arrived, I asked how to find a family doctor, and they said, "Get Harry Youngs." Turns out, Harry divorced and moved from Blue Ridge to Sarasota and served a few years as Chief of Staff at Memorial Hospital. He became our "primary caregiver" until he retired.

STONEYBROOK: A CONFRONTATION IN THE PALMETTOS

After a few years, our big house, pool, yard and landscaping became more work than I wanted to handle, so we bought a condo at Stoneybrook Golf and Country Club. It was nice there, quiet and beautiful, with a great view of trees, lake and fairway. We lived in a two-story building. One day we saw a really big alligator that had climbed up the screening on the front porch of a second-story condo! I wonder why?

One day I saw a large animal slink into the palmettos and went out to see what it was. Suddenly I was face-to-face with a kingsize bobcat less than forty feet away, and he wasn't a bit intimidated. (But I was.) We just stood there staring at each other – or more accurately, *glaring* – (him, not me!).

He seemed about to attack and I was wondering if I could run fast enough to set a new octogenarian world record for the 50-yard dash back to my patio door!

Fortunately, he decided that winning the staring contest was a victory, and he slowly returned to the deep woods. Within the next month or so – in our general neighborhood – two men were attacked, clawed and bitten by a large bobcat. The second one was a laborer who had a shovel and managed to kill the animal. Tests proved it had rabies. I know "my bobcat" was the one that attacked these men.

SMALL WORLD NOTE

At a Dinner-Dance at the Clubhouse one evening, a group of us were talking, getting to know each other, and I happened to mention having served in the Pacific War with the "hero of the Battle of Midway". One of the group then announced, *"Hey, that's my uncle!"* So I became a friend of Paul McClusky and it turned out that I knew his uncle a lot better than he did. We invited the McClusky's to visit us and see all our photos and facts about their famous relative.

A GOOD MARRIAGE THAT LASTED A LIFETIME

Laura and I celebrated our 50th Anniversary in 1992. Quite a lavish affair at the "Summerhouse" and well-attended. All my family came, plus Pep and Ruth Grawe, Derwood and Kay Johannsen (Waverly); Jack and Betty Wiles (Pangborn); John and Evelyn Mundy (USS Rapidan); Sara Bock (Blue Ridge Summit) and a whole bunch of Center Gate friends. Kris arranged everything.

Sara Bock was wearing a beautiful white fur stole. Jennifer, my granddaughter, told her it was the prettiest she'd ever seen. *So Sara gave it to her!* Sara was like that.

WEDDING IN TEXAS

After many years of avoiding marriage, Greg finally found the right gal in Texas, and we all got together in Austin and Round Rock for the wedding. Laura wasn't well but managed the trip successfully and enjoyed it. (It was her last "vacation".) Kris and Edward, of course. Edward, I should have mentioned earlier, is Kris' second husband – a great guy (man of many talents) who I'm pleased to have as a member of my family. Jennifer brought her boyfriend, Steve Tinn (also from Disney) whom she married later on. And niece Vicky and husband John came all the way from California. (They also came from Arizona to Kris' wedding years before, in Niagara Falls.)

"The right girl" Greg found was Dotty Woodard and she turned out perfect for Greg – and for me! (Our politics match perfectly!) She was a successful businesswoman (and still is). Married now for eight years, they swear they've never had even a small argument! And I believe them!

While we were there, Greg showed us a "problem lot" he had bought in Round Rock and said he knew how to design a beautiful home to fit it. He has since built a remarkable "mansion" that's full of great ideas and he and Dottie now live there in abject luxury. The videocassettes he sent us point out the many features and is truly impressive.

Daughter Kris and husband Edward

THINGS CHANGE. NOTHING LASTS FOREVER.

Retirement was great, until Kris discovered that Laura's memory was slipping, and other signs of dementia soon appeared. For the next five years, my principal activity was being a willing caretaker. I believe I became quite good at it – a surprising number of people told me that. The Alzheimers progressed and she also developed a breathing problem – Chronic Obstructive Pulmonary Disease. Hospice – a wonderful organization – became involved and was very helpful.

When I suddenly popped a hernia, I was told surgery was essential, and I would be unable to take care of Laura for a week. Hospice said they would take her. Guess who arrived at 6 a.m. to take Laura to Hospice and me to Memorial Hospital? Give up? My Certified Financial Planner, Greg Chona – with his wife, Yolanda, and kids. They got Laura checked in at Hospice, checked me in at Memorial, then drove their two boys to Pinebrook (a school for gifted children). Mid-afternoon, Greg returned to pick me up at Memorial, took me home and got me settled in. (Pretty good "financial" service!)

INTERESTING VISITOR: A WOLF NAMED WAMACI

The nurse, who visited Laura every week, soon learned about our dogs and told us about a Malamute being taken around as a "therapy dog". I asked if he could get the owner to bring the dog to visit Laura. Then one day the nurse phoned. "I was wrong. It's not a Malamute – it's a wolf!" That was even better! And Hospice arranged for the wolf to visit us. The owner wanted to learn about our Malamutes, and I've been fascinated with wolves for years.

I had read almost everything ever written about wolves and thought I knew everything about them. They don't attack people. They make terrible pets: nervous, skittish, difficult to housebreak.

But Wamaci and his partner showed me that generalizations cannot be applied to all cases. Wamaci was a big (135 lbs.) mature male wolf, and a perfect gentleman. I met him at the door, petted him, hugged him, and invited him in. We went into our living room where Laura was lying on the sofa. Wamaci greeted her and then stretched out on the carpeting near her. I sat alongside him and talked to his partner about his similarity to our Malamutes. I opened his mouth and examined his teeth. "Just like my dogs," I said.

Wamaci was not at all what I had expected. No shyness in unfamiliar surroundings, no wariness in meeting total strangers. No tail tucked between his legs. He was the picture of poise and confidence. I was greatly impressed.

I called his human companion his partner, not his owner, and I think that was the secret of this relationship, and the reason for the wolf not acting like a wolf. The man had taken Wamaci when he was four weeks old, fed him formula and foods on which he thrived. He explained: "He's 3 1/2 years old now, and we've never been apart. We eat together and sleep together. I own my own business and he goes to my office with me every day."

(I was so sure the man was not married, I didn't ask.)

When I took him into my Study for my usual dissertation on the wonders of the modern Malamute, he told the wolf to stay by Laura, and Laura told me they had a nice talk.

Our visitors stayed for more than two hours. After they left, I thought the Wamaci story would be great to run in the Herald-Tribune. But I wouldn't suggest it without the man's approval. His phone was unlisted and Hospice said they weren't allowed to give out his address or his phone number. Then I understood: the world is full of idiots and one of them might say, "God Awmighty, Jethro, sure as hell that wolf is gonna kill somebody! Maybe we just oughta shoot him first!"

That's life, I guess. Unfortunately.

Wolves don't attack people, and neither do Malamutes. But the wolf-dog hybrid (wolf-Malamute most often) is frequently a dangerous animal. Entirely different disposition, hazardous to humans, and now outlawed in several states.

NOTHING GOOD LASTS FOREVER

Laura, my best friend ever, died November 20, 2003. She was 84. We'd been married for 61 years. I've felt diminished without her, ever since.

Our marriage was as good as it gets. She was a remarkable woman, surprisingly good at everything she encountered. She handled our long, difficult wartime separations with no problems whatever, moving from city to city as circumstances required. She handled everything I couldn't, because I wasn't there. She became a wonderful mother, great with our dogs, a mighty fine human being, and loved by everyone who knew her.

And she was exceedingly happy with her life.

Without me, I believe she might have been a successful designer of ladies' wear. She made a lot of her own clothes (including tailored suits), many things for our children and even a couple of things for me. I remember, after working with a group of Powers Models at the New York Flower Show, she returned home and in three weeks was the first lady in Bucks County wearing Christian Dior's "New Look" – which, of course, she made herself!

Her death was no surprise. I knew it was imminent. She grew progressively weaker for months, and severe breathing difficulties made her life almost unbearable. Death surely was a merciful relief. I'm happy that in her last year we got a wheelchair and I was able to take her out for daily sunshine and to all the parties our condo association held at our swimming pool.

I say again: I've been lucky all my life. But the luckiest thing that ever happened to me was Laura.

Years before, we agreed we'd be buried in St. Mary's Catholic Cemetery in Waverly. (My family is there and we have no roots anywhere else.) Laura elected to be cremated, so I was able to keep her with me until September of the following year. Then I made my last trip to Waverly, attended my last high school reunion, and buried Laura in our family plot, not far from my boyhood friend, Bill Leary. I'll join her there when the time comes.

It was especially sad for me because nobody was there except the Catholic priest, the funeral director, Cousin Ruth and me. I had asked Kris and Greg not to come because of the long trips and the brief ceremony. I knew, of course, that Laura had never lived in Waverly, and I hadn't lived there for 66 years. There was no advance notice in the Waverly papers, and all of my close friends were already dead, except John Meyer – and he wasn't physically able to attend. Still, I felt this wonderful person deserved better as a final goodbye.

The new editor of the Waverly Newspapers – Anelia Dimitrova – did publish a nice feature story about me on the front page, but that appeared a week after I'd left town for the last time.

BEING LUCKY IS BETTER THAN RICH OR SMART

The major theme of this autobiography, obviously, is "Boy, Am I Ever Lucky!" I've had a great life, full of incidents, accidents and happenings that I hope make interesting stories. And I repeat for emphasis: it may read like a giant ego trip, but it isn't. *All the good things that happened to me just happened!* And you surely know that no one can take credit for being lucky.

And – I'm forced to admit – an awfully lot of my good luck happened *in bad situations I created by being stupid!* I've lived to a ripe old age, not by following the rules – I took too many chances, I smoked that damn pipe too many years, and my favorite foods have always been hamburgers and milkshakes.

Early on, I had three opportunities to die young in the Cedar River – all due to dumb things I did. (1) Being a little kid leaning out under the guard rail of the bridge, dangling my coaster wagon down to shallow water and rocks more than 25 feet below. (2) Skinny-dipping in swift waters at The Log when I couldn't swim a stroke. (3) Showing off by diving into raging flood waters during Spring Thaw when the ice was going out. (In all cases I just got lucky. Apparently, God had decided, "Not just yet.")

I remember *many* times being stupid in automobiles – excessive speed, icy hills, heavy snowstorms, zero visibility – but I survived. I think it may have been God's plan for me to die young in Colorado. "Take your pick," He may have said. "Die there on a runaway horse, or die there in a runaway car!"

CRAZY HORSE, NASTY DOG, AND BIG ROCKS

1940. Estes Park. I told Jack Wright I wanted to ride before I left Colorado. "I hate horses," Jack said. But he agreed to go along. At the stables he asked for "a horse that preferred walking". I said I wanted "a rip-snorter, loaded with git-up-and-go". The wrangler sized me up. "Can you ride?" he asked. I told him I wasn't a professional but considered myself a talented amateur. "Saddle up Cyclone," he called to somebody.

We rode up a straight dirt road that rose gently a couple miles toward the high mountains. Jack pointed out the deep ditches. "When the snow melts, the water roars down on both sides," he told me. Some twenty minutes later, he said he had reached his horseback quota for the decade of the 1940s and preferred to call it a day. "See you back there in a half hour," I said. I went on for awhile and Cyclone kept telling me he wanted to run. Finally, I turned him around and turned him loose.

Wow! This horse could run! In less than fifty yards he flattened out and was going wide open – the fastest I've ever ridden. It was scary, but wildly exciting. I crouched low like a jockey in the home stretch of the Belmont, going for the Triple Crown! Suddenly – I didn't see him until he was airborne – out of the ditch on our right, a big German Shepherd launched himself at Cyclone's head! He bounced off the horse's neck, in front of my right leg. Cyclone panicked, and still going full speed, went off the road and into the ditch on our left!

The ditch was no place for a racing horse! *Full of rocks and boulders bigger than refrigerators!* Scared to death, I hung on for dear life as Cyclone dodged the biggest boulders, but I knew he'd go down and I would catapult into the rocks at high velocity and surely die!

I tried to slow him down, but he was spooked. And then – I'm not sure why – he decided to head back up on the road, and he jumped and stumbled but didn't fall, and neither did I. But I thank God for the Western saddle, which gave me something to hold onto. We made it, and he high-tailed for nearly a mile before I could get him to slow down. When he finally did, I was able to calm down and think, and I knew I had come mighty close to death, but lucked out again.

AND NOW, THE DUMBEST THING I EVER DID!

Can you top this? Of course not. This one is in a class by itself. 1940. Leaving Estes Park for California. By the scenic route. Traveling alone. Having a wonderful time, on a great adventure, but aware that I had no job and no income, with months to go before any possibility of another paycheck. I'd have to stretch my limited funds and it wouldn't be easy.

On a high mountain road I saw the sign: TRUCKS LOW GEAR NEXT 12 MILES. Being a flatlander from Iowa with no mountain-driving experience, I saw this as an opportunity to save gas and conserve my limited funds. So I put my '39 Dodge in neutral, shut off the motor, and coasted down the winding mountain road – *picking up speed at an alarming rate and almost immediately aware that I had made a horrible mistake!*

I hit the brakes but couldn't stop or even prevent the car from going faster. I literally stood on the brake pedal with both feet and pushed with every ounce of strength I could muster! Again, nothing! In a panic, I tried desperately to restart the engine and get the car back into gear. Nothing even came close. I went faster and faster, 60, 70 miles an hour, screeching and sliding around the curves!

On my left, a rising cliff of solid rock. On my right, a sheer drop off – fifty feet to 300 feet and more! *And no guard rails!*

I was desperate to stay alive. Scared silly! I prayed out loud! Tried to figure a way out by maybe ramming into the cliff – or a tree if I could find one.

All I could do was steer, and I fought to keep the careening car on the winding road, away from the drop-offs which I knew would be the end of me. With all the high speed skidding around the curves, I came close to going over on every left turn! I was totally exhausted but I kept fighting. And praying. Fighting and praying…

Wow! Twelve miles down the road I reached the bottom and was able to get the car slowed, and finally stopped. It took me more than a half hour to calm down and stop shaking. Lucky again – and maybe even luckier, I guess, that I never encountered a single car or truck during the whole descent!

So maybe God decided, "OK, then, not in Colorado." If so, I don't know why. But later I figured He knew WW2 was coming and I'd be in it, and that could be a good place for me to cash in my chips! (Just a thought. I'll never know.)

But I do know that once again, good fortune won out over abject stupidity – and I learned a lot about mountain driving. Despite exceeding a lot of speed limits on my way to California – and all the way back to Iowa – I remained relatively safe for the next year of so of my life.

WAR, OF COURSE, CAN BE HAZARDOUS TO HEALTH

For the next few years, I had several excellent opportunities to die young – all war-related. Many months in the N. Atlantic on a slow tanker, living on top of 325,000 gallons of highly explosive, high-octane aviation gasoline. (German subs sank 3500 ships and killed 35,000 Allied naval and merchant seamen in the Atlantic war.) *The Rapidan was torpedoed on its first trip after I left it,* so I didn't get in on that. (As previously mentioned, by the unlikely miracle of paravanes, it did not sink!)

The wave that nearly washed me overboard in the middle of the stormy night in the N. Atlantic when I was on watch, alone, on the fantail, was an experience so nearly lethal it scares me whenever I think about it, even today.

Our engine's breakdown during our "Perfect Storm", our losing steering control and nearly capsizing, was a disaster nobody on board expected to survive. Then the long trip home – eighteen days of slow sailing with no escort – had us waiting for the torpedoes we expected, but fortunately never came.

(I don't even count the Salinas taking our place and getting torpedoed, because it didn't sink. Or the torpedoes fired at us near Iceland, because they missed.)

In the Pacific, the torpedoes fired at us that missed, went on another mile and blew the Liscome Bay to pieces, killing 646 officers and men, was a certain lifesaver for all of us on the Corregidor, and probably as close to death as I've ever been.

Off Saipan in 1944, three or four enemy divebombers screamed down on us from high altitude, dropped bombs and barely missed. Then, hit by our gunners, slammed into the sea, close aboard. This was scary but it got worse: the torpedo plane that roared in on our starboard beam for a "slam-dunk, can't miss, dead-center" shot! I immediately remembered the Liscome Bay and I felt sure this would be a rerun, with the Corregidor the one blown to pieces! But my gun crews really nailed him and saved all our lives.

My second "Perfect Storm" was scary and could have been lethal. We survived – no loss of life, but it did cause structural damage bad enough to alter the Corregidor's missions for the rest of the war. Later, we discovered that just west of us, this same typhoon capsized three of our destroyers – *lost, with all hands, no survivors*; "massively damaged" three other destroyers, a cruiser and five aircraft carriers; destroyed 146 airplanes – *and 790 of our officers and men were lost or killed!*

Apparently, we were saved by geography – we just missed the worst of it! (Again, I was extremely lucky.)

Our encounter with the enemy sub off Eniwetok atoll, where I got a bit too cocky and handled the situation without calling the Captain, might well be called a "sticky wicket". One U.S. destroyer, one Jap submarine, and one defenseless Kaiser Coffin seem to add up to a situation that could go either way. I like to think my skillful zigzagging – while avoiding the dangers of shoal water on one side, and getting too close to the sub on the other – deserve some credit. But my decision to do this on my own was seriously wrong and downright stupid. (What was I thinking?)

Looking back, I'd say our many opportunities for collisions at sea were extremely dangerous. The retired Admirals brought back to be Commodores of 120-ship convoys in the N. Atlantic handled them badly, especially when ordering course changes during nighttime or bad weather. And the Admiral commanding our CVE task group who wanted to change fleet axis with every change of course, invited collisions which our flimsy carriers could not have survived.

It's hard to judge these things. If you survive, they're "scary" – maybe "scary as hell". If you die, you know for sure they were authentically "life-threatening".

GOOD GRADES COULD GET YOU KILLED???

I joined the Navy more than a year before Pearl Harbor. In December 1940, along with nearly a thousand other young college graduates at Midshipman School, I was told, "Study hard. Your grade average will determine where you end up in the Navy's pecking order. And more important, the guys with the best grades will get the assignments they ask for; the rest of you will get what's left."

I had definite ideas on where I wanted to be – on a real fighting ship – battlewagon or cruiser – and I wanted the Asiatic Fleet. There were no battleships in the Asiatic Fleet, so my choice was "Cruisers, Asiatic".

I studied hard and finished high enough to be sure of getting what I asked for. But I ran out of luck on this one: just before we were commissioned we were told, "The Bureau in Washington is getting swamped. No time to honor requests. Sorry!"

This was a huge disappointment. Even worse, I was assigned to an old 10-knot oil tanker in the Atlantic! Not a fighting ship, a damn sea-going filling station! No place for the "lean, mean, fighting machine" I fancied myself to be!

However, look at what happened. There was only one cruiser in the Asiatic Fleet, the USS Houston. That's where I would have been – when, less than three months into the war, it was sunk by superior Japanese forces! *Most of its officers and men died in the battle or went down with the ship – more than 600!* All survivors were picked up and spent the entire war as prisoners, in Japan, where many died of malnutrition, or worked to death in Japanese coal mines!

Sometimes you don't know good luck until it sneaks up and taps you on the shoulder. I was mad at the Navy for changing the rules, but they saved me from probable death in early 1942 when I was 25 years old. If not then, possibly during years of slave labor and suffering as a prisoner of war.

THE BEAT GOES ON: POST-BELLUM NEAR MISSES

Life in peacetime is much safer than in war. But accidents happen – to all of us. Some are deadly, some inflict permanent damage, some are painful but we get over it and are thankful it wasn't worse. And sometimes we all find ourselves in extremely dire circumstances where "the luck of the cards" determines our fate – which could range all the way from dying then and there, through varying degrees of injury, to close calls that scare us silly but damage us not all.

A lot of these things happened to me, and I'm sure most of you who live lengthy lives have stories of your own to tell. Many of mine involved long-distance driving to and from dog shows in heavy snowstorms, and one on a freeway just outside New York City: four lanes each way, heavy traffic moving at 75-80 mph, and suddenly a fog bank, zero visibility, flashing lights, horns, sounds of collisions! (Keep going and crash into cars ahead, or brake down and get smashed from behind!) I did nothing but steer and pray, and we sailed through untouched!

Early one Sunday morning in the 1960s, I was high-balling down a two-lane highway in Indiana, en route to Chicago with Laura and our two kids on board. Not a car in sight, so I was going about 80. Suddenly, a farmer drove a large tractor from a hidden side road directly in front of me and stopped, blocking both lanes! I jumped on my brake, pushed as hard as I could and careened to a screeching halt, just six inches from disaster! When I got out to look, the farmer thought I was going to punch him. I didn't. But I remember offering a fairly vigorous diatribe that included several mentions of the word "stupid".

At 63, I was trimming a tree, 25 feet up, a limb broke and I fell and lit flat on my back. Limped for a few days, but nothing was seriously damaged.

In my mid-70s, I was in the storage area over my garage, handing things down to Edward, my son-in-law. My feet got tangled in something and I fell *headfirst* through the opening. On the way down, I yelled for help and Edward caught me six inches from the concrete floor! A twelve-foot drop *headfirst* onto concrete is surely lethal – broken neck, crushed skull. I'm grateful for Edward's quick response and sure hands – and especially for not leaving to get a Diet Pepsi at the time!

So again I got lucky, but in this case I did incur some damage which apparently will stay with me for the rest of my life. As I was hurtling down through the opening, I tried to grab its far end. I missed with my left hand but my right hand caught and held just long enough to tear up my right shoulder. The orthopedic surgeon said something about a rotator cuff, gave me a cortisone shot and told me that's all he could do and I might just have to live with it.

Unfortunately, I've reinjured the same shoulder *four times*, once in a bad fall, dislocating it at age 89. That one involved 911, the Emergency Room and months of therapy. Now it aches a lot, but I'm getting used to it. (May 2007: an orthopedic surgeon examined the X-rays and said, "It's permanently dislocated – out of its socket, because there is no socket.") Bad news, but for obvious reasons, I still consider myself remarkably lucky.

There were many other opportunities to die young. *Looking back on all these events convinces me that my greatest achievement in life is simply survival.*

SAD FAREWELLS TO LONGTIME FRIENDS

Living a long time, most people agree, is a lot better than the only alternative. But I miss old friends who left before me. Jack Wright and Fred Studier died years ago and Waverly buddies Pep Grawe, John Meyer, Derwood Johannsen and others departed recently. Except for Cousin Ruth, I have no reason to ever go back home again.

Friendships were always important to me, persisting over many miles and many years. Ed Kepler, divorced, ended up living alone in northwest Colorado, trying to write the novel that would make him famous. He told me I was the best friend he ever had, and that I had influenced his life. Merle Kepler's wife had Alzheimer's and was institutionalized. A few years ago, Ed phoned that he and Merle wanted to come to Florida and spend time with me. But Merle's wife died suddenly, so Ed drove all the way by himself, despite old age and bad health.

We talked for a week – a great reunion. Before he died a couple years later, I phoned him, but I don't think he knew who I was. Merle, in bad shape for several years, died recently. His niece notified me of his passing and said that in his last days, he told her, "Be sure to notify Bob Zoller."

Bob Harris, who became a successful CPA, stopped to spend time with us in Blue Ridge Summit en route to Washington. A couple months later, he died in a car crash.

Johnny Weires settled in Salinas, CA. I always sent him my lengthy Christmas letters. Johnny didn't write but always phoned, so we kept in touch for years. Right after his last call, Johnny died.

I began to feel like the Angel of Death.

Best college friends and fraternity brothers Lannon, Hild and Overton kept in touch and we visited for years – then all of them passed away.

I grew up, kindergarten through college, with Bob Schulze. A number of years ago, I was in Denver and decided to stop to see him in Omaha on my way home. He met me at the airport and we spent a couple days talking old times. We visited fraternity brother Phil Allen, then a radio personality in the Midwest. A few months later, Bob died. Cancer. He knew it was terminal, but he didn't tell me.

Marshall Carpenter married Johnny Weires' sister Kate, and one of their daughters married the Olympic champion wrestler Dan Gable (famous as the winningest coach *of any sport* in college history!). Late in life, Marshall wrote me, "We had great teams in 1932, and you and I and Eddie Harden are the only ones still alive." He died shortly after that, and Eddie, a year or so later.

Eddie Harden. Marshall's letter reminded me I'd lost track of Eddie and hadn't seen him for many years. But Zenobia Anderson (widow of old friend Bev Ladage) provided his address (north of Seattle) and told me he had a birthday coming up. On that day I phoned and said, "Happy Birthday", but wouldn't tell him who I was. "Guess!" He thought for a few seconds, then said, "Bob Zoller?"

Don't ask me how he did it. We talked for a long time about our lives and I mentioned our dogs. A few weeks later, the phone rang. It was Eddie. He sounded excited. "I just have to tell you," he said, "I overheard some of our staff members here talking about Alaskan Malamutes. So I stopped and asked if they ever heard of you. "Bob Zoller? Wow!" they said. In Malamutes, that man is God!" (Sorry, but that's an exact quote.)

John Mundy is one of my few friends still living. Retired Captain, U.S. Coast Guard. Goes to Colorado a couple of times each year to ski with his "Over-the-Hill Gang". Saw a Malamute there, mentioned my name and got a response almost the same as Eddie did. I've kept in touch with the Mundys for years. Still do. We attended their 50th anniversary in Slidell, LA, and they came to ours in Sarasota.

A few years ago, Scoop Rutherford phoned and, like Ed Kepler, said he'd like one more get-together while both of us were still alive. "We pretty much settled the world's problems in '44 and '45," he said. "But there are new ones and we should talk." So he and Alice flew from Oregon to Sarasota and we talked day and (most of the) night for a solid week. Scoop was badly crippled with arthritis, but his mind was still remarkable. Alice was a jewel.

Scoop had spent nearly thirty years writing the most profound book I ever read, "NO ESCAPE FROM GREATNESS". (Subtitled, "The record of a lifelong exercise in thinking. A remarkable insight into the meaning of everything".) In which he searches for answers to such questions as, "Is there really a God?" And, "Who am I and why am I here?"

He decides there is a God, and he proves it by mathematics – the laws of probability! I was impressed by the tremendous fund of knowledge this old friend had accumulated over the years – and even more impressed when a few months ago (in 2006) I read that a "think tank" of intellectuals, philosophers and scientists *had pondered the God questions for years, decided there is a*

God, and had proved it by mathematics! Scoop beat them by more than 16 years!

He died recently. Alice is in a nursing home.

A few of my old friends are still alive. Not many, and I suspect there may be fewer still when Christmas card time arrives. Besides Mundy: from Pangborn, there's Jack Wiles (near Cape Kennedy) and Bob Benner (Colorado). Monsignor Topper (Harrisburg), George Lasezkay and Irene Pizzimenti (Carborundum) and Malamute oldtimers Dot Pearson, Martha Gormley, Penny Devaney and Dick Tobey.

And a special favorite of mine, Carol Jane (Osterholm) Brown of Albuquerque – whom I talked into joining me at the Waverly High School Reunion in 2004. "CJ" and I write often and I now call her "the only girl I ever kissed who ain't dead yet".

FINAL CHAPTER: A HAPPY CAMPER

Several months after Laura passed away, I began to wonder why I was still at Stoneybrook. I never played golf, and I was tired of my own cooking. Checking a number of "retirement estates", I found Lakehouse West to be the best. Moved here in late 2004 – and never regretted it for a single minute.

Most senior citizens would like to turn the clock back to our teens or twenties, but we can't. So, at this stage of my game, I can't think of anyplace I'd rather be.

I have a very nice unit with one of the most beautiful lake views you'll ever see. I love Florida and there's no place like Sarasota. Everything is First Class at Lakehouse West and management provides more activities – theatre parties, seminars, beach picnics, tours, etc. – than I can ever use.

However, I never miss the cocktail parties. We have a reputation as "The Party Place". The ownership pops for an Open Bar on every special occasion – every national holiday, and made-up excuses like Mardi Gras, Kentucky Derby, Christmas in July, Mexican Fiesta, Crazy Hat Night and several others. The only thing missing is Ground Hog Day and I suspect we have a committee working on that.

Betty Peary, a Chicagoan born in Norway, currently heads our Hospitality Committee and does a wonderful job making new residents feel like part of the "in group". This lady became my mentor early on and now I'm on the Board of the Residents' Association – we call it The Council – and I have a large number of very good friends. I'm a regular member of the "Suss Specially Selected Sunday Seven". (Lou and Eleanor Suss entertain almost every

Sunday before dinner – cocktails and Eleanor's deluxe and ever-changing goodies.)

I'm one of the better Bocce players and the Captain of my team, "The Fox Run Road Gang". We tied for our League's championship last year, and just now won it free and clear for this year.

I could write another book about Lakehouse West, but I will say only that I'm impressed with the people who live here. As I learn more about them, I find that most have led interesting and productive lives, and many are well-known and major contributors in their special fields. All are successful ladies and gentlemen, and they look and act accordingly. We have MDs, PhDs, VPs and wealthy widows by the carload. Eva Langyel spoke with the Pope when she was a child, and later, as wife of the Ambassador to the Court of St. James (from Hungary), she was presented to the Queen of England. (Just one example.)

"SMALL WORLD" STORIES. When Paula Meikle first arrived and said she was from Cedar Falls, I told her "I'm from Waverly and I should know people you know." But I couldn't think of anyone. We kept talking and then I snapped my fingers and said, "Bob Voorhies!" She laughed. "I know him very well!" (This was a kid I knew at Scout Camp when we were fourteen years old, and I never saw him again!) Then I remembered playing basketball against a "Captain Grant", and she said, "He was my boyfriend in high school!" And when I asked if she knew Ruby Grant, his stepmother, she said, "Very well." *(Ruby was a good friend of Laura's, in Chicago, before she moved to Cedar Falls to marry Dr. Grant!)*

Norman Morris moved here – a retired Navy Commander. He told me about his war experiences and that his best friend had died in "one of the major disasters in our Navy's history." It was the Liscome Bay. I told him, "I was there. I saw it happen." His friend was Admiral Mullenix, Commander of our escort carrier group.

Recently I had dinner with a retired naval aviator my age, a man named Bill Bogg, and discovered that in the Pacific war he had served in a squadron commanded by Wade McClusky, and later in another squadron, with my good friend and Midshipman School roommate, Fred Joyce.

The Sarasota Herald-Tribune has been running a series of articles about WW2 servicemen and their war stories. They did one on Stan Chichester (shot down over France) and one about me (mainly, my Liscome Bay story.) Also, one about a Navy flyer who survived many missions in the Pacific.

I saw that article, but neither his name nor his photo rang a bell. Then I saw that all his service was aboard the Corregidor! *My Corregidor!* So I looked him up and we had a wonderful reunion. Later, I wondered if I had ever mentioned him in this book. I read through the first draft and found that when Tom Talbot and I were on Guadalcanal, trying to get back to our ship, I had written that, "Joe Cooper, one of our pilots, had a Jeep and he drove us to the dock," (to catch the How-boat back to our ship!)

When I met our LHW Marketing Director, Sue Carleton, she told me that at one time she had worked in Waverly! "Tell me where you worked and I'll tell you who your boss was." She said, "Waverly Publishing Company". I said, "Ed Droste, and a bit later he sold it to my buddy, Pep Grawe."
(By the way, Ed Droste's son was the principal founder of Hooters!)

OTHER GOOD THINGS HAPPENED LATELY. Most important, I seem to be in very good physical condition for a member of the "geezer generation". And no financial worries – pretty lucky, since I haven't earned a paycheck for twenty-seven years.
Malamute-wise, a lot of nice things happened, starting in 2003 with our 50th Anniversary Meeting and National Specialty Show in Sturbridge, MA. (Kris came to take care of Laura so I could go.) With eight other surviving Charter Members, I was a special guest, all expenses paid, and I was treated like royalty. *There was a long line of people waiting for my autograph!* Nancy Russell was one of them (more champions than anyone in our breed history). She was also the head judge of this most important Specialty Show. I told her I should be getting *her* autograph!
In early days, Dorothy Dillingham was a Seeley fan and definitely no friend of mine. At Sturbridge, she told the meeting of 250 assembled members: "It's time for all of us to acknowledge that everything good that's happened in our breed and our Club is the work of one man, Bob Zoller!" This was a total surprise and one of the nicest things that ever happened to me.

Early 2005, Nancy and Bob Russell came to Sarasota to talk dogs with me for two days and we are now best friends. (Nancy even sent me cookies!) She now judges dogs all over the world: she writes me from Australia, New Zealand and various places in Europe!
Early 2006, the top winning dogs of every AKC breed, 2,648 of them, from 20 countries, were assembled at a "World Championship" show in Tampa, and *an Alaskan Malamute called "Costello", won Best in Show! A historical achievement for our breed!* Sandra D'Andrea, the owner and breeder who also was the handler, won $80,000! She is an AMCA member, but I didn't know her. I sent her a short note and she responded: "Thank you so much for the wonderful note. Having you write such kind words was like winning the show all over again! A thrill of a lifetime. Without you and all your contributions, there would be no Costello."

Daughter Kris found a lot of things about me on the internet, including a man in the mountains of Italy who says wonderful things about me and my dogs on his website. Cesare Giammiro and I are now good friends.

A package arrived from England – the Quarterly Journal of The Alaskan Malamute Club of the United Kingdom. The fourth item in the Table of Contents was "The Robert Zoller Story". A nice surprise! This was my story "The Critical Years" which, I'm told, has now been published in six languages!

One day I received a package from an AMCA member in Virginia – a coffee can and a short note: "Is this Geronimo?" On the cover of the container was artwork of a big sled dog and a man dressed in arctic clothes. The dog shown was an exact copy of a widely published photo of my Geronimo, except they altered his face markings to hide the plagiarism. And I had been replaced by the "musher". The product was Murchie's Canadian Blend, Vancouver, B.C. (Geronimo had been dead for nearly fifty years.)

And I especially liked this one: Janet Edmonds, an English anthropologist, researched "The Origins of the Present Day Malamutes". She totally overlooked the role of the third-strain dogs (an important part of our breed's history), but I forgive her because she wrote: "I find it interesting that when the types were sensibly interbred that the resulting dogs looked the most like the original Gold Rush Malamutes. *The classic examples of this are the Husky-Pak dogs of the 1950's.*"

PROGENY

I haven't said much about my granddaughters, but again, I got lucky. Kris has two daughters, Andrea and Jennifer. I'm proud of them for many reasons – including their good judgment in choosing the men they married.

Andrea lives in the Philadelphia area where she plays an important role in an important assignment – the education of children – as head teacher and curriculum coordinator for a private academic pre-school. Her husband, Vince Coccia – a contractor and realtor, is a personality match: Mr. Nice Guy (like Perry Como). Two children – a daughter Jillian (4) and son Anderson (brand new).

Jennifer is a rising star at Disney, in Orlando. Early on, she was one of ten finalists for the role of Walt Disney World Ambassador, a singular honor, and currently serves as Manager of Sales Development – planning growth strategies for Disney's very successful Vacation Club business. Her husband, Steve Tinn, served four years as Disney's Manager of College Recruiting, heading the team assigned to recruit 10,000 college students each year to be interns at the company's theme parks and resorts, worldwide. Later he became the Human Resources Manager aboard The Disney Magic, the company's big ocean liner, in charge of the 935 Disney people providing food, entertainment and services to passengers – everyone except the officers, crew and engineers who report to the ship's captain.

What impressed me: right from the start the guy wore an officer's uniform, *with three stripes*! It took me five years in our wartime Navy, all at sea, and mostly in danger, to earn my three stripes and the "scrambled eggs" on my cap! (I told you my Navy was damn slow when it came to promotions!)

The busy Tinns have two boys – Hudson (2 1/2) and Parker (brand new). And Foster, one of the best non-Malamute dogs I've seen in years!

MONEY MATTERS. (IT CERTAINLY DOES!)

Another reason for my being a "Happy Camper" at this stage of my game is not having any financial worries. I got lucky investing, came to realize we had more wealth than we would need, and were at the point where the government was likely to get more than our kids would, when we died.

So we stepped up our charitable contributions and put everything we owned into Revocable Trusts, one for Laura, one for me. We established a large Charitable Remainder Trust to provide lifetime incomes for Kris and Greg. (After they die, the remainder will go to selected charities, including St. Mary's Church in Waverly, the Waverly Community Foundation, and the Alaskan Malamute rescue program, now called The Alaskan Malamute Assistance League.)

We also created a Principal Residence Trust that transferred ownership of our condo to our children. We paid them rent for as long as we lived there, and, of course, they received the proceeds when the place was sold. These, and several other measures we took, reduced our taxable estates and will leave more for our kids and our granddaughters.

MY WRITING AWARDS PROGRAM

Probably one of the best ideas I ever had came to me after I retired. I left Waverly for good in 1940, but I kept in touch with friends there for many years. I love my old hometown, and I wanted to give something back. I kept reading that too many high school graduates couldn't write well enough to fill out job applications properly. I believe the ability to write well can be helpful, no matter what one does to earn a living – and perhaps, in a small way, I could help.

I contacted the Superintendent of Schools in Waverly and offered to provide funds for a Writing Awards Program. Cash prizes for the best fiction, nonfiction and poetry by students in Waverly-Shell Rock high school, on an annual basis. Judging by the Editor of the Waverly Newspapers, the head of the Wartburg College English Department and a representative of the American Association of University Women.

My offer was accepted. The Waverly Newspapers liked the idea so much they donated a large brass plaque, displayed in the high school, that lists the names of the winners in all three categories for every year. I was especially interested in having the program continue many years – virtually "forever" – and we had to solve the problem of inflation: a prize worth working for in 1990 would be peanuts 30 or 40 years down the road. So my endowment would be adequate to fund the early years, with much or most of it invested to provide continuing growth in future years.

The Waverly Community Foundation and the Trust Department of the State Bank of Waverly have done a great job of managing the money. The program has gone on for 17 years, the awards have increased several times, and now include three winners in each category. It has been praised by the Superintendents, and teachers told me they consider it one of their best teaching tools.

Best of all, every year I get wonderful thank-you letters from kids who win. And it's called "The Robert J. Zoller Writing Awards Program", so, in Waverly, my name will still go on for many years after I am long forgotten – which I probably am, already.

AN ALL-TIME FAVORITE MEMORY

You know I have a lot of memories – some good, some scary. All are important to me in my final years. There is one, however, that I enjoy most of all, and I think about it often. (On purpose.)

It was probably in the early 1920's. I'm five or six years old, and it's Christmas Eve. Somebody wakes me up and tells me to get dressed – we'll be leaving soon for Midnight Mass. I get up and look out the back window of our apartment, and I see a wonderland of new-fallen snow! A foot deep and still coming down, covering everything and turning the entire neighborhood into a thing of beauty that remains in my memory after more than eighty years.

At the end of the alley, I can see the street that leads to our church, and people already heading that way, to get there early, to hear the Christmas music and get a good seat.

The memory changes and now I'm in church. The altar is beautifully decorated for the Christmas Masses. People who I remember are sitting right where I remember them sitting every Sunday. The organ is playing and the choir is singing the same wonderful songs we still sing today. "Silent Night". "Ave Maria". And "O Holy Night", so beautiful I want to cry whenever I hear it, especially when it's remembered along with the snow-covered Christmas Eve I'm writing about now.

Of all the memories of my lifetime, this is the one I recall most often. Probably because it's so beautiful and peaceful to dwell on. It's the Christmas music that gets to me.

...AND A NOTE ON DYING

When you get to be ninety, you can't help thinking about death. I don't do this often, probably because I am not aware that anything is "gaining on me" as Satchel Paige used to say. I've been healthy (lucky) all my life. I believe in God and an after-life because I was brought up that way, and nobody ever convinced me there's something better to believe.

So I go with my Catholic faith, and hope for eventual reunion with my beautiful wife. I like to think of her up there with her mother and sister, and of course, with Geronimo, Takoma, Cherokee, Sioux and all the rest of our canine best friends. (I'm reasonably sure that all our dogs had to promise "no fighting" as a condition for getting in!)

Dogs in heaven? Of course! Some Malamute owner – I have no idea who – wrote:

> "You can't tell me God would have Heaven
> So a man couldn't be with his friends.
> That we're doomed to meet disappointment
> When we come to the place the trail ends.
>
> That would be a low-grade sort of Heaven
> And I'd never regret a damn sin,
> If I'd mush up to the gates white and pearly
> And they don't let my Malamutes in!"

That would never happen. It couldn't. God created something so beautiful, so loyal, so helpful to humans, he'd want to keep it around. For our everlasting pleasure – and His.

(I'm talking all good dogs, not just my breed. Lassie, for example. And Sister Judy's little Yorkie, Joy. Maybe even Snoopy??)

The late, great Will Rogers once said: "If there are no dogs in Heaven, then when I die I want to go where they went."

*   *   *   *   *   *   *

I have many more stories to tell. But I'll stop now and simply offer a sincere "Thank You" to anyone who has gotten this far into My Life and Times.

I can hardly believe all these good things happened to me in my (brief) 90 years. But they did; *everything I've written, really happened.*

I'm sure you'll agree: I have been and still now am lucky indeed. (And exceedingly grateful!) Someone else said it first, but *if life is a journey, I've had a great trip!*

BOB ZOLLER

Printed in the United States
108822LV00002B/97-220/P